HEROES, MARTYRS,
AND POLITICAL MESSIAHS
IN REVOLUTIONARY CUBA,
1946–1958

LILLIAN GUERRA

Heroes, Martyrs, and Political Messiahs in Revolutionary Cuba, 1946–1958

Yale

UNIVERSITY PRESS

NEW HAVEN & LONDON

Published with assistance from the Mary Cady Tew Memorial Fund.

Yale University Press books may be purchased in quantity for educational,
business, or promotional use. For information, please e-mail sales.press@yale
.edu (U.S. office) or sales@yaleup.co.uk (U.K. office).

Set in Times Roman type by Integrated Publishing Solutions,
Grand Rapids, Michigan.
Printed in the United States of America.

ISBN 978-0-300-17553-0 (hardcover : alk. paper)
Library of Congress Control Number: 2017950926
A catalogue record for this book is available from the British Library.

This paper meets the requirements of ANSI/NISO Z39.48-1992
(Permanence of Paper).

10 9 8 7 6 5 4 3 2 1

CONTENTS

HEROES, MARTYRS, AND POLITICAL MESSIAHS IN REVOLUTIONARY CUBA, 1946–1958

A History That Dare Not Be Told: Political Culture and the Making of Revolutionary Cuba, 1946–1958

"IN THOSE DAYS," SAID VICENTE BAEZ, "you would go to the home of a family member who knew you had been imprisoned, who knew that [the police] had identified you as an insurrectionary. You had decided to leave the house where you slept the night before because the police had just raided it earlier that day and, well, you knew you had to leave. So then you knocked on the door of a close relative, thinking they would help you, but instead, they simply slammed the door in your face." A member of the clandestine revolutionary underground of the 26th of July Movement, Baez fought the dictatorship of General Fulgencio Batista for six years. Sighing, he paused and concluded: "You would have to experience it to believe it, to know what that is." I responded only with silence. Baez looked at me carefully. My face must have registered the horror that he had felt when his loved ones had left him to confront imminent danger alone.

"Once the underground of Havana was set up and running by the summer of 1957," Baez continued, "sometimes there was simply no room in any of the safe houses on a given night." One such evening, he had been eating a sandwich at an open-air lunch counter on the corner of Zanja and Belascoaín in Centro Habana with David Salvador, chief labor activist for Fidel Castro's 26th of July Movement and one of Baez's closest friends. Suddenly, they noticed they were being watched. Then the startling sound of gunfire from a nearby police station made them jump from their seats. Walking quickly, they headed straight for the most secure safe house they knew, one that always admitted any *clandestino*. "Take off your shoes, take off your shoes," repeated the anxious lady behind the door after they knocked a second time. "Taking off your shoes was the signal that you were in deep trouble," noted Baez. "Plus it was a good signal because you didn't want the neighbors to hear you. There were at least twenty people huddled inside. Why? Because there was no place to go in the whole city and the twenty people had said to themselves, let's go to the *emergency* safe house; there they are sure to admit us and we won't have a problem. That tells you that even those activists who lived in and had family in Havana had no place to go, no refuge because there was simply no place to hide, nowhere to go. Every safe house was full." In the end, Baez and Salvador spent the night sleeping on the house's colonial rooftop, stars overhead and shoes nearby, just in case someone sounded the alarm and they unexpectedly had to flee.

That morning in early August 2008 when I filmed Vicente Baez telling me this story, I barely knew him. By then, I had traveled to Puerto Rico twice, intent on following up on the suggestions of interview subjects that I received from Carlos Franqui, the national director of propaganda for the 26th of July Movement from 1956 to 1958 and then editor in chief of the government's main newspaper, *Revolución,* until 1963, when Fidel Castro unceremoniously replaced him with a Communist militant.[1] Unlike Baez, Franqui had written multiple accounts of his activism in the war against the regime of Fulgencio Batista (1952–1958) as well as the process of his disillusionment and ultimate break in 1971 with the authoritarian, pro-Soviet Communist state that the government under Castro had become by the early 1960s. In college and in graduate school, I had read and reread nearly all of Franqui's books.[2] Perhaps for this reason, it was easy to talk to him, and he found it easy to talk to me. I felt as if I knew him, and despite a fifty-year age gap, he told me that I thought and spoke like someone of the same generation. For a historian, this was a great compliment.

However, Baez had never written about himself or others in the war, and he had never previously granted an interview. Yet luckily for me, Baez was *muy cubano* (very Cuban): like my entire Cuban family and virtually every Cuban I knew, he was more than just "a talker." Baez was a *cuentista,* an eloquent, thoughtful, and charismatic storyteller. This was especially true when it came to recounting and explaining the unknown, unpopular history that, for most Cubans, remained taboo. In recent decades, the fact that the urban-based revolutionary underground of Castro's 26th of July Movement formed the forefront of the fight against the Batista dictatorship had become commonly accepted among scholars, including those on the island; however, promoting the protagonism of Fidel Castro and his "jungle guerrilla fighters"—once an overt strategy of members of the underground itself and their allies in the media—remained central to the legitimacy of their alleged unique heroism in catalyzing Batista's fall from power and revolutionaries' seizure of the state on 1 January 1959.

The day I interviewed Baez, both of us sat in uncomfortable chairs in the sparse, white-walled office of his publishing house while my partner Rolando operated a video camera. The interview lasted nearly eight hours. All three of us paused only for bathroom breaks, to retrieve bottles of spring water from Baez's mini-fridge or change the tape in the camera. So mesmerized were we by the project at hand—collecting and exchanging knowledge of the intense political and personal process that had ruled Baez's life and in many different ways determined the course of Rolando's life and my own—that we completely missed the traditional four o'clock *cafecito* hour that Cubans take until Baez's telephone rang. His wife was calling him. "Did something happen, Mateo?" she asked, her worried voice clearly audible in the room. "Mateo was my nom de guerre," Baez chuckled. "She probably thought we were back *en la lucha* [in the fight] because she hasn't heard from me all day."

The legacy of Mateo's years printing clandestine newspapers, meeting with fellow rebels in the urban wing of the 26th of July Movement, and living in perpetual fear of being arrested or killed by police had surely struck deep. Yet it represents one of many dimensions of this tumultuous period in Cuban history, of which historians have written very little.

Biographies and memoirs, some of them excellent, intellectually riveting pieces of analysis, still dominate the existing literature on the period from the 1940s through 1958.[3] However, relative to other periods of Cuba's history (especially the republic, for which works on the first thirty years abound), books that explain this critical period are distinctly lacking. That an increasingly sovereign electoral democracy morphed into dictatorship remains merely a fact of history rather than an easily explained process of complex societal interactions and the evolution of the culture's relationship with the Cuban state. Fiercely possessed of clear-minded visions of nation, however conflicting they might have been, Cubans had pushed, protested, and picked up arms repeatedly throughout the course of the twentieth century to force the state's accountability *to them,* the citizens.[4] Thus, those scholarly works that do exist on the 1940s and 1950s have become indispensable, despite their tendency toward a thematic focus. The best examine themes of race, cultural debates over identity, the role of the United States in elite politics, and the economy.[5] None, for example, other than books written by Batista himself, explore the policies, persona, and public image of Batista after his return to Cuba in 1948 and seizure of power in 1952.[6] Many represent Cuban history not only through the lens of Havana but do so by focusing, sometimes to the point of caricature, on its seedier side. Books on the mob, drug dealing, casinos, and their related industries of prostitution and brothels remain a pronounced subgenre of Cuban history.[7] With the exception of only a handful of books that explore the political history and culture of these years, the vast array of works on the struggle for democracy and the war against Batista examine almost solely the guerrilla experience of the 26th of July Movement and, to a lesser extent, other opposition groups, whose efforts failed.[8] With the exception of Steve Cushion's *A Hidden History of the Cuban Revolution: How the Working Class Shaped the Guerrillas' Victory* (a book whose title says it all), much remains to be examined with regard to Cuba's civil war against the *batistiano* state.[9] Among the mysteries to be fully resolved is the question of how civic mobilization contributed to Batista's fall despite a seemingly cowed rank and file and co-opted union leadership, much of it tied either to Batista or to a Cuban Communist Party and overtly accommodationist Soviet state. Like Cushion's work, this book finds evidence of a revolutionary working class unbolted to the machinery of both systems of control and ideology; unlike Cushion's work, I find workers' activism meshed together with a longer, broader chronology and tradition of protest in which class mattered less than personal commitment and serving the cause of Cuba was (perhaps idealistically) understood to serve the cause of all.

Only Julia Sweig's *Inside the Cuban Revolution* is based on the existing— although utterly inaccessible—archive originally organized by Carlos Franqui and Celia Sánchez of the 26th of July Movement, held in Cuba's Oficina de Asuntos Históricos [Office of Historical Matters] in the Council of State. Sweig's book is intrepid in its heavily documented argument that the triumph of the Cuban revolutionary forces over Batista in 1959 owed more to underground activists like Vicente Baez than to Fidel Castro's guerrillas.[10] As the legendary Comandante Ernesto "Che" Guevara himself admitted, the guerrillas' main tactic—avoiding direct military encounters with Batista's heavily equipped and professionally trained army—resulted in a minimal number of deaths—so few, he contended, that they could be "counted on one's fingers."[11] Even after Che and Comandante Camilo Cienfuegos led the troops' advance westward in the late fall of 1958, the total number of guerrillas killed probably reached no more than 250; by comparison, Batista's security forces assassinated 3,000 to 4,000 men and women of the revolutionary underground, many of them tortured to death, over the course of Cuba's two-year civil war.[12] Still, *Inside the Cuban Revolution* leaves the interested reader begging for more. As Sweig would likely agree, it touches only the tip of an iceberg when it comes to three critical but highly unexplored questions: What role did the Cuban citizenry play in creating the conditions that shaped and launched revolution in the 1950s? How did the political culture that resulted from citizen participation in public protests and debates over state policies before Batista's coup in 1952 influence the nature of Batista's dictatorship? And finally, how did citizens' aspirations for a morally just society forge a common program of change and ultimately justify support for an armed fight?

By delving deeply into scattered, newly opened, and personal archives as well as oral history, this book answers these questions in the following ways. First, in the mid-1940s, despite largely unchanging interventionist policies of the United States, popular expectations that the Cuban state would finally achieve sovereignty over its internal economy and political affairs reached unprecedented levels. Eduardo "Eddy" Chibás, a former student revolutionary in the 1920s and early 1930s, was elected to the Constitutional Convention of 1940 and became a senator. His legendary obstreperousness and uncompromising nationalism inspired Chibás to deliver an unending stream of vociferous rants and denunciations, mostly through nationally broadcast Sunday night radio shows, first on behalf of his mentors and allies in the Auténtico Party and then in protest of their ascendant corruption. Many credited Chibás with ensuring the Auténticos' landslide victory over Fulgencio Batista's coalition of parties in the general elections of 1944. Within only two years, he had become both *batistianos'* and *auténticos'* worst critic. In the early 1940s, radio transformed the political landscape in Cuba by bringing previously isolated citizens to the political table. According to Carlos Franqui, the son of a peasant himself and later a journalist as well as a leading activist of the 26th of July Movement, every session of the long-awaited contentious Constitutional Convention of 1940 was broadcast live on radio. This process made virtually all Cubans permanent protagonists of the national political scene.[13] Their history of struggle, first for abolition and independence from Spain and then for independence from the contradictory neocolonial interventionism of the United States, had made

Cubans the heirs of highly developed traditions of political engagement with the state.[14] After the radio broadcasts of 1940, they were even more involved.

Beginning in the fall of 1946, Chibás conceived the Ortodoxos, more as a social movement than a political party, in order to contest the Auténticos and the old top-down style of *politiquería* and corruption to which virtually all politicians in the republic quickly became accustomed once they assumed power. Between 1946 and his death in 1951, Chibás and his supporters tried to force the government into becoming an accountable state and a participatory nation. Radio enabled this process; articulate, irate, and critical politicians with regular radio broadcasts like Eduardo Chibás undoubtedly popularized the role of radio as an instrument of citizenship and a symbol of mutually connected national identity. In the early 1950s, a population of little more than 5–6 million Cubans owned 900,000 radios and 365,000 television sets, making Cuba the country with the greatest televisual and radio-listening audience in the hemisphere besides the United States.[15]

Perhaps more than any other party, the Ortodoxos used radio and the press to raise the expectations of the Cuban public regarding the potentially transformative role that could be played by the national state. They appealed to an increasing majority of Cubans because Chibás and his fellow leaders demanded a government that responded to the practical needs of the citizenry and embraced anti-imperialism and the goal of greater social and racial justice. They relied on a discourse that ascribed to Cuban identity an exceptional, historically rooted propensity to morality and self-sacrifice. Politicians who did not live up to such standards because of "selfish" corruption and "demagoguery" betrayed Cuba. They also betrayed all those nationalist martyrs who had given their lives for a free, democratic nation-state that promised to surpass models set by all others, especially the United States, since 1898. In that year the Spanish surrendered their colony not to the Cuban revolutionaries who had fought for their independence from Spain for thirty years but to the United States, thereby initiating a process of neocolonization and a sense of thwarted destiny from which Cuba never recovered.[16] Thus, despite Batista's coup in 1952—or, arguably, *because* of it—citizens' expectations, sense of personal duty toward *la patria* (the fatherland), and patterns of protest, including street demonstrations and the development of an activist press, never went away.

Subsequently, public and private debate became Cuba's true national pastime. Martyrdom, whether achieved symbolically or as a result of confronting state violence, emerged as the most revered hallmark of *cubanidad*. (More than just a common term for identity, *cubanidad* connoted Cuban pride, the near-obsessive conviction that one day Cubans would not only fulfill the very highest standards of human potential but that, in a way, they already had—simply by aspiring to do so.) The post–World War II context both fueled Cubans' hope and ignited debate. When Western Europe and the United States openly repudiated colonialism to endorse democracy and human rights, their claims awakened historically rooted sensitivity over the United States' role in repeatedly thwarting Cuba's path. The idea that Cuban politicians needed to live up to basic moral standards of political behavior and constitutional mandates in order to make Cuba a leading democracy in the world—one as great or even greater than the United States—seemed a viable, realistic goal. As Cuban historian Herminio Portell Vilá put it in 1949, "The first duty of every Cuban who truly wishes to rescue Cuba from the ills of today is to believe in the epic history of Cuba and in the heroes, martyrs, and patriots who created Cuba."[17] Possibly more than ever, the task of saving Cuba thus came to depend on citizens' willingness to retrieve the values of the past and actively, even forcibly, reconnect them to contemporary events. Doing so would finally set Cuba free.

This political culture of the postwar years meant that after Batista's coup in 1952, he would not be able to rule arbitrarily or militarily; he would have to respond to demands for accountability and constitutionality. He faced a context in which the legacies of heroic activism, first in Cuba's three late nineteenth-century independence wars and then in the 1933 social revolution against Gerardo Machado's neocolonial dictatorship, were very much alive. Clear to all Cubans was one unavoidable fact: U.S. policies of direct military occupation, intervention, and diplomatic as well as economic blackmail had diverted Cuba from the destiny it would have achieved at the conclusion of its wars against Spain in 1898 and repeatedly throughout the prolonged struggle against Machado in 1933. Aware of the paradox his actions had created but always convinced he could overcome it, Batista invested heavily in the construction and projection of his image as a savior of Cuba through well-crafted publicity at home and abroad as well as public welfare policies whose aims and content he carefully managed and maintained. Batista wanted Cubans to see him as he saw himself: a defender of democracy, a man of the people, El Hombre (The Man), a supremely generous individual capable of doing what institutions could not. Modernize, educate, discipline, and embrace Cuba, despite the ingratitude that so many of its citizens showed him: these were the tasks Batista set himself.

Ironically, as this work shows, much of Batista's discourse of change and his program for improving Cuba by modernizing its infrastructure, uplifting the peasants, expanding rural education, crafting a social safety net, improving conditions for national investment, supporting labor rights, and ameliorating the vast class difference between rich and poor mirrored the platforms of most Cuban political parties *before* his coup as well as those opposed to his rule after. As *Heroes, Martyrs, and Political Messiahs* demonstrates, the fact that very little distinguished the political promises and discourses of the dictator from his opponents is not surprising since a consensus on the need, nature, and pace of change had already emerged from the majority of citizens before 1952. This was a year when the elections—had Batista and the military allowed them to take place—would have brought the Ortodoxos to power and everything would have changed, or so most Cubans likely believed. As Batista discovered, however, most Cubans proved impossible to dupe. They also showed themselves impervious to the dictator's means of disciplining civil society. Unable to count on the broad complicity of most citizens, Batista increasingly failed to legitimate himself in the self-assigned role of savior to Cuba's middle and working classes.

To his obvious chagrin, Batista at best achieved only superficial legitimacy among certain sectors of citizens. Their support for him in some cases and toleration in others required constant negotiation to maintain. At best, stability came at the cost of ever-deepening dependence on overt forms of repression, bribery, and distortions of a government role in the economy so as to favor the Batista clan and its cronies. Having originally gained fame and popularity for leading the Sergeants' Revolt that consolidated the anti-imperialist social revolution against President Gerardo Machado in 1933, Batista proved reluctant to accept his image as dictator: on the very day he took command at the central military base of Camp Columbia in 1952, Batista explained his actions as "a revolution" he was "forced to make," rejecting even the idea of a *golpe de estado,* or coup.[18] He also called his first cabinet a "Junta Revolucionaria," reviving the memory of his short-lived heroic reputation in the Revolution of 1933.[19] Even Batista's own lawmakers and loyal cadres of paid journalists rarely accepted these laughable terms, preferring to call Batista's regime a "de facto government."

Ironically, the handful of scholarly works covering these years tend to reproduce the idea that Batista's coup was met with "national ambivalence."[20] Albeit unintentionally, this conclusion serves well the post-1959 historiography of Fidel Castro's regime. It has tended to gloss all political activism and protests of the Batista dictatorship as precursors to Fidel's 26th of July Movement, failing to analyze oppositional actions and unarmed organizations in their own right.[21] More recent works, such as *Batista: El Golpe,* take a more distinctive tack. Written by retired intelligence agents of the Castro government, *Batista: El Golpe* is innovative in its use of Cuban government archives open to the authors but off-limits to historians. However, while its authors recognize that the coup immediately triggered a broad panorama of opposition, they blame the highly critical public culture of denunciation for laying the groundwork essential to Batista's success. That is, rather than see citizens' will to dissent and debate as positive hallmarks of a vibrant, emerging democracy, the authors perceive the centrality of strident public critiques of the state as not only "self-destructive, uproarious," and "sensationalistic" but responsible for "undermin[ing] the foundations of a building that was never solid: that imperfect and weak building that was the republic."[22]

Here I take a different view. Critiques had become part and parcel of everyday popular and official "high" political culture since the late 1940s. Undoubtedly the fall of the Auténtico government "did not warrant public outrage," as Louis A. Pérez succinctly surmises, and few citizens wept over the departure in 1952 of President Carlos Prío Socarrás or his corrupt minions.[23] Nonetheless, Cubans' culture of outrage over political hypocrisy and their search for justice in courageous acts of unarmed civic defiance defined how they saw the crisis Batista provoked as well as its solutions. Profoundly anti-militaristic, opposition to Batista came from all sides, taking new forms, occupying new spaces, and recruiting new actors to spar in the political arena.[24]

Nonetheless, Batista persistently emphasized the idea that only *he* could "save Cuba" from the "messianic" solution that Eddy Chibás clearly tapped in mobilizing mass protests prior to Batista and in laying the groundwork for a revolution in consciousness through legislative government, even if its policies conflicted with the interests of the United States. Like U.S. officials, most of whom unconditionally supported him, Batista never recognized the unpopularity of his position and the resistance yet to come. From 1952 to 1958, top leaders of the opposition, particularly the student leader José Antonio Echeverría, urban activist Frank País, and lawyer turned guerrilla Fidel Castro, all recognized the appeal of self-sacrifice and calls for martyrdom as vehicles that could erode the foundations and operation of Batista's power. Only one of these three leaders would survive: Fidel Castro. As the sole and principal leader of the war against Batista, Castro prestaged his assumption of power in the mountain villages of the liberated zones that his guerrilla army controlled by implementing an idyllic, microcosmic version of the political program most Cubans had long waited for. He also prefaced what would later be called his "apotheosis" in the wake of Batista's flight on 1 January 1959, by crafting a narrative of salvation for Cuba based on messianic principles of loving generosity and a complete rupture with corrupt neocolonial history; in this narrative, Fidel Castro was easily cast in the starring role.

Over the past six decades, few if any Cubans have been able to escape this narrative, regardless of where we were born or where we live. Nor have we been able to avoid defining who we are and what Cuba is without referencing Castro's version of our past, present, and future. Growing up Cuban in the small town of Marion, Kansas, I always identified with the idea that Cuba needed saving, if not a savior. Despite the fact that I literally knew no other Cubans outside my own immediate family, I felt a sense of duty to learn the history of Cuba and its current struggles under the combined pressures of U.S. aggression and Communist rule. In my naive, childish mind, I always wanted "to do something about it." I surely developed this attitude because conversations with the few relatives we had in the United States and saw twice a year inevitably seemed like covert operations. When controversial topics came up or someone got too emotional, my parents always shooed me away. Back in my room, I could hear but not understand impassioned, detail-laden discussions about controversial topics, such as whether or not there could have been a land reform that "wasn't Communist" and if self-admitted Marxists Che Guevara and Raúl Castro had really run the show before *and* after Batista fled in 1959.

This happened every Christmas, New Year's Eve, and throughout the month of June, which we traditionally spent in the wholly Cuban quarters of Miami. The list of more specific topics that no one wanted to talk about nonetheless loomed large in nearly every family conversation: the husband of my grandmother's first cousin, Luis del Castillo, who owned two domestic appliance stores in Santa Clara and Cienfuegos and donated thousands of dollars to Castro's 26th of July Movement; my maternal grandfather, who aided clandestinos like Vicente Baez whenever he could and later joined the very first revolutionary militias organized after 1959; my great-uncle Dr. Eduardo Pino Vara, the last batistiano mayor of Cienfuegos, who faced execution in early 1959 until his wife relied on a past romantic relationship with Carlos Rafael Rodríguez, a prominent Communist Party militant allied to Fidel's movement, to miraculously save his life. To say the least, the history of the war against Batista, let alone its aftermath of a nationalist revolution leading to the consolidation of a Communist state, was complicated. Discussing its complexity, however, was also largely taboo.

I first learned that lesson while talking history over games of Chinese checkers with my grandfather "Chichi," Heriberto Rodríguez, as a young kid. A peasant with a fourth-grade education who, by the late 1940s, had become a top executive at Sabatés, the Cuban subsidiary of Procter & Gamble, Chichi told me that he had been a member of a radically nationalist, anti-corruption party called the Ortodoxos. It was led by a senator and radio talk show host named Eddy Chibás, he said, "a man and a martyr for Cuba" whom he clearly admired. Ashamed to discuss publicly his loyalty to the revolutionary program in 1959 despite its adoption of Communism in the years beyond, Chichi openly confessed his initial belief in the 1959 revolution's salvation once I started studying Cuba and Latin American history in college. To my surprise, I discovered that Chichi had voluntarily joined the government militias while continuing to work at his job at Sabatés even *after* the company was nationalized in August 1960.

"We were building the world that Chibás convinced us we could make. The revolution against Batista," Chichi said more than once, "would never have been possible without Eddy Chibás. Neither would the rise of Fidel Castro. No one would ever have paid any attention to Fidel if it weren't for Chibás." *Who was Eddy Chibás?* I inquired, always getting the same reply: "Eddy Chibás *was* revolution. He knew how to remind us of what it meant to be cubanos." *What does it mean to be cubano?* I would ask. "Chibás was very cubano: he yelled, he protested, he denounced the hypocrisy of politicians. He always demanded that Cuba live up to what it should have been."

Thanks in large part to constantly talking and being denied the right to talk about the enigmas and paradoxes of Cuban history, I grew up feeling very cubana. Over time, the weekly letters my mother forced me to write to my paternal grandparents in Cuba evolved into an activity I looked forward to and also feared: living in Kansas and being "American" in a Cuban family had left me bilingual but illiterate in the language I loved most, Spanish. Moving to

Miami when I was fourteen allowed me to immerse myself in Spanish classes at school. Soon I launched a voluntary letter-writing campaign to get to know my relatives still living in Cuba. In reply, great-aunts, great-uncles, and first cousins who were my age never tired of writing back, recounting details of a deliberately forgotten past, often waxing poetic in a tropical form of political Morse code. *Were the people truly apathetic when Batista launched his military coup in 1952?* I asked. *Did Cubans really not believe in elections throughout the 1950s?* To these questions, I received abrupt, formulaic answers that seemed the product of rote memorization. Given Cuba's highly politicized pedagogy and the near-constant policing of public and private speech at the time, they probably were. "The people were in shock over the coup. They didn't believe in Batista's corrupt predecessors so they didn't care about the coup," wrote one. "Cubans did not want elections because they would all be fraudulent," wrote another. "The solution started with Fidel Castro's assault on the Moncada military barracks in 1953," wrote many relatives, countless times. Family members in Havana would often write the same simple phrase that relatives in Pinar del Río did, a summary of what they could not or simply would not say: "Todo empezó en el Moncada" (Everything started with Moncada). From these exchanges, I decided that much of Cuban history in 1940s and 1950s was, quite simply, a history that dared not be told.

Quickly, I learned that some questions I asked my relatives they would never answer, at least not in writing. Ironically, none of the questions I asked had to do with current conditions. Reading books like *Cuba in the 1970s* by Carmelo Mesa-Lago and Hugh Thomas's *Cuba; or, The Pursuit of Freedom* as a teenager and then dozens of works about the rules and realities of Cuba's Communist state in college taught me not to do that: they would likely have stopped writing me altogether if I had.[25] Years later, I also discovered that Eddy Chibás had died in August 1951, having shot himself by accident or on purpose—nobody knew—shortly after one of his famous Sunday night radio broadcasts denouncing politicians' corruptions and betrayal of Cuba. So how could such a man embody "revolution"? How could a politician who had been dead for several years be responsible for Fidel Castro's rise to power and fame prior to 1959?

When I moved to Cuba for a year in 1996 to research my dissertation on Cubans' often violent struggles over how to define and consolidate the nation-state in the early twentieth century, I met and grew to love more than a hundred relatives across three provinces, many of whom had been my pen pals for years.

Few of the past struggles I studied in the archives during the day seemed resolved in the contemporary Cuba I encountered at night and on weekends. To the older ones, I posed the same questions I had asked once Chichi. Mostly, I received exasperated explanations: "Aquí no se habla de Eddy Chibás en décadas; no se puede" (Here no one has spoken of Eddy Chibás for decades; you can't). "Aquí, Eddy Chibás no existe; solo se habla de Fidel" (Here Eddy Chibás does not exist; one only talks about Fidel). To the younger ones, I asked variations on themes they themselves had once parroted in their letters to me. For instance, *Why do you think everything began with Fidel's assault on El Cuartel moncada?* Shocked by my "obsession with Moncada," everyone quite lovingly admonished me. "Niña, ¿tu estas segura de que naciste en Estados Unidos? ¡Tú suenas como militante de la Juventud Comunista!" (Girl, are you sure you were born in the United States? You sound just like a militant of the Communist Youth!) laughed my first cousin Puchito Guerra. In short, my battle to engage the history of the 1940s and 1950s, whether in heretical or authorized form, proved a formidable one I simply could not win. Yet this period seemed so critical: it was the prelude to the post-1959 revolutionary state when leaders like Fidel Castro, strategies of protest, and hopes for radical change were formed.

Like my family on the island, my professors and the predominant historiography of the late 1980s and early 1990s held to the view that most Cubans in the 1940s and 1950s were not yelling and protesting political hypocrisy as my grandfather had said they were: the majority were passive or resigned to a permanent state of frustration in the face of the massive corruption that overwhelmed all chances of reform in the 1940s, a period defined as Cuba's most "democratic era" for its successful Constitutional Convention of 1940 and two "clean" general elections. After General Fulgencio Batista's military coup of 10 March 1952, insisted the conventional view, things only got worse: then Fidel Castro, his followers, and a handful of young student radicals led by José Antonio Echeverría, the president of the Federación Estudiantil Universitaria, challenged Batista's violation of the Constitution and subsequent reign of terror. The Cuban citizens were supposedly only bystanders to this history, dominated by corrupt politicians and national sellouts. Only when Batista fled Cuba on New Year's Day, 1959, did most defend the long-sought sovereignty of the nation-state in the face of constant interventions by the United States and its backing of dictators like Batista. Only then, allegedly, did Cubans explode into action. Euphoria and total unity greeted the triumph of revolutionary forces led by Fidel. However, when I finally sat down in 2011 with a rich mother lode of documents, particularly the vast collections of Eddy Chibás and Carlos Márquez Sterling, another Ortodoxo politician, in Cuba's National Archive, I discovered that my grandfather's accounts of a populace seething with resentment of a hypocritical, increasingly violent government and a clear, preexisting revolutionary social vision proved far more accurate than the commonly accepted historical tale of a small handful of brave heroes defying public passivity and political apathy to challenge the state. In fact, the idea of an *already* prepared, *already* revolutionary citizenry made sense given the very real euphoria and near total unity that greeted the triumph of revolutionary forces under Fidel Castro in January 1959. The nature and endurance of that euphoria and unity became well-documented centerpieces of discussion in my last book, which covers the consolidation and evolution of a revolutionary "grassroots dictatorship" in the first decade following the flight of Batista in January 1959.[26]

This book, consequently, deepens arguments I have made in earlier works by demonstrating that the "New Cuba" that allegedly emerged in January 1959 did not rise from the ground up. The seeds of revolutionary Cuba were not just planted in the years before, they had sprouted and flourished: people's mass participation in supporting radical change and rejecting any U.S. role in Cuba's political affairs consolidated the view that Fidel Castro's small guerrilla army had not simply defeated an overwhelming, well-equipped military force of tens of thousands of soldiers, air force pilots, and marines; it had defeated the historical *deviation* of Cuba from what should have been its gloriously democratic, socially just, and racially egalitarian path. This was the Cuba imagined by nationalist leaders and fighters of Cuba's thirty-year independence struggle against Spain at the end of the nineteenth century. It was also the Cuba that peasants, workers, intellectuals, and enlightened sectors of the country's middle class had demanded since 1898 when the war ended and U.S. intervention began.[27] This Cuba began to flourish in the late 1940s and came to fruition in the last months of 1958 when Cubans consumed, constructed, and helped craft the image of a generous, accountable, morally pure, and messianic revolutionary state that Fidel Castro was committed to lead. When Batista fled on New Year's Day the stakes for change were already very high. The United States' immediate hostility to the revolutionary social movement that made Batista's flight both possible and inevitable drove them higher. Cubans demanded palpable evidence of a historic *and* historical break from the past.

Amid such desires, it was no wonder that Eddy Chibás's electorally grounded, financially accountable, nationalist, and anti-Soviet program for the Cuban state emerged in new form among middle-class activists eager to rebuild civil society. Equally vibrant was the echo of Chibás and other activists' rages against impunity in the public's demand for the castigation of all corrupt politicians and abusive state agents in 1959. However, Fidel Castro almost immediately moved to scuttle memories of Eddy Chibás and co-opt other movements of revolutionary opposition to Batista, precisely because they threatened his ambitious plan for managing and ultimately subverting citizens' control. Only twice during the entire six-plus decades of the Castro-led revolution did the government bother to honor Eduardo Chibás, a hero and a political mentor to whom Fidel Castro assigned himself and whom he clearly imitated (as we shall find) several times. In January 1959, Fidel paid homage to Chibás at his grave but did not personally participate in the single subsequent commemoration of him. Fidel was notably absent, in both word and deed, when the Ejército Rebelde (Rebel Army), made up of his mountain guerrilla forces, Raúl Castro's later recruits, and members of Cuba's legendary Federación de Estudiantes Universitarios (FEU, Federation of University Students), performed a march of mourning to the Colón cemetery on the anniversary of the death of Chibás, 16 August 1959.[28] From that point on, Cuba never again remembered Eduardo Chibás, just as most Cubans would never again analyze or formally study this period of their past from any perspective that might discredit, dissolve, dismantle, or simply dislodge the centrality of Fidel Castro and his guerrilla forces from a pivotal, unparalleled role. Left out of this mythology was not just Chibás himself or the Ortodoxos but, more important, the Cuban people, who undoubtedly propelled events, actions, and actors through sheer audacity, the burden of belief, and commitment alone.

This book puts the voices and experiences of average citizens at the center of its stories whenever sources and the narrative permit; my choice to do so is dictated by my astounding sense of personal responsibility for the array of documents I found in Cuba's National Archive articulating a very different view of the Cuban people than I expected. *Heroes, Martyrs, and Political Messiahs in Revolutionary Cuba* demonstrates how deeply reluctant most Cubans were to take up arms against the Batista regime in the 1950s. Yet it does *not* argue that they held to this position out of apathy, fear, or passivity. On the contrary, public protest had achieved leverage over the state and even U.S. economic controls before the Batista regime of the 1950s, both under Auténtico rule in the 1940s and after Batista assumed power by force in 1952. This remained the case at least through 1955, when public pressure and protests led by students, intellectuals, and workers forced the Batista regime to release hundreds of political prisoners whose subsequent actions clearly changed the tide of Cuban political destiny, especially that of Batista himself. The *presos politicos* (political prisoners) included not only Fidel Castro but dozens of activists from a spectrum of opposition groups. The diversity of Cuba's opposition to Batista, recognized by many previous histories, is more fully examined here. In many ways, unpacking the elements that made up this diverse and increasingly divided opposition nonetheless reveals the intensity and sincerity of most Cubans' commitment to constitutionalism, an end to the abuse of power, and *socialist*—not Communist—forms of socioeconomic democracy based on state intervention in the economy.

This book does not seek to retell old stories in new ways. It seeks to tell entirely untold, unacknowledged, and deliberately altered or forgotten stories. There is a lot of "talking" in this book because one of its goals is to recover the long-lost voices of otherwise anonymous, "everyday" Cubans who saw themselves as citizen-patriots and took on the many duties this role inscribed. Many wrote letters, sometimes dozens of pages long, filled with spelling mistakes and grammatical errors that bore witness to their socioeconomic marginality much more than to their limited literacy. Others went to rallies, sometimes walking miles to catch a glimpse of Eddy Chibás, shake his hand, and offer their advice in person. After Batista's coup, many journalists became a fearless force of the opposition. Students, workers, and young professionals suffered numerous police beatings in order to assert their constitutional rights of assembly, protest, and representation in government. Others did more: taking up arms to back what began as a myriad of organized anti-Batista groups committed to dying so that the ideals of a constitutional democracy might live.

Thus, while the first half of this book focuses on democracy's last stand in Cuba, the latter half attempts to rewrite the story of the war against Batista from multiple angles. These angles are as rooted in the personal testimonials of participants like Vicente Baez as they are in previously unused, unknown, or ignored archives. In particular, later chapters rely on the testimony of Andrew St. George, a foreign-born freelance journalist based in the United States who, like so many other journalists, became an eyewitness to Batista's carnage and a proponent of the cause of armed struggle to defeat him.[29] As Leonard Ray Teel has recently shown, these journalists represented a new breed of reporters who risked life and safety not simply to "get the story" for sensationalistic purposes or for the sake of profit, as much of the yellow press that covered Cuba in the early part of the twentieth century had; rather, journalists like St. George, Robert Taber, and others sought to rip apart the screen of censorship hiding Cuba's violent and unjust reality from the rest of the world, thereby reinforcing the rootedness of democracy in freedom of expression and access to information at a time when U.S. support for dictatorships abroad rose and domestic persecution of countercultural thinkers abounded.[30]

In addition to the questions already posed above, this book asks challenging ones whose importance few scholars or citizens have doubted—although many have thought them impossible to answer. One is the relationship of the Communist Party to the ever-hardening policies and peculiar "populism" of the Batista regime in the 1950s as well as the Communists' potentially ironic role in helping to stabilize rather than topple it. At the same time, *Heroes, Martyrs, and Political Messiahs in Revolutionary Cuba* contends that Cuba's political culture in the 1940s and 1950s was a recent invention, a product of the previous and stalled social revolution of 1933, as explained below.

Reasserting Democracy: The Political Culture of 1940s Cuba

Until the 1980s, many historians on the island and Cuban political figures alike frequently ascribed the return of revolutionary attitudes and armed struggle in the 1940s–1950s to the actions and ideas of fighters in Cuba's last independence war of 1895, from white nationalist ideologue José Martí and black revolutionary general Antonio Maceo to their mostly black troops, descended from slaves. In doing so, these historians echoed the position that Fidel Castro consistently repeated in the 1950s when he justified his own armed struggle as a return to the war of 1895; this strategy allowed Fidel to renounce any connection or inspiration in contemporary politicians who claimed an activist heritage and had cut their teeth in the most recent Cuban revolution, that of 1933. This book contends that the cradle of modern Cuba's cycle of dictatorial and anti-dictatorial processes was the presidency of Gerardo Machado from 1925 to 1933, and the decidedly unresolved revolution that ended it in August 1933. Given that survivors of the struggle against Machado, from Batista himself to his adversaries, all became central players in Cuban politics from 1933 through 1958, two generations of historians no longer dispute the significance of 1933 in shaping later discourse, attitudes, or sense of what it was possible to achieve politically. However, few have taken on the challenge of exploring these direct connections, as exemplified by the dearth of works that analyze Cuba's "democratic era" of the 1940s.[31]

Possibly the most despised of Cuba's dictators, if not the most demonized, Gerardo Machado came to power on a Liberal Party ticket that promised to overturn the continuing impact of the Platt Amendment, a U.S.-authored addition to Cuba's Constitution of 1902 imposed by force of arms. In 1898, U.S. officials reversed Congress's earlier promise to allow Cuba to enjoy its political independence after U.S. forces helped the Cuban army defeat Spain. Subsequently, the Platt Amendment represented Washington's efforts to subvert any possibility that the Cuban government might ever make decisions alone, without first accounting for U.S. interests and investments. Imposed on the Cuban Constitutional Convention of 1901—itself a result of Cuban revolutionaries' protests of the U.S. government's betrayal of its promises—the Platt Amendment gave the United States the right to intervene whenever it liked, allegedly on behalf of Cuban "independence," and to establish a military base in "perpetuity" at Guantánamo.[32]

During his first run for the presidency in 1925, Gerardo Machado pledged to create a true economically and politically sovereign state that was neither beholden to U.S. interests nor held hostage by fears of a U.S. military occupation. By 1925, Cuba had already experienced two such occupations that had profound, long-term impacts on the way in which any future freely elected Cuban government could operate.[33]

To take but one example, both the first U.S. military government of 1898–1902 and the second of 1906–1909 imposed pro-U.S. laws that could not be overturned by any future Cuban Congress or executive at the risk of provoking yet another U.S. military occupation. Under the reign of the U.S.-authored and militarily imposed Platt Amendment, the hands of Cuban statesmen seemed perpetually tied. Adding to this problem was the willingness of many administrations to use the threat of U.S. intervention as an excuse for repressing critics and opponents.

Perhaps the most dramatic case of this occurred in 1912 when the Cuban government unleashed the Cuban national army as well as volunteer militias and racist vigilantes against black Cubans, leading to a nationwide massacre of an estimated five thousand to eight thousand in less than three months. Government action was justified as a response to armed protest by the black-led Partido Independiente de Color, a party that also included progressive white members. The government had first criminalized the party in 1909; Cuban congressmen cited José Martí and Antonio Maceo's alleged idea that Cuban nationality was "raceless" and the state was anti-racist by virtue of the black-white/ former slave–former slave master alliance that proved fundamental to Cuba's independence wars.[34] When the Partido Independiente de Color responded with a show of force, the Platt Amendment and threat of yet another loss of state power to the Americans propelled officials' presumption that all blacks might be enemies of the state, the nation, and cubanidad. Notably thereafter, political mobilization on the basis of race within parties became strictly taboo. Blacks' activism demanding enforcement of constitutional guarantees of equality and nondiscrimination took place outside the supposedly "nonpartisan" spaces of mutual aid and social clubs to which blacks had been long relegated, since before the Cuba's independence wars.[35] By 1925, when Gerardo Machado was elected, however, Cubans had had enough of government hypocrisy. Cuba had become a true "neocolony," one whose officials and political elite were more accountable to foreign powers and corporate interests than they were to their own citizens. Although divided by both race and class, Cubans were also united by belief in the more egalitarian, more just, and economically nationalist "Cuba that might have been" had the United States never intervened.

Yet within weeks of taking power after campaigning on a platform of U.S. divesture from its monopoly control over key parts of the Cuban economy and government promotion of domestically driven capitalism, Machado presided over an unprecedented expansion of U.S. economic control. Then, in 1928, he arbitrarily declared the extension of his and other lawmakers' current rule. While his predecessors may have been similarly corrupt and equally, if not more, repressive, Machado surpassed any president in terms of brazen hypocrisy and police brutality against young opponents whose social and class standing seemed to have protected them before. He also shamelessly demonstrated contempt for the electoral process. Machado did not simply steal elections as Mario Menocal and Alfredo Zayas had done previously: he canceled them altogether and arbitrarily extended his rule. As generations of other historians have found, populism and pragmatism certainly characterized Machado's policies regarding certain sectors, such as smallholding sugar farmers, known as *colonos,* and middle-class, educated, and organized blacks. Yet these gestures were neither deep enough nor radical enough in their purposes and effects to warrant any broad defense of his rule by the early 1930s.[36] On the contrary, Gerardo Machado became and remains a villain in Cuba's republican-era history, one whose role in worsening Cuba's political alternatives and setting standards of authoritarian rule is both legendary and quite true. Had Machado never taken the path he took, Cuba would not have endured the bloodbaths of the counter-revolutionary rule of Fulgencio Batista in the 1930s or the twists and turns of civilian mobilization, political corruption, and repression yet to come.

Thus, a social revolution based on a year-long countrywide general strike, unarmed protests, and violent subversive groups led by mostly middle- and upper-class students brought down Machado, the most pro-imperialist president turned dictator Cuba had ever known. In 1934, the establishment of a hundred-day revolutionary government that implemented drastic long-awaited reforms gave way to mass repression and counterrevolution. This outcome was mostly thanks to a military coup led by Fulgencio Batista and the direct intervention of the United States on his behalf. Yet by 1940, the unending pressure and protest of average citizens, labor unions, and still-young veterans of the struggle against Machado seemed to have achieved the impossible. Batista unexpectedly granted major concessions, such as the convening of elections for a constitutional convention, the legalization of all political parties, including the Communist Party, and the promulgation of the very rights conceded by the 1933 revolutionary regime that he had sought to destroy. Batista guaranteed the right to strike and women's suffrage overnight. Moreover, Batista dismantled the very structures of his own "strongman" government by allowing free elections—and thereby civilian control.[37]

Still, nearly twenty tumultuous years of civic protest and labor activism against the false democracies of first Machado (1925–1933) and then Batista (1934–1944) led only to the ever deepening corruption of the revolutionaries who took power in 1944. Auténtico rule began in 1944 with the landslide electoral victory of Dr. Ramón Grau San Martín, once head of the revolutionary government that Batista deposed in 1934 and founder of the Auténticos. Nonetheless, feelings of anti-imperialist nationalism and intense commitment to building a more egalitarian, just democracy did not ebb in the late 1940s and early 1950s; they peaked. Cuba was on the verge of greatness or apocalyptic disaster, many Cubans surmised.

By the end of 1951, most Cubans believed that men like Grau and other once prestigious leaders of the battles against Machado and Batista could no longer be trusted. They had become interested merely in preserving and expanding their power, not changing Cuba. Only honest average citizens outside the structures of traditional state power and unconventional, incorruptible politicians— *locos*—like Eduardo Chibás could save the country.

High-born and privately educated by a landed family in Santiago de Cuba, Eddy Chibás descended from slave-owning sugar planters who had launched Cuba's first war for independence from Spain and famously called for the abolition of slavery in 1868. As a law student in the late 1920s, Eddy had joined University of Havana activists in the nationwide social revolution against the Machado dictatorship in 1933. Not only had Chibás and fellow student activists played a central role in bringing down Gerardo Machado in 1933, hundreds of thousands of public school students of all grade levels and thousands of teachers were responsible for launching the last general strike of February and March 1935 by walking out of their classrooms. The brutality with which Batista's armed forces repressed the strike undoubtedly matched the revolutionary threat to the military state and the U.S.-dominated economy that it represented.[38] Chibás not only supported these actions but, along with others, inspired and urged them on, no matter the bloodshed and sacrifice involved. By then, heroism, martyrdom, and messianism were deeply inscribed in the political consciousness of Cubans, born of the ideological sense of national identity resulting from decades of nationalist struggle and multiple U.S. betrayals. These ideals fused together the very soul of the Cuban people, repeatedly uniting them throughout the course of the 1940s and the struggle against Batista, much as they did once Batista had fled and the only path to liberation seemed to lay in opposition to a discredited, hostile United States and toward a future guided by Fidel.

Two years after the fall of the Machado dictatorship in 1933, as the U.S.-backed military rule of Batista struggled to fully stamp out Cuba's revolutionary nationalist movement of sugar workers, students, intellectuals, and middle-class urban radicals, Eddy served months in prison, eventually going into exile in the United States. He returned only when Batista issued a full amnesty de-

cree for all political exiles in 1937 and then surprised everyone by compro-
mising with the most far left of his opponents in 1938, the Cuban Communist
Party and the vast Communist-led labor movement in the countryside. Until
that point, Batista had been principally responsible for the massive expansion
of the army, both in terms of sheer numbers as well as authority, since seizing
power in January 1934 from the revolutionary government established earlier
under Grau San Martín.[39]

Having replaced the all-white, oligarchical officer corps with highly diverse,
highly loyal commanders (many of whom had once been no more than cooks,
blacksmiths, or enlisted men), Batista then consolidated his power at the time of
Chibás's and other exiles' return by reinstalling nearly two hundred ex-officials
of the Machado dictatorship he had once helped destroy in elected positions at
all levels of government.[40] By the end of the decade, the strategy yielded great
fruits: Batista's courting of the reactionary Right, compliance with U.S. objectives, and reliance on martial law to either annihilate or force submission of
the most unruly radical sectors gave way to negotiations and Batista's eventual
alliance with the Communist Party between 1938 and 1944. In a bow to their
newest and most unexpected patron as well as Stalin's "united front" strategy
against fascism, the Cuban Communist Party renamed itself the Partido Socialist Popular (Popular Socialist Party, or PSP) in 1938—a less radical name, to be
sure. Batista's relationship with the PSP stabilized the economy, reestablished
legal guarantees for civil society and, with the help of Communist-led labor
unions, got him elected president of the republic from 1940 to 1944. No longer
was Batista "the focal point of reaction," declared the Central Committee of he
Communist Party, "but the defender of democracy."[41] In effect, the conservative, militarized counterrevolution and highly disciplined Cuban wing of the
Soviet-led international Communist movement had joined hands.

Like most former veteran revolutionaries who fought Machado, Eddy Chibás
initially viewed these developments with horror. He remained unconvinced that
either Batista or the Communists were genuinely interested in defending democracy. Thus, upon returning to Cuba, Chibás immediately turned his energies to
unraveling and discrediting the contradictions of the batistiano-PSP "solution."
First he served as delegate to the Constitutional Convention of 1940 and then
campaigned hard in the election of 1944 on behalf of the Auténticos, especially
presidential candidate Ramón Grau San Martín, whose revolutionary government Batista's coup had deposed in 1934. Soon, however, evidence of graft

and Grau's intolerance for straitlaced, ethical rivals in his own party prompted Chibás to renounce both the Auténticos and all ties to the Grau regime.

In 1946, Chibás founded the Ortodoxos as an uncompromising, more "authentic" offshoot of the Auténticos who had led the revolutionary government of 1933, permanently changing Cuba's political fortunes and redirecting its political culture back to the citizen-based agitation that had defined his generation. Today, Eddy Chibás remains an enigma to most Cubans and historians of Cuba. Apparently, even forcibly, he has dissolved into the shadowy realms of unexplored political legend and individual memory. His work and legacy are deeply documented but barely analyzed in terms of their connection to the larger landscape of citizens' consciousness and the celebration of a renewed anti-imperialist Cuban identity that defined Cuba in the late 1940s and early 1950s. His life seems oddly exempted from the historiography of the period, relegated only to a handful of biographical books. These include a highly encyclopedic memoir published by professional sycophant Luis Conte Agüero in 1955, several anthological tomes published over the last decade in Cuba, and one genuinely well-researched, highly readable scholarly biography produced in the United States.[42]

Consequently, this book starts with the story of Eduardo Chibás's rise to prominence—some observers called it an apotheosis at the time, much as they would later do with reference to Fidel in the late 1950s and early 1960s. It does so because so much of Chibás's activism resulted from and illuminates the participatory culture of Cuban society, from Havana to the most isolated villages of Oriente, where citizens of all ages were weekly riveted as much by his political theatrics as by the sincerity they ascribed to them. Fidel Castro, an unknown and, by many accounts, unliked law student at the time, learned much from the example of Chibás and blatantly copied much more. Castro also studied and rebuked, as most Cubans did, the figure of Fulgencio Batista as one who sought to craft of himself as a peacemaker, a statesman, a modernizer and, as we shall see, even a Cuban "Abraham Lincoln."

Thus, the stories this book seeks to tell—of the views of average Cubans, the actions of civic opposition to corrupt and authoritarian states, and the multiple, often hidden heroism of activists against Batista—are sometimes intertwined and sometimes necessarily overwhelmed by the story that Fidel Castro constructed about himself, the cause of Cuba, and his own centrality in saving Cuba from Batista, if not from Cubans themselves.

Fidel was not simply an early follower of Eddy Chibás: he was a consummate imitator. Not only did he pave the way for a congressional run in 1951
by launching his own twice-daily radio show on the station La Voz del Aire in
October but he, like Eddy, relied on his father's personal fortune to free up time
for political activism during regular work hours and float his campaign.[43] Moreover, he adopted the famous phrase Eddy had used in dozens of tirades against
Auténtico politicians, "Yo acuso" (I accuse), to launch similar public attacks on
the administration of Grau San Martín's Auténtico successor, Carlos Prío Socarrás, starting in January 1952.[44] In the wake of Batista's coup in March 1952,
he also named his clandestine newspaper *El Acusador* (The Accuser).[45] Such
forgotten ironies raise the question of whether historical events or deliberate
efforts helped eclipse the importance and meaning of Eddy Chibás's popularity after Batista fled Cuba and Fidel Castro became the undisputed leader of
the revolution of 1959. Indeed, as noted earlier, Castro seems to have publicly
mentioned Chibás only once after 1959, in mid-January, when he visited his
tomb.[46] In that same month, journalists and intellectuals called him "extinct"
and began relegating him to the role of inspiring Castro and his followers in
the assault on the Moncada military barracks on 26 July 1953, or as merely
another example in Cuba's extensive history of suicide, especially in politics.[47]
Thus, with the exception of that singular homage paid, all public references and
discussion of the legacy of Eddy Chibás mostly vanished from the post-1959
political scene.

Why was Chibás so dangerous or simply so unimportant after 1959, if he had
been so important in fostering the revolutionary Cuba that triumphed over Batista in 1959? This book argues that it was *not* Chibás whom the forces of corruption, stagnation, or demagoguery considered dangerous. Rather, the threat his
name posed came from the civic activism and belief in a non-Communist but
powerful, accountable, and electorally rooted state among the Cuban people to
which the Ortodoxos' activism gave rise. For Chibás's Auténtico opponents as
well as Batista, civic activism and the nationalist consciousness that inspired
citizen control over the state were anathema to retaining power and their own
political ends. For Fidel Castro after 1959, one could easily say the same thing.

Some would argue that Chibás was always a threatening memory to Castro's
leadership after the revolution of 1959 for very similar reasons. However, the
phenomenon of Eddy Chibás is one of only dozens of factors in Cuba's political
history from 1946 to 1958 that many Cuban officials under Fidel and now Raúl

Castro's rule would rather we forget. Given all that happened *after* Chibás died, this is not surprising. *Heroes, Martyrs, and Political Messiahs in Revolutionary Cuba* shows that Chibás himself and, more important, the activist culture of the Cuban public and the many hidden rivals to the heroism of "known" heroes, embody a history that dare not be named. In the Cuba of the 1940s, Cubans from all walks of life were steeped in a culture that invited, even inspired, acts of protest that they themselves came to see as the general responsibility of all Cubans, everyday heroes. As bloody confrontations with the Auténtico government increased before Batista's military coup, opportunities for martyrdom abounded and its prestige increased tenfold. Yet beginning with Chibás and ending with Fidel Castro, Cubans searched frantically, deliberately for a political messiah who would champion the cause of sovereignty, true freedom from without and from within, as well as social justice—or die trying. These years represent a lost opportunity to escape Cuba's neocolonial past and plot an alternative, morally cleansed future without another Batista regime, without a civil war, without the need for a revolution led by armed, politically ambitious men like Fidel Castro. The memory and the history of these years are taboo because they foreshadow neither the return of Batista in a military coup that would topple the Prío government in 1952 nor the protagonism of Fidel Castro, who would launch his armed struggle for revolution in 1953. They reveal a different Cuba, one on the verge of truly dramatic, democratic change.

1

Cuba on the Verge: Martyrdom, Political Culture, and Civic Activism, 1946–1951

ON 7 MAY 1949, SIXTEEN-YEAR-OLD Ramón Rey Martínez wrote to Orthodox Party founder and recent presidential candidate Eduardo Chibás from an isolated hamlet in Camagüey. Addressing him as "Muy Admirado Paladín" (Much Admired Gentleman), Ramón's letter reflected how many young Cubans saw themselves by the late 1940s. Patriotic education in schools, contemporary events, and access to the news through radio and print media led many young people to believe that they could and should influence the actions and nature of the state. Heroism, in this sense, was a self-assigned task, especially peculiar to Cuban youth. In Ramón's letter, one of hundreds "Eddy" received in these years, Ramón urged him to live up to his promises to reform the republic, with slightly ominous warnings of a new, youth-led rebellion to come. Distinguishing himself from his father, whom he called *gobernista* (a government loyalist), the boy insisted, "I am a fervent devotee of evidently virtuous men . . . capable of raising the prestige of our humiliated Patria and the economic condition of our ruined people. And since you have been, until now, a truly incorruptible person, I am decidedly and unconditionally by your prestigious side."[1]

Echoing the former senator's go-for-broke style of speech writing and propensity to emphasize personal rebellion, Ramón drew two examples from his own life to illustrate the strength of his commitment to Chibás's cause. A year earlier, he wrote, when he was only fifteen, Ramón had convinced his mother to defy his father's loyalty to the Auténticos and vote for Chibás on the Orthodox Party ticket by hiding her voter registration card on the day of the election. In Cuba failure to vote was a punishable offense; in small-town Cuba, it was socially offensive as well. Seeking to avoid both, Ramón's mother conceded. Most recently, Ramón had broken the electrical meter on his family's home when his father refused to light the house with candles in solidarity with Chibás's call to regulate the American-owned utility company. Even as he expressed admiration, Ramón also claimed rebellious motives and the nationalist consciousness driving them as his own. "I know that some of your demoralized adversaries . . . call you *loco*," he concluded, but given the fact that nearly all of Cuba's past presidents had turned out to be thieves, "we should take our chances with a *loco* like you just in case you know how to govern with dignity." Although still far from voting age, Ramón signed off with Chibás's emotionally incendiary slogan, "Unconditionally at your side, *Vergüenza Contra Dinero*" (Humility Fights Money).[2] An awkward phrase in translation, the slogan referenced a cultural etymology inherited from Cuba's rural communities, where the term *sinvergüenza* (literally, "without shame") represented the greatest of personal insults: to be shameless meant not recognizing that one's economic power, comfort, and social prestige derived from the labor, sacrifice, and likely exploitation of others. In a context of massive government corruption where the impunity of politicians reigned, the Ortodoxos' slogan asserted that the opposite, *vergüenza*, that is, consciousness and modesty amid wealth or power (such as that embodied in Chibás himself), could defeat a political system rife with bribery, theft of state coffers, and complicity with both practices.

Far from incidental, the perspective expressed in this and other letters conveys two defining features of Cuban political culture in the 1940s and early 1950s: first, the sense that citizen participation in national politics was a personally heroic duty; and second, the role of Eduardo Chibás in setting up a standard of political engagement with the public through the media that relied on constant critique of the failings of the state. Unlike most politicians, Chibás credited the majority of the Cuban people with a deep reserve of democratic values and an innate instinct for mass acts of bravery; these qualities, insisted Chibás, had propelled Cuba forward since its founding as a nation.

At the time he received the teenager's letter, Chibás had barely begun a six-month prison sentence. Jailed for calumny, Chibás had accused three of Cuba's Supreme Court justices of accepting bribes to drop an inquiry into the legality of increasing Cuba's already inflated electrical rates by as much as 60 percent.[3] Profits from the rate increase accrued to a U.S.-owned monopoly whose name, the Cuban Electric Company, defied its neocolonial origins. A primary beneficiary of past dictator Gerardo Machado's largesse, the utility enjoyed preferential tax rates and land rights that neither the Cuban state nor its citizens enjoyed. In an aside to the gigantic United Fruit Company, or El Pulpo (The Octopus), another monopolistic company despised throughout Latin America, Chibás called the utility the Anti-Cuban Electric Company and El Pulpo Eléctrico.[4] Actions like these certainly made Chibás the central character in a political drama of failed democratic aspirations that most Cubans, especially historians of the 1940s and 1950s, have wanted to forget. Yet as this chapter shows, Chibás's popularity did not so much catalyze civic activism in Cuban society as prove a commitment to civic activism that was already there.

The reason for Eddy Chibás's appeal—indeed, the reason he was seen as a selfless loco or madman amid hordes of self-interested hypocrites—lay in the crushing weight of nationalist consciousness and anti-imperialist sentiments among Cubans at the time. Consequently, when Chibás founded La Ortodoxía as a movement in 1947, his rivals in the ruling Auténtico Party simply could not control a stage increasingly crowded by average citizens committed to this task. From the mid-1940s to the early 1950s, government-sanctioned violence and widespread corruption characterized Cuba's brief "democratic moment," but so did civic activism, unarmed struggles for political liberty, and a flourishing, expanding media. The promise that Eddy Chibás represented was only one of many solutions that Cubans found in themselves, particularly through lessons learned from a proudly revolutionary culture and recent political history of triumphant and then repressed social revolution in the 1930s. Nationalism manifested in the willingness of millions of Cubans to support Chibás in multiple, now largely forgotten, unarmed protests against political repression and the theft of public funds.

It also emerged in the unexpected theatrics of young university students and self-appointed Chibás protégés such as Fidel Castro and key allies, including covert members of the Communist Youth. Like Chibás and the Ortodoxos, Fidel, the Communists, and other young activists mobilized collective mass protests of anti-imperialism in historically meaningful ways. Meanwhile, many of Cuba's most prestigious intellectuals pioneered the use of radio as a vehicle for civic education and reforming the role of government. Average Cubans enacted everyday loyalty to the nation through street protests, personal habits such as self-conscious consumerism, and writing letters to politicians like

Chibás that demanded a response. In short, pent-up frustration with traditional politicians did not deplete activists' reserves but fueled them.

"¡Morir por la Patria es Vivir!": Political Martyrdom in the Late 1940s

As Louis A. Pérez has recently shown, Cubans dwelt in the past during the late 1940s in order to make their nation gloriously just and culturally whole amid the seemingly never ending onslaught of U.S. political and economic will. Yet it was not simply Cuban historians who studied the past with a purpose. "The past had never really passed because it had never really ended," writes Pérez. By the 1940s, the past was "a presence, an awareness of something pending" that needed to be corrected because its legacies continually impeded Cubans' ability to create "what the nation was meant to be and what it should have been—and what it was. The past developed into the adversary of the present."[5] In libraries, public plazas, conversations, and the press, Cubans of all social classes did so as well. Surely, the opposition of investors to Cuban government initiatives to protect local interests and multiple U.S. military interventions had fragmented the narrative of Cuba's march to stability, sovereignty, and democracy since the first (1898–1902) and second U.S. military occupations (1906–1909) of Cuba. For this reason, Cubans took seriously a past that united the generations. "Morir por la patria es vivir" (To die for the fatherland is to live) was not simply a line from the national anthem taught to schoolchildren, it was the central thesis of Cuba's national existence. For citizens who supported or participated in the ever-increasing number of street protests and the island's expanding press, civic activism had become a way of life. Having "liv[ed] with a wrong that needed to be righted, as both a state of mind and a condition of the heart" for so long, citizens in these years recalled repeatedly Cuba's history of "thwarted nationhood" and defied its continual betrayal as much by self-assigned "allies" in the United States as by generations of their own republican leaders.[6] Few seemed more aware of the sins of Cuban leaders and the anger that knowledge of them could ignite than Eduardo Chibás.

Before founding his own party, the Partido del Pueblo Cubano-Ortodoxo (the Orthodox Party of the Cuban People), Eddy Chibás had served as delegate to Cuba's Constitutional Convention of 1940 as well as congressman and then

senator for the Partido Auténtico. However, he was best known for his irrever-
ent, impassioned weekly radio address delivered on CMQ Radio virtually every
Sunday night since 1944. So popular was his show among Cubans that those
as far away as Ohio tuned into short-wave radio every Sunday so they could
be part of the one-man movement, one-man show that was Eddy Chibás.[7] As a
former student rebel himself, Eduardo Chibás knew all too well the power and
the pride that Cuba's youth and intellectuals had taken in galvanizing protests
in the past. Indeed, if Batista emerged from the 1930s and early 1940s as a favorite of U.S. business and consular officials alike, Cuban youth consolidated a
proprietary grasp on concepts of purity and martyrdom for the sake of the nation.
For the next two decades, every successive generation of youth not only inherited
the mantle of heroic defenders of national ideals of justice, liberty, and political morality; they assumed the mandate of reminding past young rebel leaders
who had become elder statesman that they needed to honor their own personal
pasts and the martyrdom that many leaders, especially Auténtico Party founders
like Ramón Grau San Martín, Carlos Prío Socarrás, and Eduardo Chibás, had
barely escaped. The best example of just how far Cubans took their belief in the
cleansing power of martyrdom could be found in the emerging acceptability of
suicide as a politically legitimate and socially galvanizing act.

Echoes of this view resonated in the introductory remarks that a young Ortodoxo named Fidel Castro made in Santiago when Chibás announced his presidential bid in May 1948: "This lunatic, out of sublime craziness for the sublime
ideal of an improved Cuba, values the recognition of his own people above all
else. . . . The day Chibás senses a reduction in citizens' affection he would put
a bullet through his heart, not out of cowardice in the face of failure, but so that
his self-sacrifice ensures the victory of his disciples."[8] Although Castro was
only a twenty-two-year-old law student at the time, his words represented Cubans' long-standing cultural endorsement of the idea of suicide as a political act
that could break down walls of censorship and public apathy, especially amid
civilian struggles for justice and in the absence of a national war.[9]

As Louis A. Pérez has persuasively revealed, Cuba had the highest suicide
rate in the world by the late 1940s and 1950s for reasons that bore little or no
relation to those prevalent in other countries with similarly high rates, such as
postwar Germany, Japan, or France.[10] Certainly, the cult of death as the highest
symbol of selfless patriotism had been inscribed in Cubans as early as the 1860s
by way of the national anthem: have no fear of a glorious death, repeatedly in-

toned the chorus, for "morir por la patria es vivir!" Long after Cuban independence was formally established with the end of the first U.S. military occupation in 1902, however, an exemplary death *without* the benefit of "pure" martyrdom that nineteenth-century independence heroes enjoyed was still unusually valued. Importantly, some of the most prominent civilian allies of independence leaders José Martí and Antonio Maceo killed themselves in the wake of peace after the 1895 war against Spain and the start of U.S. interventionist policies in Cuba in 1898. Subsequent decades brought generations of citizens to a "consensus of remarkable endurance . . . around the efficacy of self-immolation in defense of patria, as a source of national pride and illustration of what it meant to be Cuban. The duty to sacrifice and to die became deeply embedded in the dominant formulations of nationality, where it acted to influence the character of national conduct."[11]

Only a few months before Fidel Castro dared Eddy Chibás to live up to his promises or die by his own hand for not trying hard enough in May 1948, the mayor of Havana had done just that. After more than a year of struggle, mostly against fellow members of the Auténtico Party, Mayor Manuel Fernández Supervielle had been unable to secure funding for a much needed aqueduct due to the obstructionism of corrupt allies, including the Auténtico president Ramón Grau San Martín. In a suicide note, Fernández Supervielle minced no words in citing his "political failure" to fulfill campaign promises and his betrayal of the people as the reason for his death. "As a man with a conscience," he wrote before shooting himself, "I prefer suicide."[12]

In response, *habaneros* (Havana residents) and politicians alike announced the glory of his martyrdom and erected a monument to the mayor celebrating his personal honor and selfless political creed. Ironically, the man most responsible for Fernández Supervielle's failure, Grau San Martín, delivered his eulogy, an act that garnered further prestige for Fernández Supervielle even as it increased the public's disdain for the hypocrisy of Grau.[13]

Given this background, it is perhaps not surprising that Eddy Chibás *did* shoot himself as Fidel Castro had seemingly predicted—not once but twice, neither time in the heart. Utterly lost to public memory, Eddy first shot himself in the arm while running as delegate to the Constitutional Assembly of 1940. Ostensibly an accident, the act garnered him only a few headlines at the time and enduring public ridicule in *Política Cómica,* a satirical newspaper that prophesied Chibás would surely do it again (figure 1).[14] After his successful senatorial

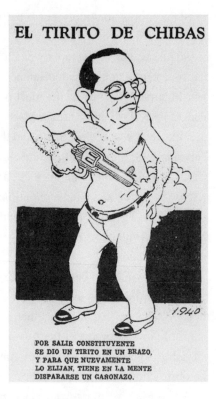

EL TIRITO DE CHIBAS

POR SALIR CONSTITUYENTE
SE DIO UN TIRITO EN UN BRAZO,
Y PARA QUE NUEVAMENTE
LO ELIJAN, TIENE EN LA MENTE
DISPARARSE UN CAÑONAZO.

Figure 1. This political cartoon satirized Eduardo Chibás for his self-inflicted gunshot wound to the arm as a show intended to serve his bid for election to the Constitutional Convention of 1940. (*Política Cómica*, 2 June 1940)

run in 1946, the pro-Auténtico newspaper *Prensa Libre* satirized Chibás's 1939 "accident" as a vehicle for gaining free publicity and national sympathy with the radio play *The Suicide of Chibás (A Horrifying Drama Banned for Minors of Less Than 40 Years of Age).*[15]

A one-man show starring Chibás himself, the drama made fun of Cubans' national obsession with martyrdom as the most genuine proof of nationalism. In it, the character Eddy admits to having failed in his quest for political perfection, unable to extinguish all corruption and all political violence generated by the "gangsterism" of the time. "I am going to commit suicide in this radio broadcast, killing myself before this radio audience, before this invisible public, kill myself in the presence of my radio listeners," gushed the parodied Eddy. "May no one detain my hand, may no one get in the middle. . . . Attention: I am going to shoot . . . (an explosion is heard. The body falls along with the microphone. Shouts. Panic. Tears. The suicide of Chibás is announced over the very same broadcast. The republic, from one end to the other, dissolves into vast pain, immense commotion)." Act 4 ends with the embarrassing revelation that Eddy had been treated for only a tiny wound to the "tippy-tip tip of a finger on his left hand."[16]

Incredibly, almost five years later, Chibás staged an eerily similar scene on his national radio broadcast after several months of launching attacks and counter-attacks against possibly the only uncorrupted member of President Carlos Prío Socarrás's cabinet, Aureliano Sánchez Arango, a fellow veteran of Chibás's own anti-Machado activism of the 1930s and Prío's minister of education. In response to Eddy's claims that he was hiding millions in investments abroad, Sánchez Arango in turn accused Chibás of the moral crime of secretly exploiting *campesinos* (peasants) on isolated family estates. In the end, neither man provided clear-cut evidence of the sins of the other and each hardened his position, organizing Ortodoxo and Auténtico youth rallies that competed for public support.[17]

Then, on 5 August 1951, after reiterating his accusations against Sánchez Arango, the real Eddy shot himself in the lower part of his abdomen, shouting, "¡Pueblo de Cuba, levántate y anda! ¡Pueblo de Cuba, despierta! ¡Este es el último aldabonazo!" (People of Cuba, get up and walk! People of Cuba, awaken! This is the last knock on the door!)[18] With the radio transmission cut after this final phrase, most of Eddy's half-million listeners remained unaware for hours that he had shot himself. Rushed to the hospital by fellow Ortodoxos, Chibás responded to the question of where he had been shot, "In the belly. . . . What a shame it wasn't in the heart!"[19] In the days that followed, Chibás monitored the effects of his actions on the public. Requests to be fulfilled in the event of his sudden death included asking party stalwarts to organize a rally to celebrate a rural school he had built with money from the sale of a coffee estate; he also expressed pleasure that Catholic masses were being offered for him across the island.[20]

Eleven days after his last radio broadcast, Eddy Chibás died. Now more than ever, he assumed the status of selfless patriot, victimized martyr, and would-be messiah in the eyes of millions. Embalmed and displayed at the University of Havana's Aula Magna, where hundreds of thousands of mourners wept and prayed for the republic by his side, the body of Eddy Chibás rode to its final resting place in Havana's Cementerio Colón on an unprecedented crest of over three hundred thousand agonizing souls (figure 2).[21] Apparent to all was the fact that not only did the mourners outnumber those who attended the burials of greats from the independence struggle but that the massive crowd's presence was entirely voluntary, not the result of favors dispensed, jobs in the civil ser-

Figure 2. Hundreds of thousands of Cubans paid their last respects to beloved leader "Eddy" Chibás in August 1951. Laid out in an open casket at the University of Havana's Aula Magna, Chibás's body featured a commemorative edition of *Bohemia* honoring his lifelong activism on his chest. His funeral procession following this public wake drew nearly a million mourners, paralyzing Havana. (Courtesy of the Archivo Nacional de Cuba)

vice, or membership in labor unions. Cubans were grateful to Chibás for who he was, not what he offered them in material terms.[22]

Yet the impact of Chibás's suicidal publicity stunt of 1951 makes sense only when seen against the backdrop of the real-life national drama that he, other Ortodoxos, and student activists of varying political stripes had carefully played out in the previous five years. While Chibás was its central star and other Ortodoxos a supporting cast, the protagonists he invited to join him on-stage were the majority of the Cuban people. This began in the closing weeks of 1946 when Chibás broke with previous allies of the 1933 revolution in the Partido Auténtico. A decidedly rich man who appointed himself spokesman for the people, Eddy Chibás enticed followers by arguing that a shared impeccable heritage of political ideals inherited from *los mambises,* nineteenth-century nationalist revolutionaries, trumped age, class, race, and to a certain extent gender in uniting Cubans in one task: saving Cuba.

To Build a Civically Responsible State:
Patriotism as Personal Duty

Cuba's top intellectuals and political commentators shared many of the same convictions young student activists claimed as their own in the late 1940s. Above all, outrage, pride, and belief in the need for change united the views expressed by Cuba's top political analysts and intellectuals Rafael García Barcena, Raúl Roa, Francisco Ichaso, Jorge Mañach, Ramiro Guerra y Sánchez, and many others at the time. Soon to form the core leadership of Chibás's Orthodox Party, they were all members of the generation that lived the initial idealism, violence, and social revolution of the Machado government as well as its slow demise between 1925, when Machado was elected as an anti-imperialist candidate, and 1933, when he was brought down after multiple general strikes and mass protests for betraying the very nationalism he espoused. By the late 1940s, these intellectuals often joined forces in publishing dialogic opinion pieces analyzing Cuba's current affairs. They also revived the strategy of bringing intellectual discourse to the masses that legendary anti-Machado student leader and Communist Party founder Julio Antonio Mella had launched in the early 1920s.

Called La Universidad Popular José Martí, Mella's project combined a public lecture series with an open public forum that invited workers, professors, and affluent students to engage in face-to-face discussions about the economic, social, and political issues facing Cuba. In many ways, Mella's Universidad Popular recalled José Martí's network of "revolutionary clubs" of the 1890s among exiles in the United States and night school for black "Antillean" workers, La Liga Antilla. In the name of reviving revolution, they strove for the same thing: cross-class communication, mutual political radicalization, the building of trust in political leaders and, above all, national unity. Although far from advocating armed struggle, the CMQ radio station claimed the mantle of past revolutionaries Martí and Mella when it launched a series of educational courses and informative follow-up debates among invited guests called La Universidad del Aire (University of the Air).

Starting in October 1949 and ending in 1950, the title of the course spoke to the urgency with which Cubans increasingly perceived their political moment: Actualidad y Destino de Cuba (The Current State and Destiny of Cuba). In its inaugural session, Goar Mestre, general director of the radio station, recognized that because most Cubans owned or had access to radios, its power was nothing short of "atomic." The time had come to use radio in order to inspire Cubans to act now and forever change Cuba, before it was too late. Despite the relative prosperity that World War II sugar prices had brought to the island economy, "there is, without a doubt, a great sense of discontent in Cuban life. We gain nothing from ignoring it, nor by resigning ourselves to it. We have to ask why that discontent exists and how we can remedy the ills that cause it."[23] Immediately following Mestre, Jorge Mañach put it even more bluntly. Mañach's reputation preceded him: admired statesman for his contributions to the Constitutional Convention of 1940, graduate of Harvard University in 1920, professor at the University of Havana, and director of the University of the Air. Author of Cuba's first best-selling biography of José Martí in 1933, Mañach only broadened his notability by reaching across class and educational divides by intellectualizing radio.[24] One would be hard-pressed to find a Cuban today, Mañach remarked, who is satisfied with the republic: the *fauna parasitaria* (parasitic fauna) of the political class "are the only Cubans for whom Cuba does not seem a pained and painful *patria*."[25]

In subsequent radio classes, veteran of the 1895 war General Enrique Loynaz del Castillo echoed these views even more dramatically: the promises of the Manifesto of Montecristi that launched Cuba's last war for independence reflected the moral teachings of Jesus Christ.[26] Rebuking those who doubted the power of moral righteousness in politics, Loynaz del Castillo argued that citizens should not invert the word order of the Ortodoxos' slogan to see the struggle as "dinero contra vergüenza," because calculating it in such terms ensured they would lose. Nor could they define the battle for salvation cynically as a matter of "dinero contra dinero" (money fighting money) because doing so reinforced the power of the rich and left average citizens out.[27] While private capital gave Cuba the illusion of progress and development, the reality of progress and development could only be achieved through honest use of Cuban state coffers, the richest of Latin America.[28] In other words, Loynaz del Castillo called for state intervention in the amelioration of poverty and historically rooted inequalities. This principle would become part and parcel of the Ortodoxos' political creed.

"Vergüenza Contra Dinero" marked the Ortodoxos' official ideology of "socialism." Endorsed by Eddy Chibás himself, Ortodoxo socialism stood in direct contradiction to the policies and practices of the Soviet-led Cuban Communists and his own former allies in the Auténtico Party such as Grau San Martín. *Socialism,* like *revolution,* was a catchword emptied of any content by the PSP Communists and the Auténticos' distorted appropriation and overuse.

Similarly, other lectures and discussions of the Universidad del Aire argued for a stronger civil society. Cross-class pressure groups, the act of listening to radio itself, autonomous labor unions, and civic mobilizations broadened Cuban democracy by catalyzing separate spheres of political power *outside* the state and forcing the state to respond.[29] Carlos Márquez Sterling, president of the Constitutional Convention of 1940, even called for public financing of all political campaigns.[30] Rubio Padilla went so far as to challenge the unwritten rules of Cuban political discourse. "One has to guard against a permanent revolutionary psychosis," he said. Overreliance on the term *revolution* not only emptied it of meaning and condemned Cubans to repeat failed formulas for change, it reduced democracy to demagoguery. A new vision and model of civic activism were required.[31]

While intellectuals saturated the airwaves with political theory using plain, unembroidered language, they also wrote more formal essays in popular magazines. Often dialogic pieces, these essays meant to provoke public discussion.[32] Former student leaders of the revolution of 1933 who were now university professors and writers used the opportunity to trace Cuba's recent political history. This exposed the highly checkered past of former *machadistas* who had quietly reentered the political fold. For example, Raúl Roa dredged up the pro-

Figure 3. Presented in the guise of a sample ballot for the election of 1948, this propaganda flyer allegedly promoted Liberal candidates for president and vice president. Yet photographs depicting Batista's origins and long political career as Cuba's "strongman" at the bottom left little doubt who was really running behind their bid for office: "If I now reincorporate myself into politics, it is for the purpose of continuing my struggle for the worker, the peasant, for he who has little or nothing," the banner quoted Batista.

Machado roots of the revived Liberal Party, particularly those of its presidential candidate, Dr. Ricardo Nuñez Portuondo, Batista's choice and, according to campaign propaganda, a clear political stand-in for El Hombre (figure 3). Putting people like him back in power, argued Roa, was like returning Louis XVIII to the throne of France.[33]

In a similarly impassioned opinion piece, Lucilo de la Peña summed up how most intellectuals viewed Cuba's options in much starker terms: "Cubans! Now! Now or Never! Either a Cuban Revolution or a Communist one! *There is no other choice.*"[34] Importantly, de la Peña's essay was not written in the hyperbolic style so typical of Cold War–era opinion pieces in the United States at the time. Nor was he rattling the skeleton of Cuba's Communist Party in order to spark electoral panic. Rather, de la Peña recognized that the PSP gained adherents in Cuba because it spoke in a unified voice for radical social equality and did not quibble over the role of the state in being the primary instrument for achieving it. However, the PSP had gained traction over the years since its legalization in 1938 because of its pragmatism and willingness to work with enemies of democracy—namely, its own primary enemy, Fulgencio Batista and the Cuban army—in exchange for power. The frustration of poor sectors of Cuban society with an electoral system built on vote buying, fraud, and the influence of wealthy donors was, according to de la Peña, going to implode their faith in constitutionalism if something was not done.

Arguably, Cubans *had* waited for the state to implement a nationalist agenda of public works, education, guarantees against racial discrimination, labor rights, and agrarian reform that would transform Cuba's socioeconomic landscape since the independence wars. Today, de la Peña's warning reads like an uncanny prediction of events that lay ahead. In the late 1940s, however, the sense of urgency to save the republic was fueled, many Cubans felt, as much by the brazen behavior of Auténticos, once heralded as revolutionaries, as it was by the raw outrage that Eduardo Chibás unleashed in denouncing their most shameless moves.

The Insanity of Chibás and the Impact of Auténtico Corruption

More than just a national celebrity or a popular statesman who candidly censured former allies as crooks, Chibás strove to embody the slogan of the Orthodox Party that he formally founded in 1947, "Vergüenza Contra Dinero." He did this by financing his own campaigns through the sale of his family's palatial Vedado mansion and much of his personal inheritance rather than compromise his ethics to rich donors.[35] With less than a month to campaign for president after announcing his candidacy in May 1948, Eddy also famously invited every Cuban household to see itself as collaborating with Ortodoxo goals by publicly displaying a broom—a symbol of sweeping away political corruption—on front porches and doorsteps as a mark of universal public scorn.[36] He also collected almost $4,000 in spare change from supporters in less than three days.[37] In this, Eddy Chibás clearly broke the mold of Cuban politicians, embracing his reputation as "el loco," the lunatic, among detractors and supporters alike. The term proved fortuitous: in the same company were none other than Cuba's great martyrs Antonio Guiteras, "el muchacho loco," assassinated on Batista's orders in 1935, and before him, José Martí himself.[38]

As his leadership in the Orthodox Party subsequently showed, Eddy Chibás believed that the Auténticos' willingness to form pacts with other parties in order to secure dominant voting blocks in Cuba's semi-parliamentarian system sharply undermined long-awaited concrete goals, in addition to the problem of increasing corruption. Batista had earlier set this pattern by allying with his former archenemies the Communists in 1938. Through their leverage with labor unions, he had won the presidential election.[39] Yet it was the very public fight against graft that made Eddy distinct in the eyes of Cubans. This was especially true during and after the pivotal year of 1946, when Auténtico corruption reached new heights and levels of bravado, mostly facilitated through the Presidential Palace.

By many other measures, 1946 should have marked an auspicious, pivotal year in Cuba's political economy. As World War II drew to a close, food shortages ended and prices stabilized in Cuba. Yet citizens seemed increasingly convinced that their country was on the edge of either total moral collapse or democratic transformation. Once considered the greatest hope for the consolidation of sovereignty, clean politics, and positive social change, the youthful, educated revolutionaries who made up La Generación del 33 quickly became known as La Degeneración del 33.[40] After two years of Auténtico rule under Grau San Martín, Cubans could not help but conclude that the great democratic era of social justice, national sovereignty, and prosperity for all was being obstructed daily by those once considered its heralds in the Auténtico Party. As Chibás repeatedly pointed out, no better example existed than the system of public education.

Even during the worst years of Batista's de facto military rule in the 1930s, citizens' long-standing belief in education as a great social equalizer persisted, especially in Cuba's neglected rural areas: schools and dedicated teachers would make up for what government could not or would not do to improve social mobility and level the playing field. Ironically, Batista had played a central role in catalyzing the educational system's transformative potential in 1936 when he dedicated a large portion of the military budget to the creation of civic-military academies in far-flung reaches of the nation. Staffed by 750 military instructors, the schools provided basic scholastic training as well as classes in health and agricultural techniques to an estimated thirty-five thousand children and twenty thousand adults. The program soon proved a genuine and tactical success. For Batista, its populist dividends more than compensated for the expense. In order to fund it, Batista had instituted a 9¢ tax on each one-hundred-pound sack of sugar Cuba produced, famously known as Inciso K. While Batista's handpicked president at the time balked (a position that soon contributed to his impeachment), mill owners "accepted the sugar tax as a sort of insurance against labor trouble" and an opportunity to end funding of small, private schools on their own plantations.[41] Ironically, Raúl Castro, Fidel's younger brother, was a product of one of Batista's escuelas cívico-militares, located near their father's massive farm.[42]

By the early 1940s, access to education was widely seen as more than a panacea for ideological division or a substitute for genuine social legislation; it had become a constitutionally guaranteed right that could not be ignored. Yet in 1943, after decades of posting declines in the illiteracy rate, the Ministry of Education revealed that the trend had been reversed: illiteracy was once again on the rise. Ten years later, it remained at the same stagnant level of 23 percent nationally, and in remote rural areas long dominated by U.S. companies like Oriente, the rate was twice as high as the national average.[43]

Against this backdrop, Grau San Martín appointed Luis Pérez Espinos, a former member of Antonio Guiteras's Joven Cuba, his first minister of education in 1944. Impeccably honest and energetic, Pérez Espinos ordered the construction of two thousand new classrooms and admirably expanded breakfast and lunch programs, institutionalizing them in new dining facilities and state-provisioned dispensaries.[44] Deeming him "too popular for his own good," Grau forced Pérez Espinos to resign. Replacing him as minister, Diego Vicente Tejera, the son of a famous socialist and independence activist whose fame once rivaled Martí's, fared no better. Tejera's "popularity" stemmed not from effective policies but his distribution of thousands of sinecures to allies and enemies alike.[45] Known in Cuba as *botellas,* this early twentieth-century term for sinecure referenced the idea that babies born to mothers who lacked sufficient breast milk would survive only if they had access to milk in a bottle. Although the term conveyed collective recognition of just how tempting theft of public coffers could be amid an environment of scarce resources, Cubans' universal resentment of the practice lay deep.[46]

While distributing botellas was nothing new, Grau forced Tejera to resign on these very grounds, only to appoint José Alemán his new minister of education. Known for outright thievery and ostentatious real estate investments that included the purchase and profitable resale of Florida's Key Biscayne, Alemán took the use of sinecures as well as flattery for Grau to unprecedented heights. A "golden accountant" with twenty years' experience at the ministry before he headed it, Alemán "knew where the money was and how to tap into it."[47] Because the Constitution of 1940 protected current officials from prosecution, Alemán operated with total immunity, and therefore total impunity. Alemán even had the audacity to take over and shut down La Escuela Normal José Martí, the country's sole training school for rural teachers, an act that slammed the door on improving literacy where it was most needed.[48]

When the Senate passed a no-confidence vote against Alemán in October 1947, Grau refused to dismiss him, appointing him to the vague, even less accountable position of cabinet minister without portfolio.[49] In response, Alemán staged his own "pro-confidence" rally and refused to cancel it even after an altercation between an armed Alemán supporter and a student protester left the high-schooler dead only minutes before the event was scheduled to begin.[50]

With Alemán's appointment and apparent impenetrable permanency, Grau established a pattern that extended well beyond the education ministry into other branches of government. This included the army, where Grau fired Batista's most despised generals, such as Franciso Tabernilla, only to promote a mediocre, obese officer named Genovevo Pérez Dámera five times in less than six months in order to justify making him chief of staff.[51] To cement loyalty and ensure power, Grau also sought to co-opt armed gangs, euphemistically called *grupos de acción,* tied to factions of the Partido Auténtico and structures of law enforcement. The most important of these were the Movimiento Socialista Revolucionario (MSR), headed by cabinet minister José Alemán, police chief

Mario Salabarría, and ex-Communist Rolando Masferrer, a congressman from Holguín; and the Unión Insurreccional Revolucionaria (UIR), led by Emilio Tro, director of the National Police Academy and backed by politically ambitious university students such as Fidel Castro. Whether out of a desire for revenge and control over lucrative coffers or as a reaction to the culture of impunity that Batista had cultivated for nearly a decade, these groups warred with each other, to the horror of citizens, especially in the capital. Nighttime shootouts and at times spectacular hours-long standoffs involving police became commonplace. Inevitably, civilians were often caught in the crossfire.[52]

For most youthful observers like Lionel Soto, a literature student at the University of Havana, elected leader of FEU, and a secret militant of the Communist Youth, it was important to stay out of the fray. Like many opponents of the regime, Soto believed that Grau saw his hands-off approach to political violence as a means for engendering peace through the gradual extinction of one side by the other.[53] Nonetheless, many politically active male students at the University of Havana felt they must carry weapons. In fact, Soto first met Fidel Castro when he came by Soto's apartment to retrieve a pistol Soto had taken from him during a dispute with a fellow student before it was broken up by police.[54]

By December 1946, one major event made the sincerity of Grau's approach to eradicating political violence downright laughable. In that month, Havana's Hotel Nacional hosted the world's greatest "mob summit." Organized by Meyer Lansky, a notorious former rum-runner in the United States during Prohibition (1913–1934) and Mafia chieftain, summit participants gathered in Havana to plot new business strategies in addition to celebrating the arrival of mobster Lucky Luciano to Cuba, recently released from ten years in a U.S. prison. Delegates to the mob convention took over the top four floors of the Hotel Nacional, feasting and conspiring for days. Apparently bored by the local talent, they even flew in Frank Sinatra for additional entertainment.[55]

Like Lansky, who had been Batista's "personal banker" during the 1930s when Batista amassed a fortune of $44 million and stashed much of it away in Swiss banks, Luciano had been able to secure legal residency in Cuba because of his ties to the Presidential Palace.[56] In Luciano's case, however, it was not Batista who helped gain him legal entry to Cuba but a host of Batista's enemies close to Auténtico Party bosses, including Paulina Alsina de Grau, the president's widowed sister-in-law, Auténtico Senate president Eduardo Suárez

Rivas, and Francisco Prío Socarrás, brother of Grau's prime minister and eventual successor, Carlos. As part of the deal, General Pérez Dámera, Grau's chief of staff, generously agreed to sell Luciano his own opulent residence on favorable terms.[57]

Indeed, the selection of Cuba as headquarters for the U.S. Mafia capped off a year in which the public's ability to change or even influence the behavior of public officials seemed to wane by the second. Apparently, neither Grau nor the leaders of his party seemed to care how profoundly their actions had dashed the hopes of millions of Cubans who had granted the Auténticos a landslide victory in 1944. Articulating public disgust with Grau, Cuba's most popular magazine, *Bohemia,* lauded his presumed successor, minister of labor Carlos Prío Socarrás, two years early.[58] Caricaturists, whose profession was always a profitable one in Cuba, parodied the futility of public protest and the greed that motivated aspirants to power within the Auténtico Party. On a single day, one satirist reported, a plethora of (useless) organizations had protested before the Presidential Palace, including La Unión de Jóvenes con Novias Pero Sin Empleo (The Union of Young Guys with Girlfriends but No Jobs) and La Sociedad de Ciudadanos Enemigos de las Motonetas (The Society of Citizen-Enemies of Uncomfortable Bus Seats). In addition, quipped the satirists, fifty-five thousand members of the Association of Auténtico Youth, all between the ages of eighteen and seventy, had paraded before the Presidential Palace to demand the government add another "K" to the Inciso K sugar tax—making it the Inciso KK—since the wealth it currently produced was not enough to go around.[59]

Against this background of shameless fraud, flagrant hypocrisy, and growing (if humorous) fatalism, Eddy Chibás launched a moral tirade against Auténtico corruption via radio in December 1946. On the twelfth of that month, Chibás broadcast the most famous and riveting speech of his political career. Focusing his rage on the betrayal of minister of education José Alemán as symptomatic of the sickness of the whole administration, Chibás demanded,

What have you done, bandit, with the funds destined to buy paper, pencils and other material for public schools? What have you done, bandit, with the 400,000 pesos conceded by the Council of Ministers . . . so that there would be breakfast in all of the public schools of Cuba? What are you doing, bandit, with the 100,000 pesos you have robbed on a monthly basis from the account of the Ministry of Education using made-up names? Where are the funds going, bandit, that belong to the Escuela Normal Rural José Martí, that despite its great utility to the peasant class, you have arbitrarily closed, violently expelling its teachers and students with your pistol-wielding gangs? . . . You are, Alemán, the greatest scoundrel of a Minister of Education that the Republic has ever known. You are even speculating with the breakfast of school kids. To think that I have spent 20 years making revolution only to contemplate things like this now![60]

Although well known for his inflammatory style, Chibás exceeded the normal bounds of oratory in calling Alemán what he was—a shameless bandit—not once but several times in the course of his radio broadcast.

Five days later, *Prensa Libre*'s editor and director Sergio Carbó, a prominent member of the deposed revolutionary government of 1933 headed by Grau, published a reaction whose sentiments many surely shared. "One might call him *loco,* now that speaking all the truths that so many officials once said in order to gain their political posts has apparently become a form of insanity . . . but no one can accuse Chibás of having ever compromised nor clumsily watered down [his values]."[61] Like Carbó, journalist Guido García Inclán urged Chibás to embrace his "insanity," despite the fact that the epithet was originally the work of his detractors. "Those who have stolen and destroyed the republic are called *vivos* [the live ones]. Those who have the opportunity to steal from the state and refuse are called *bobos* [fools]. You, Chibás, they call *loco*— precisely for having always defended decency and honesty. They call you *loco* for having known how to bravely insert yourself into that struggle between *vergüenza* [humility] and *desvergüenza* [shamelessness]."[62]

In the wake of Chibás's extraordinary radio address, virtually no one in the Auténtico camp who had previously stood with José Alemán subsequently supported him publicly. Unwilling to accept the reality of his declining popularity and naively hoping for a reelection bid, President Grau San Martín subsequently struggled to revive his own history as an anti-imperialist revolutionary and symbolically shore up his government's contributions to education through two means. First, he launched a publicity campaign in favor of his educational policies and, second, he sanctioned a wildly ill-conceived expedition of Dominican exiles and young Cuban recruits to topple Rafael Trujillo, longtime dictator of the Dominican Republic. Grau funded both moves through Inciso K, the million-dollar fund supposedly reserved for Cuban children's education. He also appointed the minister of education, Alemán—rather than a military officer—to head the armed liberation of the Dominican Republic. These efforts ultimately revealed the fragility of Grau's revolutionary resolve. Yet they also energized the public's willingness to back and legitimate radical measures for the sake of change, whether or not Grau and other politicians endorsed them. As the following discussion reveals, many citizens considered the *cause,* rather than the leader, the most important instigator of change.

Galvanizing Anti-Imperialism and Grau's Effort to Retake Center Stage

In order to provide a positive report on his administration's contributions to public education, Grau commissioned Emma Pérez to write a book. A professor of education at the University of Havana, Pérez was better known for her superficial if entertaining contributions to the gentlemen's society magazine *Gente de la Semana*. True to form, Pérez peppered her otherwise thin coverage of Grau's educational achievements with catchy chapter titles such as "To Make Rather Than Theorize" and "Toward a More Democratic Humanism" as well as many phrases authored by the famously less-than-self-critical Grau himself.[63] These included the slogan of the Cuban delegation to a recent international education congress in Geneva, "Le hemos perdido el miedo a la libertad" (We have lost our fear of liberty). The slogan was an inexplicably odd choice given Cubans' deep-seated view of their history as propelled by a unique commitment to love—not fear—of liberty.[64] Real-life delegates to the congress and readers alike must have wondered who Grau was talking about: *when* and exactly *which* Cubans had ever feared liberty? The answer might have been none other than Grau himself: few Cuban presidents, with the exception of Grau's own nemesis Gerardo Machado, suffered such deep unpopularity at the end of his term.

In her efforts to shore up Grau's image, Pérez had to come up with what the Grau administration could not: clear evidence of improvement. Contradictions and halfhearted explanations abounded. For example, the book included a picture of a thatched hut described as "the most common rural school before the government of Dr. Grau" but the adjoining photo of a new rural school built after Grau gave no impression of being either common or even more numerous now: it simply *was*.[65] Recent history, it seemed, could not be pinned down. Moreover, Pérez justified the continued building of tiny schools in isolated hamlets rather than large, consolidated and more effective schools with the flimsy argument that the "montuno" [mountain] schools better reflected peasants' way of life, while the latter, the "progressive model" typical of U.S. rural schools, remained a foreign import.[66]

The book's actual cost to taxpayers and the educational budget far outweighed the cheapness of Grau's "anti-imperialist" shot at U.S. rural schools. The glossy 142-page edition had a whopping print run: forty-five thousand paperbacks and five thousand hardbacks.[67] Adding insult to injury, the book even included a laudatory portrait of increasingly despised education minister José Alemán alongside former FEU president and fellow MSR gang member Manolo Castro, described in Spanglish as "el *leader* revolucionario."[68]

Still, the heroic claims Grau reserved for himself and other administration officials were directly related to an unfolding plan to restore Grau's anti-imperialist revolutionary credentials by assaulting the long-standing U.S.-backed Dominican dictator Rafael Trujillo. Appointed chief of the project, minister of education Alemán purchased an unprecedented arsenal of weapons, jet bombers, and fleet of seven war ships for the invasion with $3 million of his ministry's funds. He also offered school buildings, trucks, and buses otherwise reserved for educational purposes to the movement.[69]

Significantly, public response to rumors of the invasion plan proved overwhelmingly favorable. For the first time in a long time, it seemed that Grau had tapped Cubans' nationalist pride. The idea of putting one's life on the line for hemispheric liberty against the forces of dictatorship and the hypocrisy of the United States quickly set ablaze young men's wildest political desires. Although recently heroic in its wars against European and Japanese fascism, the United States had once again turned a blind eye to its role in maintaining and supplying similar dictatorial regimes on which U.S. business interests depended in Latin America and the Caribbean. For those who eagerly backed Grau's anti-dictatorship plan, the staggering burden of Cubans' thwarted history and the chance to set aright Cuba's destiny proved an irresistible call to unite the older generation of revolutionaries with young would-be rebels.

Best known by the name of the quay where Cuban recruits awaited authorization from the Cuban Navy to depart for Dominican shores, the Cayo Confites expedition drew an extraordinary array of patriot volunteers. They were willing to put aside their enmity with the Grau administration and disgust with its lackeys in order to participate in the Liberating Army of America. Military invasion represented the first step in the Auténticos' broader scheme to found a multination Cuba-led Caribbean Legion. Although the plan was originally conceived by Dominican leaders of the anti-Trujillo opposition exiled in Cuba, Alemán sidelined Dominicans from their own war front and recruited members of the infamous MSR *pistoleros* (gun brandishers) he headed to top ranks. These included Eufemio Fernández, chief of the secret police, and Rolando Masferrer, current owner of the newspaper *El Tiempo en Cuba* and a former army commander of the socialist Republic of Spain that had been defeated by Franco's fascists a decade earlier.

Together with Alemán, Fernández and Masferrer enlisted nearly thirteen hundred young university students, workers, and professionals through Manolo Castro, former FEU president and Grau's current national sports director. Hardly a secret and now mostly a Cuban affair, the Liberation Army of America trained at the José Martí Sports Park and other arenas where members of high society, such as José Luis Wangüemert, son of the director of *Carteles* magazine, and even rival pistoleros in the UIR gang, joined ranks.[70] These included the nineteen-year-old Fidel Castro, a UIR member and legendary foe of Manolo Castro (no relation). When his sisters attempted to persuade Fidel not to go, he replied dramatically, "To topple Trujillo is a mission for democracy and if the price to pay is one's life, then all of us here are ready to pay it. . . . Only dead will I desist in my plan to go!"[71] However overstated his testimony might sound today, Fidel surely spoke for the mass of recruits. In this respect, Fidel Castro did not stand out from the crowd of his peers but represented it. Indeed, the opportunity to join and fight in the Caribbean Legion offered everything a young Cuban steeped in the post-1933 nationalist culture could want: the badge of heroism that mere membership conceded, the chance to prove one's patriotic stripes by risking martyrdom, and the opportunity to replace Trujillo, a demagogue often equated with the devil himself, through the unified actions of committed, anti-imperialist messiahs.

The fact that recruits came from all social classes and not just the traditionally politically active elite of Cuba's national university in Havana further confirms this. As Carlos Franqui, a self-taught journalist of peasant stock, later explained, the sheer audacity of the expedition sparked the imagination of so many in so little time precisely because it was the kind of thing young Cubans had been hearing and dreaming about all of their lives. While on his way to joining combatants at Cayo Confites as a volunteer through the eastern city of Holguín, Franqui encountered only an opposition group of wives and mothers, marching down a street in silence. "Estos muchachos están locos" (These kids are crazy), one told him when he asked why the women marched. "*Carajo* [damn it], don't you know that Trujillo kills everyone? This town is going to be left without men because all the *muchachos* want to go!"[72]

Indeed, had the expedition advanced, let alone succeeded, it would not only have targeted Trujillo but encompassed larger plots to eliminate every dictatorial regime in the region, all of which were U.S.-backed and some, as in the case of both Trujillo and Nicaragua's Anastasio Somoza, U.S.-trained.[73] However, after months of planning and amassing a well-equipped army that was more than ready to go, in mid-September Grau suddenly sent the Cuban Navy to halt operations. Three factors combined to change his mind: the protests of U.S. officials, the anger of the army chief of staff whom Grau had tactically excluded from the plan, and a three-hour shootout in Marianao's Orfila neighborhood between the MSR and the UIR, the two rival Auténtico political gangs. The shootings injured a ten-month-old baby and left six dead, including a woman and her unborn child.[74] Happening only hours before Grau's order to cancel the invasion plans, events at Orfila were captured live on camera and radio before millions of horrified Cubans. From every angle, top leaders in the national police and the Presidential Palace appeared to blame. Not surprisingly, Grau's abandonment of the anti-imperialist cause evoked sighs of relief from Washington and incremented nationalist frustrations at home.[75] As with so many of Grau's policies, the project to liberate the Dominican Republic from Trujillo's grip had produced far more smoke than fire.

However, if the Cayo Confites fiasco was an "irreconcilable breach" in people's view of Grau and the Auténticos, it also galvanized Cubans' faith in the idea that "true" Cubans' selfless, anti-imperialist commitment to personal heroism and nationalist martyrdom could not be tarnished, no matter how traitorously they might be denied. Welcomed as heroes in Havana, the expeditionaries were released from confinement by order of the Supreme Court, while Grau, Alemán, Masferrer, and other leaders' public personas sank further.[76] Thus, in many ways, Cayo Confites proved how easily Cubans could respond to a seemingly ingrained call to defend Caribbean freedom and shared national sovereignty even to the point of arms when the opportunity came knocking. In much of the public's imagination, citizens' will to fulfill their country's imagined destiny as a global leader of democracy in the region more than made up for the hollowness of Auténtico support.

Thus, civic activism took center stage back from Grau and evinced a variety

of forms. Even Eddy Chibás, who had made little comment on events at Cayo
Confites, seemed to recede into the wings before an onslaught of highly orches-
trated political high jinks arranged by militants of the Communist Youth and
Orthodox Youth under the guidance of University of Havana law student, Fidel
Castro. At the heart of multiple protests and mass spectacles was Fidel Castro's
plot to bring a 380-pound bell, a national relic of Cuba's first war for independence, all the way from Oriente province to the Hall of Martyrs at the University of
Havana. Born of historical frustrations and the urgency that came with believing
that Cuba stood at the crossroads of its development, stunts like this and other
efforts discussed below served to rival as well as undermine seasoned political
figures' attempts to dominate public discourse and monopolize policy-making
authority through traditional structures of power.

The Lessons of Cuba's Liberty Bell and the
Challenge of Cuban Youth

On 6 October 1947, Grau's minister of governance Alejo Cossío del Pino arrived in the colonial city of Manzanillo, Oriente. He wanted to persuade the city
council and the local branch of the Veterans' Association to loan the Grau administration a bell from the Demajagua plantation, now a national relic, for the
upcoming seventy-ninth anniversary of the launching of Cuba's first independence war on 10 October 1868. As generations of schoolchildren had learned in
classrooms and popular legend, white planter Carlos Manuel de Céspedes, El
Padre de la Patria, had famously rung his plantation's giant bell on that day for
an entirely different purpose than usual. Rather than gather the slaves together
before sending them off to work, Céspedes had called Cuba's first national assembly: addressing his slaves as "citizens," he granted them freedom in return
for fighting for the liberation of all Cubans from Spain. Decades later, the bell
was more than a symbol of the independence struggle. It represented Cubans'
original pledge to sacrifice their lives for the sake of a republic founded on freedom, justice, and equality for all. Morir por la patria es vivir, in other words.

Had the councilmen and local veterans of Manzanillo consented to Grau's
plan, the bell would have formed the centerpiece of a mass celebration in Havana, complete with a twenty-one-gun salute, a military parade, and an act
commemorating the Day of the Veterans of the Independence Wars presided
over by President Grau and other speakers. However, to the shock and horror of

Minister Cossío del Pino, not only was his request rejected by César Montejo, a fellow Auténtico member of Manzanillo's municipal assembly, it was greeted by jeers. "Thieves!" members of the audience cried. "You have already stolen everything and now you even want to steal the Bell! . . . Where are the funds for the [public] works in Manzanillo?" Forced to leave immediately amid what he later characterized as a "screaming mob," Cossío del Pino returned to the capital. His mission and the Auténtico government were thoroughly humiliated.[77]

Coming only weeks after Grau's "betrayal" of expeditionaries at Cayo Confites, this reaction of Manzanillo's local representatives to Grau's envoy as well as the recent killing of a high school student by police at Alemán's personally organized "pro-confidence rally" prompted palpable outrage among young university students. One of them was Fidel Castro.

Politically ambitious at a precocious age, the teenager had been an observer of politics from the rural margins of Cuban society as a child. Born to a wealthy but only semi-literate sugar planter in Oriente province and shipped off to boarding school in Santiago at the tender age of five, Fidel suffered constant rejection from class peers, who pejoratively called him a "Jew." In large part, his social alienation derived from the fact that his uneducated mother did not marry his father or baptize her son until he was seven. Indeed, the family was apparently prompted to do so only because baptism was a prerequisite for admission to Catholic schools. Yet once Fidel was admitted to Cuba's top Catholic schools, first the Colegio de Dolores in Santiago and then the prestigious, breathtakingly monumental Colegio Belén in Havana, the combination of Jesuit educators' rigorous academic training, his intelligence, and the survival skills he had developed early in life served him well. Never popular enough at the University of Havana to be elected to represent the law students in FEU, Fidel was nonetheless acknowledged as a brilliant and mesmerizing public speaker.[78] Like many law students, he was also an aspiring politician: Grau's bell debacle got him thinking. *What if the University of Havana students could achieve what Grau had not?* On a personal level, the opportunity clearly gave Fidel Castro his first chance to ignite the public's admiration and to take a visible spot on Cuba's national stage.

Rather than allow Cuba's sullied and sinful politicians to bask in the historical glow of the bell on Veterans' Day, Fidel suggested that a delegation of students and veterans convince *manzanilleros* to lend *them* the bell and take it back to Havana. There it would be exhibited at the University's Hall of Martyrs, a space dedicated to commemorating slain student revolutionaries, and serve as the centerpiece for a mass demonstration on 6 November, Cuba's National Day of the Student, against Grau and his fellow *politiqueros*. The change of venue and holiday would signal the consent of the older generation of veterans to passing the torch of heroism and revolutionary mission to young university patriots. Moreover, Fidel believed, the dramatic spectacle of the bell's arrival in the capital would help wake up other Cubans from their slumber to demand the resignation of Grau and other money-grubbing leaders. Indeed, there were no limits to the excitement that the bell might bring: after "agitating the masses" with a series of speakers, Fidel planned to ring the bell "just as it had been rung to initiate the war for independence." As a result, "the masses of partici-pants, now filled with patriotic fervor, would march to the palace to demand the resignation of Grau and, after the fall of the regime, establish a revolutionary government."[79]

According to his close friend and covert Communist Lionel Soto, Fidel first proposed this plan to Alfredo Guevara, president of the literature department's branch of FEU, a popular student, and a publicly known member of the PSP's Communist Youth. Guevara, in turn, sought the approval and, more important, behind-the-scenes support of the Communist Party before finally presenting the idea to the directorship of FEU, none of whose members had any idea that the national leadership of the PSP were involved.[80] In fact, the role of the Commu-nists proved integral to the plan's success. As Castro, Soto, and Guevara well knew, Manzanillo had been a hotbed of popular support for Communism for decades. In the 1920s, FEU president Julio Antonio Mella and socialist veteran of Martí's PRC Carlos Baliño held the first congress of Communists at an old plantation in Manzanillo in order to constitute Cuba's first Communist Party and call for its recognition from Russia's Comintern. Manzanillo also had the distinction of electing Francisco "Paquito" Rosales Benítez, Cuba's first Com-munist mayor, in 1940; by 1947, he was a PSP congressman.[81] Moreover, at the time of Fidel's proposal, the vice president of Manzanillo's town council, Juvencio Guerrero, was also a Communist. "Who oriented the Party in Manza-nillo and its numerous allies to facilitate our plan?" Soto proudly remembered years later. "The directors of the Partido Socialista Popular and the Socialist Youth oriented all their entities in Manzanillo to organize and support, with all their forces, the action we proposed to carry out."[82]

Why did Fidel Castro rely on the support and guidance of the PSP if he was,

by 1947, an aspiring Ortodoxo and admirer of Eddy Chibás? After all, the Ortodoxos were sworn enemies of Communism in general and Cuba's PSP Communists in particular. One answer is clearly that Alfredo Guevara, Lionel Soto, and
others were loyal and genuine friends. They occupied a special place in a landscape that Fidel himself described as more harrowing and emotionally raucous
than that of the Sierra Maestra range, where he would later wage a guerrilla war
against Batista.[83] Another answer is that Fidel's political ambitions surpassed
any ideological proclivities—as much then as they did in later years when the
stakes were higher and the potential reward of state power loomed large on his
personal horizons.

More to the point, however, was the extreme, legendary discipline of local
Communists in following the party's official line and the secret activism of
members close to Fidel such as Soto. These factors ensured that the public and
university students would buy the story just as organizers wanted it told. After
all, the legitimacy of FEU rested on its political autonomy from the state; any
sign of infiltration or manipulation of FEU-backed events by political parties
would inevitably have crushed the selfless, untarnished image of Cuban youth
so critical to student activists' influence over the state and the public. In the end,
the support of the PSP on the ground and behind the scenes in both Havana and
Manzanillo ensured that Fidel's plan went like clockwork. Understood and promoted as a purely FEU-authored and FEU-sponsored tactic, the reception of the
bell by *la juventud cubana* (Cuban youth) seemed stripped of any political ambitions. In addition, the demonstrations that they had planned appeared spontaneous, purged of the very deliberate coordination of the PSP Communists that
had actually taken place. This was important, for unlike the Orthodox Youth,
to which many FEU leaders like Fidel formally belonged, the PSP seemed,
because of its earlier entanglements with Batista, like a highly self-interested,
even ruthless political party.

Importantly, *Noticias de Hoy,* the PSP's national newspaper, offered a moment-
by-moment account of the bell's arrival in Havana on 4 November in the hands
of none other than Fidel Castro and Lionel Soto, two delegates Guevara had
"suggested" to FEU's leaders and they had approved. On the train with Castro
and Soto came Hilda Necolar de Rojas, the president of Manzanillo's town
council, and the elderly president of the local veterans' association. Importantly, *Noticias de Hoy* was the only print publication to run images of the bell's
arrival that did *not* show Fidel Castro at their center. The strategy was undoubt-

Figure 4. "Stick your face to the bell!" Lionel Soto advised young and ambitious law student Fidel Castro when they arrived at Havana's train station in 1948, carrying Cuba's historic liberty bell. Rung to inaugurate Cuba's first war for independence in 1868, the bell seemed a perfect symbol of Cuban youth's aspiration to free the country from political stagnation. Its transfer to Havana also served to place Fidel Castro on the national political stage. (Courtesy of the Fundación Antonio Nuñez Jiménez)

edly meant to ensure that Fidel could never be accused of covert militancy in the PSP or complicity with its equally covert activities, including the delivery of Céspedes's bell. For the regular media, however, Soto himself remembered instructing Fidel to "fuse" himself to the bell in every frame taken by reporters' cameras.[84] Published decades later in *Bohemia* and *Granma,* collections of these images from *El Mundo* and other newspapers show Soto, Guevara, and other covert militants standing next to a fresh-faced Fidel, barely out of his teens, hardly able to contain the euphoria of his victory.[85] One picture shows Fidel posing for the cameras, embracing the bell with one arm and holding the clapper with his other hand (figure 4).[86] One can only wonder what the ghost of Céspedes might have thought.

"It would have been an outrage for the bell and for the veterans had the government been able to use this patriotic symbol for its sectarian and electoral propaganda," declared Necolar de Rojas to a massive crowd that gathered when students finally transported the bell from the train station to the university. To shouts of *Down with Grau!* she continued: "and for that reason, we *manzanilleros* resolutely refused such a pretension from Grau and Cossío del Pino." FEU president Enrique Ovares went further, accusing Grau and all his ministers of having "betrayed the Revolution," "ridiculing the University and the *pueblo cubano*." The only solution, he said, was to force new elections.[87] After speeches by Fidel, invited guests, and others ended, thousands of students filed reverently past Céspedes's liberty bell of Demajagua, now carefully ensconced in the Hall of the Martyrs, just as Fidel and his Communist allies had first imagined.[88] The next day an even greater demonstration awaited, or so they thought.

Incredibly, though, by dawn, the bell that Céspedes had used to free the slaves and that Fidel would have used to call for a new revolution was nowhere to be found. Left unguarded by the very students who claimed to be the relic's only just and rightful guardians, the bell had "disappeared" in the middle of the night, likely by order of President Grau and carried out by complicit university police.[89] In its absence, Fidel and others rallied the crowds anyway, accusing Grau of "stealing" the national icon and refusing to return it to the people. According to *Noticias de Hoy,* twenty thousand to thirty thousand demonstrators gathered in response to the bell's disappearance, with student leaders demanding a general strike.[90] Meanwhile, hundreds of miles away in Oriente, outraged manzanilleros rioted.[91] The bell only reappeared days later when it was anonymously delivered to the home of General Enrique Loynaz del Castillo, long-admired veteran of the 1895 war and radio commentator for University of the Air. When Loynaz del Castillo promptly had it sent to the relatively more responsible generation of "patriots" at the Presidential Palace, Fidel, FEU, and other students were left with the task of salvaging the wreckage of their own prestige amid obvious evidence of arrogance, laziness, or worse, sheer stupidity.

In public speeches, however, the students showed no remorse and chose not to play the card of political innocence. Instead, Fidel insisted that nothing of their public image had changed, not even among veterans: "The freedom fighters of yesterday trust the young students of today; thus we are continuing their task of achieving independence and justice."[92]

Much *had* changed, however. Humbly, Grau had ordered the bell returned to Manzanillo by General Loynaz del Castillo and chief of staff General Pérez Dámera in a public ceremony to be held on the main plaza. The national government spared no expense. Accompanied by a huge military escort, the same veterans who had brought the bell to Havana with the students by train now boarded a government plane to take the bell home alongside many of the very political enemies they had recently denounced.[93] Met at the airport by an enormous crowd, the two generals then presented the bell in Manzanillo's principal square amid cannon fire and the national anthem played by municipal band. The sight of the relic understandably provoked tears from elderly mambises and "frenetic" women; it also calmed the "state of veritable insurrection" gripping the community. Whether scripted by local Auténticos or generated spontaneously, the crowd's reaction reversed Manzanillo's image as a hotbed of incipient revolution and hostility to Grau. Not only did attendees cheer Grau but, amid deafening applause and chants, they barely allowed Pérez Démara to leave.[94]

In many ways, the primary lesson of the battle between Auténtico officials and the younger generation of activists who wanted to claim the revolutionary mantle for themselves was that neither succeeded. What emerged in the end was simply one set of actors theatrically fighting the other while the public threatened to storm the stage.

Notably *off*stage and actively preparing for a very different struggle that might yield concrete change was Eddy Chibás. From 1948 to his death in 1951, Eddy Chibás and the older generation of still-untarnished revolutionaries of anti-Machado, anti-Batista battles who formed the Partido Ortodoxo rode a wave of building nationalist preoccupations and expectations. More than simply use the elements of a national culture that glorified revolutionary activism against seemingly invincible adversaries, Chibás and the Ortodoxos augmented its dimensions, empowering citizens against contemporary day-to-day economic and political foes. The true enemies of la patria were not just corrupt Auténticos in the Presidential Palace and apathetic congressmen, but the complicity of citizens themselves. More than simply inspire or incite, Chibás and his party proved that civic action, not just civic protest, could democratize the state and potentially save Cuba.

"Vergüenza Contra Dinero" in Action and the Triumph of Chibás

Far from dead or sidelined, senior Ortodoxos flew into life in the months that followed the ruckus over Cuba's Liberty Bell, gathering funds little by little and then finally fielding candidates for the 1948 general elections under Eddy Chibás's increasingly effervescent direction. Grau's personal publicity machine notwithstanding, the formerly pro-Auténtico press remained at best guarded about Grau's choice of a successor, minister of labor Carlos Prío Socarrás, and concerned at worst. Magazines such as *Carteles* shared the view of most patrician politicians and conservative members of Cuba's educated society. While some Cubans appreciated Eddy's "vehemencia" (vehemence), others considered it an embarrassing and dangerous form of "demencia" (dementia).[95]

However, the upper ranks of the Partido del Pueblo Cubano-Ortodoxo defied this assessment by including icons of respectability such as Eddy's cousin, the dour and demure Professor Agramonte, as well as a woman, María Teresa Freyre de Andrade, the eloquent founder and director of Cuba's Biblioteca Nacional José Martí.[96] Their collaboration clearly deepened the party's seriousness and prestige. Both relatives of legendary mambí generals, Freyre de Andrade was the sister of three brothers famously murdered in their own beds for revolutionary activism by Machado's goons. Like Eddy's own heritage, the top ranks of the Ortodoxos were human embodiments of a past betrayed and a present that, with citizen support, might be redeemed. But the ranks of the Ortodoxos did not just commemorate the past in human form, they pointed toward a progressive and modern future: all of Cuba's top radio talk show hosts were leading Ortodoxos, including José Pardo Llada, host of *La Palabra,* Manuel Bisbé, and Guido García Inclán, director of Radio COCO.

The seal of the party also spoke to the nationalist idea of supporting local business and entrepreneurialism: along with the majestic Royal Palm and classic *sombrero guajiro* (peasant hat) adorned with the mambí insignia, the Ortodoxos' main symbol was that of a cogged wheel like that of the Rotary Club, a local branch of which Eddy's father had headed in Santiago.[97] Importantly, however, the Ortodoxos' earliest explanations of this symbol ignored all mention of the Rotary movement, probably due to its foreign roots and personal connection to Chibás. Instead, the twenty-cogged wheel evoked "the last twenty years (1927–1947) of the fight of the people for economic independence, political freedom, and social justice." It was also a complete version of the half wheel that symbolized the Auténtico Party. The cogs on the Ortodoxo symbol also clearly referred to Chibás's own twenty-year history of political activism: "This symbol represents our firm decision to place justice, as Martí wanted, as high as the palms. With Chibás, we will save Cuba!"[98]

In fact, as hundreds of letters in Chibás's personal archive attest, few *co-religionarios* (co-religionists), if any, disagreed with this point of view. On the contrary, Chibás's defenders ridiculed critiques of his "bad taste" and "acidic vocal tone." They loved Chibás's irrepressible instinct to call a spade a spade. "What do you want?" asked one citizen in a four-page typed letter to Carlos Lechuga, editor of the prestigious and widely read newspaper *El Mundo*. "Is Chibás supposed to call Batista anything besides a thief and the assassin of [Antonio] Guiteras? What do you want Chibás to say about Grau? That great faker, deceiver and fox?" For heavens' sake, continued the writer, who signed himself El Mazo de Hábanos (A Handful of Cigars), without that kind of language, Cubans with any self-respect would get nowhere.[99]

As Ortodoxo president and top spokesman, Chibás countered critics who contended that he proposed to substitute the structures of government and constitutional order with "the power of the microphone" and demagogic displays of supporters: "Nada de eso" (None of that), he told a reporter for the right-wing *Diario de la Marina*.[100] On the contrary, he defined "the revolution" not as a past event or series of events but as a process of implementing "economic, social, political, and cultural justice." Although Chibás had never held a job other than an elective office, he refuted the charge that he was a professional politician. Inspired only by "quijotismo desinteresado" (disinterested quixotism), he undertook his job "like a man and like a revolutionary, as a member of a generation that imposed upon itself the task of saving Cuba; I have a sacred debt to those who gave their lives for that task and the principles that they served until their sacrifice." In Cuba, he added, no one has the right *not* to be a patriot.[101]

Rounding out Eddy's philosophy of good government were three practical priorities: the creation of a Tribunal de Cuentas, a special court for trying cases of corruption committed by otherwise constitutionally immune government officials; the fulfillment of the 1940 Constitution's mandate that the executive submit an annual budget for negotiation and approval by Congress (rather than simply rule by decree with congressional approval always pending, as Grau and Batista had done); and the reform and professionalization of the civil service so as to expunge Cuba of botellas, the practice of distributing jobs in government bureaucracies in return for votes and complicity with corruption.[102]

The specificity of these principles alone made the Ortodoxos stand out among a crowd of parties reliant on similar-sounding but vague appeals to nationalism. In addition, the Ortodoxos' party platform confirmed an overall commitment to "nationalism" as a priority. They defined this as "effective elimination of

racial discrimination"; improvements in the working conditions of civil servants and teachers; diversifying agriculture and industry through government
support; nationalization of all public utilities (including Cuba's electrical plant,
trains, telephones, and streetcars, all of which were owned by private U.S. companies); an agrarian reform profound enough to transform landless plantation
employees into property owners; and cancellation of all special tax holidays
and other concessions made to foreign corporations at the cost of developing
Cuba's own national businesses.[103]

Finally, Chibás clarified that while Batista relied on the Communists to rule
and Grau tolerated the legacy of their control over the island's largest labor
union, La Confederación de Trabajadores Cubanos, or CTC, he considered
Cuba's Communist Party, the PSP, "a gear in the vast imperialist organization
of the Soviet. We are a party of pure nationalism." Members of the PSP called
themselves "socialist," but they referred to an internationalist and totalitarian
socialism, clarified Chibás: by contrast, "the socialism" of the Ortodoxos was
utterly distinct—nationalist, democratic, and anti-imperialist. Always one to
make his point as sharply as possible, Chibás asserted that his party backed the
independence of Indonesia from Holland, Puerto Rico from the United States,
and Czechoslovakia from the Soviet Union.[104]

By the time Chibás made these announcements, the legitimacy of the PSP
and its popularity, even among workers, were in sharp decline. Postwar inva-
sions of Eastern Europe proved the Soviet Union's hypocritical embrace of
imperialism, once seen as a political staple of U.S. and Western European cap-
italist states alone. Moreover, the PSP's opportunistic relationship with Batista
shook workers' confidence in its goals and "real" intentions for the island. Able
to easily and accurately exploit the PSP's top leaders' pro-Stalin views, the party's political rivals reflected an anti-Communism that was clearly homegrown,
sinking deep roots in sugar sectors of the labor movement, some of which created their own "Pro-Democracy Associations" with membership open to all.[105]

In 1947, workers had thrown the Communists out of the top echelons of most
unions by election, a process undoubtedly aided by minister of labor Carlos
Prío Socarrás's campaign of violent intimidation against pro-Communist unions. With a viable Ortodoxo option still absent, workers tied to the Auténticos
were clearly divided over the meaning of this outcome. In Camagüey, CTC delegates rightly worried that unions affiliated with an Auténtico-led state would
corrupt or water down their effectiveness; worse yet, *pandilleros* (gangsters for

hire) or even the associates of Lucky Luciano might fill their ranks.[106] Other workers in Oriente were happy to be rid of PSP founder and the party's long-time labor czar Lazaro Peña and his "Soviet lackeys." These workers went so far as to chastise Eddy in an open letter for giving *any* positive acclaim to the Communists in one of his recent radio addresses. At Central Palma, they wrote, most workers considered the Communists self-interested "vulgar criminals associated with Batista and Saladrigas's followers." Carlos Saladrigas had been Grau's opponent in 1944 and Batista's handpicked successor.[107]

Disagreements among organized workers over how to keep the dictatorialism of Communists at bay while augmenting union autonomy from government control opened up a vast field of opportunity for Eddy Chibás and the Ortodoxos. This field had only widened with the unexpected assassination in January 1947 of PSP congressman and beloved defender of sugar workers Jesús Menéndez. An army captain had shot him in the back for resisting arrest—despite Menéndez's immunity as a public official. In light of what was clearly an assassination, Eddy Chibás joined hundreds of thousands of mourners at a massive funeral procession in Havana and denounced Menéndez's killer. Defended before reporters by Grau's chief of staff General Pérez Dámera, however, the murderous army captain ultimately got off scot-free.[108]

In addition to reaching out to workers, Eddy Chibás addressed poor voters directly in every campaign poster and speech by pledging never to buy votes or "consciences" as other parties did. Ortodoxo propaganda castigated voters for complicity, a tactic that confirmed the power of each and every vote. If you refused to vote, sold your vote, or paid off a favor to a friend by giving away your vote, concluded an Ortodoxo political ad published in *Bohemia,* "you lose your right to happiness. . . . Do not accept coercion!"[109]

While this "do or die" strategy for convincing voters might have seemed both ill advised and over the top, Eddy Chibás and the Ortodoxos pulled off what election observers considered nothing short of a miracle in only three weeks' time: they collected 320,929 votes in the national election of June 1948, almost double the number of Ortodoxos registered. Rallies held to support Chibás were massive in size (figure 5). Symbolic of the guarantee that Chibás would sweep away corruption, supporters carried brooms and posters in support of Ortodoxo candidates on the streets (figure 6). With unlimited resources at their disposal, the Auténticos won all six provinces but garnered only 45.83 percent of the vote, while the Liberal Democrats, widely considered the "Machado-

Figure 5. While the Auténticos won a clear victory in the national elections of 1948, Eddy Chibás's last-minute campaign for president and fielding of congressional candidates on an Ortodoxo ticket yielded astonishingly massive support during its short three-week run. (Courtesy of the Archivo Nacional de Cuba)

Batista Party," received 30.42 percent.[110] No longer able to take their popularity for granted, Auténticos breathed a sigh of relief as Carlos Prío Socarrás, Grau's relatively clean minister of labor, took the presidency. Left without a seat in Congress but armed with a microphone, Eddy Chibás became more than a thorn in Prío Socarrás's side. In many ways, he championed the role of the media and helped make journalism what came to be known by the early 1950s as Cuba's "fourth power," just as influential as the executive, judicial, and legislative branches, if not more so.[111]

In the first few months of his administration, Prío Socarrás tried to steal the Ortodoxos' thunder and replace rancor with what his campaign called "the politics of cordiality." Given Grau's record of preventing Auténtico congressmen from attending congressional sessions and thereby impeding the passage of legislation for lack of quorum, virtually *any* collaboration with Congress might

Figure 6. Citizens were quick to improvise symbols, like their own household brooms, in shows of public support for Eddy Chibás and the Orthodox promise to prosecute and punish the many national leaders responsible for well-documented cases of graft, abuse of public coffers, and acts of political violence. (Courtesy of the Archivo Nacional de Cuba)

have been considered a triumph.[112] By contrast, Prío not only passed Cuba's first congressionally approved budget in years but appointed honest men to key cabinet positions. Carlos Hevia became foreign minister and Aureliano Sánchez Arango accepted the previously infamous post of minister of education. In addition to firing hundreds of employees with botellas and histories of corruption en masse, Sánchez Arango actually enforced certification processes for teachers and piloted his own plane to all parts of the island in order to carry out on-the-spot inspections of school facilities.[113]

Making good on a campaign promise to put an end to political violence, Prío engineered a legislative ban on "gangsterism." Known as the Anti-Gangsterism Law, it created a special court to prosecute pistol-packing members of the Auténtico-linked political action gangs affiliated with law enforcement, especially Masferrer's legendary MSR and its rival, the UIR, backed by the national police. However, only two weeks after Prío had declared that law against gangsterism a success, his crowning achievement made him a laughingstock. On 12 January 1949, MSR gunmen under orders from Masferrer gunned down a national police sergeant and UIR member while he was drinking in a bar, riddling his body with seventeen bullets.[114] The murder sparked a renewed cycle of revenge killings among rival gangs, student strikes to protest the deaths of fellow youths, and general public outrage. Word on the street declared that Prío's law targeted only "innocent citizens [with] hunting rifles," not politically connected and police-protected gangs.[115] When Jorge Mañach's Amigos de la República arranged a nationally televised debate on what to do about political violence, debaters Rafael García Bárcena and Bernal del Riesgo made common cause: *pistolerismo* was not a faceless crime; what Cuba needed were not new laws like Prío's anti-gangsterism ban, just men brave enough to enforce the existing ones.[116]

Despite the auspicious beginnings of Prío's presidency, its legitimacy and popularity seemed to be on the skids by the end of his first six months. For Chibás, now free of his senatorial duties and focused entirely on his radio show, the case against Prío and other "sinners, apostates, and thieves" was easy to make: they needed to be "expelled from the temple."[117] In fact, concern regarding Prío's willingness to root out crime and corruption in his own party increased dramatically at the start of 1949. Then Ortodoxo senator Pelayo Cuervo Navarro filed a meticulously researched legal brief with the criminal division of the Supreme Court against Grau, Alemán, and other officials, accusing them of embezzling $174,241,840.14 from the national treasury.[118] In an apparent effort to establish order even as the foundations of his legitimacy were slipping away, Prío took a number of unpopular steps that prioritized control of public opinion over rule of law. One of these was to resurrect the Servicio de Inteligencia Militar (SIM), a Batista creation of the 1930s that operated at executive discretion outside the confines of public accountability. Another was to order the silencing of popular radio shows hosted by Ortodoxo leaders Guido García Inclán, Juan Antonio Márquez, and Eddy Chibás himself, ostensibly for security reasons. Such actions were not only intolerable but unbelievable, coming from a president who had once been a member of the student-based Directorio Revolucionario of 1930. They seemed to augur, wrote one fellow veteran of the Directorio to Prío in May 1949, "a return to those times that we thought long forgotten, of the tyrannies of Machado and Batista."[119]

At the same time, Prío inaugurated his presidential tenure by making an official state visit to the United States, something that Gerardo Machado had memorably done as well. While Prío's trip might not have ruffled many feathers at the time, it took on special symbolic significance only a few months later, when an entirely unexpected diplomatic crisis rocked Cuba.

With disgust over Prío's self-described "cordial" approach to governing and *gangsterismo* brewing, four gallivanting U.S. Marines nearly provoked their own lynching in March 1949 when one of them climbed to the top of the national monument to José Martí in Havana's Central Park and urinated on his head. In response, the already unpopular national police found themselves in the ironic position of having to defend the Marines from a seething nationalist crowd.[120] Incredibly, the moment was captured on camera by photographer Fernando Chaviano and published in *Alerta* the very next day.[121] Recognizing the seriousness of the crisis, U.S. embassy cars made the rounds of Havana on the night of the incident, offering $2,000 to anyone who could deliver the incriminating negatives and prevent the photos' release.[122] Once again led by Fidel Castro and Communists Lionel Soto and Alfredo Guevara, university students protested at the U.S. embassy. Although the ultimate goal of the three young men was to set the building ablaze, they only managed to inflict permanent damage to the shield emblazoned on an outside wall before being attacked by club-wielding police.[123] The unanimity of public fury, evident across the press, left U.S. ambassador Robert Butler no choice but to issue a nationally televised public apology and a second one at the feet of the monument, site of the imperialist "crime."[124] Lost on no one was the mildness of the penance paid by Marines or the United States.[125]

Throughout all of this, Eddy Chibás's radio broadcasts blasted Prío's weak-kneed complacency with increasing U.S. domination of Cuban industries and moves to indebt the Cuban state through loans as a means to strengthen U.S. control. "Every day, the government of Carlos Prío tries to imitate some aspect of the government of Machado."[126] Public indignation over the actions of U.S. Marines—whom Chibás called "savage beasts" who "do not even belong to the human race"—demanded more than symbolic responses.[127] Meant to stoke the fires of pent-up nationalist expectations, Chibás's radio broadcasts also prophesied a new Ortodoxo front in "the great battle against imperialist corporations."[128] Acting behind the scenes, Chibás allied with Pelayo Cuervo to yield a civic victory.

At the time, *Bohemia* magazine declared Chibás and Batista the only leaders of the opposition formidable enough to defeat the Auténtico political machine.[129] Yet in the lead-up to the partial elections of 1950, Chibás and the Ortodoxos continued to show an unwillingness to reproduce the Auténtico or Liberal parties' tit-for-tat networking schemes to secure votes or create disciplined party cadres to propagate the party line at workplaces and social venues. As Jose Pardo Llada described it, Chibás's refusal to play political games, let alone abide by their traditional rules, continued to set him apart: "Eddy Chibás is practically a man without a party."[130] Chibás likely felt he did not need one: after all, he had the people.

For at least some Ortodoxos, putting vergüenza contra dinero into action as an organizational tactic without enforcing discipline among the rank and file seemed far too naive.[131] Others clearly chafed at what they construed as the tendency of their party to call for open political rallies that anyone could attend without anyone bothering to note *who* was in attendance. More scripting and staging was necessary. "With anonymous mass rallies and no coordination, we can't build an organization," warned Havana businessman Victor del Pino in a private letter to Chibás. "Our party has to stop being the party of noise to become by steps a true organization."[132] Eddy was their "general" in an unarmed moral army; he had "to order the troops." [133] However, as thousands of letters in Eddy's private archive can attest, voices such as these were few and far between. It was Eddy's genuine spirit of spontaneity that made the Ortodoxos different.

In the spring of 1949, when the U.S.-owned Cuban Electrical Company suddenly raised its rates, Chibás and the Ortodoxos launched their battle. Almost immediately, *Bohemia* magazine called on President Prío in the name of the Cuban people, refusing to mince words: "The voracity of the *pulpo electrico* has grown to such an extent that the entire Cuban population repudiates it and is ready to combat it *mano a mano,* without worrying about the consequences." The goal was not simply to lower the rates, "a typical measure taken by government," but to nationalize the utility company: "a revolutionary determination that, once undertaken, would be embraced by the nation."[134] A month later, the Supreme Court rejected the Consumer Association's challenge to the legality of the government's approval of a rate hike. Chibás then used his radio show to denounce the Supreme Court. Cubans already paid almost double the cost per kilowatt that customers did for the same service in neighboring Puerto Rico. Claiming that the judges had been bought off by bribes totaling $300,000, Chibás followed up his accusation with nighttime candle-lit rallies and a motion to the Senate calling for the impeachment of the three judges who sided with the company.[135] In fact, according to one of Eddy's confidants, a Catholic priest in Fomento, the electric company's "donation" was higher: $500,000 in total, although one judge cheated the other two and kept $300,000, the lion's share, for himself.[136]

Highly metaphoric of how little Cuba had changed since the time of Machado, Eddy was brought up on charges by a *tribunal de urgencia,* or emergency court, part of an extra-constitutional judicial system of trial by judge rather than jury. Originally created in the 1920s and shored up by Batista in the 1930s, emergency courts ensured conviction and imprisonment of critics, political activists, and labor organizers deemed a nuisance or threat to the current regime. Despite the efforts of Cuba's top lawyers in arguing for the courts' elimination before the Supreme Court in 1947, their political utility to the executive and other special interests ensured that they endured.[137]

Adding insult to injury in this case, Chibás was not simply tried before an emergency court; he was tried in exactly the same court and forced to face exactly the same judge who had convicted him to six months in prison for revolutionary activism in 1935 during Batista's counterrevolutionary reign of terror. Dressed in an immaculate white linen suit and tie, Chibás sat tensely on the edge of his seat this time, listening as Judge José Cabezas convicted him again in 1949 and sentenced him to six months in prison (figure 7). Taken to one of Havana's oldest dungeons, El Castillo del Principe, Chibás became prisoner no. 982.[138] Not surprisingly, the response of the Cuban public was instantaneous and fierce. In its first edition documenting events and reactions, *Bohemia* offered a stunning two-page spread of photographs showing José Pardo Llada, a top radio journalist and fellow Ortodoxo, leading mass protests held on the night of Eddy's verdict in multiple provinces. The images showed crowds of citizens, young and old, rich and poor, holding candles, torches, and portraits of martyred revolutionaries José Martí, Antonio Maceo, and Antonio Guiteras in protest. "Cuba Entera Contra El Pulpo Eléctrico" (All of Cuba Is Against the Electric Octopus), the headline read.[139] "¡Hay que apretar las filas!" (We have to close ranks!) editors urged in a separate statement.[140] A subsequent survey showed that 76 percent of Cubans sided with Eddy Chibás against the imperialist Pulpo.[141]

Letters of support from Cubans of all social classes, educational levels, provinces, and ages poured into the prison, which soon became known as Eddy's "castle."[142] These included a letter from a thirteen-year-old boy who said that he had been tying his shoes in the double-knotted "Ortodoxo style" since he was eleven and would have written earlier except that he had failed two courses in

Figure 7. The trial of Eddy Chibás on charges of having "insulted" Cuba's Supreme Court judges by accusing them of taking bribes from the U.S.-owned electrical company, popularly known as El Pulpo Eléctrico, outraged the Cuban public. Listening to the judge sentence him to six months in prison, Chibás, dressed in impeccable white linen, appeared ready to spring into action at any moment. (Courtesy of the Archivo Nacional de Cuba)

school and the make-up process had slowed him down.[143] A self-declared avid listener of his radio show, four-year-old Marucha wrote to Eddy: "I send this letter because I want you to know that I love you very much and I send you a photograph of me so that you can get to know me. . . . I pray to God for you and I made a promise to the Virgin of Charity [Cuba's national patron] so that you can get out of that cell soon and that nothing may happen to you."[144] Most writers affectionately addressed him as "Our President," fudging whether they referred to the party or the nation, even though Eddy ran for president only once, lost, and his campaign had lasted less than a month. Rife with spelling errors and poor penmanship (proof of their writers' lower-class status), many letters ended with apologies for their flaws and requests that Eddy write back so that the writers could know for sure how he was doing.[145] "You," wrote a man from Cienfuegos, "far from being a politician, are *very* Cuban and above all, you are always with the truth and for the truth."[146]

Virtually no one asked for aid or favors, unusual for the time. Exceptions included autograph seekers, a woman who hoped to acquire a wheelchair so she could register to vote before the deadline, and a teacher who asked to see Eddy's personal doctor gratis in order to cure her anxiety-driven dyspepsia, a request with which Conchita Fernández, Eddy's personal secretary, readily complied.[147] A surprising number of folks sent Eddy something, such as a box of ripe mangoes from Santa Clara or a spectacular watermelon from the Isle of Pines.[148] A Cuban in New York City offered himself for whatever Eddy needed and threw in access to his brand-new car as part of the deal.[149] Indeed, one can only imagine the excitement these writers must have felt when they received Eddy's responses to such intimate missives—which they almost all did. Eddy marked up the top and main points of each letter in wax pencil and meticulously made carbon copies of responses for his files.

When legal authorities refused to allow Chibás to transmit his regular radio show on Sunday from a prison cell, Guido García Inclán, director of Radio COCO, broadcast a special thirty-minute show on 19 May, the anniversary of the death of José Martí, Cuba's greatest martyr and would-be messiah, comparing Eddy Chibás to Martí himself. Addressing Chibás directly throughout the show, García Inclán also explained that when Eddy published a long opinion piece in *Prensa Libre* as a substitute for what he might have said over the live airwaves, the government shut down the newspaper for three days. "But we are marching upward, whatever happens . . . and the struggle for *vergüenza* has been forged, and friend, we have a whole people to whom we must respond," he concluded.[150] In the wake of these events, Cubans did more than compare Eddy Chibás to José Martí; many now saw Eddy as Martí incarnate.[151]

These included the son of a mambí who, like Eddy and Martí, had also languished in a prison cell for the sake of Cuban sovereignty.[152] As many secularists as spiritualists believed in Chibás's "apostledom." For instance, the director of a Cuban institute for the study of the popular pseudo-science of spiritualism declared that since he first heard Eddy speak against the Machado regime in the Workers' Theatre in Tampa, "I realized then that there was the soul of an Apostle in you, and a defender of truth and freedom."[153] Similarly claiming that Chibás was one of a handful of divinely appointed "predestined ones," the president of Los Hijos del Cosmos Institución Científico-Místico (The Sons of the Cosmos Mystical-Scientific Institute), a sister organization, went further: "My dear admired Teacher of Humility: To the revolutionary, the tree of life, the Apostle of Dignity . . . we contemplate in you a Rebel, a Mirabeau, a Martí, a man who sincerely loves his Patria."[154]

The more secularly inclined were no less hyperbolic. Middle- and upper-class activists saw themselves as "sergeants" in Chibás's moral army but also echoed Eddy's unwavering convictions in spiritual or religious terms. "The Triumph is ours," top-ranking Ortodoxo leader Benito Castillo wrote Eddy from Trinidad. "God willing, because with that we can save the Patria."[155] Chibás's rank-and-file supporters, by contrast, reveled in what they perceived as their party's lack of hierarchy, writing Eddy using the informal Spanish form of address *tú* and frequently declaring themselves "loco como tú" (as crazy as you are).[156] Mario Ribadulla claimed to speak for many when he wrote, "When a man is nick-named '*loco*,' it is generally because he is a genius. And you are. . . . Columbus was called *loco* and so was Copernicus and Magellan and Tesla and an infinite number of sages and geniuses, of heroes. Let them keep calling you *loco*, because of all of them, you are the most sublime. United we shall triumph."[157] Devoted listeners to his radio show in Miami advised Chibás to keep a cool head and demeanor: "Don't give cause to those hungry rats who call you *loco* and bellicose and plant hatred. Keep your spirits high for the good of Cuba—the hour will come to balance out pending accounts and bring to justice all of those delinquents with ties; on that day, they will understand that simply wearing a robe does not a monk make."[158]

In many respects, Chibás was already heeding his Miami listeners' advice. Having traded in his usual white linen suit for pajamas, he filled his days at the prison reading torrents of correspondence, writing, and greeting supporters during visiting hours.[159] Within a month, public responses and universally favorable media coverage forced Liberal Democrats and Auténticos in the Senate to join forces and request a presidential pardon that would free Eddy.[160] Realizing how badly Chibás's "martyrdom" affected his own party's standing among voters, Prío Socarrás reluctantly complied with the pardon and then yielded to public and press demands: suddenly, the president lowered electricity rates to previous levels by decree.[161] Prío then followed up that act by lowering the U.S.-owned Cuban Telephone Company's rates as well.[162] To everyone's amazement, it seemed that vergüenza contra dinero had actually won.

Undoubtedly, Chibás's actions and regular weekly radio shows democratized and transformed public culture in palpable ways. Eddy lowered the bar on the acceptability of launching attacks on politicians and dropped traditional standards of censoring one's language in formal writing and public spaces as opposed to private speech. Although Cubans of all social classes were accustomed to using far saltier language in private, many also let loose when writing to Eddy. All used strong language to denounce "the terrible paradox that the scoundrels [*los pillos*] are out on the street and *la vergüenza* and honor are in jail."[163] By the time of his release from prison, Chibás was not just a man of the people, he was the very personification of the Ortodoxo slogan. One letter, written by a resident of the largely black barrio of Jesús del Monte, peppered his encouragement of Eddy's work with denunciations of "the government of bandits and traitors" and called for the Ortodoxos to "exterminate the pirates of Cuban politics . . . and a tyrannical government that is worse than that of Machado."[164]

Chibás's unflinching and unvarying sense of outrage made him many things to many Cubans: an embodiment of José Martí, yes, but more important a vehicle and voice for their own empowerment. Apparently attempting to capitalize on Chibás's fame and align himself with the new politics demanded by the day, even Fulgencio Batista got into the act, preparing voters for a presumed electoral bid in 1952, in which he and Chibás would spar away. He did this in Holguin through a comedic public spectacle that matched a fighting cock owned by Batista and named after himself against one named Chibás owned by a local Ortodoxo. The contest was allotted a two-page photo spread in *Bohemia* titled "'Chibas' Pecks Batista's Eyes Out." Spectators clearly delighted in watching Chibás's cock defeat that of Batista, who famously campaigned on his supposedly proven commitment to the working man and the slogan "Batista es El Hombre" (Batista Is the Man).[165] However, if Batista intended the stunt to demonstrate that Chibás represented little or no threat to him, the same could not have been attempted by either President Carlos Prío or Grau, equally committed to ensuring a continuation of Auténtico power. Thus, Prío adopted new tactics meant to silence Chibás and other unarmed critics; much as Chibás charged, they showed Prío to be little better than their once mutual enemy, Gerardo Machado.

From the summer of 1950 through the first weeks of 1951, Chibás increasingly focused his assaults on rising incidents of gangsterism, a fact that seemed only to embolden Auténtico-affiliated gangs, especially MSR pistoleros connected to Rolando Masferrer, now an elected Auténtico congressman. No longer content simply to get away with murder, Masferrer began providing interviews to the media in which he scarcely denied his guilt, admitting in one case that he would have preferred to "scare" rival gang members rather than kill them. Masferrer then went so far as to plant a bomb below Ortodoxo founder and legal scholar Roberto Agramonte's library.[166] President Prío followed up on Masferrer's declarations and actions not by condemning them, but by ordering his minister of communications to assign the first ten minutes of Eddy Chibás's Sunday night radio broadcast to none other than Congressman Rolando Masferrer himself.[167]

On 18 February 1951, shortly after Batista's cockfight with "Chibás," these events came to a head. Hours before Chibás was scheduled to deliver his regular weekly radio broadcast, the army and the national police cordoned off the area in front of CMQ radio station to prepare for the government-ordered radio address of Rolando Masferrer. Meant to intimidate the hundreds of Chibás fans and supporters who normally accompanied Chibás as he walked the short distance from his penthouse apartment at La Focsa (then and now Havana's only skyscraper) up the hill to CMQ, the militarized show of force predictably ended in violence. When the army opened fire and police battered fleeing protesters with machine guns, dozens were injured. One Ortodoxo, a young man named José Otero Ben, lay dead.[168] Later, Chibás visited the wounded in hospital. Both he and José Pardo Llada were pallbearers at Otero Ben's funeral.[169] *Bohemia*'s lengthy five-page photographic report revealed dozens of armed military personnel flooding the area near Eddy's home, guarding Masferrer and intimidating, if not outright provoking, unarmed Ortodoxos, Eddy Chibás in particular.[170] Highly symbolic of what many observers took as a radical turn in the nature of politics, Prío's use of military tactics rather than police controls prompted *Bohemia*'s editor and owner, Miguel Angel Quevedo, to pen a prophetic editorial. "Faced with the events of last Sunday," he wrote, "the people are asking themselves in alarm: Will this open yet another tragic cycle for *la patria?*"[171] Under the title "Toward the Dictatorship!" Herminio Portell Vilá prophesied that Prío's actions laid the groundwork for a new authoritarian state yet to come.[172]

Chibás's survival of what appeared to have been a government-sanctioned assassination attempt seemed no less than miraculous. Perhaps in desperation, the beleaguered Prío administration then decided to exploit Chibás's propensity to accuse others of wrongdoing and turn his best weapon against him. Possibly in an effort to distract attention from his own flagging popularity over the mass firing of teachers and closure of normal schools linked to his predecessor Alemán, the minister of education Sánchez Arango picked a fight with Chibás in June 1951. On more than one occasion, Sánchez attacked him as a hypocrite who exploited peasants on his family's coffee plantation and speculated in coffee prices. Within hours of Sánchez Arango's most damaging attack, Chibás responded in kind, first declaring him culpable of graft in the purchase of real estate in Guatemala and then focusing on his alleged poaching of precious hardwoods in Guatemala for resale on the black market. The ensuing back-and-forth between the two men quickly acquired all the earmarks of a useless dispute between two Cuban *machos*. Neither of them could claim sufficient evidence against the other; yet the absence of such evidence only fueled each man's need to discredit the other publicly and thereby "win" the debate.[173]

Undoubtedly, the day that Chibás decided to charge Prío's only clean and effective cabinet minister with corruption, he took the Auténticos' bait: Sánchez Arango had picked a fight with Chibás in order to whip up publicity at a time when Prío did not favor him as a potential successor in the next election cycle.[174] Given that Sánchez Arango's approval rating hovered at only 2 percent, most Cubans might have wondered why Chibás bothered to respond at all. In 1951, with the possible exception of Sánchez Arango's education ministry, political immunity reigned supreme under Prío, despite nearly three years of promising otherwise. The greatest proof of that lay in the fate of his legendarily corrupt predecessor, Grau San Martín: amid public amazement, a meticulously crafted indictment of the former president, the former education minister Alemán, and Havana's customs house director was dismissed. Why? The Auténtico Party machine simply forced the consecutive recusals on scant pretenses of three courageous judges who had initially supported the indictment. Among the charges documented in the indictment was the "bacchanalia of thievery" that had characterized Grau's final days in office, when nearly 21 million pesos disappeared from the national treasury. Apparent was Prío's refusal to see his Auténtico patrons investigated, fearing that the trail of stolen pesos would inevitably lead back to his own administration.[175] Indeed, in his last interview with the prestigious *Visión,* a glossy Latin American magazine edited in New York, Chibás noted that just as Batista had begun his career with a monthly salary of 36 pesos but managed to cede over 18 million pesos to his first wife along with a magnificent apartment building adjacent to the Presidential Palace in 1945, so Prío had ensured his family benefited from his own political fortune, making his brother Francisco one of Havana's premier real estate magnates. It was not so much the immorality of these acts that "nauseated" the Cuban people, said Chibás, as the "cynicism" they demonstrated on a daily basis.[176]

In short, at the time of Chibás's standoff with Sánchez Arango, la patria had clearly had enough. For many, all that was left to do was wait for Chibás to be elected president in 1952. A peasant from Oriente's Central Estrada Palma said as much when he wrote to Chibás to share his father's last words, issued from his deathbed. "My only regret was that I won't live to see *Chibás Presidente*."[177] Tragically, this was a destiny that no Cuban lived to see.

The Destiny of La Patria and the Legacies of Eduardo Chibás

Whether it was undertaken by accident or by conviction that martyrdom was the only way open to him, Eduardo Chibás's decision to shoot himself in the stomach on 5 August 1951 radically transformed Cuba's future. In many ways, his actions robbed Cubans of the glorious, democratic, and just destiny that he had inspired them to believe he and they could fulfill. In a bizarre twist of fate, Cuba's most beloved and promising political messiah had killed himself. To the millions of Cubans who mourned him and then witnessed the violent struggles of the 1950s that followed, it may have seemed that Chibás's greatest legacy could not be found in any one leader or any subsequent revolutionary movement but in Cuban history itself after his death in 1951. After all, everything might have been different if Chibás had truly *lived* for la patria and not died.

Or would it? The following chapter reveals a society whose citizens did not give up the commitment and belief in electoral democracy that Eduardo Chibás had undoubtedly revived. Cubans' belief in their destiny as a sovereign and uniquely democratic republic remained unwavering, even in the face of an event that few Cubans could have predicted: the military coup that Fulgencio Batista launched on 10 March 1952.

2

El Último Aldabonazo: Fulgencio Batista's "Revolution" and Renewed Struggle for a Democratic Cuba, 1952–1953

IN THE FINAL SECONDS BEFORE HE FATALLY shot himself after his live radio broadcast on 5 August 1951, Eddy Chibás had announced dramatically, "¡Pueblo de Cuba, levántate y anda! ¡Pueblo de Cuba, despierta! ¡Este es el último aldabonazo!" (People of Cuba, get up and walk! People of Cuba, awaken! This is the last knock on the door!).[1] Whatever he hoped Cubans would make of his self-assigned martyrdom, Chibás surely believed that his role in national politics lay beyond that of winning the presidency. As he had said only days earlier in a final press interview, "Here in Cuba, anyone can be president. . . . What is more difficult is to head a movement whose primary purpose is to moralize [moralizar] the state and the government."[2]

The shock of Chibás's suicide only deepened the commitment of Ortodoxos at all levels of the party to ensuring that his life's work would not be lost. Scarcely a month after Chibás's death, Dr. José M. Fadraga, the superintendent of Matanzas's public schools, told top Ortodoxo leaders that it was still Chibás who would win the elections for the Ortodoxos, not anyone else. "The people . . . demand, at the top of their voices, substantial changes in the socioeconomic order. . . . Chibás and the party are the same thing. The party without Chibás is nothing. The party will triumph to the degree that his figure and his ideals grow within it."[3] Attesting to this, there was surprisingly no dispute over who should inherit Chibás's candidacy for president. After making a graveside pledge to maintain the independence of their party platform from interparty pacts, the party's executive committee unanimously selected Roberto Agramonte, Chibás's own choice of a running mate and his intellectual (if dour) cousin, as the presidential nominee for the upcoming election on 1 June 1952. Rank-and-file members followed their leaders' example, promising unity behind whomever the party chose.[4]

In the last months of 1951 and first weeks of 1952, Ortodoxos fanned the flames of Chibás's memory, keeping hope in participatory democracy alive. *Bohemia* ran a special commemoration of Chibás's armed revolutionary activities against the unofficial military rule of Fulgencio Batista in 1935.[5] Election campaign placards featured Agramonte's portrait framed by a large doorknocker, or *aldabón*. Backed by two criss-crossed brooms, symbols of the need to sweep away impunity and injustice, placards repeated the Spanish rhyme: "Con Chibás en la mente [With Chibás on our minds], Agramonte Presidente." Prospective voters further embellished the placards with an additional smaller broom carrying Eddy Chibás's face.[6]

In the long run, however, it was not unity but partisan fragmentation that characterized Cuba's political scene in the years after Chibás's death. Foremost among its causes was General Batista's unexpected seizure of power on 10 March 1952. With the near full support of Cuba's armed forces, Batista's coup led to the subsequent cancellation of the election that, by all accounts, the Ortodoxos would have won by a landslide. Indeed, Eddy Chibás's final public words were a prophecy: el último aldabonazo turned out to be the blow to democracy that the coup represented. Batista's actions quickly became a wake-up call to fight for what generations had longed for and believed in: a different, better, socially just, and more egalitarian Cuba.

In the days that followed the coup, President Prío sought political asylum in the Mexican embassy before settling in Miami. Meanwhile, Batista forcibly dissolved Congress and censored the media. He also imposed his own version of "constitutional" rule by decree and crafted an eighty-member Consultative Council of sugar magnates, secretaries-general of Cuba's labor unions, and representatives of key professional organizations, including the bar and medical associations.[7] Other means of governing included violence, intimidation of vocal opponents, and legal maneuvers that facilitated graft and thereby cemented his rule from 1952 to 1953. At the heart of this chapter, then, is the untold story of how Batista consolidated a stable, if illegitimate, rule, and how historically dismissed opposition movements articulated deeply rooted beliefs in electoral democracy as well as constitutional freedoms of assembly, expression, and citizens' control over government. Cubans did not endure the new anti-constitutional order of Batista passively. On the contrary, for Batista, that was precisely the problem. Cubans repudiated what the dictator saw as his political destiny. Repeatedly, Cubans refused to surrender aspirations for participatory, accountable, and clean politics that the Ortodoxos, Cuba's watchdog press, and civic activism had restored so decisively in the recent past.

10 March 1952: Ground Zero of Fulgencio Batista's "Revolution"

The first months of 1952 found Cubans expectantly readying for elections and the Prío administration enveloped in an ever rising tide of public scorn. Apparently hoping to convince voters that Auténticos had turned over a new leaf, the party's 1952 platform promised to put the treasury to work for citizens in radical ways. To carry out "the socialization of the economy," Auténticos would "empower the State . . . to intervene directly in the production, distribution and consumption of wealth."[8] The pledge was also a subtle tactic aimed at enticing the highly dependable, if minority, PSP voting bloc to pact with the Auténticos and edge out the Ortodoxos to win. It failed. Instead, the PSP offered the Ortodoxos a formal alliance. This proposal the party of Chibás promptly rebuffed. Still suffering the sting of rejection, PSP cadres nonetheless instructed militants to vote against the Auténticos in favor of an Ortodoxo slate.[9] If Ortodoxos were privately pleased with the news, publicly they ignored it; doing otherwise would have undermined Eduardo Chibás's founding principle of *anti-pactismo* with other parties.

Not surprisingly, the campaigns of most Ortodoxos were less about what they expected to achieve and more about whom they hoped to remove from power. They also guaranteed that a resounding Auténtico loss would expunge corruption and impunity from Cuba's future political record. Naturally, Auténticos anxiously viewed this position as a promise to prosecute and jail Grau, Prío, and others for graft as soon as Ortodoxo lawmakers assumed power.[10] The campaign of Fidel Castro for a seat in the Cuban House of Representatives typified the general Orthodox position. Echoing Chibás's famous "Yo acuso" style point-by-point, Castro attacked Prío with a long list of accusations. Among them were Prío's recent decision to issue a presidential pardon to an associate found guilty of raping a child five years earlier and his use of military recruits as field laborers on the farms of friends and allies.[11]

Importantly, given the Auténticos' pathetic levels of popular prestige, Batista, a candidate for the Partido de Acción Unitaria (PAU), was running dead last among the top three contenders, far behind both Ortodoxos Agramonte and Auténtico nominee Carlos Hevia, Prío's foreign minister.[12] In the months leading up to the anticipated June election, the national press regularly revisited Batista's checkered past, focusing especially on the history of revolutionary consolidation that Batista's coup of 1934 had stolen from Cuba. Singled out for particular scorn was Batista's reputed order to assassinate revolutionary social-ist Antonio Guiteras during the military repression of a general strike in 1935.[13] Hoping to cast a positive light on his image as Cuba's U.S.-backed "strongman" of the 1930s, Batista's campaign posters exhibited a full-size, civilian-suited Batista next to the slogan "Él es El Hombre."[14] To ridicule Batista's version of *hombría,* citizens joked about PAU, Batista's party abbreviation, pronounced *pow* in Spanish: What did the letters P A U *really* stand for when it came to Batista's method of winning votes? asked the joke. "Por Asalto Únicamente" (By Assault Only), answered the punch line.[15]

While Batista's own interest in gaining the presidency through force rather than votes might be obvious, historians have conventionally identified the idea for a conspiracy among a small circle of officers who, they claim, invited Ba-tista to join them in the coup. Known as *los septiembristas* for their alliance with Batista against Machado's generals in the 4 September revolution of 1933 and their continued allegiance to him in the years after, this group supposedly chose Batista over other candidates.[16] Since most of the officers had been forci-bly retired by Grau, Prío paid little attention to this group, focusing whatever concerns he had of a possible conspiracy against him on *los puros.* "The pure ones" were a group known for their clean reputation and amenability to three key Ortodoxo leaders, all of whom taught classes at Cuba's top military acad-emy, La Escuela Superior de Guerra: sociologist Roberto Agramonte, historian Herminio Portell Vilá, and philosopher Rafael García Bárcena. In the rush to block his rivals through any means available, Prío assigned most of los puros to posts abroad or in remote locations of the interior.[17] This strategy ultimately backfired as Prío inadvertently dissolved one of the few obstacles to a broader scheme hatched among septiembristas to overthrow Prío as early as January 1952.

In many respects, historical accounts of the events leading up to the conspir-acy echo Batista's own version, namely, that he was invited at the last moment and that a coup was inevitable.[18] As the son of Batista's chauffeur and bodyguard to Batista's second wife Marta Fernández, Alfredo Sadulé recollects that the inevitability of a coup meshed well with the notion that Batista did not *choose* power but *was chosen* for it by circumstance. This only added to Batista's self-inscribed mystique as a humble man who always put Cuba first. Sadulé summarized the prevailing official view: "On the 10th of March Batista was simply someone who jumped on the bandwagon [*Batista fue uno que se montó en el tren.*] The 10th of March would have happened with or without Batista. . . . So true was this that he didn't choose the date, it was chosen by *them* [the military officers]."[19]

However, a confidential military intelligence report preserved among the personal papers of Prío's foreign minister turned presidential candidate Carlos Hevia reveals a significantly more complex story. Acting on Prío's orders, SIM had conducted secret surveillance on Batista as well as his retired army associates with ties to active-duty officers for over a year.[20] According to high-level informers and SIM agents, Batista had met with a group of retired officers in late January, including old favorites Francisco Tabernilla, Ugalde Carrillo, and Manuel la Rubia, at PAU headquarters in Vedado. Arriving at a consensus that Batista's candidacy was doomed, they agreed to "stay in touch and explore the environment" for possible signs of support for a coup among existing military ranks.

That very night, Batista then gathered all of his publicity agents at his large estate, known as Kuquine, to modify the plan of propaganda for dissemination over radio and printed media. The group designed three new messages, ostensibly to prepare the public psychologically for a coup: first, to condemn the Prío government as incapable of maintaining order, public peace, and property guarantees; second, to convince the public that "only Batista could reestablish an equilibrium"; and third, to drop "Batista Presidente" in favor of two telltale slogans: "Batista irá a dónde el pueblo lo lleve" (Batista will go wherever the people take him) and "Batista hará lo que el pueblo reclame" (Batista will do whatever the people demand). The author of the report and head of Prío's secret national intelligence service, Salvador Díaz-Versón, noted that a leaked account of this meeting explained why the journalist Mario Kuchilán related rumors that Batista would seize power by force in *Prensa Libre* on 30 January.[21] Indeed, Kuchilán was not alone in his fear for the future of the republic. In *Bohemia,* Mario Llerena sounded alarm bells, warning not of a possible coup but of a return to a dictatorial situation in which citizens' choice might be merely between Batista and Grau—neither of whom, Llerena declared, had ever been trustworthy revolutionaries.[22]

As of 7 February, the night before Díaz-Versón penned his report, the urgency of the situation had increased considerably. At another nighttime meeting on the Kuquine estate, Batista concurred with the retired officers that they needed to "shake things up" if the public was ever to believe that Cuba's national security was at stake and that control over public order was slipping away from Prío. Aside from "intensifying the propaganda," the men decided to recruit young members of PAU to agitate the public by "carrying out personal assaults and promoting all manner of alterations in the public order." They hoped that Cuba's national holiday of independence on 24 February would be celebrated "in a state of alarm and disturbance, and in this way justify the taking of power through illegal and anti-constitutional means."[23] Given all of this, Prío's security chief concluded that the nation faced a crisis: Batista and his retired generals were carrying out a conspiracy that had to be stopped. With the greatest urgency, Díaz-Versón recommended that Prío order the chiefs of Cuba's three most important regiments to prohibit all contact between active military personnel and retired officers.[24]

Why did Díaz-Versón not simply order the arrest of Batista and his co-conspirators? As he respectfully noted in his report, the security chief did not yet have concrete proof that the retired officers had already tapped and secured compliance from the active armed forces. Lacking this, it would have been impossible to justify their arrests.[25] In other words, what Díaz-Versón did *not* say mattered more than what he said: that is, in the absence of convincing proof, ordering the arrest of Batista, a rival candidate whom Prío himself had allowed to return to the country in 1948, would have made Prío more of a laughingstock in the eyes of the public and media than he already was.[26] Another explanation is that Prío simply decided to allow the coup to happen in order to avoid the inevitability of arrest and potential jail time that Grau's administration had barely escaped months earlier. As discussed previously, thieves stole the evidence against Grau from Supreme Court offices and then, after Ortodoxos assembled a new case, officials successfully engineered the resignation of three presiding justices in 1951.

Regardless of what might have happened if Prío had chosen to arrest the conspirators rather than wait out the storm, there can be little doubt of the extraordinary coordination with which Batista carried out el golpe and, contrary to standard accounts, of the resistance that greeted this act. Famously dressed only in his "shirtsleeves" (*mangas de camisa*), Batista and sixteen uniformed officers arrived at Camp Columbia in the predawn hours of 10 March. Once he entered, he announced, "Yo soy Batista, ayúdenme a resolver el problema de Cuba" (I am Batista, help me solve Cuba's problem).[27]

However, as island-based Cuban historian Gladys Marel García Pérez documents, Batista's entrance was far from pacific. As he and companions announced their arrival, fifty conspirators blocked access to the base with tanks and another group of young officers imprisoned army chiefs in their homes. In all, the insurrectionaries arrested one thousand officers at Camp Columbia alone, most of whom were subsequently dismissed for refusing to join the coup. Once notified of events, Prío had machine guns placed on the roofs surrounding the Presidential Palace and raced to Matanzas, where he hoped to persuade Cuba's second most important military base commanders to reject Batista's entreaties. When the head of the base, Colonel Martín Elena, sided with the constitutional government, officers arrested him and raised Batista's 4 September flag.[28] Mass purges soon followed, as did the dissemination of raises for all members of the armed forces, promotions in rank, and other material benefits meant to consolidate the support of the army.[29]

Back in Havana, the standoff had not ended. By midmorning, students at the university organized a mass meeting on the grand entryway and staircase, known as *la escalinata*. There, FEU leaders delivered a string of denunciatory speeches over loudspeakers, breaking the silence of the radio and television airways, now under Batista's control. Both before and after the rally, a group of students led by FEU president José Antonio Echeverría arrived at the palace and offered to defend the republic with their lives. By noon, two bodies lay at the feet of reporters outside, and the entire military command of the island had already ceded control to Batista.[30]

As FEU activist Jorge Valls Arango recalls, Rolando Masferrer, the congressman from Holguin and former member of the MSR political gang involved in the failed assassination of Eduardo Chibás, arrived at the university early in the morning. He offered to supply arms, a thinly veiled tactic meant to cause confusion among the students and seek their entrapment. Valls and others quickly surmised that Masferrer was already in cahoots with Batista. "I remember I said, 'With this guy we are going nowhere; he is going to sell us out'" (*Me acuerdo que yo dije que con ese no se iba a ninguna parte, que nos embarcaba*).

Knowing that Batista's slogan was "Batista es El Hombre," the students raised a long banner reading, "Este es el hombre que asesinó a Guiteras" (This is the man who killed Guiteras). They hoped to remind the public of who Batista really was: not a liberator but an assassin.[31] Meanwhile, military and police surrounded the unarmed students on all sides and arrested Valls along with others. "There, as soon as I arrived at the police station [no. 3], I received my first beating [*cogí mis primeras entradas a patadas*]. Later they pulled me out [of my cell] in the middle of the night and beat me to a pulp again."[32]

Other citizens also refused to give up. On the day of the coup, Huber Matos, a prestigious high school teacher and educator at the Escuela Normal, a teacher-training college, mobilized a student walkout. He then improvised several rallies to condemn Batista's coup, culminating in Manzanillo's town square. Although soldiers dispersed each one, Matos held out hope for their superiors' refusal to back the coup and for a violent reaction from what seemed likely sources of opposition among the Auténtico-dominated labor unions. To his disgust, the powerful stevedores' union and small-business owners vacillated; local political leaders conveniently "disappeared."[33]

Back in the capital, educators and Ortodoxos continued to protest. Led by the chancellor, the faculty from all thirteen departments of the University of Havana assembled publicly to announce their opposition to the coup and "any government that does not achieve power through election."[34] In addition, the entire national directorate of the Ortodoxos protested, first to the Court of Havana, then to the Organization of American States (OAS), and finally to the United Nations. Their efforts came to no avail. The legitimacy of the coup was recognized by twenty countries before the United States conferred its diplomatic blessing; its global acceptability to the UN, OAS, and highly U.S.-dominated international agencies made its initial stabilization a diplomatic fait accompli.[35]

Although he was a leading Ortodoxo and a candidate for Congress on the party ticket, Fidel Castro reacted alone. He issued a mimeographed denunciation in his paper *El Acusador* ridiculing Batista's seizure of power as "a coup not against Prío but against the people" and called on "courageous Cubans to sacrifice and fight back! *Morir por la patria es vivir!*" Never one to fear hyperbole, Castro also delivered a brief to his local Tribunal de Urgencia, one of the extra-constitutional courts normally reserved to try insurrectionaries that Machado had created and Batista had used so strategically during his earlier periods of rule.[36] After outlining the myriad ways Batista flouted key articles of the Social Defense Code prohibiting attempts to change the Constitution through violent means, Fidel counted up the penalty that each violation incurred. He challenged the court to issue Batista the maximum sentence of over one hundred years in prison.[37] Not surprisingly, his brief was unceremoniously ignored.

In the days following Batista's coup, student strikes consumed Havana and Matanzas high schools as well as national universities. In both provinces, a total of thirty thousand electrical, textile, and department store workers joined a mass strike. Mass detentions followed. However, intervention on behalf of the government by trade union representatives under the leadership of former PSP militants inclined to aid former ally Batista and the decision of Auténtico-affiliated labor leader Eusebio Mujal to support the coup soon quelled union protest.[38] Although he initially condemned the coup, the legendarily opportunistic Mujal had quickly turned an about-face when Batista invited him to remain as head of the CTC, Cuba's confederation of labor unions, a position he relished.[39] FEU also released a statement of principles claiming its commitment to defending the sovereignty of the Constitution against all odds and without considerations of party or ideology. "We are a pure force," wrote José Antonio Echeverría.[40] Students then staged a four-day "wake" at the University of Havana before burying the 1940 Constitution, symbolically enacting what Batista had done but refused to admit.[41]

According to Ruby Hart Phillips, a resident of Cuba and correspondent for the *New York Times* for nearly twenty years at the time, many businessmen, Cuban and foreign alike, were secretly pleased by the coup. Batista had immediately promised to protect all foreign investments in Cuba and patched together a plan with CTC chief Eusebio Mujal that included the cessation of strikes. He also imposed regressive policies of taxation such as a beer tax and higher postal rates in order to raise revenues without touching the profits of big business. Moreover, the U.S. government gave diplomatic recognition to the government in the same week that the Soviet Union took it away.[42]

Symbolizing the high elite's initial support for Batista, the Bacardí family had the leather bomber jacket that Batista had worn the night of the coup on 10 March ceremoniously placed in a glass cabinet at the heart of their famous national museum in Santiago de Cuba.[43] Batista also relied on young admirers, such as Rafael Díaz-Balart, the president of PAU Youth. A graduate of the

University of Havana, brother-in-law to Fidel Castro, son of the Liberal mayor of Banes, and onetime instructor at Princeton University at the tender age of twenty-one, Díaz-Balart possessed great political ambitions, pristine academic credentials, and a social pedigree. He became Batista's first vice minister of governance immediately after the coup. Interviewed in April 1952, Díaz-Balart explained his reasons for supporting Batista on moral grounds. Batista would promote young people like himself without putting them through the paces of political gangsterism as the Auténticos had: "Now the thug ceases to exist, with an official government check, gun, and the impunity to spill fraternal blood. Moreover, [our] effort will displace audacity, and gangsterism will give way to work and the conviviality of the Cuban family."[44]

Nonetheless, enthusiastic endorsements of Batista's coup, even from a privately pleased business community, were as limited as the protests. The reasons most citizens seemed to have stayed at the margins of protests and that most historians do not know about them are related. Fear, censorship, and most of the armed forces' betrayal of the republic in favor of military rule combined to temporarily limit awareness of the protests that *did* take place. By default, this blocked knowledge of them and therefore hindered their ability to spread.

From the moment Batista seized power, army units controlled the Cuban Telephone Company and all radio communications, the primary means by which millions of Cubans in remote rural areas of the island were connected to events in the capital as well as the politics of urban society.[45] Clearly outgunned if not outnumbered, citizens who turned to the mass media also found efforts to launch a war of words against Batista annulled before they began. A day after the coup, Batista's minister of information Ernesto de la Fe instructed the press that "private individuals" would not be allowed to take to the microphones.[46] The category included opposition politicians, who were no longer permitted to broadcast their radio commentary shows through party-affiliated stations like the Ortodoxos' CMQ. Until then, Cuba had never had an official censorship or propaganda office. Curiously, however, it was to Minister de la Fe that Batista left the distasteful task of announcing the official dissolution of all political parties until further notice.[47] The statement constituted a thinly veiled threat against the many "individuals," particularly Ortodoxos José Pardo Llada, Luis Conte Agüero, Fidel Castro, and others, whose editorial broadcasts dominated the airways. Among the direct targets of Batista's censors were CMQ-TV's *Ante la Prensa,* a popular nighttime talk show based on interviews with national politicians, and Jorge Mañach's Ortodoxo-staffed radio program to educate the public on civil and human rights, *Universidad del Aire*. By May 1952, Batista had institutionalized government censorship, subjecting to potential closure all news outlets and public affairs programming that criticized the state.[48]

For Batista and his supporters, the military's violation of constitutional rule fulfilled the will of the people, desperate for liberation from the conditions of "chaos," "incivility," and "unconstitutionality" created by the Auténticos.[49] "The people seconded [the takeover] through their absence," contended Batista's publicity agents. "The people approved and approve, every time they acclaimed and acclaim, en masse, the word of the Leader of March."[50] Never one to underestimate the role of media and imagery in shaping citizens' will to protest or conform, Batista took unprecedented steps to extend the reach of his publicity machine beyond the borders of Cuba to the United States. There he found a loyal base of supporters, both in Washington and on Wall Street. "A revolution is under way [in Cuba], yes," contended the Cuban Ministry of Information in an English-language pamphlet titled *Batista—Some Call Him a Dictator. The Cuban People Tell Their True Story,* "but it is a peaceful revolution of progress and work—a revolution which is necessary for the survival of democracy."[51] The pamphlet also echoed Batista's claim that President Prío, cognizant that he would lose the June 1952 election, would have carried out a "self-coup," allegedly planned for April, a little more than a month after Batista beat him to it.[52]

From the moment he seized power, Batista consistently maintained that the complete absence of "blood or revenge" from his "Civic-Military Revolution of March" had not only legitimated it as a patriotic act but also "restored in the shortest time possible the order and guarantees which were denied the Cuban people" under Prío.[53] Although the apparent lack of popular resistance was partly the product of censors and partly the result of good planning, Batista also regularly relied on it as evidence that the people recognized Cuba's military was "radically opposed to demagoguery . . . to resentment and hate among brothers."[54] The same love of country and of liberty that motivated Batista also motivated "*la gran familia militar*" (the great military family) through which he reigned.[55]

Arguably, Batista's concern for crafting a civilian-anchored self-image had everything to do with why stability and selective repression rather than insurrection and mass violence characterized the first three years of his regime. Famous for shunning military dress in favor of an impeccable (usually white) business suit and ending his speeches with the phrase "¡Por Cuba! ¡Por el pueblo! ¡Salud! ¡Salud!" (For Cuba! For the people! Health! Health!), Batista saw himself as a benevolent ruler whose humble roots could and should inspire Cuba's poor, especially from rural areas, to pull themselves up by their boot-straps as he had done when he had first enlisted as a stenographer in the military decades earlier.

In the latter years of his 1950s administration, Batista resorted to mass spec-tacles on the order of neighboring Dominican dictator Rafael Trujillo, including rallies that enlisted tens of thousands of civil servants as a ready-made audience of supposedly willing participants. Yet in the early part of the regime, cele-brations of Batista's self-designated national holidays on 4 September and 10 March were relatively low-key, if opulent, affairs, with a banquet and military parade held at Camp Columbia. As such, they symbolized the paradox that lay at the heart of Batista's style of rule: on the one hand, he invested much ego and energy in projecting himself as not just "a man of the people" but as *El Hombre,* the only man Cuba needed to progress. On the other hand, Batista could simply not afford to rely on image making and heavy-handed tactics alone, whatever the cost to constitutionality. Imposing Batista's vision of Batista as reality may not have meant less corruption than that of previous Auténtico governments. But it did mean limiting the anarchical street violence of political gangs connected to the Auténticos and the armed forces. It also meant that co-optation, persua-sion, and valuable policy making in the most visible social arenas became in-trinsic to enforcing order, discipline, and complicity among citizens with anti-constitutional, undemocratic rule.

The Early Stability of a (Mostly) Illegitimate Military Regime

In many ways, the self-congratulatory view Batista repeatedly expressed in the early years of his rule echoed point for point the arguments that he and fellow septembristas had made in the late 1930s in order to explain their re-versal on calls for the restoration of constitutional rule and an end to military repression, which they had previously embraced in response to labor protest or demands for civic freedom. When he took control of the government with the support of the military and the United States in 1934, Batista had chosen, in his own words, "to embody" the revolution that "was conceived and materialized within the army." Feeling "personally responsible for Cuba," Batista explained his actions then in ways that easily applied to his coup of March 1952: "I believe that I have been appointed by destiny to do my utmost for the republic."[56] According to Batista, Cuba's revolutionary impulse tended to make citizens victims of despotism. "I saved that impulse from its own errors. I saved it from its own deformations," he announced in 1939.[57]

Yet fifteen years later, Batista ignored utterly his betrayal of the revolutionary government he had helped install on 4 September 1933, and years of "strong-man" rule. Instead, he claimed a continuous historical trajectory that represented the authentic revolution against Machado as a continuing fight for true democracy. "The 10th of March 1952 . . . is the consequence of the fortunate tying together [anudamiento] of the program of 4th of September," he argued, a moment that had "rescued [Cuba] from the insatiable beast of chaos."[58] Batista also imagined the military as Cuba's greatest civilizing force in combating politicians' "incivilidad," one that threatened to spill over into barbarity. In fulfilling his self-assigned destiny, Batista "saved" Cuba from the likes of voters who might otherwise have elected irresponsible officials in 1952.[59] Now, as in the past, Batista promised to establish a state in which "the masses . . . [would] be taught a new idea of democracy and learn to discipline themselves" based on "authority" and not "force."[60]

Publicly and privately in the early 1950s, Batista carefully cultivated his image as a civilian leader who overcame his working-class origins, humble upbringing, and the racial prejudice of others. He allegedly achieved this through sheer personal will, hard work, and the acquisition of a skill set that allowed him to meet the social protocols set among Cuba's political elite and lily-white high society. Hoping to convince postwar, dictator-wary Americans of this, Batista employed former Latin American bureau chief for the Associated Press and recent senior vice president of CBS Edmund Chester to craft a succinct and appealing biography. It neutralized doubts by co-opting them from its very first page. "Maybe Batista is a dictator," wrote Chester. "But if he is, he certainly is a new kind of dictator. . . . If Batista were just a Latin American copy of the dictators of Europe there would be little reason for writing the story of his life."[61]

Batista, Chester wrote, was possessed of great charm and a sparkling personality, "one of [his] best assets." Chester argued that only "patriotism" could have motivated a man of Batista's wealth and stature to carry out a coup.[62] Why had Camp Columbia "opened her gates to receive the message of the revolution of March 10"? The answer lay in the will of the people and the persona of Batista, the man of destiny who had once been a "restless little farm boy from a hut on a hillside in faraway Oriente province."[63] Other leaders "could never enter Columbia as we did," Batista told Chester, "because when you enter Columbia you must enter more than its gates and its barracks. You must enter the hearts of the soldiers."[64] Safely established at the center of state power when Chester interviewed him for the book, Batista was preparing to preside over Cuba's long-planned and costly celebration of the centenary of José Martí's birth. Amid the festivities, he took time out to dine with friends in the library at Kuquine. Pointedly, he ended the evening by opening a large edition of the Bible and, to the understandable surprise of his guests, read passages aloud. When Chester asked why he read the Bible at all, Batista declared it relaxing, educational, and a primary inspiration for many of his speeches.[65]

Both an accomplice and a witness to virtually all dimensions of Batista's Batista was Captain Alfredo Sadulé. His father was the son of a truck driver who became Batista's personal chauffeur in 1934 and later, in 1952, the head of Batista's personal bodyguard. Thanks in part to his father's connections, Sadulé got a job working for one of Batista's sons, then the mayor of Marianao when Batista himself returned to Cuba with Prío's blessing in 1948. After installing himself at Kuquine, his suburban estate, and assuming his role as senator, Batista hired Sadulé to manage appointments, appearances, correspondence, and his famously large library.

After the coup of 1952, Sadulé served as First Lady Martha Fernández's personal bodyguard and first assistant, positions that required nearly around-the-clock availability, whether at Kuquine or the Presidential Palace. Commonly held negative views of his past were always a sore spot for Batista, noted Sadulé. In fact, one of the first things Sadulé remembered Batista telling him when he started working at the Kuquine estate was that he had never ordered the murder of Antonio Guiteras in 1935.[66]

According to Sadulé, Batista employed a wide array of personal tutors over the years. In the years he worked at Kuquine and Batista served as senator, these included stellar scholars of the political opposition such as Jorge Mañach, who instructed him in literature and philosophy, as well as others hired to teach table etiquette, standards of taste, and appropriate modes of dress. However, Batista viewed the acquisition of such knowledge and skills as a political necessity; he did not try to be something he was not. A French chef hired at the Presidential Palace "lasted less than six months." Batista also preserved a taste for foods associated with the lower class, such as *cascos de guayaba* (guava shells). Yet Batista was anything but a country bumpkin, Sadulé remarked carefully. Batista was a "chess player when it came to politics" whose greatest talent was playing both sides of the chessboard.

Batista strictly prohibited the photographing of his wife in the presence of uniformed personnel. These orders involved more than simply a concern for "demilitarizing the government" in the public's eyes. The first lady's presence implied Batista's own: she, according to the ethos of Cuban masculinity, was an extension of him and a piece of personal property to be claimed by her husband alone. However, Sadulé insisted that this had nothing to do with *celos* (jealousy). Participation in any political event was made to appear apolitical, *desinteresado,* as if the First Lady, like the president, responded only to the people's needs, not the partisan desires of whoever might have invited her: politicians' whims could never be their own. In this sense, Batista wanted to make his rule seem as far from the patron-client model developed by his Auténtico predecessors as possible. As Sadulé explained: "If the colonel of a province wanted to be photographed with her, then she would no longer appear as the First Lady but as the First Lady *who had been invited by the colonel.* So [Batista] would say to me, 'No, no: neither the colonel nor the senator nor the governor.'"[67]

Ironically, despite these gestures and public performances, Batista's reliance on political clientelism was legendary. While septembristas ran the most lucrative parts of the government, Batista relied on similarly loyal associates such as his personal secretary, Lieutenant Colonel "Silito" Tabernilla Palmero, son of General Francisco Tabernilla Dolz, chairman of Batista's joint chiefs of staff, to determine how much should be paid out in bribes and to whom. For example, "Gonzalito" García Pedroso headed the national lottery, a fund Batista personally controlled, mostly for top officials' own profit. Batista also charged Sadulé with the delivery of bribes to the homes of recipients who demanded discretion as well as to journalists who frequented Kuquine on assignment and needed to maintain a fair and balanced image.

Depending on the importance of the journalist or the post a particular recipient occupied, bribes ranged from as little as $500 to as much as $5,000. Although *Bohemia*'s editor Miguel Angel Quevedo and *Prensa Libre*'s Sergio Carbó never took a penny, Sadulé remembered handing over envelopes of cash at Kuquine to several journalists who became virtual celebrities and spokespeople for Fidel Castro's Communist regime in the years after 1959.

These included Marta Rojas, hailed for her detailed coverage of Castro's surprise assault on the Moncada Barracks in July 1953, and Enrique de la Osa, a PSP affiliate who often wrote for *Carteles* in the 1950s and was best known for taking over the editorship of Cuba's government newspaper *Revolución* from Carlos Franqui in 1963. In other words, journalists later seen as unconditional revolutionaries in the cause against Batista were actually on the take from Batista. Given that historians have no access to Batista's records, Sadulé's account is easily subject to question. However, Rojas and de la Osa might have had good reasons for taking Batista's bribes other than the obvious ones of greed and moral decay. Taking his bribes gave Batista the impression that journalists were playing by his rules. Certainly, it gave Rojas exclusive professional access to Batista at key moments, as noted in subsequent chapters. In addition, de la Osa's secret PSP militancy might have explained his toleration of Batista since the PSP and Batista's pragmatic interests had once gone hand in hand. Nonetheless, according to Sadulé, the refusal to take Batista's money made *Bohemia*'s owner Miguel Angel Quevedo and *Prensa Libre*'s director Sergio Carbó special and, in Batista's eyes, particularly formidable foes.

Rarely did Batista or his assistants instruct journalists on how to craft the news. Although he reportedly paid a monthly stipend to publicity agents like the powerful Edmund Chester to influence press accounts in the United States, Batista's "natural warmth" and attentiveness helped gain the sympathies of most foreign journalists. Some, like otherwise tough-as-nails Ruby Hart Phillips of the *New York Times*, tended to trust Batista. "His friendliness was absolutely sincere, not only to me, but to everyone he spoke with. For exactly this reason few people could resist his charm. Foreigners, especially Americans, always left his presence favorably impressed and convinced that he was doing everything possible for his country. He must have believed this himself."[68]

Domestic journalists also needed little advice from Batista on what to say or write about this regime. They followed the cultural logic of a popular Cuban saying, *Lo que se sabe no se pregunta* (What is known is not asked). However, Sadulé recalled at least one exception. When a journalist of *La Campana* complained that the bribe would not cover a trip to Spain, Sadulé reminded him, "Look, we are not giving you this help so you can go to Spain. We are giving you this help so that you can help *us* in politics. Spain is not part of the program, at least as far as I know. Or did you speak to the President and did he say that he was going to pay for your trip?"[69]

Batista's strategic largesse led him to fund a diverse spectrum of actors who had not previously benefited from government graft. To do so, Batista not only overturned many of Prío's legislative victories, such as the government accountability that came with Prío's passage of congressionally approved and publicly recorded national budgets. He also distorted irreparably the parts of Prío's 1948 banking law that required the representatives of private banks to be members of the National Bank's board of directors. Meant to check opportunities for public officials to line their pockets at the expense of Cuban taxpayers, this measure had previously inhibited the government from making loans to itself. Knowing that a government without transparency or accountability would easily flout these safeguards, Felipe Pazos, the Banco Nacional's highly regarded first director, resigned as soon as Batista seized office.[70]

Within fifteen months of taking power, Batista had modified aspects of the banking law with respect to loans and the printing of pesos no fewer than eight times. These changes formed part of a larger package of eight hundred law decrees and six thousand executive orders that had utterly disorganized the national treasury and enabled precisely the kinds of policies to which the private sector had traditionally objected. Yet not once did the watchdog members of the National Bank's board complain, object, or even bother to comment. Where had so much of the $7.2 million in commemorative currency that Batista printed to honor the 1953 centenary of the birth of José Martí gone? What about the National Bank's justification of a government loan of $20 million to cover expenses for the 1952–1953 fiscal year? How was that money spent? In successive public letters "to the nation" as well as the domestic and foreign banking community, a group of prestigious lawyers, most of them former Auténtico officials, pondered these questions. One could only imagine possible answers, they noted, but never really know.[71]

Still, Batista tended to combine bribes with surveillance as mechanisms for managing complicity rather than enforcing total compliance with or endorsement of government demands. One example of this lay in how Batista dealt with Congress. From 10 March 1952 through February 1955, when Batista seated a new legislature based on fraudulent elections, he suspended Congress and surrounded the Capitol building with military guards to impede the reentry of any congressmen or staff. Nevertheless, he did *not* eliminate members' salaries, a fact that undoubtedly softened the blow of the coup among statesmen who, under Auténtico rule, had rarely met to discuss legislation anyway.[72]

Importantly, Batista unilaterally raised his presidential salary from $2,000 to $12,000 a month upon taking office.[73] But Decree 2185, passed in 1954, also gave him complete discretion to fund institutions and programs at will. By his own account, Batista gave $63 million to specific organizations over the course of his administration, including $1.3 million to labor unions and $3.6 million to labor's social security funds. Ignoring the secular nature of the state as set forth in Cuba's two previous constitutions, Batista also distributed over $1.6 million of lottery funds to the Catholic Church, much of it to bishops who, despite their criticism of him, happily accepted the money.[74] First Lady Marta Fernández, who ran her own charity office, was known for taking individual destitute families under her wing, finding the recently widowed reputable forms of employment, and even paying for children's boarding school tuition.[75]

In order to deal quickly and surgically with internal threats to his power, Batista counted on SIM, the secret service, army informants, and the CTC in constructing his internal intelligence network during the early years of his regime. "The best [sources] came from the CTC," explained Sadulé, "because the CTC was town-by-town, union-by-union . . . in general the CTC had the best political information, not us."[76]

On the other hand, Cuba's police officers, arguably a better bet for information gathering since they operated block by block, were less reliable. Poorly paid and lacking even the benefit of full medical coverage, the national police force had been notorious since the 1930s for padding salaries with a system of kickbacks gleaned from casinos and prostitution. Every patrolman had to give a peso to his captain for every *puta* (prostitute) in the area he patrolled.[77] Batista's relatively light approach to controlling the police meant that in the course of the 1950s, police raids on brothels became increasingly rare.[78] The autonomy that this long-standing practice of taking commissions from streetwalkers and sex workers gave police might explain not only Batista's reluctance to rely on the police for intelligence but also Grau's and Prío's increasing use of military units as a supplement to—or at times substitute for—regular police forces in repressing political events staged by the opposition, such as Chibás's infamous standoff with Rolando Masferrer in February 1951. Moreover, lines for promotion in the national police force did not automatically extend down from the executive office of the Presidential Palace. In the military, by contrast, one always knew that the leverage lay in the chief executive's chair.

Nonetheless, one of Batista's greatest strengths in the first two years of his regime was precisely his denial of military rule and promise to hold and respect elections. In this sense, history was on his side: no voter alive at the time could have forgotten the landslide victory Batista had shockingly conceded to Grau in 1944, or Batista's willingness to leave the island shortly thereafter. Batista exploited that memory. On the first anniversary of his 1952 coup, for instance, he announced that even if the opposition parties had not yet accepted his proposal to hold elections in either June or November 1954, he was not planning to run for office.[79] At the time, the possibility that Batista would willingly stay out of politics undoubtedly whipped up flagging hope for a return to constitutional order among some sectors.

In addition to promising elections, central to Batista's efforts to legitimate his rule were much-needed public works and concern with taking back his mantle of patron to rural education that Grau's administration had so notoriously destroyed and Sánchez Arango, as Prío's minister of education, had struggled to recover. Batista centralized expenditures of public funds in the absence of congressional vigilance and a press still largely packed with ombudsmen. Consequently, he substituted accountability for his policies and expenditures with annual commemorations of 10 March and 4 September. On these occasions, he issued a "state of the union" address publicly specifying the achievements of his administration in the realms of housing, road building, and the like. Importantly, it was to these topics rather than the rising crest of civic opposition that Batista devoted most of his early speeches. With few exceptions, Batista dismissed partisan opponents, depicting them all as if they were disgraced Auténticos whose corruption gave them no authority to accuse Batista of violating the 1940 Constitution in the first place. That, he said, was like the pot calling the kettle black.

However, in two years Batista could rightfully claim to have inaugurated and built more public works than the previous two Auténtico administrations combined. These included the Ciudad Deportiva, a massive sports arena, the modern market on Havana's Carlos III street, Cuba's national Museo de Bellas Artes, an eight-hundred-bed hospital for tuberculosis patients in the mountains of El Escambray, thousands of kilometers of new roads, and new agencies of government charged with alleviating the conditions of previously neglected populations such as "invalids" and slum dwellers.[80]

While it is difficult to assess what portion of public funds destined for a particular public works project actually went to that project as well as its success, the visibility of many of Batista's constructions lent credibility to his promise to modernize infrastructure. This was especially true of the underwater tunnel connecting the Bay of Havana, designed by engineer Manuel ("Manolo") Ray, road repair in pothole-pocked Havana (which Batista claimed "resembled a bombed city" in 1952), and La Via Blanca, an eastern highway to Havana's beaches.[81] Claims that Batista built and repaired more than sixty thousand rural homes for peasants and eliminated thirty-four shantytowns over the course of his administration, mostly found in the pro-Batista press, often raised more doubt than confidence.[82]

Still, the Comisión Nacional de Vivienda, founded by Batista and charged with slum clearing, seems to have experienced unprecedented success. Using social workers, the commission achieved more or less voluntary removals from insalubrious slums like El Fanguito. The lands to which the government removed residents remained peripheral and underserviced, a problem that tended to reproduce the very conditions they hoped to flee. However, one major difference was that residents became titled owners of their plots, meaning they were finally safe from eviction.[83] Batista's version of an FDR-style housing authority did replace hundreds, if not thousands, of peasant-style huts with small cottages, most of which still line the national highways connecting Matanzas to the southern coast and from there to Camagüey. Their proximity to roads was undoubtedly of benefit both to the image of the government and the low-wage homeowner who could set up stands selling hand-crafted cheese and home goods to passersby, tourists, and other interprovincial traffic.[84]

Achieving social peace through government programs was a constant concern that Batista thought best addressed through initiatives in education. Indeed, Batista rarely responded directly to the rising chorus of oppositional voices and protest in the political realm, choosing to toot his own horn and thereby better control the frame for debate. For example, Batista's educational ministry reached out to rural teachers with the monthly magazines *Educación Rural* and *Orientación Campesina*. With much coverage devoted to Batista as Cuba's "primer sargento-maestro" (first sergeant-teacher) and to photographic rather than statistical documentation of advances, these magazines tended to replicate similar propaganda produced by Grau.[85] Accordingly, they showed government officials bestowing prizes on their own appointees, wrecked classroom furniture as evidence of past state neglect never to be repeated, and recently arrived busts of José Martí to schools in towns whose residents had never seen one before.[86] The campaign must have proved effective. Indeed, the revolutionary regime of Fidel Castro after 1959 would rely on many of these very same images, particularly of damaged or unusable school furnishings and the "first-time" arrival of patriotic images such as Martí's bust or the flag, to demonstrate Batista's neglect and the current government's pledge of radical change.[87]

Yet Batista also appointed the well-regarded lawyer Dr. Andrés Rivero Agüero to be his minister of education and created a new department answering to the needs of rural schools. Given that graft famously overtook the functioning of all other ministries in Batista's administration, the fact that Rivero Agüero ended his tenure in 1958 with a positive reputation and largely clean record speaks to the management of his ministry. As we shall see, the combination of economic stagnation, corruption, and civil war undoubtedly sank the chances of Rivero Agüero's rural educational programs to succeed in the long term. However, several of his programs clearly served as unacknowledged models for post-1959 educational projects on a much larger and more effective scale. For example, he opened thirty-four Hogares Infantiles Campesinos for uniformed peasant boys under the same military discipline as Batista's original civic-military schools of the 1930s and inaugurated 5,092 new rural classrooms.[88] Rivero Agüero also carried out Cuba's first mass literacy campaign and claimed to have taught seventy-three thousand adults between the ages of eighteen and ninety to read in one year.[89] In 1954, the ministry even began sending shock troops of doctors, dentists, lab technicians, and midwives to select rural areas in *unidades móviles de salud* (mobile health units) equipped with X-ray machines, rudimentary labs, and much-needed information on how to prevent and treat infections.[90] Fidel Castro's regime would later copy and expand this same set of programs, particularly the literacy campaign and use of portable or mobile clinics to reach neglected rural populations. Ironically, both Castro and Batista's programs were highly influenced by PSP advisors.[91]

Perhaps most impressive, however, was Batista's competition for the best rural students, called El Saludo Anual de la Flor Martiana (Annual Salute of the Flower for Martí). Dressed in blue overalls or skirts, white shirts, and straw hats emblazoned with the Cuban flag, more than five thousand peasant children traveled without their parents from the far reaches of the island to meet Batista personally in Havana. Each represented a different rural school.[92] In the city they lay flowers before the statue of José Martí in Central Park, attended an awards ceremony in El Palacio de los Deportes, the new national sports arena,

Figure 8. One of the hundreds of children selected from remote rural schools to represent their classmates during a week-long visit to Havana, this sharply uniformed black girl, shown shaking the dictator's hand, exemplified the vision that Fulgencio Batista wanted for himself and his administration. (*Orientación Campesina,* May 1954)

and enjoyed an all-expenses vacation that included a trip with the first lady to Havana's version of Coney Island.[93] Needless to say, the experience undoubtedly inspired this select group of elementary schoolchildren in unique ways. Not only a trip that their parents could never afford, the vacation was probably the first that most of them had ever taken so far from home. Meeting the president, the first lady, and other important officials made each child and possibly the community he or she hailed from feel special. The children also served as witnesses to the reality of Batista's rural education program in the court of an increasingly cynical public opinion. Government handlers distributed a photograph, for instance, of Batista greeting recipients of the Flor Martiana prize, showing him smiling and warmly shaking the hand of a visibly impressed, meticulously uniformed black girl (figure 8).

Given the often well-deserved demonization to which Batista's administra-

tion has long been subject, the existence of these programs, let alone their success, might seem surprising. Central to their importance was the fact that access
routes to improving one's life conditions in the countryside were few and far
between, if available at all. For instance, Cuba did not suffer from a shortage of
teachers at the time but a shortage of classrooms. Getting a teaching job in the
public sector was not guaranteed even before the 1952 coup and was sometimes
subject to the clientelism of Auténtico rule.[94] Moreover, Batista's established
reputation for championing the cause of blacks in the army and civil service
garnered him enthusiastic support from large swaths of the black and mulatto
community across the island. Significant in this regard was the almost immediate official backing Batista received from the national association of veterans
of Cuba's independence wars, a disproportionate number of whom shared Batista's peasant background and African-descended roots. Their support, particularly that of Generoso Campos Marquetti, the association's longtime president
who continued to befriend Batista and correspond with him for years after his
fall from power and grace, proved shocking to many patriotic white elites. La
Unidad Nacional Constitucional, for example, descried the veterans' endorsement as a betrayal of their own role in Cuban history, contrasting it with the
protest of FEU, an almost all-white middle- and upper-class organization.[95]
Questions of race, racial discrimination, and the relationship of both to class
mobility rarely, if ever, seemed to enter into citizen calculations of Batista's
potential to rule. Yet perceptions of Batista's attitudes toward black Cubans and
his own "race" clearly lay on his side: they worked as unspoken advantages.

Carlos Moore, who grew up in the black quarter of the U.S.-owned Central
Lugareño, the son of sugar workers, recalled scenes of jubilation and camaraderie among Rural Guards and local townspeople upon hearing the news that
Batista had taken power in March 1952. Shouts of "¡Pa'lante, Indio!" (Charge,
Indian!) and "¡Arriba el Mulatón!" (Mulatto on top!) expressed admiration for
Batista in hyper-masculine terms. Locals considered him an inspiring fellow
black endowed with the spiritual power of African deities and capable of turning the tables on racist white folks and exploiters. However, Batista himself
never manifested pride in his perceived blackness, and rumor had it that he
straightened his hair so as to look "less black." Nonetheless, the mere fact that
"Cuba's blue bloods hated the mulatto intruder ardently" gave him credibility
in the eyes of those who endured both daily denigration and, in Cuba's peculiar
political culture, widespread denial of that denigration.[96]

Indeed, after four years of utter neglect of race issues and no semblance of racial equity in government under Prío, Batista's coup generated great expectations as well as highly visible positions in government for blacks. In addition to appointing a black lawyer as minister of justice and Santiago's mayor as advisor to his cabinet, Batista included veteran Generoso Campos Marquetti, journalist Gastón Baquero, *Diario de la Marina* columnist Gustavo Urrutía, and other Cubans of color to his Consultative Council. More than symbolic, these appointments ensured patronage to followers, support for black societies, and a clear guarantee that racial concerns would not simply be ignored or swept under the rug.[97]

True to form in this respect, Batista granted half a million dollars for the founding of a national association of Cuba's societies of color so that they could construct private beach and recreational facilities. He awarded the elite Club Atenas the Order of Carlos Manuel de Céspedes for its efforts to combat racial stereotypes and service to the nation on behalf of blacks. His Council of Ministers also issued a decree penalizing discrimination "on grounds of sex, race, color, or class." However, the decree, like article 20 of the 1940 Constitution before it, failed to define discrimination and lacked the provisions for implementation that black congressmen and activists had been demanding for years. Although head of a government that was apparently "friendly to black people," Batista refused to take the bull by its horns. After all, he funded a beach *for* black Cubans rather than order the desegregation of all existing beaches as the Constitution of 1940 demanded. Despite repeated lobbying, moreover, his government never condemned, let alone legally banned, other de facto forms of racial segregation that dominated Cuba in the face of clear evidence that such segregation had worsened over the course of the previous decade.[98] In the 1940s, the Auténticos' infamous educational policies had led white middle- and upper-class families to abandon the public education system altogether in favor of Catholic and other private schools. This social stampede left already vulnerable state schools in the hands of Cuba's most politically and economically disadvantaged constituents.[99] It also left a generation of young white kids culturally and socially isolated from peers whose social experiences and perspectives reflected many challenges and contradictions to which white Cubans were never subject, regardless of their class.

According to historian Alejandro de la Fuente, in the 1930s and 1940s white elites and intellectuals came to value "blackness" as a cultural inheritance and element of racial synthesis in creating a distinctive Cuban ethnicity. Yet, ironically, the embrace of *mestizaje* and the idea of Cuba as a mulatto nation served to entrench racial hierarchies in new ways. While this process provided blacks the opportunity to participate in the construction of Cuban identity through art, music, literature, and politics, it did so on *white terms,* that is, in ways that did not displace whites from either structures of power or positions of cultural authority.[100] In other words, Cuba remained a country committed to paradoxical discourses of national inclusion and social practices of *anti-racism* rather than guarantees of racial equality and desegregation.[101] Black and mulatto Cubans were thus subject to the daily hypocrisy of neighbors, teachers, and co-workers who lauded "the Cuban race" but refused to swim, dance, or socialize with them. To explain this phenomenon, politically progressive Cubans in the 1940s and 1950s often joked that there were two things no Cuban in the world could stand: first, racism; and second, blacks.[102]

Nonetheless, in the early years of his rule, the racial visibility of Batista might have prompted greater possibilities for the publication of race-based social analysis than had been the case in the recent past. This seems as true of pro-Batista black intellectuals as it was of his black critics. For example, journalist and press secretary for Club Atenas David Grillo published two editions of *El Problema del Negro Cubano* in which he argued that blacks had wasted much time in the frustrating search for legal remedies: economic autonomy and education, argued Grillo, were the answers.[103] Revolution in Cuba, he contended, was born of blacks, not whites, including slave leaders like José Antonio Aponte, who led the mistakenly demonized black rebellion of 1812.[104] Yet after the revolution of 1933, from which Cuban blacks gained little more than the promises of the Constitution of 1940, white Cubans still believed that blacks could only represent blacks politically, never whites. Despite all the historical hype about the color blindness of cubanidad, in other words, the racial standard for elections always worked the other way around.[105]

Significantly, Grillo called on Batista's "Revolutionary Government" to fulfill the hopes of the "descendants of Maceo." If constructive revolutions transform societies, he wrote, "the 10th of March, for its *physiognomy* . . . has to distinguish itself from all others in its just application of policy." Thus, "the Revolution of the 10th of March" should not only enforce article 74 of the Constitution, he urged, but roll back the historically accumulated disadvantages facing blacks by providing government loans to help them establish commercial and industrial small businesses.[106] Unlike other governments staffed and backed by whites, Grillo implied, there was nothing that could block this one from advocating directly for blacks. The reason was clear: in effect, it was headed by a man most Cubans saw as black.

Far more radical than Grillo, anti-Batista critic Juan René Betancourt held out little hope for a government solution given that the government had always been the primary discriminator in the country, regardless of who ran it.[107] Urging blacks to shake off the racial inferiority complex that made them ashamed of their appearance and willing to accept the terms white racism had burdened them with, Betancourt blamed black societies for dropping their original practical functions of providing education to members in favor of a white model of "social club" concerned only with frivolity, hierarchy, and fashion.[108] Moreover, Betancourt contended that harsh legal measures sanctioning white racists for discrimination might only make matters worse: "Today in Cuba [people] discriminate because they can, because it is in the climate; fortunately, we have no creole Klu Klux Klan, but the promulgation of a penal law against those who discriminate would lead to such extremes."[109] In other words, he endorsed the age-old accommodationist logic that punishing racists would just harden other racists' resolve. Cooperatives, economic autonomy, and self-reliance were the means to improve black lives and to demand, from a position of economic and social strength, total equality.

Batista's perceived race and amenability to the poor made him symbolically important to many citizens who lent their support because they trusted Batista's form of politics and possibly gained something from it, even if they did not condone his forced ascent to rule. Batista's form of politics also garnered him the favor of others *despite* their perceptions of his race. Thus, patronage and clientelism not only appealed to blacks and some poor citizens because such a system provided them with few other means for social and political mobility; it also resonated with the values and practices of the wealthiest sectors of Cuba for entirely different reasons. Batista might not have been socially or racially acceptable to them, but the policies he espoused and his style of dealing with the ever widening gap between financially secure Cubans and the poor through charity and traditional discourses made Batista's top-down form of rule pleasing to the richest and whitest citizens.

Sources of Supremacy: Batista's Common Ground
with Cuba's Top Elite

In the late 1940s and 1950s, patronage and clientelism were part and parcel
of who wealthy Cubans perceived themselves to be and how they justified their
position at the pinnacle of a society whose national myths proscribed discrimination and racism as antithetical to cubanidad. For them, charity, benevolence,
and personal gifts served as appropriate vehicles for alleviating potentially immoral extremes of class, opportunity, and experience among Cubans. The state
and their own corporate fiefdoms should mirror one another. In many ways,
during Batista's reign of the 1950s, they did.

Such values were especially dear to the highest elite in the land, such as
the Braga, Rionda, and Fanjul families, who in 1909 founded the Czarnikow-
Rionda Company and Cuba Trading Company sugar conglomerate in New
York, with affiliated plantations in Cuba. The descendants of Spanish immi-
grants, Manuel and his brother Francisco Rionda, who were among the very
first to establish plantations and grinding mills, known as *ingenios,* in Cuba
funded through corporations in the United States, gave rise to a clan that considered itself deeply Cuban. Among them, George and Bernardo Braga, principal heirs of the business, framed their lives within the tumult of Cuban politics,
defining an identity that was transnational, bicultural, and bilingual long before
such terms entered common parlance. While these families were not friends
or necessarily fans of Batista, their comfort with the regime had everything to
do with the facts that its policies guaranteed their wealth and that its leader's
approach to the needy sectors of Cuban society imitated their own.

At its height of success in the 1910s, the company owned seventeen ingenios
and was a major stockholder in five more through the Cuba Cane Sugar Corporation. Together these plantations produced over 30 percent of the Cuban sugar
crop.[110] By the late 1940s, the total number of mills in the hands of the Bragas
had dropped to eight. With a total extension of half a million acres, an area
two-thirds the size of Rhode Island, some forty thousand people lived on these
lands, although only five thousand worked in the sugar mills, cane fields, ports,
railroads, sugar warehouses, and the like.[111] These investments proved highly
profitable. Francisco Sugar Company encompassed two sugar plantations, Central Francisco and Central Elía, consisting of approximately one hundred thousand acres of land, located in Camagüey province.[112] Along with Central Manatí

(worth $4 million in liquid assets alone), Central Francisco and Central Elía were top producers, grinding more than a million 250-pound bags of sugar per harvest and worth $3 million in cash by the late 1950s.[113] Thanks in part to the perceived stability of Batista's regime, the Bragas' total investments in the Francisco Sugar Company reached nearly $27.5 million by 1959.[114]

In these years, the Bragas also began to diversify Manatí plantation production by partnering with Texan cattleman Robert Kleberg, owner of the extraordinary million-acre King Ranch in Camagüey. To do so, they needed to locate and forcibly remove thousands of *precaristas,* underemployed and landless squatters who fed their families by growing crops on the companies' unused lands. Because these areas were suitable for cattle raising, Kleberg and the Bragas ordered a complete aerial mapping of Ingenio Manatí in late 1952 and early 1953: the only thing that stopped the process of eviction was the triumph of revolutionary forces over Batista in late 1958.[115]

Yet despite their extraordinary privilege, the Bragas assigned themselves a role similar to Batista's in Cuba. Taught to speak always in the plural ("*I* and *my* should always be substituted by *we* and *ours*"), the Bragas saw themselves destined by their wealth, much as Batista was destined by power, to improve the lives of citizens whom they considered their charges rather than their equals. "It was ingrained in us that it is the obligation of the owner to expand and to provide work for succeeding generations. This the family had done in Cuba over a period of 200 years. The head of the family often said, 'The day will come when it will be considered as immoral to be within a mile of someone who is hungry as we now consider it to have been to dine over a dungeon.'"[116]

Although no Braga or Rionda ever dined over a dungeon, Bernardo Braga Rionda, the nephew of company founder Manuel Rionda, claimed that his uncle would have been much richer if he not been "so selfless in giving away to each member of the family," a group that numbered fifty-one heirs.[117] However "selfless" company founders may have been within the family, outright charity contributions were pitiful, particularly when compared with the lavish entertainment expenses allocated to company executives. For example, records for the Francisco Sugar Company indicate that charity contributions from 1955 to 1959 totaled only $1,125.[118] Meanwhile, for the five-man executive board of Manatí, entertainment expenses incurred outside company business for opera tickets and club dues totaled $3,640.36 for one year alone.[119] Perhaps shallow paternalism might best describe the family's form and style of espousing "social welfare." Yet it was precisely in the realm of person-to-person relationships of patronage that the Bragas excelled, and they did so proudly.

By tradition, the Bragas ritually mixed with their own impoverished employees every Christmas when the grinding season began. Just as Batista and his wife held toy drives, visited country towns, and sponsored thousands of peasant children's trips to Havana for the Flor Martiana prize, the Bragas went door to door, meeting with and listening to the stories of plantation workers. "We visited little houses, some with dirt floors. Always we were given a drink. Sometimes there was only one glass," recalled George Braga, "which we shared with our hosts."[120] The Bragas also sponsored elementary schools on their plantations, but Central Manatí offered the greatest variety of schools to the greatest number of school-age residents: hosting four public schools and a kindergarten that served 268 students as well as seven private religious schools with 533 students, some run by Catholic nuns, Manatí offered primary education to 801 of 1,260 schoolkids in the 1950s. Much of it lay in the area of agricultural and technical training useful to the plantation.[121]

The Bragas also boasted about sending the very best students to college in the United States. However, according to company records, the company actually sponsored only one such student, twenty-two-year-old Juan Nicholas Evans, the son of a Jamaican-born carpenter at Central Manatí, who had already achieved a high school education. Company president George Braga, vice president Michael Malone, and the company's board of directors took on the case of Juan Nicholas, described as "a bit on the sleepy side but [having] a fairly good command of English," as a personal matter. Relying on Dana McNally, the owner of a summer hunting lodge the family frequented, Braga and Malone pulled strings so that the University of Maine would not only waive all admission exams but provide a scholarship reserved for foreign students in order to remit tuition.[122]

As the only black student on an all-white campus in Orono, Juan Nicholas braved near-arctic winters, suffered from what he called "a language barrier," and generally had his work cut out for him. This he made clear in typed progress reports that he consistently submitted on a midterm and semester basis to company president Braga, vice president Malone, and vice president–treasurer John González.[123] Nonetheless, company executives' personal and financial interest in Juan was exceedingly light. Basic room, board, and books were $650 a year. While the company covered most of this cost, it also withdrew $40 from the monthly salary of Juan's father, a man whom Central Manatí's general manager recognized as being employed for only eight months out of the year. Moreover, when Juan proudly reported grades in the A to B range during his second year and declared an economics major, it took a memorandum from a college official to prompt a brief congratulatory note from his sponsors: "Regarding Juan Nicholas' letter of November 19th, don't you think it would be good if someone wrote a congratulations to the boy on his good marks?" wrote H. S. Schneider to Malone.[124]

Nonetheless, the Bragas and their associates likely understood their efforts to go as far as they did on this boy's behalf as altruistic. Central Manatí's own general manager had clearly warned them that giving a poor black kid a four-year degree was useless to the company and possibly even to Juan himself: "As to first call on his services, we can not conceive of any circumstances under which Juan Nicholas could even be of any use to Manatí as an engineer. We know our people here and we know that they would not accept working under or with a colored engineer."[125] By the winter of 1960, Juan shamefully reported that despite his best efforts, his grades had slipped from a 3.00 average to 2.50, putting his scholarship and the Bragas' support at risk.[126] Although it is unclear whether the Bragas continued payments for Juan's education beyond 1960, the year when Fidel Castro's government confiscated all their properties, Juan Nicholas managed to graduate with his class from the University of Maine in 1962 and returned, perhaps not surprisingly, to Central Manatí, now under Communist state ownership.[127]

Thus, in many ways, the Braga family's approach to charity and shallow paternalism was about fulfilling certain social obligations expected of the rich and powerful and boosting their own self-image. Similarly, despite deficit spending and annual budgets of some $300 million during the first three years of Batista's regime, social welfare, housing, and other programs fell far short of his own officials' assessments of national need. The well-intended hand of charity reached only so far because it was never meant to transform the structures that determined poor Cubans' life chances, only the quality of the lives of individuals who, by chance, design, or convenience, happened to get lucky.

In this sense, the most common kinds of patron-client activism of middle- and upper-middle-class professional Cubans differed little, as did the discursive expressions through which they attempted to give voice to the poor. For example, since the 1940s, *Bohemia* regularly pioneered a column featuring articles on the poor that was meant to evoke sympathy, not a radical critique of the structural causes behind their predicament. Typical of this, an article titled "Niños de la Patria" (Children of the Fatherland) offered a heart-wrenching, three-page photo essay focused on child beggars, homeless kids sleeping on the streets, and rural workers under five years old.[128] Beginning in 1943, regular *Bohemia* columnist Guido García Inclán featured photographs and accounts of poor families with a sick or deformed child in desperate need of medical care they could not afford. Sometimes he quoted directly from the letters of precarista families who had lost their land and despaired before the eyes of their starving, swollen-bellied children. And for all the hype about Batista's wife's personal investment in the treatment of tubercular patients, García Inclán reported that the patients at Ambrosio Grillo asylum threatened a hunger strike if they did not get their medicine and care. "Years ago, when Prío was in charge, something similar happened. We thought this social ill had been mitigated but . . . everything is the same! It's as if it were yesterday," he wrote.[129] Always, Cubans responded, sending 5 pesos or more for the rescue of those featured. Notably, by the late-1950s, García Inclán retitled his column "¡Arriba Corazones!" (Lift Up Your Hearts!), a highly Catholic reference to the idea that in lifting up one's heart for the sake of others, one raises it up to God through the sheer joy of giving.[130]

Independently wealthy and upper-class Cubans also differed little in the high value they placed on social prestige or the question of who could achieve it and how. A quick glance through Havana's social registry of 1946, for example, reveals a tightly woven network of social power central to Cuba's political system, long before Batista's coup or even Chibás's suicide: there, alongside debutantes, wealthy magnates, scientists, and esteemed physicians, were not only Fulgencio Batista (despite his continuing exile in Florida at the time), his former vice president Gustavo Cuervo Rubio, and batistiano military ideologue Dr. Arístides Sosa de Quesada, but Eduardo Chibás, Carlos Márquez Sterling, and even the son of hated U.S. consul Frank Steinhart, architect of the second U.S. military occupation of 1906–1909. Needless to say, dark faces did not abound in the registry's hundreds of pages.[131] Absent major differences of class, Havana's social registry thus expressed a very entrenched Cuban ideal of "race-less" national harmony.

Yet behind the veneer where sociability reigned supreme, Batista's racial and class origins as the son of a cane cutter made him socially unacceptable to the country club elite of Cuba. In fact, Havana's top social clubs, the "Big Five," famously barred him from membership altogether. Cuba's top elite tolerated Batista, even supported him, because his socioeconomic and political policies appealed far more than the "wild-card" reforms popular among professional and educated classes. Importantly, though, Cuba's upper crust put up with Batista because they saw his policies as necessary to life not only as they knew it, but to *life as they enjoyed it*. By contrast, the political calculus to which most professional, educated, and salaried Cubans ascribed was entirely different, based on less pragmatic ideals that most of them would probably have qualified as patriotic.

The highest elite of Cuba attended events such as a Christian Dior fashion show at the Havana Country Club and considered, like the Bragas, open endorsements of any politician bad for business.[132] Meanwhile, salaried professionals, small-business owners, and others formed the bulk of the politically active and activist class who read newspapers, attended rallies, and ultimately participated in the wide spectrum of actions that repudiated the regime beginning in the summer of 1952. Pride in their own patriotism and the idea that they, as a second-tier elite, were closer to the struggles of Cuba's workers and poor classes had everything to do with the diverse forms that opposition movements to Batista took from late 1952 to early 1955—and, potentially, why they failed to mobilize Cuban society as a whole.

In Defense of Cubanidad

From May 1952 through the summer of 1953, forms of resistance to Batista's regime were characterized by diversity, disorganization, and a lack of coordination among activists. During that time, the term revolution became ubiquitous, possibly metaphoric of a generalized effort to reclaim the truth of Cuba's historical past from Batista, who seemed daily to undermine its meaning. Suddenly, the idea of "revolution" was not only on the lips of every politician, as it had been since the 1940s when revolutionary credentials became essential to election—it was also used to sell everything from Cristal beer to a new Cuban dance craze known as el meneíto, often simultaneously (figure 9). On a practical level, though, *revolución* was not an empty term: Cristal beer used it to capitalize on the unpopularity of its notorious, self-assigned claimant, that is, Batista himself. "The word 'revolution' became associated in everyone's mind

Figure 9. A short-lived but wildly popular dance craze, the meneíto, involved an independent, zigzag movement in which the woman appeared to avoid/tease her macho pursuer. Not surprisingly, Cuban companies, officials, and citizens alike adopted it as a metaphor for Cuba Libre, the traditional female image of the Cuban nation, constantly persecuted by her would-be rescuer, the self-serving masculine state. (*Bohemia,* 1954)

with an ideal yet attainable state," recalled Mario Llerena, a Presbyterian minister and regular columnist for the national newspaper *El Mundo*. "For the great majority . . . revolution meant simply getting rid of Batista."[133] The question was not whether to do so but whether or not Batista's ouster could be achieved through unarmed means.

Among Ortodoxos, arguably the most united political party until the coup, generational differences emerged regarding how best to topple Batista. At first, Orthodox Youth converged almost nightly on the homes of Agramonte and Pelayo Cuervo, "waiting for some kind of reaction" or simply an order to do something. "But nothing worked," remembers Jorge Valls, then a university student. Society, like its leaders, who had once been firebrands, appeared stuck in a condition of "perplexity. . . . They simply didn't *move* [*Aquello no se movía*]."[134]

In June 1952, Max Lesnik, national secretary-general of the Orthodox Youth, issued a declaration denouncing the two options proposed by party leaders: first, to unite with all other political parties in a single electoral slate of candidates that could defeat Batista in any upcoming election; and second, to opt for "static isolation" which, Lesnik noted, "does nothing and resolves nothing." From the perspective of young members, "We are for the line of revolutionary action, that of combat in the street, of open struggle against the de facto government, that will cultivate the conditions necessary for the Cuban people to shake off the weight this government installed by force represents. Batista today, like Machado yesterday, cannot be overthrown with 'tiny bits of paper' [*papelitos*]."[135] For many, Chibás's successor, Roberto Agramonte, exemplified inaction. Fat, balding, and dispassionate, Agramonte became known as La Masa Boba (the Dumb Blob) among impatient young activists.[136]

Two months later, as a guest on CMQ Television's *Ante la Prensa,* national president of the Orthodox Party Emilio Ochoa appeared to endorse a position closer to that of younger Ortodoxo protégés: the idea that mass unarmed civic activism could spark a general popular uprising against the government or, at the very least, force the government to reveal its true martial colors and drop the act of protecting "peace" and democracy. For all Batista's talk, Ochoa pointed out, the government had already spent nearly $5 million on tanks, bomber jets, and weapons but only $4,500 on a polio epidemic gripping the country.[137] "The party should launch its masses and its men onto the street and in all ways attempt . . . to force the government either to agree to proceed to elections or cover the republic in blood from one extreme to another." Specifically, Ochoa called for a demonstration of five hundred thousand citizens at the gates of Camp Columbia.[138] Upon completing his televised appearance, however, Ochoa was promptly arrested by SIM agents before he could even leave the building. Ochoa was tried, convicted, and sentenced to twenty-one days in prison, and his proposal for a confrontation between hundreds of thousands of unarmed civilians and the military never came to fruition.[139] Nonetheless, in a dramatic show of support, thousands of Cubans donated pennies, nickels, and dimes to a fund that paid for the thousands of dollars in fines to which Ochoa was also subject.[140] By October, *Ante la Prensa* was shut down altogether, accused of providing a permanent venue for opposition figures to slander the regime.[141]

Unbeknownst to the public and most members of both the Auténtico and Ortodoxo Parties at the time, however, were their leaders' secret plots to overthrow Batista by recruiting adherents from within military ranks and supporting counter-coups behind the scenes. In December 1952, for example, after weeks of surveillance and infiltration, authorities quietly arrested retired soldier and bank guard Tomás Martín y Sánchez in the process of recruiting financiers as well as other active-duty soldiers in a conspiratorial movement to overthrow the government with the backing of Aureliano Sánchez Arango. Unfortunately for the movement, two of Martín y Sánchez's principal collaborators turned out to have been secret agents of SIM. Moreover, for his cooperation in ratting out fellow conspirators under interrogation at military headquarters, Martín y Sánchez was set free, a strategy that clearly diluted chances for a second Auténtico try.[142]

Far more famous but less likely to have succeeded was the conspiracy of philosophy professor and national poet laureate Rafael García Bárcena. A former instructor at Cuba's top war college, La Escuela Superior de Guerra, Bárcena cut a dynamic public figure whose leadership credentials only increased when police arrested and jailed him without charge in August 1952, either as a preventive measure or an intimidation tactic.[143] Gathering together leaders of the politically activist organization Acción Católica, university students such as Danilo Méndez, and prestigious intellectuals like Mario Llerena, Bárcena founded the Movimiento Nacional Revolucionario (MNR). The term *humanism* served as the MNR's sole programmatic ideology for returning Cuba to electoral democracy and addressing the social injustice defining its landscape. Known for his extreme asceticism (Jorge Valls recalls that one could only sit on the edges of his couch since Bárcena would never have thought to get its sunken center fixed), Bárcena easily relied on his reputation for "obsessive purity" and valiant demeanor to gather adherents.[144] Then, on Easter Sunday, 11 April 1953, Bárcena himself led an armed attack on Camp Columbia that, according to supporter Llerena, "fizzled miserably" from the start. Along with dozens of followers, Bárcena served a six-month sentence at the notoriously insalubrious La Cabaña prison.[145]

Yet armed movements like these were exceedingly rare in these years. On the contrary, citizens participated in a spectrum of unarmed protests whose creativity and bravado galvanized disdain for Batista and united the public amid an indisputably *disunited* opposition. Importantly, despite all Batista's efforts to control and imitate the press through "gifts" and charm, journalists became the primary targets of his repression in the months following the coup precisely because they reported on civic protests as well as their own repression at the hands of police.

In August 1952, Aracelio Azcuy, an Ortodoxo and staff writer for *Prensa*

Libre, published a detailed "list of attacks on freedom of expression of thought" since the March coup. Highlights included the prohibition of a May Day parade by workers anywhere on the island; the use of force to prevent public gatherings on 1 June, the date that would have been national election day had it not been for Batista's coup; a ban on commemorating the first anniversary of Chibás's death; the arrest of FEU activists collecting signatures for a pledge of loyalty to the 1940 Constitution; persecution of potential rabble-rousers among socialist exiles from Spain; the closure of Chibás's preferred newspaper *La Calle,* among others; journalist Jesús Melón Ramos's detention; and, most recently, the savage assault on *Prensa Libre*'s Mario Kuchilán Sol, author of the popular column "Babel."[146] Kidnapped by police demanding to know the whereabouts of former education minister and now suspected insurrectionist Aureliano Sánchez Arango, Kuchilán was beaten unconscious by police, tied up, and left for dead on the side of the road. He was eventually picked up by a passing public bus. Newspapers bravely circulated photographs of Kuchilán's deeply bruised and wounded back, crisscrossed by the marks of *fustas,* leather-bound whips made from the long leg bones of goats traditionally used by Cuban police.[147]

Yet, as the most outspoken reporters like Azcuy had to admit, times had clearly changed from the days of Auténtico rule when journalists had stood shoulder to shoulder in defense of civic freedoms. In the wake of the police's stunning assault on Kuchilán, the Colegio Nacional de Periodistas called a general assembly to propose a twenty-four-hour media strike, as it had done a year earlier when Prío's government had detained two journalists. On this occasion, however, the result was not the same, even though the atrocities committed by Batista's forces were far worse. Of 370 journalists who attended the assembly, only 92 voted in favor of a protest strike. Ernesto de la Fe, Batista's top censor, had coerced the rest into obeisance, concluded Azcuy. Given journalists' previously heroic defense of constitutional rule and an end to the impunity enjoyed by politicians and security forces, this reaction clearly demonstrated the success of Batista's carrot-and-stick tactics. He combined methods of intimidation with financial subordination, managing perceptions of the republic while simultaneously terrorizing his enemies and detractors.[148]

While Azcuy's assessment may have been accurate when it came to much of the press, citizens became increasingly emboldened rather than cowed with the passage of time. Indeed, despite the ban on commemorating the death of Eddy

Chibás, thousands, if not tens of thousands, of habaneros marched in solemn procession from the University of Havana to the Cementerio Colón, preceded by women holding the emblem of the Orthodox Youth. The parade "constituted the most exceptional proof of public memory of 1952," declared *Bohemia*.[149] Batista did not deal so generously, however, with Ortodoxo party leaders: in advance of meeting for an official public act in Santiago, Chibás's birthplace and the cradle of ortodoxía, top leaders were all summarily jailed.[150] Batista followed these spectacles with spectacles of his own, such as a massive display of civil servants and CTC workers "organized by the government" before the Presidential Palace on the oddly insignificant date of 12 September 1952. Their purpose was to express "the backing and gratitude of peasants to General Batista."[151]

If repression over the course of Batista's first year as dictator had been bad, the first half of 1953 proved far worse. The long-planned (originating in 1939) and long-anticipated jubilant national celebrations of January, a month marking the hundredth-year anniversary of José Martí's birth, seemed to many to be Batista's alone, although these celebrations were mostly planned in his absence from power. However, Batista silenced that fact in order to take credit for inaugurating a massive new national monument to Martí, a new national library, the restoration of his childhood home (now fully outfitted with relics from Martí's life), issuance of commemorative coinage, and a gala at the Presidential Palace.[152]

While already announced, the year-long series of events had not been fully funded until Batista took charge in 1952, a point of pride he was loath to let citizens forget. To orchestrate matters, Batista appointed loyal batistiano intellectuals and officials such as his own minister of education Andrés Rivero Agüero, the Academy of History's Dr. Emeterio Santovenia Echaide, and engineer Gastón Baquero Díaz, a mulatto, to head the national commission responsible for all the acts, commemorative publications, and monument to Martí. This commission invited one hundred intellectuals from across the Americas whom Batista planned to fete and feast at the Presidential Palace. He also paid for Cuban embassies in Mexico, Haiti, the Dominican Republic, and the United States to hold concurrent ceremonies and celebrations.[153] In addition, the commission devised a national unified curriculum on "the meaning of Martí's birth" for use in all public schools and the making of a personal album honoring Martí by each schoolkid.[154] Largely devoid of content actually drawn from Martí's

body of political works and social commentaries, except for a series of morality tales for children known as *La Edad de Oro,* the curriculum centered on
themes of love. Students were required to memorize musicalized versions of
Martí's poem about friendship, "La Rosa Blanca." They were also required to
recite and write the phrase "Yo quiero a Martí" (I love Martí) as well as discuss
the apparently vexing question, "¿Por qué yo quiero a Martí?" (Why do I love
Martí?)[155]

To launch the week-long series of events, culminating with a banquet at the
Presidential Palace, the commission organized a team of runners who raced
from Santiago to Havana carrying a torch: notably, the runner who traversed
the final lap and brought the torch to the Central Park monument to Martí was
black.[156] However, while Batista may have highlighted Martí's anti-racist call
for "a nation for all," he silenced other aspects of Martí's political biography.
Notable among these was the fact that Martí was "first chained, jailed, subjected to forced labor and eventually exiled as a teenager for words" the Spanish considered revolutionary, a focal point of the speech President Prío had
delivered two years earlier upon the inauguration of Martí's mausoleum in the
cemetery in Santiago de Cuba.[157]

Hoping to prolong for more than one year the legacy of his nationalist largesse as both the principal patron of Martí and his natural partisan, Batista also
commissioned a full-length feature film based on Martí's life. Incredibly and
somewhat ironically, the author of the biography on which the script was based,
the scriptwriter, the film director, the cinematographer, and the actor playing
Martí were all Mexican rather than Cuban. Félix Lisazo, Batista's point person
for most centenary activities, justified these choices based on Batista's view
of their alleged talents rather than their distance from the obviously burning
political contradictions and thorny historical questions at which an all-Cuban
production team might arrive.[158] Moreover, the storyline focused on Martí's
alleged love for a long-dead girl, the subject of a famously popular poem "La
Niña de Guatemala," rather than his incessant political work denouncing U.S.
imperial intentions toward Cuba and the exceptional revolutionary potential he
ascribed to a free Cuba.[159]

Conspicuously absent from the affair was the family of Martí's legitimate
son, José Martí Zayas Bazán. Raised with the values of his pro-Spanish mother
rather than those of his father, José Martí Jr. began a military career shortly after
the 1895 war, serving first as U.S. military governor Charles Magoon's personal

assistant (1906–1909), then as an officer involved in the Liberal government's massacre of blacks following the protest of a pro-black rights political party in 1912, and finally as an officer in Machado's army.[160]

Considering all of this and Batista's obsession with denying his own militarism, it comes as no surprise that his administration focused on persuading María Mantilla, officially Martí's goddaughter but publicly known to be his illegitimate daughter, to attend the ceremonies.[161] Born and raised in the United States, Mantilla was the widow of the legendary Mexican-born Hollywood star César Romero Sr. She accepted the all-expenses-paid visit and donated the precious ankle chains that the Spanish had forced Martí to wear during his time as a teenage political prisoner working in the rock quarries on the Isle of Pines. Although Mantilla willingly shared the limelight with multitudes of batistiano luminaries, she made no political comments on Cuba's current state of affairs throughout the duration of her stay. Significantly as well, while she handed over her father's ankle chains to Batista's national commission for permanent display, she kept the keys.[162]

Separately from Batista's celebrations, diverse sectors of civil society chose to honor Martí's legacy on their own. Boasting one of the most gender and racially diverse workforces in the country, the Cuban cigarette manufacturers' union, for example, celebrated Martí with special columns on his thought in its monthly magazine. They also sponsored an exhibit of Martí memorabilia collected from tobacco workers who had once suffered exile in the United States and collaborated with Martí in founding Cuba's last revolution against Spain as well as poetry recitals by the children of union members in honor of Martí.[163]

Still, union-affiliated activities were for the most part politically neutral in terms of rivaling or challenging the *conciencia martiana* (Martí-inspired political conscience) conveyed by Batista. In this regard, student effort took a radically different turn. FEU inaugurated a pedestal and bust of Julio Antonio Mella in early January 1953. Founder of FEU and the Communist Party, Mella was best known for pioneering the fight against the dictator Machado in a series of actions that culminated in a hunger strike he staged while serving time in Machado's prisons and a wave of national protests on his behalf. Forcibly exiled to Mexico as a condition of his release, Mella was later assassinated on Machado's orders. During his years as a law student in Havana, Mella had also founded and led La Universidad Popular José Martí, which brought together students and workers. Mella particularly focused on the cigar-making sector because cigar makers had played such a vital role in José Martí's activist network supporting Cuba's final, 1895 war for independence and subsequently, in the mythification of Martí as a selfless, raceless, and classless messiah.[164] However short-lived La Universidad Popular's existence might have been in Cuba, its very name was enough to contest how Batista conceived the role of intellectuals and treated the legendary political "purity" of Cuban students. Honoring Mella also implied a comparison between Batista and Mella's nemesis, the detested dictator and onetime enemy of Batista himself, Gerardo Machado. Because Mella was also widely credited with achieving the university's political autonomy and freeing campus grounds from the authority of the police and armed forces, honoring him allowed students to express all they despised about Batista without doing so overtly.

Of course, for Batista and his supporters, the meaning behind such an homage rang loud and clear. Five days after the monument to Mella went up, they responded. On 15 January 1953, students awoke to find the bust vandalized and covered in *chapapote,* a heavy black tar. Immediately, the news set off a firestorm of protest as dozens, then hundreds of students gathered in an impromptu demonstration. By ten thirty in the morning, they had hung a giant effigy of Batista from a lamppost on the corner of L and 23, a major Havana thoroughfare near the university. Bombarded with water from fire hoses and then gunshots, the students threw rocks, cans, debris, anything they could find at police and continued to march down San Lázaro, a street that leads directly from the university to Central Park. Under a hail of bullets, the students urged one another on to the Presidential Palace, repeatedly screaming "¡Abajo Batista! ¡Abajo la dictadura!" (Down with Batista! Down with the dictatorship!) and, most ominously, "¡La cabeza de Batista!" (Off with Batista's head!) Confronted by a wall of police, soldiers, and marines carrying long firearms and even Thompson machine guns, José Antonio Echeverría, Juan Pedro Carbó, Rolando Cubela, and others linked arms and attempted to push their way through. In the end, mass arrests ensued. Bloodied protesters littered the streets and byways. Five students had been shot. Ruben Batista Rubio, a student who coincidentally shared the dictator's last name, sustained wounds so severe that he died within a month of the protest.[165] Fearful of the inevitable public outrage over the student martyr's death and possible repercussions, Batista ordered all newsreel footage of the demonstration confiscated from director Manuel Alonso: it showed the armed forces pointing machine guns at unarmed young protesters. A string of reporters, including sports commentators who denounced government actions, found themselves jailed, harassed, or beaten; some saw their homes raided. Not even NBC's Ted Scott or Ruby Hart Phillips of the *New York Times* escaped the campaign of violence and intimidation although, by Hart Phillips's own account, she and her team quietly weathered the storm.[166]

Confrontations over both the legacy of Martí and the meaning of present-day repression were only getting started, however. At the end of the month, while Batista toasted the birth of Martí on 28 January 1953 with guests at the Presidential Palace, FEU organized a silent march by torchlight down San Lázaro Street to the original monument to Martí erected in Central Park in 1905. Clear to everyone was the dual significance of the act: not only were they honoring Martí, they were commemorating their own heroism in having confronted the militarism of government forces on that very street two weeks earlier. SIM then raided the studio of sculptor J. M. Fidalgo, destroying his work and charging him with subversion for producing eighty statuettes of José Martí inscribed with the phrase "Para Cuba que sufre" (For Cuba who suffers).[167] On 14 February, when Ruben Batista Rubio died, mourners, including Fidel Castro, walked from his funeral at Cementerio Colón to the nearby home of Luisa Margarita de la Cotera, one of Batista's publicists. There they pelted the illuminated billboard of Batista's image that decorated her front lawn with rocks and overturned her car before being dispersed by police.[168] Then came 24 February, anniversary of Martí's Grito de Baire and the launching of Cuba's 1895 war for independence, followed by 20 May, official birth date of the Cuban republic. On all these dates, from Guanajay, Pinar del Rio to Sagua la Grande, Santa Clara, and the far eastern towns of Camagüey, commemorations led by teachers, schoolchildren, and even La Juventud Católica Cubana (Cuban Catholic Youth) ended violently with arrests and assaults on participants by army soldiers, police, or both.[169]

According to the pioneering work of Michelle Chase, women figured prominently in early acts of protest and resistance, acting on their own or through groups not led by men. On the first anniversary of the coup, groups of young female students stood at major intersections in downtown Havana handing out black armbands as a sign of collective bereavement. When Batista's CTC held an official Labor Day rally in May 1953, an alternative celebration held at the University of Havana attracted mostly women. Sometimes women dressed up for protests in the Cuban flag or wore the iconic costume of "Cuba Libre."[170]

Seared into the memories of generations of Cubans who had grown up surrounded by patriotic memorabilia of the independence wars, this image of a flag-adorned woman signified the eternal struggle of the nation to break the chains of slavery and colonialism, whether Spanish or American.

Moreover, the earliest sites of resistance included private places where middle-class women championed the cause by exploiting stereotypical aspects of social acceptability, such as being stay-at-home housewives, to protest through "phone chains" in which one woman called ten others, denouncing the dictatorship in a few rapid-fire lines and inviting each one to call ten more. Women also countered the very values of leisure, modernity, and material consumption that Batista promoted in the 1950s by embodying asceticism: refusing to wear lipstick (a staple in any self-respecting bourgeois Cuban woman's performance of femininity and aesthetic), wearing black to symbolize a national state of mourning, and refusing to patronize movie theaters, cabarets, and other places were only a few methods of protest. Enjoying oneself implied denying the suffering of others, argues Chase. Women led men in regularly remapping lively Havana into one of many "dead cities" whose empty streets denounced individualist forms of escapism and collectively embraced a consciousness of Cuba's violent political reality.[171] Women may also have staked a greater claim to the mantle of moral righteousness and authority early on, simply through their disproportionate membership in Eddy Chibás's Orthodox Party movement and their reputation as central participants.[172]

Undoubtedly, these unarmed challenges to Batista and even the armed movements led by students, Castro, and others that followed sought to gain the support of citizens. They did so because the facts of history stood on their side. Bottom-line logic dictated that while Batista could claim to be a constitutionalist, the very nature of his government could not show it, whatever his words, good deeds, or patriotic acts. However, the often-cited disorganization of early struggles to topple Batista was perhaps less important at this stage than most citizens' apparent aversion to armed insurrection as a response to Batista's *marcismo* (martialism), a double entendre that implied his militarism as much as his constant referencing of his successful "Diez de Marzo" (10 March 1952) coup, subsequently decreed a patriotic national feast day. Other factors weakened the legitimacy of those who might otherwise have inspired legions of followers. Perhaps the least recognized and possibly most central of these was race—or, more specifically, racism.

Hidden Weapons: Race and Racism
Among the Opposition to Batista

The visible face of the opposition to Batista, as Alejandro de la Fuente has written, was not only middle to upper-middle class, it was also almost invariably white.[173] At the same time, however, the visible face of the enemy—Batista—as depicted by vocal and publicly renowned opponents, was not just black but savage, animalistic, perverse, and antithetical to the norms of civilization as defined by cubanidad. Thus, the most prominent and consistent features of Auténtico and Ortodoxo Parties' anti-Batista propaganda in these years were overt references to Batista's race. For example, Luis Ortega, respected director of the newspaper *Pueblo,* wrote in 1953:

> The bestial Fulgencio Batista, *mono encaramado* [perched-up monkey], the great brake holding back Cuba, sergeant of the lowest form of shorthand, chief of an Arab emirate of bandits, always nourished his goal of rubbing up against the precarious marquises and countesses of Cuba. . . . [Yet] he has three other goals he wants to hide: the goal of aristocratizing himself, the goal of straightening his hair, and the goal of being able to pronounce correctly the rebellious word "doctor." Useless, always useless, uselessly useless always. What is inherited cannot be stolen or hidden. [*Lo que se hereda no se hurta.*] It is the only thing that he has not been able to steal or hide.

Batista could not pronounce "that traitorous c" in the Spanish word *doctor,* noted Ortega, because he was black. Batista "struggled, bravely, to push into his small brain that pesky word" (*luchó, bravamente, por meterle en el poco seso la palabreja*). He could and would never achieve it, concluded Ortega sarcastically, because he always tripped over that "ancestral obstacle" (*el obstáculo ancestral*).[174]

Stripped of their journalistic credentials on Batista's orders, Luis Ortega and José Luis Pardo Llada, Eddy Chibás's former right-hand man at CMQ Radio and the Orthodox Party, nonetheless attended the ninth annual convention of the Inter-American Press Society, headed by Jules Dubois of the *Chicago Tribune,* in Mexico. Allowed to speak, they denounced nearly case by case the atrocities committed by Batista's henchmen. They also distributed sixty-five thousand copies of their speeches in a thirty-one-page pamphlet replete with astonishingly racist political cartoons that portrayed Batista as a fur-covered, sword-, club-, and pistol-wielding beast with a vulture for a pet.[175] Illustrator Salvador Cancio Peña used every possible racial stereotype to portray Batista's face with enormous, protruding lips, slanted slits for eyes, pointy ears, and a gorilla's low, furrowed brow. Occasionally garbed in an overly decorated, unbuttoned army jacket while at other times shown in his naked "fur," the Batista that these leading opposition figures imagined wore a striped, homespun *taparabo,* the kind of loincloth Cubans disdainfully presumed was donned by pre-Columbian Indians.

More powerful perhaps than the pamphlet's printed words, its images accused Batista of raping the press much as he raped the nation. Two cartoons showed Batista leading a muzzled and chained woman wearing a banner with the word "Press" on it; another portrayed him hovering over a scantily clad, apparently violated Cuba Libre. With a knife in her back and her French-style revolutionary cap lying on the floor, the victim covered her face in shame with her long hair. Another illustration showed a brutalized and whipped white man, his back to the viewer, head hung in shame, ropes still dangling from each limb as he sat, stunned, on the floor.[176] Adding to the idea that Batista's limitless brutality might extend even to sodomy, the very next cartoon portrayed him proclaiming to the people, "¡Yo soy el hombre!" (I am the man!), right paw over his chest (figure 10).[177]

In depicting Batista in such terms, early opposition movements curried favor with those who detested Batista more for his race than for constitutional reasons. Yet they also turned Batista's discourse of military order and civil discipline on its head, framing his rule within the more basic dyad of militarism and racial savagery. Quite possibly, given the paradoxical racial consciousness so typical of white Cubans at the time (and, I would argue, common even today), opposition activists like José Pardo Llada and Luis Ortega would not have recognized their denunciations as racist; indeed, on the contrary, they might well have argued that *because* Cubans were supposedly "above" black and white, as Martí contended, their portrayal of Batista was not about evoking stereotypical ideas of blacks as monkeys, gorillas, or the like but about denouncing Batista as anti-Cuban, the antithesis of cubanidad, as well as the subhumanity of the Batista regime itself.

Indeed, perhaps it was Batista's very rejection by great swaths of the mostly white, middle- and upper-middle-class opposition on racial grounds that made

Figure 10. Since the 1930s, Fulgencio Batista's dark skin, lower-class roots, and successful manipulation of power had angered Cuba's politically progressive middle class. Auténtico propaganda like this relied on whites' deeply embedded racism to denigrate Batista for his anti-constitutional rule and brutality. The tactic doubtless inspired few blacks to join the opposition, whatever they thought of Batista's rule. (Aracelio Azcuy, *Cuba: Campo de Concentración* [1954])

¡YO SOY EL HOMBRE¡

him so powerful to those in the army who owed their positions to earlier moments of valor in 1933 or to later moments of strategic clientelism after 1933. In any case, Batista was clearly not supported by the army alone. United to the army were clients of the lower class but also unmistakably important supporters of the professional and rising upper class such as Rafael Díaz-Balart.

When asked in an interview filmed in 2002 to explain the origins of his relationship to Batista, Díaz-Balart noted that he became a "sympathizer" of Batista, without ever having met him at that point, in 1945 when he entered the University of Havana and Batista was still in exile in Daytona Beach, Florida. Recognizing that it was largely under Grau that massive corruption and political gangsterism had begun to grow, Díaz-Balart saw Batista as the only Cuban leader who had presided over an "exemplary democratic transition from 1933 to 1944" and handed over power peacefully. Why, then, did so many Cubans openly reject him out of hand by the end of his first period of rule, when they should have supported Batista more than ever before? Díaz-Balart asked.

Effectively, they say to me, "You are right. He is a man who handed over power but he is a shitty nigger" [*Me dicen tienes razón, es un hombre que entregó el poder pero es un negro de mierda*]. That's when I realized that there is a ferocious racial ingredient at work here. It started back in 1933 with a classist element. . . . When suddenly Cuba awoke on the 4th of September with new leaders, leaders who were army leaders . . . and when in Havana, which is where the head [of state] is visible, they wake up and start reading the newspapers, they see that there are these new leaders named Ruperto [Ruperto Cabrera], Fulgencio Batista, Ulciceno, Euterio—and they say, What the hell is that? Where are these people coming from? [*¿Esto qué cosa es? De dónde sale esta gente?*] They were *guajiros*. Humble people. There you get a classist shock to the system. *Never has Cuba been cured of that*. But then later, it gets worse. They find out that in addition to the fact that [the new leaders] are *guajiros*—el Euterio, el Fulgencio and el Ulciceno, el Ruperto—that aside from [their rural origins], *their leader is a mulatto!* And so you get the racist element added to the classist element. From that Cuba has never been cured. As Gastón Baquero says in his great essay, *El Negro en Cuba,* because there he explains the inexplicable, he says, Cubans have a racist element but they want to think that they are not racist. *They need to think that they are not racists*. But let me tell you, a ferocious racial element was at play there.[178]

Rafael Díaz-Balart's perspective clearly reflected his experience and position as a white, blue-eyed, wealthy, socially well-connected young lawyer with political ambitions. It also reflects his identity at the time of his interview in 2002: an ardent opponent of the Cuban revolutionary regime of Fidel Castro known for his batistiano roots, Díaz-Balart had reason to depict both himself and Batista as more enlightened than their opponents on issues of race in the 1950s. Still, according to Díaz-Balart, Cuban racism *and* anti-racism meant that if Batista had played by the rules in politics after 1944, he would never have had a chance.

Perhaps for this very reason, the forces of the opposition that *would* prevail were those who made neither class nor race an issue. Indeed, the discourse of revolution ignored matters of race, whether in the movement of Fidel Castro, Díaz-Balart's brother-in-law and Chibás's onetime protégé, or that of its primary rival, FEU, led by José Antonio Echeverría. Within and across these movements, raceless and classless cubanidad joined hands. These ideas combined within a long-established nationalist cultural milieu of politics that conceived activism among Cuban youth as naturally desinteresado (selfless) and pure. Cubans of all walks of life, like the young activists they admired and sometimes joined, continued to hope for a state whose morality, altruism, and justice matched the needs of its people.

The Crossroads Between 1952 and the Start of a Civil War

As resistance increased and repression grew in tandem over the course of 1953, the opposition gained credibility regardless of its own clear organizational disunity, even among partisan ranks. In the all-too-common discourse of the day, the equation of political backwardness and an uncivilized reliance on violence with race was also perhaps the easiest to make. "[We must] never appeal to the system of tribes and the physical elimination of the individual," wrote J. M. Cruz Tolosa to Ortodoxo leader Carlos Márquez Sterling. Invoking the ongoing, bloodily repressed rebellion of native Kenyans against the British Empire at the time, Cruz Tolosa continued, "That is the system of the Mau-Mau that the hypocritical revolution of 1933 has badly left in its wake."[179]

Yet calls for peaceful solutions and civic activism to defeat a militarily imposed dictatorship in the name of preserving civility and rebuking savagery, whether racial or otherwise, was more than just a racist strategy. It was a racist strategy unlikely to inspire a collective uprising on the part of Cuba's poor masses and, quite simply, a cop-out. By the summer of 1953, more and more young Cubans recognized this: without the empowerment and participation of the masses in favor of armed struggle, there could be no revolution against the state. Among them were Fidel Castro and the soon-to-be-elected president of FEU, José Antonio Echeverría. Nonetheless, most citizens' commitment to constitutional democracy and a return to electoral restraints without the same old politicking and corruption of the past simply refused to go away. Between 1953 and 1955, the struggle for such a democracy—the bloodless "revolution" that Batista falsely claimed and that many Cubans still hoped would take place *against* Batista—took its last stand. Ironically, the unarmed opposition that rejected violence, called for a just government, and demanded morally driven social reforms also laid the ground rules for how *armed* groups, like those led by Castro and Echeverría, would shape and justify their use of weapons and violence to defeat Batista. As Batista's repression increased, so did the use of violence among those who defined their responses as defensive maneuvers intended to save Cuba from its attackers. This clearly masculinized the movement against Batista, as Michelle Chase has shown, both in terms of tactics as well as participation and leadership.[180] However, this did not mean that putting one's body on the front lines of the struggle in near weekly street protests or protesting through highly visible, if symbolic, methods ended. On the contrary, opening the eyes of citizens to the prospect that one could defeat Batista's war on Cuba's constitutional state only through war remained foundational to legitimating the cause of armed struggle as the ultimate solution.

3

Los Muchachos del Moncada: Civic Mobilization and Democracy's Last Stand, 1953–1954

IN THE SPRING OF 1953, TWENTY-SIX-YEAR-OLD Mario Chanes de Armas was the secretary-general of a large union of commercial workers covering the municipalities of both Havana and Marianao. Known for successfully combatting Communist control of union leadership through clean, persuasive electoral campaigns against the PSP, Mario had joined the Ortodoxos and regularly attended the Juventud Ortodoxa's weekly meetings at Prado 109 in Centro Habana, national headquarters for the party. There, a fellow labor activist introduced him to the young lawyer Fidel Castro Ruz.

Almost immediately, the two of them hit it off. Like most members of the Juventud Ortodoxa, Mario and *compañeros* from his union were fed up with the failure of party stalwarts to endorse armed struggle. Every weekend, when Fidel, Mario, and other *jovenes* (young people) got together in the absence of elder Ortodoxo statesmen, recalled Mario in 2002, "We criticized every type of dictatorship and the one that we most criticized was that of the Soviet Union. . . . Russia had enslaved half of Eastern Europe." United by the common Orthodox values of anti-imperialism, opposition to dictatorship in all forms, and interpartisan pacts, Fidel easily persuaded Mario and other close labor activists to start organizing secret armed cells in the Marianao neighborhoods of Ceiba and Puente Grande.[1] Their goal, although Fidel did not disclose it at the time, was to assault the Moncada military barracks in Oriente, Cuba's second-largest military base.

In organizing his own armed network, Fidel nonetheless faced stiff competition from other Ortodoxos with simpler plans. Among these, Fernando Aranda and Blanca del Valle, relatives of Jorge Valls, turned down Fidel's offer to collaborate in favor of an effort to assassinate Batista during a regatta at Varadero in late July.[2] However, the fact that Rafael García Bárcena had been arrested three months before Fidel began his recruitment drive aided his efforts to create the commando team: surviving members of the MNR quickly joined Fidel.[3]

Within a short time, Fidel counted on the solid support of 159 followers, most of them skilled workers or, like Chanes, seasoned unionists. Only four of the total held university degrees.[4] Two were women, Haydée Santamaría, the sister of Abel Santamaría, whom Fidel first met at an Orthodox Party protest in May 1952, and Melba Hernández, a young lawyer.[5] Timed to coincide with Santiago's annual carnival and Catholic feast day, 26 July 1953, the commando assault was ambitiously planned but disastrous in its outcome. In the end, Raúl Castro and Abel Santamaría's units successfully captured only two key sites on the Moncada military base, the courthouse and the hospital, as planned. Yet these minor victories mattered little once soldiers opened machine-gun fire and Fidel called a sudden retreat of the main force. Dozens lay wounded or dead on the ground.

Government forces sustained nineteen killed and thirty-one injured; vengeful officers carried out a bloodbath over the next four days, capturing, torturing, and murdering more than fifty rebel prisoners and dumping their bodies in garrisons or along roadways to simulate death in combat. As Antonio Rafael de la Cova writes in his definitive history of the assault on Moncada, "It was the largest mass killing of prisoners since the War of Independence. The slaughter, halted after civic and religious leaders appealed to Batista, allowed Castro to turn a military disaster into a political victory."[6]

Surely, the history of the struggle against Batista did attest to the accuracy of this view: the real purpose of Moncada lay far beyond its stated goals of sparking a national uprising. Indeed, Haydée Santamaría would say as much when asked in 1966 how she and others dealt with the horror of the attack's failure: "You might think that this is not true—I tell you in all sincerity—it's true. We never thought that the attack on Moncada had failed!"[7] After Batista's flight in 1959 and Fidel's assumption of power as head of a Communist state between 1960 and 1961, Moncada's meteoric rise in the discourse of official state media and Cuba's new pedagogy had no rival. It was often described as "one of the greatest heroic acts" ever carried out by young people "anywhere on the globe" by both official analysts and surviving participants alike. The event was also celebrated annually on its anniversary after it was designated a national holiday in July 1959. On its tenth anniversary in 1963, the Soviet Union and many countries of Latin America held their own commemorations.[8] Haydée Santamaría believed that the assault on Moncada proved its importance with each year that Fidel Castro remained in power.[9]

Nonetheless, the assault on El Cuartel Moncada was seen very differently at the time it occurred. Viewed in the historical context of prevailing political conditions, the event that launched Castro's revolutionary movement emerges less as a turning point in the embrace of armed struggle than as a confirmation of the public's continuing, if temporary, opposition to it. The Moncada assault was diminished by allies and patrician politicians alike as only one of many attacks on the regime; its failure added to the relative legitimacy of popular mobilization and the possibility of forcing Batista to concede genuine electoral victories or simply cede power to opposing sides. As one manifesto of a civic group put it at the time, "Minorities need weapons. United majorities do not."[10] As Fidel Castro, Moncada assault veterans, and dozens of other political prisoners languished in jail for more than a year, Batista's promise to return to constitutional rule with a general election in 1954 primed the pump of civic activism. In the months after Moncada, Batista remained more concerned with Rafael Bárcena's potential for agitation from behind prison walls than he was with Fidel Castro. Indeed, no other president, Batista declared, had lost as much sleep. But it was Bárcena's Movimiento Nacional Revolucionario and not Fidel's 26th of July Movement that he blamed.[11] Batista's statement speaks to how many people dismissed Castro's leadership, believing that his Ortodoxo roots and connection to Eduardo Chibás's vision of a participatory, bottom-led democracy for Cuba was questionable.

When Batista betrayed hopes by resorting to fraud and intimidation to win the election in 1954, this civic consciousness shifted into high gear. Disappointment in the outcome enervated citizens' belief in both electoralism and constitutional democracy as paths to freedom. By the beginning of 1955, civic pressures appeared to be succeeding. Protests on the street, in the media, and in private garnered both an important cessation of censorship as well as the release of all political prisoners, including "los muchachos del Moncada" (the kids of Moncada) as Fidel and his followers became known. In fact, the release of political prisoners in the early spring of 1955 represented a new beginning in the public's unification behind a common discourse of unarmed struggle, despite the disunity of partisan opponents even within their own parties. Consequently, as the public increasingly united behind the slogan "Fuera Batista" (Out with Batista), would-be insurgents would have to contend with what one observer called citizens' desire for "a revolution without revolution" and "politics without politics."[12] The challenge of the opposition, including Castro's 26th of July Movement, the Ortodoxos, and a markedly activist FEU, would be to address this desire. They had to win a moral war among themselves before a real war against Batista could begin.

The Impact of Moncada and the True Face of Batista's "Revolution"

Conceived in December 1952 but prepared in only a matter of three months, Fidel set the assault on the Moncada military barracks for late July 1953, during the carnival of Santiago. Then the presence of dozens of visitors to the province would raise less suspicion and the soldiers themselves would either be drunk or nursing hangovers.[13] While most of the participants provided their own transportation, the operation proved costly. To fund the operation, including weapons, army uniforms to be used as disguises, bribes, pre-assault surveillance trips to Santiago, bus and train tickets for many participants, and the rental of Siboney, the farm where the rebels planned to gather, Fidel needed $6,000. Refused by his father and provided with only a measly $116 from his mother, he financed the plot through the personal bank account of Naty Revuelta, his married lover. A largely unsung hero of the early struggle, Naty also pawned precious jewels to cover deficits.[14]

The largest single group from outside Havana hailed from Pinar del Rio: thirty-five from the bustling commercial town of Artemisa and five from Guanajay.[15] Of these, a handful belonged to Acción Católica, the most socially engaged wing of Juventud Católica, and the rest were young Ortodoxos. As Andrés Candelario, a principal leader of Juventud Católica in Artemisa, remarked in 2008, his uncle's farm had served as a training camp for several secret conspirators to practice shooting .22 caliber rifles. This was the primary weapon with which they would later confront soldiers armed with submachine guns and hand grenades—soldiers who would outnumber the rebels four to one.[16] "Ciro Redondo, for example, was someone I knew personally," remembered Andrés Candelario, "because he worked in a shoe store in front of the town's central park. And no one could have imagined that he was involved in that . . . that is, no one could imagine that such a regular kid [*un joven común y corriente*] who had never expressed any type of patriotic concern [*inquietud patriótica*] until that point would have gotten himself involved."[17] The same might have been said of a great many of the conspirators.[18]

While 135 of the group were to assault Moncada, Fidel assigned 24 to attack the much smaller Rural Guard barracks at Bayamo. Both sites held deeply symbolic historic meaning. El Cuartel Moncada was the very same military base where beloved revolutionary Antonio Guiteras had planned a similar commando raid almost exactly twenty years earlier during the revolution of 1933. Like Castro's attempt, Guiteras's assault had also failed, largely before it even got started. Yet as Castro's attack on Moncada would also confirm, the political legacy of Guiteras's effort transcended its immediate result. The sheer suicidal bravado of both assaults seemed to prove the selfless political innocence that lay behind young heroic Cubans' ambitions. What was entirely new about Castro's plan was its inclusion of an operation in Bayamo. The military complex at Bayamo mattered only for Bayamo's legendary status as the cradle of Cuba's first revolution against Spain. The leading verse of the national anthem, written in 1868, inscribed this point in Cuban consciousness: Morir por la patria es vivir. The anthem addresses the townspeople of the city, *los bayameses*, effectively Cuba's first nationalist revolutionaries, demanding that patriots race into battle and defy death.[19]

Echoing Guiteras's belief that a successful rebel takeover of Moncada could inspire a national strike against then dictator Machado, Fidel thought that the people of Santiago and Bayamo would rise up against Batista along with legions of his own military personnel at the bases. In deference to José Martí's *natalicio* (yearlong birthday commemoration) of 1953, they called themselves La Generación del Centenario (The Generation of the Centenary). So great was the rebels' conviction of the pivotal importance of their action that "The Hymn of the 26th of July" was composed to honor the movement three days before the assault actually took place.[20]

In May, Havana recruits began weapons training at the university in anticipation for *la citación*, the day Fidel would announce that they would launch the armed struggle. "But we only learned how to handle weapons," Chanes noted with some irony. "We didn't actually shoot."[21] Although Mario already considered himself a good shot, there were many other aspects of the plan that

Fidel expected would spark the fall of Batista that Mario later regretted not questioning. One was the group's general lack of knowledge of the area, and Santiago in particular. Ignorance cost many their lives. Aside from Fidel and his brother Raúl, a startlingly small number of the participants were from eastern Cuba, and hardly any of them had visited Santiago, let alone the focal point of the operation: El Cuartel Moncada. Indeed, Fidel and his second in command, Abel Santamaría, did not fully inform the vast majority of the group of this key factor or the precise details of the operation until only hours before they left for Santiago and gathered at Siboney.

Chanes and other participants in the Moncada attack never questioned its validity as a method to renew the association between armed struggle and the *desinteresado* political purity of youth in Cubans' national imagination. It was through this association that they wanted to pull citizens back into the fight. "There was a declaration that was going to be read over the radio in case we took the Cuartel," said Chanes, "—*and we believed we were going to take it*." While the rebels did have a backup plan of heading back to Siboney and then to the hills in case of a retreat, they did not perceive that even a failed assault would lead to political failure.[22] In Havana, Naty Revuelta was the only person who knew the plan in advance. Assigned to distribute a manifesto addressed "to the nation" among reporters, to the U.S. embassy, and to the homes of top Ortodoxo leaders on the very day of the attack, Naty completed her task early, apparently never imagining the bloodshed that lay ahead.[23]

Soon after the assault, Castro himself contended that it was never the group's intention to assume power on that day but rather to incite average citizens to battle so that el pueblo might achieve state power. This latter goal he portrayed as inevitable: whether the *moncadistas* lived or died mattered little. The act itself ensured that the revolution launched at Moncada, whose "intellectual authorship" he ascribed to José Martí, would eventually win.[24] In rare public testimony before University of Havana students years later, Haydée Santamaría concurred. The rebels' greatest fear was not dying in the assault but surviving it and consequently not fulfilling its goal: to topple Batista. "We felt the pain of remaining and of not being understood; we felt the deep pain of remaining and that our children would remember us as insane, as a group of crazy people [*de que nuestros niños nos recordarán como una locura, como un grupo de locos*]."[25] This near complete absence of doubt in the validity of the assault, in the idea that that they could achieve the impossible, united the hearts and minds of almost all of Fidel's co-conspirators.[26] This conviction—that one way or the other, success or failure, Moncada would matter—is perhaps the only factor that explains the breadth of the rebels' ambition as well as their insistence that even a fiasco would be an inevitable success in the long term. What they had on their side that remains unmentioned in accounts of the event is the Cuban people's time-tested cultural propensity to support, justify, and participate in revolt. Although badly conceived against all odds, the assault would spark popular sympathy for the rebels and galvanize further support for armed attacks on the Batista regime. Despite the attack's bravado, the fact that it seemed designed to fail spoke to its youthful organizers' presumed selflessness, will to martyrdom, and political innocence. The rebels knew this and counted on it to propel their cause's prestige and, if he survived, Fidel Castro's leadership forward.

In military terms, the assault was a disaster. Shortly after midnight in the predawn hours of 26 July 1953, Castro and his followers disguised themselves in standard-issue military uniforms and proceeded to command post 3, the main entry point to the Moncada base. The first car in the rebel caravan successfully surprised the guards and penetrated the post, removing the chain restricting access and allowing the remaining cars to pass. Hoping to confuse other guards into believing that Batista himself was paying an unexpected visit, the assailants then drove on, yelling, "Clear the way for the general!" Yet almost immediately everything went awry.[27] A specially trained guard unit known as the Guardia Cosaka gave the alarm. Only forty-five of the ninety-five men under Fidel's command managed to arrive at the barracks. The rest mistakenly took a side road, got lost, and were later arrested or killed.[28]

The death of sixty to seventy of the rebels and the subsequent gory display of corpses for the benefit of reporters who entered the military base on the following day outraged citizens.[29] Carlos Franqui, a television reporter for Channel 2, was in Santiago that weekend to cover an unrelated student protest at the University of Oriente organized by Frank País and Vilma Espín. Franqui had been in communication and collaboration with these activists since May 1952 when Bárcena's MNR took root at the University of Havana. In addition to filming and photographing the gruesome scenes at Moncada, Franqui confirmed the singular horror that Haydée Santamaría had suffered: soldiers presented Haydée with her brother Abel's eyes and her boyfriend Boris Santa Coloma's testicles on a tray.[30] Privately, in a letter written from prison a few months later, Fidel Castro attested to further atrocities: none of the more than thirty assailants whom Batista's soldiers arrested and murdered the first night were buried with their eyes, their teeth, their testicles, or even their personal effects.[31]

Franqui's films and detailed coverage never reached the airwaves or the print media, however. Once back in Havana, his visual record and written accounts in hand, Franqui was summarily fired by the TV channel's owner and director of the widely read national newspaper *El Mundo,* the Italian Amadeo Barletta, whom Franqui viewed as a fascist and a Batista fan.[32] However, Batista treated Barletta's news outlets no differently than those of his regular nemeses and promptly installed censors at *El Mundo, Prensa Libre, El Pueblo,* and *Bohemia* in the wake of Moncada.[33]

In fact, only in Oriente, where reporters were allowed to photograph and interview the rebel prisoners in Santiago's jail, did citizens hear something of the rebels' goals and plans. On 1 August, Fidel and the remaining six assailants, including Mario Chanes, had been captured at a local farm. They were rescued from certain death thanks to the locally powerful Castro clan. Their appeal to Santiago's archbishop resulted in Monseñor Enrique Pérez Serantes accompanying the arresting army unit into the field. His presence and the ethical character of the arresting officers ensured that the prisoners were taken to Santiago's regular prison, El Vivac, rather than to the closed military base, where they would likely have been shot.[34] Shortly after his capture, Fidel gave a twenty-minute address to the news media from prison, eight minutes of which military officers edited for broadcast over Cadena Oriental de Radio and quoted in *El Crisol,* a Havana paper.[35] Only in the United States did the assault on the Moncada Barracks make headlines, but even there none of the assailants' names, including that of Fidel Castro, were released.[36]

Still, perhaps the most important aspect of Fidel's speech might have seemed the least significant at the time. Much as he would do consistently from that day forward, Fidel appropriated and adapted Batista's idea of a bloodless coup giving way to an authentically revolutionary form of rule—in Batista's words, "una revolución sin sangre" (a revolution without blood).[37] Fidel discursively transformed this paradox into a historically awaited dream of true liberation and a fraternal nation under his command rather than Batista's. "I did not go to Moncada to kill soldiers," declared Fidel on the day of his arrest. "We revolutionaries are not against the army, but we are against Batista. . . . Batista forces you [soldiers] to fight against the people. Batista is the main enemy of the army and of the soldiers."[38] In a message he echoed in many subsequent speeches and writings, Fidel articulated the notion that Batista alone was the enemy of change and that his supporters were simply victims, not culpable collaborators. He also implied that revolution could be achieved without violence even as he embraced, instigated, and justified violence in its name. Cuba's revolutionaries were not attacking the state, according to Castro: they were defending it for the sake of the nation.

Naturally, Batista took a contrary view. At his annual address at Camp Columbia that September, the dictator awarded the regiment that had defended Moncada with the Maceo Cross, the highest honor conferred on members of the armed forces. He also called the events of the 26th of July "a hard experience for those who believed in the atonement of the repentant." In other words, Batista lumped together all of his opponents, strategically naming none and condemning all as responsible for the "chaos" and crimes he attributed to the republic he had rescued from Auténtico hands on 10 March 1952 (figure 11).[39]

By identifying his enemies as having "repented," he glossed all the opposition as not only cognizant of their guilt in corrupting the republic and forcing him—reluctantly—to take power but secretly grateful for his generosity in "forgiving" them for their sins. After all, he neither subjected Auténtico officials to court for graft as an Ortodoxo-led government would have done, nor did he shoot any of them for treason as a more traditional military dictator could have. However, Batista did not extend the paternalistic logic of "forgiving his enemies" to the practical and legal responses of his regime to opponents in the weeks following Moncada. In other words, no blanket forgiveness would be forthcoming. The assailants' "betrayal" of his kindness and of the republic's political traditions as he saw them forced him to trade the forgiveness and generosity that had allegedly characterized his rule for a system of discipline, new mandates, and unremorseful punishment in the near future. Starting the very day of the assault on Moncada, Batista's security forces carried out sweeping raids on the homes of leading Ortodoxos and Auténticos alike, arresting and jailing men and women indiscriminately without charge. On 28 July, censorship extended to all print media in Cuba.[40]

Between 26 and 29 July, thirty political leaders were confined to a single five- by three-meter cell. Left without food or water for the first twenty-four hours, the prisoners also had to take turns sleeping on the floor because of the lack of space. Only former military officers suspected of sympathizing or aiding in the attack were held separately, presumably under better conditions.[41]

Figure 11. In 1938, the Cuban Chamber of Congress in New York feted Batista. Flanked by steadfast supporters Rafael Guas Inclán and Carlos Saladrigas Zayas, who later lent their legitimacy to his 1950s dictatorship, Batista focused on the script of a radio address to the U.S. public. (Donated by Elena Doty Angus, Braga Brothers Collection, courtesy of Special and Area Studies Collections, University of Florida)

At two in the morning on the third day, the SIM transported all of the leaders arrested in Havana to La Cabaña prison; officers chose the predawn hour to ensure that no one would see the "caravan of such prestigious men," exhausted, smelling badly, and under mass arrest.[42] Not until 4 August were relatives informed of their location. After fifty-three days spent in La Cabaña, the groups were then transferred to El Cuartel Moncada and finally to the infamous Boniato Prison near Santiago. Tried at the end of September alongside the little more than two dozen surviving assailants of the attack on Moncada, Aracelio Azcuy, an Ortodoxo and good friend of MNR founder Rafael Bárcena, whom he encountered for the first time at La Cabaña in the first weeks of his detention, recalled the horror. The military's occupation of Santiago wreaked revenge on residents. "The capital city of Oriente . . . gave the impression of being under siege [*una plaza sitiada*]. All the avenues and streets were patrolled by pairs of soldiers; the sidewalks were deserted and there was barely any automobile traffic. The residents of the city remained in a state of terror, despite the time that had transpired since that frightful slaughter of the 26, 27, 28, and 29 of July."[43]

On those days, the army had killed a still untold number of citizens in Santiago indiscriminately.

To facilitate this process of repressing all opposition and justifying atrocities in defense of nation, Batista also issued a new Decree of Public Order with unprecedented restrictions on Cubans' civil rights on 6 August 1953. Ironically, the decree prohibited citizens from "disobeying," "harming," or even "disparaging" the 1940 Constitution, despite the fact that the decree itself, not to mention Batista's anti-constitutional regime, already did all of these things and far more. Consequently, the August decree stuck to Batista's script of saving the citizenry from itself and restoring order for the sake of present and future generations. In practical terms, the law criminalized any act that subverted or destroyed the "political, social, economic, or juridical organization of the state as it is currently constituted." The first articles of the law defined such acts of subversion in extremely broad terms, encompassing the transmission of false, misleading, or tentatively verified news; this definition went so far as to include rumors.[44]

Propaganda that subverted the legitimacy of the state and therefore "endangered" government security was not confined to "newspapers, magazines, books, pamphlets, flyers, signs, placards, publicly placed posts, letters destined to various people" or radio, television, and movies: the decree's definition went so far as to define propaganda as "word of mouth."[45] Creatively, the law also criminalized "propaganda" that jeopardized the financial well-being of the country, an addition that hinted at prosecution if economists or reporters rendered less than positive assessments of the economy in the mainstream media.[46] Sanctions for all of these "crimes" were stiff, mandating fines of $500 to $5,000 and minimum jail sentences of three months to one year for first-time offenders and one to three years for repeat offenders.[47]

Yet by far the most stringent part of the law expanded the definition and meaning of *desacato,* literally, disrespect for public figures or state authorities: "Those who defame or injure in any form the powers of the state or any of its agencies, armed forces or police, or any class of civil servants" as well as any "authority" of the state, including a military leader, police officer, or bureaucrat, committed a crime, whether through word or deed. The same sanctions applied to those who "defamed, calumnized, injured, or provoked" not only Cuba's head of state but "the head of any foreign state with which Cuba maintains diplomatic relations." Given Cubans' increasing contempt for U.S. support of Batista, this part of the law clearly aimed to undercut open declarations of anti-imperialism.[48] Parody and satire were also banned, whether expressed in the media or the theater.[49]

Batista's draconian Decree of Public Order had swift and profound effects. If journalists "not on the take" from Batista had already found themselves in dire financial straits before Moncada, now they were far worse off. One example was Antonio Zamora Hernández, a frequent writer for *Bohemia* and *El Mundo* already under heavy censorship before the new law. A good friend of Carlos Márquez Sterling, Zamora wrote to "Carlitos" to request a loan of $12.39 to help him cover three months of back rent for a tiny one-room apartment in Old Havana.[50] After passage of the law, Pedro Revuelta, a well-known humorist, told Márquez Sterling that he was in an untenable position. Unemployed since Batista's coup, he could not get even a mildly ironic cartoon titled "Ode to Uncle Sam" published "absolutely anywhere in Cuba."[51] Although enclosed with Revuelta's letter, the "ode" mysteriously disappeared from Márquez Sterling's otherwise extraordinarily complete personal archive of correspondence. Did he himself or his secretary throw it away out of fear of repercussions? Regardless, the message was clear. After the Moncada attack, Batista was no longer in the mood for humor or for being humored, no more than the head of any other military regime in Latin America at the time.

Although the national suspension of constitutional guarantees and the imposition of censorship were set to end by 28 October 1953 (when, theoretically, all the truly "guilty" would be imprisoned or subject to trial), Batista generously lifted the ban four days earlier. He also made light of his own severe policies, insisting that they had been a "temporary emergency measure." Cuba was in no more danger of seeing "permanent restrictions on the basic freedoms of democracy" than the United States.[52]

Such sentiments provided little comfort to those already disdainful of the United States' long-standing disrespect for Cuban sovereignty and democracy in promoting its own interests. Batista's words were even less convincing when the power of security forces to persecute critics and opponents expanded by leaps and bounds with the issuing of yet another decree a month later. Critically, Batista titled it La Ley Anti-Comunista (Anti-Communist Law), a title designed to create the illusion that *only* Communists, that is, card-carrying PSP militants, would be surveilled and subject to prosecution for endangering the powers of the state. However, the first to argue that Batista's law had little or nothing to do with actually persecuting international Communism or its local adherents were Cuban Communists themselves. On behalf of the party, Juan Marinello, president of the PSP and a longtime Communist who had befriended Márquez Sterling during the constitutional convention of 1940, declared this in no uncertain terms: "It is blatantly clear that the so-called Anti-Communist Law is an instrument that appears to be solely directed against 'the interference of international Communism'; but in reality it is disposed to persecute, at whatever time the caprice of government may dictate, any institution, group, or party that the government cares to harm. The character of the law, its intended generality, and possible reach signify a flagrant threat to all who show any inconformity with the current government."[53] The nature of the law necessitated condemnation by all and a unified repudiation, concluded Marinello. "We do not ask for any identification with our ideals; we exhort only that you understand that ideological differences [between the Ortodoxos and the PSP] should not present an obstacle . . . for this law is directed against all of those who figure in the anti-government camp."[54]

In fact, with the exception of the Moncada attack and continued unarmed protests of university students, there had been little reason for Batista to fear either a coordinated surge of civic activism from the political opposition or even the sense that Cuba was on the precipice of a new insurrectionary age. On 2 June 1953, only weeks before Moncada, deposed Auténtico president Carlos Prío Socarrás, other Auténticos, and many top Ortodoxo leaders including Emilio "Millo" Ochoa had gathered in Montreal to sign a pact endorsing patriotic unity and cooperation for a return to constitutional, electoral rule to defeat Batista; the pact said nothing of supporting armed struggle. Outraged, stalwart Ortodoxo founders Roberto Agramonte, Manuel Bisbé, and Carlos Márquez Sterling declared the pact a betrayal of principles. Ortodoxo defenders of the pact saw the latter's denunciation in equally black and white terms: they accused them of committing either the greatest mistake in Cuba's political history or treason.[55]

Privately, however, Ortodoxo associates of the Agramonte-led faction opposed to establishing a pact with Prío and other Auténticos pled for some middle ground. "The immediate Cuban solution, Carlos," wrote a friend to Márquez Sterling, "cannot come from a party that hoists intransigence as a flag. . . . I believe that you could have a great historical role. Acting like a Cuban and serving *La Ortodoxia despite La Ortodoxía*." He begged Márquez Sterling to embrace unity. After all, he prophesied, as military dictatorship after military dictatorship swept Latin America, it was clear that the age of revolution had ended in Cuba and elsewhere.[56]

This writer could not have been more wrong. However, in the heat of the moment, he appeared right: rather than foster unity, the Auténtico-Ortodoxo deal in Montreal undercut the Ortodoxos' legitimacy and divided the party permanently. Until then, not only were the Ortodoxos the most popular political party, they were still seen as the true victors of what should have been the 1952 general elections. After Montreal, however, the Ortodoxos slowly began to lose their place as the centrifugal force behind any majority political movement to topple Batista through peaceful means.

Meanwhile, Fidel and his surviving followers faced the possibility of decades in prison. There was a total of 122 defendants at trial, only 48 of whom had actually attacked Moncada or Bayamo; 25 pled guilty. However, only 98 of the 122 defendants were present; 24 of them were absentees. Three of the latter formed part of Fidel's group, including Gustavo Arcos, who remained hospitalized. The court designated the other 21 absent defendants "fugitives," a category so haphazardly drawn that it included at least one defendant living in the United States.[57] The court proceedings were a drawn-out affair, mostly because police and the SIM netted dozens of PSP activists, Ortodoxos, and Auténticos who had had nothing to do with the attack. Fidel Castro was quickly excluded from the general trial. Tried alone but allowed to act as his own attorney, wear an attorney's robe, and occupy a seat in the defense section, Fidel delivered an undeniably brilliant performance, one subsequently documented blow by blow by Cuba's journalists turned revolutionary spokespeople after the fall of Batista in 1959.[58] At the time, though, the trial received relatively undetailed press coverage. *Bohemia,* for example, did not publish a full account of the proceedings until the Moncada prisoners' release. However, Jules Dubois, editor of the *Chicago Tribune* and president of the hemisphere's largest press association, meticulously and fearlessly documented the subversive speeches of the Moncada defendants, especially Fidel Castro's.

Uncharacteristically brief but persuasive, Fidel conceded his "guilt" by turning its meaning on its head: he indicted the legal validity of the entire proceedings. The prosecutor's accusation did not apply to him or anyone else, argued Fidel, since he and others were being accused of revolting against the constitutional powers of the state. "In what country are we living, Mr. Prosecutor?" asked Fidel. "Who has said that we have promoted an uprising against the *constitutional powers of the state?*"[59] He also celebrated the "attitude" of his forces, saying that they could have taken the regiment by arresting the top officers in their quarters, "a possibility that we rejected because of the very human consideration of avoiding scenes of tragedy or fighting in the family quarters." He then added that they also chose not to announce their actions over radio until victory was secure: "This attitude of ours, seldom seen because of its gallantry and grandeur, saved the citizens a river of blood. With only ten men, I could have occupied a radio station and hurled the people into the fight. It was not possible to doubt their spirit: I had the last speech of Eduardo Chibás in CMQ transcribed in his own words."[60] Once again, he praised the armed forces, predicting that the navy would have joined them and even Batista's soldiers would have changed course had the citizens risen, refusing to treat their own people as the enemy.[61]

Fidel then addressed the glaring class inequality of Cubans and the need for a state committed to sovereignty and social justice. "We call on the people," Fidel declared. "Fight now with all your forces so that liberty and happiness may be yours!" Most significant were the heartfelt, precise terms he used to define Cuba's people. They were, intoned an impassioned Fidel, the hundreds of thousands of industrial workers whose union funds were regularly embezzled by government officials; the underemployed or landless, hardworking peasants "who dwell in miserable shacks, who work four months of the year [during sugar-harvesting season] and are hungry the rest; the thirty thousand teachers and professors so devoted, sacrificed, and necessary to the better destiny of future generations and who are so badly treated and paid"; and the tens of thousands of small businessmen and young professionals whose skills and services could not compete in an economy of markets colonized by foreigners and neglected by the state.[62] Left out of Fidel's portrait of a suffering, struggling, and often starving Cuba was virtually no one except Batista himself. Fidel's speech ascended to the status of myth when he elaborated it further from prison in April 1954. With the help of his wife, Mirta Díaz-Balart, he smuggled it out to followers who famously printed thousands of copies for clandestine circulation throughout the island.[63] The title of the resulting fifty-nine-page pamphlet came from Fidel's closing argument to the court. His final words said it all: "Condemn me! It doesn't matter! History will absolve me!"[64]

The Recasting of Fidel Castro, 1953–1955

In the end, nineteen of the Moncada assailants were freed for lack of evidence; sixty were acquitted. Among them were top Cuban Communists from Santiago who had gone home for the carnival and were found innocent; their political activism on behalf of the party opposed strategies like that of Moncada and their presence there proved unrelated to the attack. The rest served jail time.[65] The court condemned Fidel Castro to fifteen years in prison, his brother Raúl and Ernesto Tizol Aguilera to thirteen. While Ciro Redondo, Ramiro Valdés, Mario Chanes, and Juan Almeida each received a ten-year sentence, others received far less. Melba Hernández and Haydée Santamaría were sentenced to serve only seven months each at the women's prison in Guanajay, Pinar del Río, partly because they were women and partly because they claimed to have played a minor role or none at all in planning the attack (Haydée said she had simply gone to Santiago to visit her brother Abel).[66]

Beginning in October 1953, Fidel Castro found himself confined to a cell in the hospital wing outside the Isle of Pine's famously circular Presidio Modelo prison, where he endured solitary confinement for more than four months. He estimated that he had spent a total of three thousand hours alone except for visits from his wife and son, in addition to the three months he had already spent in Santiago de Cuba in similar isolation.[67] Fidel suffered greatly from having no access to nature, the lack of light, the absence of books, and the wasteful sense of endless waiting.[68] Nonetheless, the conditions were in keeping with the patriarchal pattern of deference to his class and his family's background that Batista's military had established from the time of his arrest. Allowed to live in larger quarters than other prisoners during and after his period of solitary confinement, Fidel was also subsequently granted special, if not consistently better, treatment.

According to Fidel himself, Batista once sent his own minister of governance Ramón Hermida Antorcha to check on his conditions. Hermida knew what Castro's experience was like: after all, during the struggle against Machado, Hermida had also been imprisoned twice for repeatedly attempting to assassinate Machado and other officials. "You are a young man," he told Fidel. "Be calm; all these things will one day pass."[69] Although Fidel was allowed only two family visits per month and regular conjugal visits like everyone else, the warden eventually authorized him to share the same cell as his brother Raúl. This gesture signified special treatment, if not outright sympathy for the young men's hopeless but admirable cause. The two also fraternized in common areas with their former Moncada collaborators for at least part of their stay. Mario Chanes warmly recalled Fidel's group cooking for themselves, and Juanita Castro remembered Raúl and Fidel spending much of their time reading and making spaghetti, although she never tried any of it herself.[70]

Undoubtedly, Fidel found profound pleasure in the passionate letters he exchanged with his lover Naty Revuelta as well as in the short visits he enjoyed with his wife Mirta.[71] However, jail time was still jail time, regardless of the special status accorded to "political prisoners" like the moncadistas and other conspirators by the always image-wary Batista. When Mirta eventually discovered Fidel's affair with Naty, he deemed his wife a traitor, accusing her of accepting a botella in one of Batista's government ministries. The episode left Fidel not only heartbroken and outraged but deeply depressed.[72]

As Mario Chanes recounted, things were not easy for any of the group, even when prison officials allowed them to reunite and the Castro brothers' period of isolation ended. Circumstances turned markedly, albeit temporarily, worse when Batista visited the prison to inaugurate structural improvements to the facility. Upon hearing the news, Fidel proposed that the group wait until Batista was in hearing range and then regale him with an a capella rendition of the hymn of the 26th of July Movement.[73] When two of the men objected, Fidel suggested a vote: embarrassed into unanimity, the men sang the tune at the top of their lungs. Later, Batista jokingly remarked to the guards, "Oye, ¡qué bien alimentado están todos ellos por lo fuerte que cantan!" (Hey, aren't they well fed! You can tell by how strongly they sing!).[74] Starting the very next day, prison officials punished the group with bad food; Fidel himself was separated from the rest.

Yet Chanes and others were still able to communicate with him via *balitas* (little bullets), messages inscribed on tiny bits of paper, shaped into the form of bullets, and wrapped in a cement-like material concocted from the husks of beans. When the guards took Fidel out of his cell at sunset for fresh air, his comrades tossed the balitas at him. "People would ask themselves how we managed to smuggle out documents that were *signed* by all of us," laughed Chanes. Few could have imagined that the moncadistas kept the balitas out of the guards' hands by hiding them in their anal cavity until the messages could be smuggled out on visitors' day, he added.[75] The term "little bullets" clearly served to mitigate the indignity that having to engage in such acts represented for moncadistas who adhered to customary heterosexual understandings of what it meant to be a macho by linguistically representing these acts as audacious, risky protests. The muchachos del Moncada, in other words, were still fighting the dictatorship with the fusion of "bullets" and words, both meant to weaken the hyper-manhood Batista projected of himself and his regime.

A selection of letters written by Castro during his imprisonment and published in early 1959 by his then secretary and confidant, Luis Conte Agüero, reveals the depth of strategizing that took place among the men inside the prison and their loyal outside organizers. These letters also reveal the heroic exceptionality that Fidel ascribed to his and his followers' actions as well as the alleged historical uniqueness of their suffering under Batista. In a letter to Conte Agüero dated 12 December 1953, Fidel expressed anger that the public remained so silent over the soldiers' actions at Moncada, particularly once the initial period of terror had past: "History knows no massacre like it, neither in the colonial era nor in the republic."[76] Moreover, whereas Fidel had publicly adopted a generous pose, glossing Batista as the only villain, alone responsible for the atrocities and constitutional violations of the regime, his private writings exposed a far less generous view. Railing against the opposition, he accused them of being accomplices of Batista for failing to protest sufficiently the abuses sanctioned under the August Decree of Public Order. Fidel also minimized past tyrannies as well as the experience of their victims. Singled out for particular disdain were the eight medical students whom the Spanish state had executed for treason on 27 November 1871, later commemorated annually as Cuba's first student martyrs in the republic. "The students of '71 were never tortured, they were subject to apparent trial, they were buried in known locations, and those who committed such horrors believed themselves in possession of divine right," wrote Fidel. "Nine times eight were the number of youth who fell in Santiago de Cuba under torture and lead bullets, without any kind of trial, in the name of an illegitimate and hated usurper government of sixteen months' time, without God and without law."[77] The bones of all the martyrs of Moncada should one day be united in the same grave as Martí, he concluded.[78]

Yet for all of this vociferating and complaining, Castro's missive to Conte Agüero had the political objective of convincing the top brass of the Orthodox Party that the moncadistas' actions were in no way intended to undermine their leadership. "Talk to Dr. Agramonte," Fidel urged. "Show him this letter, expressing that our feelings are filled with loyalty to the most pure ideals of Eduardo Chibás."[79] Indeed, as time dragged on, Castro saw himself left off the stage of political and civic responses to Batista's call for open national elections in 1954. The privately manipulative but publicly conciliatory approach to rival leaders reflected in his letter to Conte Agüero only deepened. Cubans needed and wanted, Castro sensed, "the right to be men" again.[80] The regime denied men this identity through emasculating forms of repression, censorship, and the paternalistic rhetoric of Cuba's self-appointed paragon of democracy, Fulgencio Batista.

The Search for a Different, Better "Hombre" and the 1954 Elections

At the dawn of 1954, Cubans perceived themselves on the cusp of a return to constitutional order. Even if at one point most had seen that order wrecked and disparaged by eight years of Auténtico rule as well as the superficiality of popular "democracy" under Batista a decade prior to that, now a return to the Constitution seemed not only possible and within reach, but necessary and unconditionally good. In 1954, voters and parties of all persuasions, including PSP Communists, embraced the notion that it would be not a party but a man who would save Cuba from Batista and from a cycle of violent, unpredictable revolutionary history few wanted to repeat. Briefly, optimism seemed to overwhelm the cynicism most had derived from recent events, particularly the split among Orthodox Party leaders between the Montreal *pactistas* and the anti-pact *chibasistas* whom Carlos Márquez Sterling and others claimed to be. "'The street' is still genuinely 'orthodox,'" opined Jesús Rodríguez, resident of the small Santa Clara town of Encrucijadas, "when considered against the national panorama of the future." In an impassioned handwritten letter to Carlos Márquez Sterling, president of the Orthodox Party, Jesús pleaded: "Oh, for God's sake, Carlos, don't leave us—that's all I hope for—don't get disillusioned; help us save Cuba."[81]

Indeed, Márquez Sterling's election as president of the Orthodox Party in March 1954 signaled renewed hope across the country that Chibás's program for radical change through citizen mobilization and an accountable, representative government was still alive.[82] For José V. González Hernández, a telegraph operator, the fragmentation of the party since the summer of 1953 had proven more harmful to la patria than even Batista's coup itself.[83] What was needed was an honorable man willing to step forward and lead, despite their apparent scarcity and the reigning climate of *confusionismo* created by Batista.[84] "Carlos, I tell you as a man of the people and as a friend, *se necesita un hombre* [a man is needed], and for me that it is you," wrote Miguel A. Matos from Antilla. "So tighten your belt, convoke that meeting, and together with Pardo Llada, Miranda Cortez, and other many good Cubans who still exist, La Ortodoxía under your leadership will rise again to what it used to be."[85]

The people were "anxious for a radical change in procedure," agreed Félix Barreto, writing from the small fishing village of Caibarién: if, as Batista repeatedly claimed, Cuba needs El Hombre, "they believe that 'El Hombre' is really you." Moreover, he added, there could be no better choice for vice president than Guido García Inclán, the university professor made famous by his *Bohemia* column advocating for the needs of the poor, "¡Arriba Corazones!"[86]

The fact that Barreto addressed Márquez Sterling as "Future President of the Republic" was significant. It was intended as much to pressure as to flatter. Ortodoxos everywhere—and perhaps most Cubans—knew that after two years of relative stability under Batista's dictatorial regime, the stakes were high. Freed to operate legally for the first time in two years, political parties had to decide how to respond to Batista's official call for national elections that fall, including for congressional and municipal-level offices, or whether to do so at all. Yet as early as February, faithful Ortodoxos in the far reaches of the island were already reporting batistiano efforts to engineer electoral fraud. On the Isle of Pines, one of the party informed Márquez Sterling that Batista's navy and police had been dispatching their wives to collect voter registration cards door to door for later use in elections that would force citizens to vote by party, rather than by direct vote for individual candidates. Proudly, the Ortodoxos boasted of using batistiano intimidators' own tactics against them by placing a giant portrait of Eduardo Chibás on the wall facing the front door and proclaiming it "the mirror of this household."[87] Pedro Revuelta, the unemployed political cartoonist and friend of Márquez Sterling, predicted a much simpler method for how Batista would steal the elections. He would simply rely on the local electoral councils to stuff the ballot boxes and either "bribe or kidnap" Grau's representatives on the councils to ensure that the stuffing process went off without a hitch.[88]

If elections were held, even if the process was clearly fraudulent, a vote of the people would apparently confirm Batista's tenure in the eyes of the world, especially to officials of the U.S. administration, who for decades had proved to be content with the mere appearance of electoral democracy in Latin America (from Guatemala, Nicaragua, and El Salvador to Haiti and the Dominican Republic) in exchange for support for U.S. investors and corporate monopolies. Given this backdrop, the consequences of a "successful" election of Batista and a pro-Batista Congress would surely be dire. Cuba was bound to explode in revolution. "The pseudo-legalization of the 10th of March would place our *patria* politically and economically on top of a volcano. . . . We can be certain that what gave validity to the 10th of March was the Ortodoxos' excision. Batista would not have been able to rule for so long if the Ortodox movement had maintained itself invulnerable," wrote Luis Fernández from the small town of Joliet, Illinois.[89] From Las Villas, another man agreed. In a personally penned public manifesto, he said that the only solution for Ortodoxos and all Cubans desperate for change was to "think in Cuban." The government and the opposition needed to put their differences aside and commit to letting the people decide Cuba's fate.[90]

Why did so much hope rest on Carlos Márquez Sterling? In part it was due to his reputation as the great compromiser, facilitator, and president of the 1940 Constitutional Convention who had refused to run for any office since then.[91] Viewed as politically objective and cleansed of the selfish ambition that now seemed to taint other members of the Orthodox Party, Márquez Sterling was admired even among currently beholden and employed civil servants of Batista's regime. One of these, Silvio Lubián Muro, a "journalist" at the Ministry of Information, Batista's censorship office, went so far as to apologize privately to Márquez Sterling for his inability to vote for him should he run for president. Pragmatism and his own self-acknowledged client status with regard to Batista overruled the good that offering his support would do. Patron-clientelism was still the key to Batista's success: "This continues to be a land of *caudillaje* (strongmanism); if that were not true, Batista would not be still be in the presidency."[92]

Moreover, Márquez Sterling was seen not only as the legitimate heir to Eduardo Chibás; he was seen as the *only* legitimate choice among three possible contenders: Batista, the embodiment of "brutal force"; Grau, the epitome of "demagoguery and disorder"; and Márquez Sterling, "the firm hope of a secure future."[93] Inconceivable to many was the bizarre historical twist that the Auténtico Party's candidate—despite Prío's Montreal pact with wayward Ortodoxos against Batista—was none other than Grau San Martín. The year 1954 suddenly seemed a repeat of the election of 1940 but without the faith, the excitement, or the possibility of radically changing the nature of government from patterns already established by both candidates in their respective tenures. Even if the people wanted renovation, not revolution, how was it possible that conditions in Cuba could have so conspired to shoot the nation back to the past and leave it with no other future than one of a return to tragedy?[94]

Ironically, even as both Batista and Grau claimed the mantle of having once returned Cuba to democracy (in 1940 and 1944 respectively), they both benefited from the extra-constitutional way in which Batista planned to run the election: not by guaranteeing citizens a direct vote for candidates but by giving them the option to vote only for a full party slate of candidates. This tactic allowed Batista effectively to block off the means by which Grau had defeated him in the landslide Auténtico victory of 1944. Given Batista's control over the bureaucratic and military machine in 1954, the only way to defeat him was through direct vote, and everyone knew it.[95] It was for this very reason that Márquez Sterling insisted on providing citizens with a direct vote as a precondition to holding the election. On the other hand, Grau initially could not insist on strict adhesion to constitutional rules governing elections because technically, they would have banned him, a former president, from being able to run again until 1958.[96] Too much complaining from Grau was therefore once again akin to the pot calling the kettle black when it came to the corrupt Auténticos' ability to attack Batista for corruption.

Outside the solitary column of strength and popular trust embodied by Márquez Sterling, however, opportunism seemed to have taken over the highly fragmented Orthodox Party. With excitement building around Márquez Sterling's run for the presidency by April 1954, Roberto Agramonte, once a stalwart ally and longtime friend, suddenly broke with the majority wing of the remaining Ortodoxo establishment to oppose participation in the elections altogether. Yet he immediately called into question the sincerity of this position by following it up with a multistop, multicity tour of the provinces.[97]

Probably intended to drain popular reserves of support away from Márquez Sterling, Agramonte's tour quickly earned him almost universal disdain. Uncharismatic, overly scholarly, and famously *un*endowed with the passion of his incomparable cousin Eddy Chibás, Agramonte appeared as nothing more than an opportunist in the eyes of many voters. In Camagüey, a radio show devoted to workers' unions affiliated with the Ortodoxos asked, "Dr. Agramonte, are you with the bullets or with the votes?" The same could be said of Emilio Ochoa, who had entered into a pact with Prío and later attacked Márquez Sterling. "I say you are with General Batista, Agramonte," the radio talk show host continued. "From your crystal chapel you softly attack Batista and harshly condemn the Great Pilot of STORMS [Márquez Sterling]. Let's take off our mask. Let's not keep bringing up the name of Chibás. Enough with the pledges before his tomb in order to profane the clean and combative leadership [of Márquez Sterling]." People needed to take to the streets to denounce the mass layoffs Batista was authorizing, he contended, the forced payment of dues to batistiano-controlled labor unions, and dozens of other economic problems that directly resulted from the unaccountability, censorship, and extra-legality of government.[98]

Unable to secure guarantees of a direct vote from Batista and facing opposition even from his own longtime ally José Pardo Llada, Carlos Márquez Sterling was deeply disillusioned by the summer of 1954. "La Ortodoxía no hay quien pueda unirla" (There is no one who can unite the Orthodox movement), he ominously stated to the public.[99] Then Márquez Sterling suffered the unexpected: an assassination attempt by an allegedly disgruntled twenty-four-year-old Ortodoxo named Luis López Pérez. On the morning of 9 July 1954, López Pérez fired on Márquez Sterling just as he entered his law office on Amargura Street in Old Havana.[100] The attempted murder shocked and moved the public. Letters of condolence, sorrow, and solidarity immediately poured into Márquez Sterling's mailbox from Cubans of all political views, social classes, and points on the island.[101] Even political prisoner Francisco Cairol Garrido managed to get a heartfelt letter of relief over Márquez Sterling's survival past prison censors on the Isle of Pines.[102] But the attempted murder also had its desired effect: few believed that fellow Ortodoxos were behind the act. Echoing his class peers on the relevance of the much-demonized anti-colonial uprising of Kenyans against the British state at the time, J. M. Cruz noted privately, "This is the system of the Mau-Mau that the disgraced hypocritical revolution of 1933 left us in inheritance."[103] The racial slur evoked Batista's alleged barbarity as "black" and his consequently savage culpability in preferring violence over pacific, "civilized" solutions such as genuinely democratic elections.

Tragically, Márquez Sterling's survival only served to intimidate Batista's pacific, pro-electoral opponents all the more. If men as prestigious and respected as Márquez Sterling could be targeted, who was next? asked one rank-and-file party organizer from Lawton, a working-class suburb of Havana. After all, at the time of Batista's coup, Márquez Sterling had been the first to back *only* nonviolent protests to combat the dictatorship; then most Ortodoxos did not agree. One could only imagine how liberally Batista defined his enemies now and what he was willing to do about them.[104]

Famously serene under political fire, Márquez Sterling addressed the nation less than a week later on the popular television show *Ante la Prensa* to announce his definitive resignation as a candidate in the presidential campaign.[105] Privately, he confessed that his fatalism about Ortodoxo reliability had only grown since the assassin's attack. "As you have seen, all of my efforts to produce the unity of the Orthodox Party have proven useless." He had run for office in a vain attempt to keep the ideals of Chibás alive, or at least undiluted by "those who have no other occupation than that of exploiting the memory of that great combatant and who, in the end, are responsible for all that has happened in the last years."[106]

While understandable on a personal level, Márquez Sterling's renunciation of his candidacy proved devastating to the majority of Ortodoxos. Somehow he seemed unable or unwilling to assume the mantle of martyr, let alone political messiah, that Cuba at that moment clearly needed. The decision narrowed the field of candidates to only Batista and Grau San Martín. By October, a month before the election, both Batista and Grau were campaigning much as they had in 1940, each claiming greater responsibility for restoring Cuba to elections and therefore "democracy."[107] The course of Cuban history seemed to have turned back on itself. Agramonte and other founders of the Orthodox movement, as it was still called, reiterated abstention from the election as an allegedly radical position.[108] While others adopted a sympathetic if horrified view of the inevitable outcome of Márquez Sterling's withdrawal from the race, important sectors of La Juventud Ortodoxa could barely contain their outrage. In a letter dated 19 July 1954, the Holguín delegation demanded that Márquez Sterling, "the leader of the Constitutional Convention of '40, not abandon us [but] launch himself definitively onto the battlefield." Insisting that they knew "como piensan los orientales" (how the people of Oriente province think), the young activists declared, "Cubans want elections with Agramonte and Millo [Emilio Ochoa] or without them. Alright, clearly, we need to vote against Batista and not for Grau."[109] They only way they could do that, however, was to convince Márquez Sterling to step back into the race, something that he proved entirely unwilling to do.

The Election of 1954

At the national level, Max Lesnik, president of the Juventud Ortodoxa, was beside himself over the impasse that an election involving only Grau and Batista represented. "The Great Pretender of the Revolution [Grau] cannot deceive the people of Cuba again. Fulgencio Batista represents now, just as he did in '34, the denial of citizens' rights, imprisonment, and exile, not to mention the corruption that has surpassed even that committed by the two previous Auténtico administrations. Grau and Batista are not a dilemma, they are two negations that Cuban youth repudiate equally." To combat the legitimacy of both candidates, the Orthodox Youth launched a campaign intended to persuade voters *not* to vote, an illegal act under Cuban law.[110]

Undoubtedly, the media took advantage of Batista's temporary show of openness and constitutionality to publish an unprecedented number of critical articles addressing Cuba's problems of increasing poverty as well as the failure of government to adequately finance public welfare programs, including schools. *Bohemia*'s editors proved the boldest. In October 1954, edition after edition featured critical photo essays and articles on poor socioeconomic conditions attributed to state neglect. One described life amid the filth of workers' barracks on sugar plantations as "hell."[111] Another reported that prioritized spending on war materials over the needs of the public health system had become so extreme that electricity to a public hospital was regularly cut even when doctors were in the middle of surgery.[112] Others compared barren rural schools deprived of basic materials such as paper and pencils with street scenes illustrating massive expenditures on campaign posters, particularly by Batista's party, PAU, now renamed El Partido de Acción Progresista, or PAP (Political Action Party).[113]

Yet it was not simply the media that sought to press Batista's promises for a return to the constitutional rule of law as far as possible. Unlike Ortodoxo and Auténtico leaders, citizens saw the fact that an election would be held *at all* as a unique opportunity to voice their protests. Shockingly, many did so by turning out en masse to receive and cheer Grau on his final swing through Cuba's far eastern provinces before the election on 1 November. Indeed, thousands of peasants and others showed up to hear Grau speak, packing streets and plazas to capacity. In Bayamo, police detained trucks filled with supporters at the city's limits because the city was already overflowing with spectators and supporters.[114] In Santiago, however, when Grau took the podium, "thousands of throats, in one voice, chanted the name—not of the old professor of physiology [Grau] but of the solitary prisoner on the Isle of Pines, Fidel Castro."[115]

No one was more surprised at these astonishing scenes than the Ortodoxos themselves. Bewildered, Mario Rivadulla wondered why no one in the party seemed willing to mobilize massive crowds on the streets as Eddy Chibás would have done. Only such means would "force the Batista government to remove its mask," return to the repression on which it relied, and thereby galvanize the citizenry's commitment to revolution.[116] After witnessing the crowds at multiple stops on Grau's campaign tour, an equally stunned R. Alvarez wrote privately to Márquez Sterling in Havana:

> As you know, the trip that Grau made, giving a final touch to his campaign, through the provinces of Camagüey and Oriente, was the most extraordinary demonstration yet of repudiation of the regime, that never in Cuban political history has been achieved to the same degree, in any epoch, against the force and the imposition of those who pretend to perpetuate themselves in power and to whom the masses of citizens deny all popularity. . . . I repeat, never have I seen the degree of collective effervescence with which a candidate of any party, in any age, has been received. . . . But all one could say pales by comparison with the spontaneous manner in which all those towns filled with people poured out onto the streets, everywhere but particularly here, in Santiago de Cuba.[117]

And yet, despite the mass outpouring of hope that so many Cubans willingly offered Grau San Martín and his obvious desire to stoke its flames, Batista refused to admit any possibility of losing to Grau. Denying that martial law was still effectively in place, Batista promised to restore the 1940 Constitution and allow the return of all political exiles so they could participate in a new democracy.[118] He also opened the doors of his estate to the minority group of Auténticos who sided with Grau and backed the elections. Noting that most of these men represented marginal figures within the pro-election Auténtico minority, *Bohemia* sarcastically labeled Kuquine "the Switzerland of America," a comment that mocked the Auténticos' lack of influence and neutrality vis-à-vis the disgrace that Batista's version of a "democratic" regime represented internationally.[119]

Still, signs abounded that Batista would not take chances should the tide of votes turn against him and so laid the groundwork, should he need it, to declare the elections null by providing preelection evidence of a government under siege. Thus, two weeks before the elections, Batista claimed that a "vast terrorist plan" had been arranged against him by brothers Armando and Enrique Hart, Alonso and Mario Hidalgo, Faustino Pérez, and others. Armando Hart was already known to the public; he had served as Dr. Rafael García Bárcena's attorney in his earlier trial for conspiracy to topple the government. To substantiate the arrests and thereby justify greater vigilance and control at the polls, the regime made photographs of huge caches of weapons available to the media and claimed that the places that the "terrorists" had planned to bomb included a Presbyterian meeting hall, a kindergarten, and a medical clinic.[120] Rather than targets, these very places were likely spots where Hart, Pérez, and the others—all future leading members of the 26th of July Movement—stashed weapons for a potential uprising, with the complicity and collaboration of each institution's staff.

In addition, Batista's police provided full-page spreads of photographs of hundreds of pounds of hand grenades, ammunition, rifles, and automatic weapons manufactured in far-off locales such as Germany.[121] As Carlos Franqui, Manolo Ray, Vicente Baez, and dozens of other early activists later told me, Batista's opponents, including the 26th of July Movement of which they soon formed a part, only dreamed of having that kind of massive stockpile on hand. The reality—of continually suffering a paucity of weapons and often having to steal or manufacture their own—was not only quite different from Batista's trumped-up portrayal, it plagued every movement of his opponents, not just the 26th of July.

Yet perhaps most threatening to Batista's plans for a successful electoral confirmation of his leadership of Cuba was the unexpected and startling bravado of the FEU. Hoping to announce their break with a "civic dialogue" of any kind with the dictatorship and their opposition to the elections, FEU president and architecture student José Antonio Echeverría and FEU's two vice presidents, Fructuoso Rodríguez and José "Pepe" Puente Blanco, both law students, organized a mass rally at the university's escalinata. There they planned to read an open letter explaining FEU's position. Police almost immediately dispersed the crowd, beating leaders and sending those with less severe injuries, like Echeverría, straight to El Principe prison. Rushed to the emergency room and hospitalized for severe trauma to the head, Fructuoso nonetheless inspired a bold new plan. When Pepe Puente visited him, he casually remarked that Luis Blanco, another FEU member, had a very long piece of cloth at his home and that the nationally televised baseball game between the legendary rival teams of Havana and Almandares was coming up.

Pepe swiftly moved into action, gaining the support of Echeverría at el Principe through José Antonio's sister Lucy, and ultimately recruiting twenty-two students for a protest. Their goal was to unfurl a sixty-foot banner reading, "ABAJO LA DICTADURA—FEU" (DOWN WITH THE DICTATORSHIP—FEU). José Smith, a first-year law student, was selected for the dangerous task of carrying the banner: a chubby guy, he could easily wrap the banner around his middle, wear a jacket over it, and thereby disguise the insurrectionary sign as a simply another layer of belly fat. Certain they would all be arrested if they appeared to arrive en masse, Pepe told the twenty-two to arrive on their own. At some point, José would go to the bathroom, divest himself of the banner, and hide it under his coat. During the third inning, at the third out, all twenty-two would rush onto the field, unfurl the banner, and chant, "Down with Batista! Down with the dictatorship!" at the top of their voices.[122]

The plan worked like a charm. It was a propitious moment, recalled FEU's second vice president Pepe Puente Blanco, organizer of the act. Not only could the whole nation watch or hear the reaction of the crowd and broadcasters by television or radio, but the night of the game coincided with a convention of mayors from Florida, all of whom were invited to attend. The protest itself lasted only minutes, but the live broadcast of police violence against the young students lasted several more. According to José Antonio's younger sister Lucy, the act of protest was greeted with roaring applause, followed by equally loud boos and denunciations against the police.[123] "The people started to shout in favor, *¡Abajo la policía! Abajo Batista!*" remembered Pepe, chuckling. He could hear them even as he was being beaten by police at second base. "There were even some sportscasters who expressed outrage and sympathy, along with the crowd. That is, it was a great success." Beaten twice more, once in the passageways of the stadium and once upon arrival at the nearest police station in El Cerro, the boys were nevertheless jubilant. When transferred to El Principe the next day and received by Echeverría and other arrested student activists, all of

Figure 12. Despite extreme police repression and heavy censorship, José "Pepe" Puente Blanco and other members of FEU organized a successful protest against the regime during a baseball game, televised nationally and witnessed in person by thousands of spectators. Only *Bohemia* had the courage to publish a tiny image of the high point of the protest, accompanied by a brief factual description. (*Bohemia,* 1954)

them cheered and chanted anti-Batista slogans upon first sight.[124] Only *Bohemia* carried the news and a small, blurry, but dramatic picture showing the banner fully unfurled (figure 12). The brief caption nonetheless stated that the protest, for the few minutes it lasted, "caused a great sensation among spectators."[125] Police charged the boys with violating Batista's Decree of Public Order, despite its official suspension in anticipation of the 1 November election.[126]

In the end, Batista enjoyed the unexpected luxury of running for office un-opposed: literally at the last minute, Grau pulled out of the election. Citing "a climate of violence" and the fact that Batista was stationing both police and military at polling stations in flagrant violation of Cuba's electoral rules, Grau initially demanded a postponement of elections in order to secure legal guarantees for voters forty-eight hours before the polls were set to open.[127] When Cuba's Electoral Supreme Court, stacked with Batista appointees, refused to concede, Grau simply withdrew his candidacy and called on fellow Auténticos to do the same.[128] From Kuquine, Batista decreed that the elections would go on as planned.[129] Public enthusiasm declined.[130] Max Lesnik, president of the Orthodox Youth, declared that Grau had "proved" what they had said all along, both in the press and on radio: that the government would not respect the will of the people and there were never any "guarantees" from Batista regarding the elections. Grau's last-minute discovery of this was laughable.[131]

To the surprise of nobody, Batista won election to the presidency. Voter participation was easily attributable to the use of the military, police, and other intimidation tactics to force people to the polls. In Cienfuegos, the Auténtico Party candidate for mayor declared to reporters, "The climate of violence began forty-eight hours before the elections. . . . The citizenry has been obligated to vote for Batista. . . . In the nearby municipality of Rodas, the violence was even worse."[132] Dr. Alicia Hernández de Barca, the Auténticos' candidate for governor of Camagüey, characterized the election of 1 November in no uncertain terms. "It has not been a genuine election, but rather a new 10th of March."[133] Only in Havana did voters shock authorities by managing to elect popular Auténtico politician Nicolás Castellanos as mayor despite the overwhelming support his rival, Justo Luis Pozo, received from Batista.[134] Other former Auténticos, such as deposed chief of staff Genovevo Pérez Dámera, denounced Grau vociferously for abandoning ship after Pérez Dámera, by his own admission, spent $400,000 securing loyalty to the Auténtico Party in the province of Camagüey.[135]

Importantly, while *Bohemia* dutifully published images of long lines of voters and a jubilant Batista, it also produced a supplement to its regular edition that detailed the waves of arrests and persecution that made Batista's "victory" possible.[136] Unopposed elections were elections in name only, stated editors.[137] Although the periodical issued solid denunciations, its sparse photographic coverage of the anti-constitutional, heavy police presence around the polls revealed that *Bohemia*'s editors could take their critique only so far: revealing images would have further endangered the temporary "pass" to report that Batista's electoral moment gave the Cuban media. Nonetheless, exact figures released a year after the election revealed an extremely low voter turnout. Of 2,768,186 potential voters, only 1,451,763 actually voted and of these, only 1,262,587 voted for Batista.[138] The others likely annulled their ballots; 188,209 voted for Grau anyway despite his withdrawal from the ticket.

Ignoring the facts that Batista ran unopposed and that less than half the electorate actually voted, election analyst Mario Riera noted that Batista had achieved the highest number of votes of any presidential candidate in the history of the republic.[139] Similar results obtained in every province: less than half of those Cubans who could vote, did vote. Still, Batista's party officially won by a landslide.[140] Voter inaction stood in clear violation of the constitutional mandate requiring electoral participation by all eligible citizens. For all intents and purposes, voters' absence constituted an electoral strike of national proportions. One particularly direct political cartoon titled "Political Geography" reflected the public's view. "What is the population of Cuba?" a grammar school teacher asks a little boy. "Before or after the election?" he answers.[141]

Ironically, a month after the elections, Carlos Márquez Sterling seemed to experience a change of heart, calling them—as Hernández de Barca had the night before they were held—even more shameful than the 10th of March. More to the point, he demanded the unification of all opposition: "The ideal [goal] of the people lies in realizing the revolution that will redeem for us the past as much as the present."[142]

Laying the Groundwork for Legitimating Armed Struggle and Civil War

Needless to say, Márquez Sterling's fighting words seemed far too little and far too late for a growing number of Cubans. These included founding members of his own party such as Jorge Mañach: the Ortodoxos had no one to blame but themselves for the pathetic condition in which their party found itself.[143] More important, "the spectacle of a constant polemic among the very elements" of the opposition was the primary reason that Batista had been able to consolidate his power since 10 March 1952.[144] By March 1955, principal Ortodoxos Mañach, José Pardo Llada, Justo Carrillo, and others abandoned Márquez Sterling altogether, refounding Bárcena's Movimiento de la Nación, this time as a political party rather than an insurrectionary group.[145]

Others were more forgiving. At the law school of the University of Havana, when Márquez Sterling arrived to pick up his son at the end of a long day of final exams, students hailed him with a reverent standing ovation all along La Colina, the hill that skirted the giant stairwell at the entrance to the university.[146] Many proved full of advice. Almost immediately after Batista's 1 November election, stalwarts began writing Márquez Sterling frantic letters, urging him to found his own party, run in 1958, contest the election results—*do something*.[147] If Martí or Maceo were to come back to life, the horrors of contemporary Cuba would send them back to their graves, declared one Ortodoxo in Santiago. For him, the lesson of the 1954 election and Chibás's style of campaigning through popular street protests was obvious, although party leaders refused to recognize it: the Ortodoxos needed to be the "bottom-up" party of Chibás that represented the working class and empowered the peasants. Currently, these groups were noted only for their absence.[148] Grau's unprecedented reception by lower-class voters in the far-eastern provinces had clearly shown that.

In a last-ditch effort to unite the party, Márquez Sterling resigned his presidency and Raúl Chibás, Eddy's brother and founding director of the Havana Military Academy, a private school, was unanimously elected. Raúl Chibás committed to the position until mid-1956 when he, like Márquez Sterling, realized in exasperation that nothing he did united the party's eighty-member national directorate behind a single strategic line of action.[149] Still, Márquez Sterling ultimately rejected appeals to make up with Roberto Agramonte and in the summer of 1955 removed himself from the intransigent Ortodoxos led by Agramonte to found his own wing of the party, La Ortodoxía Libre, while Agramonte began calling his faction La Ortodoxía Histórica.[150] In these months, Agramonte's image fell even further, earning him the nickname of *burro* [donkey] for his stubbornness.[151] Yet never again would Márquez Sterling or the Orthodox Party command the love, respect, prestige, or even attention that many Cubans lavished on them in the lead-up to Batista's fraudulent elections of 1954. The Ortodoxo rank and file were angry and fed up with "knowing nothing" from the leadership.[152] Indeed, in early 1955, founding member Manuel Bisbé even seemed to concede the legacy of Eduardo Chibás and his undiminished "cult following" to a younger generation of leaders. If Chibás had been alive, he concluded, there would never have been a 10th of March. Refining this point, he wrote, "There is no basic difference between the character and the thought of a student leader and the character and the thought of *the* political leader [Eddy Chibás] of recent times."[153]

By the time Bisbé wrote this editorial in the winter of 1955, the Ortodoxos were already falling into utter disarray. Yet Bisbé's call for a changing of the guard and a handing over of Eddy Chibás's mantle to the young proved prophetic: the student leader José Antonio Echeverría had already heeded Chibás's message to bravely confront and fight the dictatorship on the street. In the coming year, he would emerge as the most dynamic central figure in civic mobilizations to confront Batista and to force unprecedented political concessions from the dictatorship. Ironically, in the long run, the primary beneficiary of Echeverría's and other civic leaders' success would not be civil society, desperate for a constitutional state, but the road to revolution led by Echeverría himself along with Fidel Castro and los muchachos del Moncada.

4

Civic Activism and the Legitimation of Armed Struggle Against Batista, 1955–1956

THE YEARS 1955 THROUGH THE END OF 1956 marked a new era in Cuban political culture, although few leaders in the top political establishment seemed aware of it. Emblematic of this, Batista's vice president, Rafael Guas Inclán, wrote a conciliatory private letter to Carlos Márquez Sterling in which he lamented the masses' allegedly natural propensity to "line up behind the men-flags [hombres-banderas], the paternalistic myths" that made up all political parties in Cuba's republican history. "Neither you nor I are supporters of strongmen and warlords [caudillistas]," he wrote. Yet, whether Márquez Sterling admitted it or not, he had to agree that recent public excitement over the Movimiento Nacional Revolucionario's reorganization under the ortodoxos Pardo Llada, Bárcena, and others was just another example of this tendency, nothing more than a dance craze, like el meneíto. Citizens were like sheep that could be led anywhere, insisted Vice President Guas Inclán. The only factor that united them politically was Cubans' inclination to the left. This had reached such extremes that even those on the far right were "so cowardly that they don't dare show themselves as on the right, but rather disguise themselves hypocritically as leftists."[1]

At the time, Márquez Sterling was toying with the idea of calling for a new constitutional convention rather than either endorse civic struggle or make another bid for new elections, even though he himself did not believe that changing the current Constitution would grant much traction to the opposition.[2] In short, partisan political enemies though they were, Batista stalwart Guas Inclán and his public political enemy and Ortodoxo founder Márquez Sterling shared

Figure 13. José Antonio Echeverría giving a victory speech on the night of his election as president of the FEU, a position he won four consecutive times. Echeverría received the honor in the presence of Dr. Cosme de la Torriente Brau, a venerable scholar and veteran of Cuba's 1895 war for independence. Unaffiliated with any political party, together they embodied the idea that true patriotism called for Cubans to be selfless fighters—even martyrs—for the cause of national sovereignty, rule of law, and a socially just democracy. (Courtesy of Lucy Echeverría Bianchi and family)

much pessimism about the potential impact that a mobilized citizenry might have on the stability of the Batista regime. As events would bear out over the following year, neither of these men's assessments of citizen attitudes could have been further from the truth.

Indeed, citizens joked about the MNR as the political fad of the month and compared it to the meneíto on purpose: both the dance and the MNR shared a *línea zigzagueante*, a zigzag pattern of steps.[3] Moreover, the adoption of leftist discourse that Guas Inclán described was not merely an opportunistic move by great hombres seeking to satiate popular caprice but a necessary response to growing public knowledge of a crisis of conditions in Cuba that citizens acquired daily, despite Batista's censors. Proof of this lay in the rising tide of support for leadership of a new generation of activist leaders like FEU's president José Antonio Echeverría to combat the inertia, unaccountability, and growing arrogance of the Batista regime (figure 13). Since 1953 Echeverría

Figure 14. From 1953 through 1957, nearly every week University of Havana students staged secretly announced protests against Fulgencio Batista's regime. They often began their protests on the outskirts of campus, racing up the stairs at the university's entrance in the attempt to flee police or military forces and to invoke the university's constitutionally guaranteed freedom from political intervention. (Courtesy of Lucy Echeverría Bianchi and family)

had led nearly weekly street protests in which students found the traditional sanctuary of university grounds violated by police. His public prestige soared as repression of FEU protests intensified, as did concerns over just how far Batista would go to impose his will (figure 14). "The FEU knows only one path to peace in Cuba," Echeverría declared at a mass rally at the University of Havana in December 1954. "No one believes that the 10th of March was legalized on the 1st of November. . . . The dictatorship continues to be illegal, and regimes that rely on force can only be toppled by force. Of course, that force is not necessarily military. And as we have said many times, the revolution is not only insurrection."[4]

Shortly after Echeverría uttered these words, Cubans faced possibly one of the most absurd political proposals ever launched by any administration in Cuban history. Shortly after his annual distribution of toys to destitute children on 6 January, the Catholic holiday known as Kings' Day, Batista announced vast plans to construct a transoceanic canal right through the central geographic axis of the island. Running north to south and cutting for hundreds of miles along-side the Escambray mountain range, El Canal Via-Cuba would have required draining the Zapata Swamp in order to open a new trade route between North and South America. The canal was estimated to cost between $400 million and $500 million. Batista pictured the project as the linchpin of a new plan to de-velop Cuba according to the values of "March 10th," a plan that also invited all political exiles to return to Cuba without fear. "I have never tired of doing good and will never tire of it ever; but have I not repeated ad nauseam that all can return; who wants them to return more than I?" Batista declared.[5] Immediately, the defeat of Batista's canal project became FEU's primary concern.

Speaking on behalf of Cuba's university youth and surely many more, Echeverría contended that Batista's real objective was to establish the basis for a permanent U.S. military presence on the island, similar to the occupa-tion of Panama, on the pretense of defending hemispheric and trade security. Moreover, he rebutted Batista's claim that the canal would be financed solely through locally acquired loans and therefore not degrade Cuban sovereignty further by making the country beholden to foreign investors. If it had not been possible for Cuban capital to fully fund the construction of the tunnel uniting the Bay of Havana at a cost of $30 million, how could anyone think that local investors could fork over fifteen times that amount for a canal? "The construc-tion of the so-called Canal Via-Cuba," he stated, "constitutes a direct attack on our sovereignty. There are no historical, economic, or moral reasons to justify that idiotic scheme. For more than thirty years, the people of Cuba fought to free themselves from the Platt Amendment, and now the regime of the 10th of March intends to impose a new Platt Amendment on Cuba." "The usurpers," he concluded, meant to divide the island for the benefit of foreigners precisely at the time Egypt and Panama were reclaiming rights over their canals from the imperial powers of the United Kingdom and the United States.[6] In other words, Batista wanted to surrender Cuban nationhood to U.S. interests just as so many of his neocolonial predecessors had: now he had gone too far.

Recruiting hundreds of supporters from Cuba's professional associations of engineers, architects, doctors, lawyers, and "numerous other institutions" for a mass march and rally, FEU also called on Freemasons, Catholics, veterans, Rotarians, Lions' Clubs, and the unions of industrial and commercial workers. The date of the protest was set for 28 January 1955, José Martí's birthday and, in a repeat performance of FEU's torch-lit demonstration on that same day in

1953, marchers would proceed from la escalinata at the University of Havana to gather around the Central Park monument to Martí.[7] The support of Max Lesnik, president of the Juventud Ortodoxa, and Jorge Mañach quickly added to the growing tide of negative public opinion regarding the canal and the increasing esteem of FEU's new president.[8] *Bohemia* itself joined the chorus of protest with an article asking, "What else could we do with $400,000,000?"[9] The Cuban state needed to prioritize always the development of national capital by providing incentives to national investors over foreign ones, argued Echeverría. It should also promote industrialization and support the university training of more technical personnel, including awarding scholarships to study in foreign countries to acquire the latest skills and knowledge.[10]

In the end, Batista dropped plans for the Canal Vía-Cuba by December 1955. Credit for the victory accrued to FEU's brilliant strategists for leading thirty-five civic associations into an unarmed war of attrition that, for once under the Batista regime, citizens had won.[11] The events that transpired between Batista's announcement of the canal project and its demise, however, were clearly responsible for facilitating this civic victory. None were more important than FEU's and the opposition's unified demand that Batista free all political prisoners, including los muchachos del Moncada, as a prerequisite and prelude to negotiated change. Previously, works on this period have tended to dismiss or isolate the civic activism of FEU and Echeverría from the process of radicalization among Cuban citizens. FEU's unflinching activism in the early months of 1955 lent greater and greater weight to the push for amnesty for all political prisoners, including the Moncada assailants, a goal achieved by May 1955. Yet despite the unarmed character of such activism, this chapter argues that public pressure and organized challenges played a major factor in leading citizens to endorse armed struggle as the only means for toppling Batista.

As civic activism shifted into high gear in the two years between January 1955 and December 1956, when Castro launched his guerrilla war in Oriente province, citizens' successes and shows of unified opposition revealed how little Batista would budge when it came to loosening his grip on state power. Nonetheless, events themselves not only shaped the evolution of public attitudes in unexpected ways but ultimately yielded political outcomes favorable to Castro's movement and its emerging rivalry with FEU, especially as Echeverría further cemented a position at the center of the public stage.

To prepare the public to back the violent overthrow of the regime that he and his FEU allies were secretly plotting by 1956, Echeverría appealed to Cubans with the claim that an *armed* challenge to Batista's power could only renew and refresh the national collective union. Castro and his supporters took this argument several steps further, couching their own movement's already proven commitment to violence in discursive histrionics of "making love, not war" in defense of la patria. In adopting the prose and pose of reluctant revolutionaries who *loved* rather than hated, Echeverría, Castro, and their respective movements attempted to undercut the very claims Batista had made all along, since the very day of his coup. Batista, Castro had remarked in his 1953 defense speech and widely circulated pamphlet *History Will Absolve Me,* victimized both victims and perpetrators alike: Batista alone represented the true enemy, not the army and certainly not the cowed or even cowardly public.

Effectively then, all three sides, most especially Batista, contended that peace would and should come through war; the difference lay, however, in citizens' willingness to believe in the greater purity, patriotic authenticity, and political credibility of the armed opposition.

Amnesty and Competing Claims to a Democratic Peace

Batista followed up his January proposal for a canal by sparing no expense in celebrating his own inauguration as president for a "third term" over the course of four days. Events began with the representatives of forty-eight countries presenting their diplomatic credentials to him on Wednesday, 23 February, and continued with his swearing in, a military parade, and a reception for the diplomats on 24 February, anniversary of El Grito de Baire.[12] The inauguration also included a "gala" featuring a performance by Alicia Alonso, a Communist Party militant and Cuba's most famous ballerina. Ironically, she would later preside over the ascendance of Cuba's Soviet-style ballet company in the post-1959 era, becoming just as symbolic of the unchanging monopoly on power over a key sector of Cuba's cultural field as Fidel Castro himself was of the political direction of the Communist state. In 1954, however, Batista patronized Alonso's international premiere. Diplomats dominated the guest list for both her ballet performance and the lavish banquet that capped off Batista's inauguration on Saturday, 26 February.[13] The inauguration served as a metaphor of how Batista would increasingly come to rely on external supporters and a positive international image as substitutes for genuine popularity in his own country.

Nonetheless, he kept up the appearance of born-again democrat, vowing to "work and study all the time" so that he could be the best president possible.[14] In his first meeting with reporters after his inauguration, Batista promised to "obey" the Cuban Congress and fulfill citizens' desire for "peace." Going further, he even announced that deposed president Prío could not only return to Cuba with his protection but *should* return. When pressed by reporters, Batista said he would back an amnesty law for political prisoners with congressional approval if he could negotiate terms with the opposition.[15] Flanking *Bohemia*'s exclusive report was a manifesto signed by thirty-six of Cuba's most prestigious Ortodoxo leaders and intellectuals, including Carlos Márquez Sterling, Manuel Bisbé, youth leader Max Lesnik, José Pardo Llada, Fidel Castro's unofficial personal secretary Luis Conte Agüero, and perhaps Cuba's most revered living veteran of the independence wars, Dr. Cosme de la Torriente.[16]

From their jail cells on the Isle of Pines, Pedro Miret and Gustavo Arcos sent a hand-drawn Christmas card on behalf of "all of us" to Jorge Mañach. Writing in *Bohemia,* Mañach explained that "all of us" referred to those political prisoners jailed for "political acts," a phrase that deliberately avoided endorsing the charge that their armed revolt was a crime. "They are," he wrote, "los muchachos del Moncada." Featuring the face of Antonio Maceo surrounded by a rifle, a sword, and the Cuban flag, the card included one of Maceo's most famous quotes: "Whoever tries to possess Cuba for his own uses will collect the dust of its ground soaked in blood."[17]

In a reply to Mañach that reproduced his article's title, "The Accord and the Political Prisoners," as well as the card's hand-drawn image, one of the two muchachas del Moncada, Melba Hernández, gently revised Mañach's interpretation that its authors sent the card on behalf of *all* political prisoners on the Isle of Pines. According to Melba, the card represented *only* those of Fidel's 26th of July Movement. In making this case, she heralded a new and effective political discourse for the movement. The moral purity of its members and goals, she implied, were unique: "With greater *love* than the sentiments of war, we gave ourselves over to the task," she insisted in January 1955. "That was the conduct of an idealistic youth, eminently Cuban, selfless [*desinteresada*], among which there were neither mercenaries nor foreigners; that could act with purity because we aspire to nothing, because we only thought of Cuba and in the rescue of her institutions, indispensable for the peaceful coexistence we deserve."[18]

When Melba published her response to Mañach, little more than twenty days of her and Haydée's sentence at the Guanajay women's prison remained. Upon their release, both women immediately began work on crafting the longer version of Fidel's defense speech, *La Historia Me Absolverá*. Characteristically ambitious, Fidel ordered one hundred thousand copies printed. As Melba later admitted, the actual number they achieved fell far short (probably reaching only twenty thousand copies), mostly because the tiny group of seven urban activists affiliated with the 26th of July, including Fidel's sister Lydia, counted on only one small press to produce the copies.[19]

As Fidel's brilliantly persuasive speech began to circulate clandestinely, an unvoiced but apparent public consensus in favor of blanket amnesty for political prisoners and exiles emerged. Until late March, the sticking point for Batista was his unwillingness to include Castro and the other jailed assailants of Moncada.[20] However, two of the most powerful members of Batista's now renamed Progressive Action Party (Partido de Acción Progresista, or PAP), Senator Andrés Rivero Agüero and Representative Rafael Díaz-Balart, Fidel's former brother-in-law, defied this view. They then joined an array of other batistianos, Ortodoxos, and radical youth activists Max Lesnik and José Antonio Echeverría in endorsing amnesty for los muchachos del Moncada.[21] The call for blanket amnesty was not only "the slogan of the moment," it was the singular most unified call made during the three-year tenure of the Batista administration thus far.[22] Echeverría summarized the moment best when he concluded, "Only two political parties can exist: those who are with Cuba and against Batista, and those who find themselves with Batista and against Cuba."[23] Importantly, the appeal of the push for amnesty rested on its promise of securing greater steps toward "peace," a line that inadvertently united Batista's own discourse of legitimacy to that of the opposition's charges of his regime's *illegitimacy*. It was probably for this reason that spokesmen and consummate defenders of the dictator like Díaz-Balart and Rivero Agüero felt the need to step forward in support of amnesty; doing otherwise would have cost them the bit of validity they believed the reinstallation of a legislative state in 1954 had augured.

Among citizens, support for amnesty and hope for "peace" was easy to find. Yet many ascribed a very different definition to it compared to Batista. In Matanzas, Heriberto Corona Pérez reported to Márquez Sterling on the success of *radio-mítines,* that is, radio-transmitted calls for spontaneous rallies against the regime that hundreds of people attended. If citizens kept up this strategy with a mass surge of radio-mítines on a designated date, he suggested, Batista's police would be forced to arrest two thousand to three thousand people on one day, thereby provoking ever greater public outcry.[24] Even more to the point, *Bohemia* reported an increase in weekly sales, despite the high cost of the magazine and the rising cost of living. With a sold-out circulation of 255,000 copies in April 1955, *Bohemia* became, the most popular and successful magazine in all of Latin America.[25] Editors attributed this to the high level of political consciousness on the part of readers as the national crisis of Cuba deepened. Reading *Bohemia* itself had become an act of citizen defiance.

Examples of the bold political intervention typical of *Bohemia*'s editors and owner Miguel Angel Quevedo abounded throughout the magazine's history. They undoubtedly reached a crescendo in the 1950s, particularly after Chibás's death. A copy of *Bohemia* was buried with him, apparently at his request, and *Bohemia* dedicated three consecutive issues to honoring Chibás and the legacy of his activism.[26] Such instances go far in explaining the magazine's rising popularity and prestige. In March 1955, *Bohemia* published an exchange of letters between Fidel Castro and Luis Conte Agüero, his confidant and unofficial publicist. Calling himself and fellow moncadistas "hostages" of the regime, Fidel compared the actions of Batista to those of Hitler and his own situation to that of Jesus Christ when the Pharisees questioned him as to whether he should pay tribute to Caesar. The Pharisees knew that whatever Jesus said, it would amount to subversion of either Caesar or his allies, the Pharisees themselves. Like Jesus, Fidel adopted a path of total disinterest and noncooperation, characteristically punctuated with notes of hyperbole and hubris: "I am totally uninterested in demonstrating to the regime that it should dictate amnesty. . . . We do not want amnesty at the cost of our dishonor. . . . A thousand more years of imprisonment before our humiliation! A thousand more years of imprisonment before the sacrilegious loss of our self-respect! We proclaim this serenely," he added pointedly, "without fear nor hate."[27]

Like Castro, both *Bohemia* and its readers seemed to concur with the idea that amnesty for all of Cuba's presos, especially its most vocally radical ones, would contribute to the fall of Batista. *Bohemia*'s staff said as much in an editorial published 10 April 1955. Although likely written by the magazine's owner-director, this editorial, like others, implied a collective rather than individual rebuke of the dictatorship because of the constant intimidation and regular detention by Batista's SIM and national police that *Bohemia* staff endured. "The people will never consider delinquents those who have been exiled or jailed for defending liberty and democratic institutions," they stated flatly. On the contrary, Cuban history itself designated them revolutionaries and national heroes, not criminals.[28]

Neither fear nor hate but only love of patria motivated los muchachos del Moncada, Luis Conte Agüero had written a week earlier. Importantly, he also revealed the source of their public appeal. Contrary to expectation, he argued that it was the *absence* of a systematic program, the apolitical character of the moncadistas' politics, the sheer value of their moral consciousness, and the purity of their spirit that validated Castro and his followers in the eyes of the public. "*El pueblo* appreciates them dearly as people, but loves them as symbols. The palms will shake with the thunder of joy to see them freed from the unjust prison, but the people would also reject that jubilance if it came at the cost of *your* honor," he said addressing himself to the moncadistas directly, "because you are the embodiment of rebellious *cubanidad,* of youthful heroism, of the unwavering soul of the unchained revolutionary Cuba of the independence wars, *Cuba mambisa.*"[29]

On 15 May, Mother's Day, 1955, amnesty for all political prisoners finally arrived to all the main prisons in Cuba, from La Cabaña to El Principe and, of course, the Isle of Pines. Those released included Armando Hart, Faustino Pérez, dozens of the Triple A, an Auténtico organization that had attempted to launch a movement on 24 February, anniversary of the Grito de Baire, would-be revolutionaries who had stashed caches of arms in their homes, and Fidel Castro, Raúl Castro, Gustavo Arcos, and the entire Moncada crew.[30] The freed prisoners were met by their loved ones at the entrance to the National Prison at the Isle of Pines; joy and relief united all involved.[31] Unable to contain himself, the son of Jesús Montané raced toward his father, a member of one of the first groups exiting the main gate. "¡Papi, papi, qué bueno!" (Daddy, Daddy, I am so glad!), he yelled, jumping into his father's arms. Fidel, Raúl, Mario Chanes, Gustavo Arcos, and Juan Almeida came next. When Fidel spotted the stoic Haydée after embracing his own weeping sisters, he called to her and she burst into tears in his arms. "Everyone knew her tragic story," chronicled *Bohemia*. "Neither her brother nor her boyfriend numbered among the liberated ones, because both perished in the great effort of the 26th of July."[32]

Similar scenes of love and collective national reunion continued as Fidel praised and then publicly embraced Lieutenant Roger Pérez Díaz, one of the officers charged with supervising their imprisonment. "From him we have received only acts of kindness. . . . I want you to know, Lieutenant, and may all the members of the military know, that we are not enemies of the armed forces but adversaries, and that only because of the circumstances that exist today in the country." Returning Fidel's embrace, Batista's officer exclaimed, "¡Ojalá que estás cosas traigan mejores días para Cuba!" (God willing, things like this will bring better days for Cuba!). Before leaving the crowd and departing for Havana, Fidel stopped once again, this time to comfort a grieving mother who cried that she did not know where her son was buried. "Help me, Fidel!" Holding the distraught woman, Fidel wept with her for several minutes, saying finally, "We will find him, *viejita* [my dear old lady]. We will find him together."[33]

Later, Fidel took a plane back to the main island, arriving at the train station in Havana to be hailed by José Antonio Echeverría, crowds of young people, reporters, and Ortodoxos of all generations. Claiming that the "program of Moncada cannot be other than that of [Eduardo] Chibás," Fidel then met with both Raúl Chibás and Roberto Agramonte at a relative's home in the presence of reporters. Keeping to the line that his interest lay in uniting Cubans with love of patria, he declared, "I am a warrior without hatred and without resentments" (figure 15).[34]

Clear to officials of the Batista regime was the power that the 26th of July Movement's line of "making love, not war" and its promise of peace with liberty held for the Cuban people. Demonstrating this was Colonel Alberto Del Río Chaviano, chief of the Moncada barracks at the time of the attack and after. If Melba Hernández's and Fidel Castro's justifications of their attack on Batista's soldiers as an act of national defense and "love" were undeniably paradoxical and hyperbolic, Del Río Chaviano's efforts to explain the regime's reaction to the assault were equally so—and strangely similar. In stating that the army had "never" acted with greater "serenity" nor shown greater restraint in its responses, Del Río Chaviano turned moncadista discourse on its head. "Charged with sterile hatred," the criminals under the command of Castro never suffered any abuses at the military's hands. On the contrary, he claimed, the army "neither employed fascist methods nor gave recourse to violence." In every case, the assailants were subject to a fair trial.[35]

Not surprisingly, a now liberated Fidel Castro lost no time in issuing a rebuke, imbuing it with images of Christian martyrdom and moral hyperbole. Del Rio Chaviano's denials of the truth of his own savagery had only one goal: to

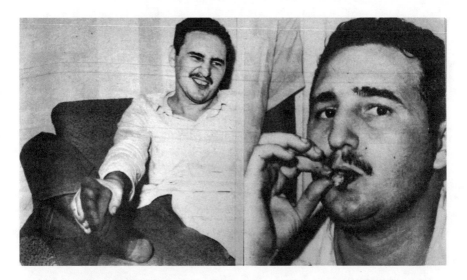

Figure 15. Looking like the average middle-class professional home from a long day at the office, Fidel Castro offered *Bohemia* the opportunity to interview him only hours after his release from the Isle of Pines. (*Bohemia*, 1955)

discredit "the heroism" and to "drown in terror and mud the idealism of a youth that refused and is not wiling to be the slave of anyone." Nero, the infamously brutal Roman emperor, acted no differently when he tried to justify the assassination of Christians, accusing them of setting fire to Rome, an act he himself had ordered.[36]

The triumph of civic groups, the press, and political figures in calling for amnesty miraculously, if temporarily, healed all the divisions among Orthodox Party leaders. In a joint manifesto issued by Raúl Chibás, they made plain the three conditions on which they were willing to arrive at a "national solution" with Batista. These were first, effective implementation of the 1940 Constitution; second, complete guarantees of protection for the return of all exiles; and third, a total cessation of authorities' attacks on citizens, arbitrary arrests, censorship (including that of mail and wiretapping), and "all violations of human rights."[37]

The problem with the Ortodoxos' position, as well as that of much of the rest of the organized opposition, was simple: it remained comprised mostly of words. As Batista quickly demonstrated, as soon as activists attempted to put their words into action, their protests would not be tolerated. Within a week of the national jubilation that the total amnesty of all political prisoners sparked, events proved that there would be no change in the terms of Batista's vision for "peace." When Echeverría and FEU attempted to organize a mass rally on 20 May 1955, the anniversary of Cuba's independence from its first U.S. military occupation in 1902 and the inauguration of the republic, the government cut all electricity to the University of Havana campus, a police cordon restricted access, and shots were fired. As if through divine intervention, the gunfire killed a dove flying overhead. Echeverría and fellow students gathered round the body of the dove killed by Batista's agents, a powerful symbol of the political death of peace and love in Cuba.[38]

FEU Takes Center Stage

On 3 June 1955, the indomitable elderly veteran Dr. Cosme de la Torriente announced that he and the twenty-three-man, two-woman directorate of La Sociedad de Amigos de la República, or SAR (Society of Friends of the Republic), a historically apolitical intellectual organization with eighteenth-century roots, would unify the opposition. They planned to negotiate a concession of immediate and fair elections from the Batista regime. Composed of the sons of Máximo Gómez, Antonio Maceo, veterans such as General Enrique Loynaz del Castillo, and others of equal social rank and prestige, SAR epitomized cubanidad and a separation from the traditional fold of self-serving, demagogic politicians. In its opening statement, SAR identified three law decrees (issued in January 1953, long *before* the assault on Moncada supposedly justified martial law) that formed the foundation of state repression and anti-democratic activities by the government. Decrees 648, 649, and 650 created a *fuero,* that is, the legal privilege of being *above* the law to all armed forces of the state, thereby allowing them to treat citizens however they wanted. These laws stood in flagrant violation of all Batista's verbal promises of promoting "peace" and on-again, off-again grants of press freedom. The first step to reconciliation, declared SAR, was the elimination of these laws on Batista's part and, on the opposition's part, a good-faith commitment to talks with Batista, despite the virtual certainty that neither side would achieve all that it wanted.[39]

In response, the presidents of every major political party, wing of a political party, and the MNR, including Ramón Grau San Martín, Raúl Chibás, and José Pardo Llada, wrote letters of cooperation and support.[40] Proof of the urgency felt on all sides emerged in sharp relief as it seemed clear that amnesty or not, the death of Cuban democracy, if it had not already taken place, was surely just around the corner. Many saw that death to lie as much in Batista's continuing grip on power as in the probability of violent revolution.

Among the chorus of voices prophesying this point, de la Torriente stood out most clearly, particularly with regard to what SAR's and the opposition's objectives should be. He confessed in September 1955 that on the day of Batista's coup, "I saw the revolution coming. What's more, I was sure that it was advancing fast and so from that first day, I moved to avoid it." He had done so immediately after the coup by convoking the country's surviving veterans of the independence wars, hoping to block Batista from continuing in office by sheer dint of the veterans' public prestige and ability to mobilize palpable citizen outrage. He did not succeed. To his shock, the veterans, led by the National Council of the Veterans' Association, accomplished nothing—Batista preempted any moves by buying most of them off. Given that the veterans were living witnesses to Cubans' decades of sacrifice to achieve independence from Spain and victims of the theft of their victory by the United States after 1898, de la Torriente considered their collaboration with Batista nothing short of treason. "They were the ones who did the least to defend the independence and freedoms of Cuba."[41] Now, Cuba had reached a historical precipice from which there was no turning back.

Indeed, Cuba would not turn back, despite months of work on the part of SAR and the multiple letters de la Torriente wrote directly to Batista, inviting him to meet with the group. Ignored, he accused the dictator of taking on a "tremendous historical responsibility" for which Cubans would never forgive him.[42] Not only did Batista simply refuse to meet with him, the opposition, or even SAR members, he even refused to write to them. De la Torriente received only one polite note reminding SAR that elections would be held in 1958, just as they had been in 1954: this represented all the proof citizens needed that democracy existed in Cuba.[43] The only concession Batista would give was the right of the opposition to meet in a mass public forum presided over by de la Torriente and SAR.

That forum took place on 19 November 1955 in Old Havana's Plaza de la Luz before an estimated crowd of one hundred thousand.[44] Importantly, only the PSP Communists were excluded, a fact they protested, because SAR considered them former and potentially current clandestine allies of Batista. Angry at being excluded, PSP militants led by Salvador García Agüero attempted to sabotage the event by putting up graffiti denigrating SAR and interrupting speakers. Almost immediately, fighting and the throwing of chairs broke out between members of FEU and the PSP.[45] When SAR'S own security forces succeeded in detaining the PSP protesters, SAR's case against the PSP was proved right: one of them was found carrying the identification card of Batista's national police. In other words, being Communists did not preclude them from becoming covert members of Batista's security forces; on the contrary, it seemed to enhance the likelihood. For their part, stalwart supporters of Castro's emerging independent wing of opposition, already known as *fidelistas,* later joined the SAR's voluntary honor guard charged with keeping order and security in expelling the Communists.[46]

Yet, importantly, the first and most effectively planned PSP-led fracas did not take place when any of the other speakers—all of them opponents of armed revolution—took the stage: rather, the disruption commenced only when the FEU president, Echeverría, began his speech immediately after the opening remarks of de la Torriente, the master of ceremonies.[47] The PSP did not disrupt speakers for the unarmed opposition because their party condemned any violent movement they could not control and whose victory would not be theirs: after all, it might spell doom for any continued activities. FEU, by contrast, was a certain enemy to PSP ends.

Recognizing that the PSP agitators' choice to interrupt *him* was no coincidence, Echeverría demanded "respect for this venerable *mambí*" and asked el pueblo to "throw out these saboteurs and agent provocateurs in the service of Batista!"[48] As he had already made clear over several months in student rallies constantly repressed by police, Echeverría was the only speaker on the dais who, along with FEU, categorically rejected the idea that *any* accommodations, negotiations, or agreement regarding elections could be made with the dictator.[49]

Once free of interruptions, Echeverría defined the position of the majority of university students and possibly his generation nationwide:

> We maintain that only a profound transformation in our political, social, and economic reality can cure of the ailments of our *Patria*. The immediate problem in Cuba is toppling the usurper Fulgencio Batista and establishing a democratic government that can carry out a revolutionary project that will solve the problem of the unemployed, the landless peasants, the exploited workers, and the [educated and professional] youth [who find no work here] condemned to economic exile....

Fulgencio Batista, the Cuban people meet here today to say: *¡VETE!* [GET OUT!] Or are you going to wait till they throw you out like they did to Gerardo Machado? With Martí, it was proclaimed: "The people's rights are not begged for, they are taken. Nothing is conquered with tears but with blood." *El pueblo de Cuba tiene la palabra*. [The Cuban people have the word].[50]

In short, Cuba's principal and most revered student leader left no doubt what path he and others like him intended to take. The crowd greeted José Antonio's fury with thunderous applause.

Nonetheless, while no other speaker, including Grau or Prío, invited revolution, pro-Batista congressmen accused them all of endorsing Echeverría's radical position and "unfurling the flag of war," declaring that SAR had even "recognized Fidel Castro as a leader."[51] These interpretations were not entirely exaggerated. Clearly inspired and emboldened by Echeverría, young people in the crowd frequently chanted, "¡Revolución, Revolución!" during the rest of the evening, for which Grau San Martín admonished them in paternalistic, authoritative terms.[52] José Miró Cardona, a respected professor and Ortodoxo, similarly dismissed the chant as the words of "kids." Like the assault on El Cuartel Moncada, remarked Cardona, any call for "revolution" could not be seen as anything more than evidence of young Cubans' naiveté.[53]

Still, it was not just revolution for which young Cubans called. Clearly audible on a rare recording of Echeverría's speech made and distributed in early January 1959 by La Corona, one of Cuba's oldest tobacco companies, are the chants of a small group of activists gathered near the stage and identified as PSP: "Fidel! Fidel! Fidel!"[54] Were they PSP members? If so, why did they call on Fidel? Did they consider Castro's relative independence from ties to other movements a possible entry point for their own agendas? These questions, however challenging they may seem, are primary concerns of the next chapter. Castro, like Echeverría, constituted a formidable threat to Batista and all old-guard politicians, whether or not they sided with the opposition. Apparently attempting to capitalize on the crowd's enthusiasm for Fidel, the deposed president Prío went so far as to ask where Fidel was and to wish he were there.[55]

Absent from Cuba since July 1955, when he left for Mexico and then the United States to organize support and drum up financing for armed revolution, Castro represented a path to change that many other young activists, such as Echeverría and a growing number of middle-class and upper-class professionals, recognized as the *only* way open to Cuba: warfare against the state. With faith in the power of civic activism and popular mobilization exhausted after nearly four years of struggle against the dictatorship, vast swaths of the Cuban people increasingly agreed.

Tapping Cubans' Revolutionary Potential

Under titles like "Yo Acuso," a phrase made famous by Eddy Chibás and then taken up by Fidel Castro, *Bohemia*'s coverage of child laborers and shoe-shiners selling their services to U.S. Marines represented an effort to grow ever bolder and more blunt—less sensationalistic—in the magazine's reports on poverty. Every year, García Inclán also added greater punch to the column "¡Arriba Corazones!"[56] As the media market for consumer products expanded, consciousness of a contrast between rich and poor also grew. Bright new shopping malls such as El Mercado Carlos III opened in Havana.[57] The number of U.S.-made products inviting Cubans to whiten their skin and straighten their hair increased.[58] A rising number of corporations, foreign and domestic, also began selling their products, from Fab dishwashing detergent to Adams Chiclets gum. But even they recognized the need to appeal to consumers by recognizing the unaffordability of their wares to most Cubans. For this reason, soap and other products were often sold with lottery-style tickets for bicycles, cars, or even homes.[59] At the same time, political cartoonists developed a new, apparently censor-proof style of parody that helped to normalize criticism of the state in the public sphere, despite its illegality. For example, in a two-page spread of cartoons, "Arroyito" showed a group of three men, one holding his toddler before the desk of a civil servant. "What do you say? Your kid needs a birth certificate? No problem! At the very entrance of the municipal courthouse there are two 'briefcase witnesses' who, for a pittance [*una basurita*], will certify that they saw your child born as easily as they will swear they witnessed the death of Christopher Columbus!"[60] Cartoons like these spoke to and for a citizenry exasperated with corruption, visibly deteriorating economic conditions for the majority, and the unfulfilled promise of a "political solution." These feelings inspired a growing public appetite for a fight against Batista, which some favored whether led by organized insurrectionists or not.

One focus of revolutionary potential was undoubtedly organized labor, especially among sugar workers. In fact, a little-known black leader from the Central Santa Clara, Fernando Rodríguez Abreu, may have offered the best assessment of sentiments among workers in the period between 1955, still defined by civic optimism, and 1956, the start of civil war. In a report to the Ortodoxía Libre, Márquez Sterling's wing of the party, Rodríguez Abreu predicted that Cuba was on the brink of all-out war because Cubans demanded a response to injustice, just as they had in 1868, 1895, 1933, and 1940. In the "fatherland of Eduardo Chibás," the constitutional promise of racial equality was "an infamous lie"; women committed suicide in the countryside rather than watch their children starve; peasants lived in hovels that resembled pre-Columbian times; and in the palaces of Miramar, Havana's richest neighborhood, "two thousand millionaires turned their backs on the needs of 1 million Cubans."[61] The absence of justice was annihilating the nation. To demand justice, he warned, workers would begin acting alone.

Some workers carried out arbitrary acts of sabotage resembling those later coordinated by guerrillas and the urban underground of the 26th of July. Although nonworkers and, later, historians seldom recognized these acts as political protest, the owners of sugar mills clearly saw their political motivation at the time. Having learned many harsh lessons from earlier experiences during the 1933 social revolution that crushed profits and led to worker takeovers of mills, the Czarnikow-Rionda Company, principally owned by the Braga and Fanjul families, had since taken out millions of dollars in insurance policies against "riot and sabotage" from the world's largest insurers in the United States and Great Britain. Beginning in the winter of 1955, the company increasingly needed them. That February, "a person or persons of malicious intent" placed a bomb on a three-hundred-thousand-gallon oil tank at the Tuinucu sugar mill. By chance, the tank was empty at the time and the explosion resulted in minimal damage and no loss of life. Keeping the incident out of the press, owners filed a claim for only slightly more than $1,000 against the company's $706,111 total insurance policy for Tuinucu at the time. Had the tank been full, however, it would likely have caused massive damage, especially since another tank, filled to the brim, was located only a hundred meters away.[62]

Unknown culprits set fire to fifty-eight crossties in late August and two days later, eighty-eight more, putting the principal rail line at the Manatí plantation in Las Tunas, Camagüey, out of commission.[63] Both events set the stage for a mass general strike of the Federación Nacional de Trabajadores del Azucar (National Federation of Sugar Workers, or FNTA), possibly the country's most powerful labor union. The FNTA was known for its ability to bring Cuba's single-crop-oriented economy to a halt at the most critical time of year, the start of harvest season. In December, FEU reached across class lines in a show of public and material support for FNTA strikers. The move did not broaden the strike to other labor sectors, as FEU had hoped, but it did push owners and key ministers in Batista's cabinet to the negotiating table for successful payment of *la diferencial,* a bonus paid to workers based on the difference between the previous and current year's price of sugar.[64]

Although la diferencial had been previously mandated by law thanks to the efforts of labor leaders turned congressmen like Communist Jesús Menéndez, assassinated in cold blood and broad daylight by police in 1948, Batista's arbitrary approach to law enforcement encouraged owners not to pay it. Undoubtedly, the FEU's actions and its leaders' very public appearance in the University of Havana's Salón de Mártires (Hall of Martyrs) with top labor activists Conrado Rodríguez and David Salvador had everything to do with the strike's resolution through government intervention by early January 1956. Ominously, José Antonio Echeverría declared the unity between radical students and labor against the forces of oppression an inevitable success.[65] However, the very fact that sugar workers had gained concessions from owners through Batista—in the person of CTC Batista stalwart Eusebio Mujal—also spoke to the opposite conclusion: that workers would play it safe and stay out of the struggle so long as they gained something of what they needed from existing structures.

Despite or perhaps because of this very real possibility, the late fall of 1955 and early winter 1956 were busy ones for Echeverría, the FEU's popular new president. When the strike formally began, he led the federation's directorate in a closed-door debate and vote on the organization of an armed wing of the FEU, the Directorio Revolucionario (DR). The proposal rested on allowing Echeverría the exclusive liberty to recruit members, including former members of FEU whom other members trusted but were no longer students. The measure was approved by a majority of delegates. The DR counted on recent graduates as well as politically reliable "hombres de acción," older veterans of earlier struggles who knew how to handle weapons and form commando units.[66] On 24 February 1956, the anniversary of El Grito de Baire, the DR made its purposes of insurrection known, issuing a manifesto declaring its connection to the historical legacy of the FEU and its position as sole representative of that organization's continuing cause: a definitive Cuban revolution to establish a democratic republic and end all need for revolution in the future.[67]

In addition, Echeverría traveled to Costa Rica with a handful of founding DR members, including FEU first vice president Fructuoso Rodríguez and Juan Pedro Carbó Serviá. They went to help the national army of Costa Rica's democratically elected president José Figueres combat an armed incursion across the border by forces of Nicaraguan dictator Anastasio Somoza.[68] Over the next six months, Echeverría continued to expand his place on the world stage as the increasingly politicized and anti-imperialist youth of Latin America conceived it.

Thus, on 28 January, he and other students placed a crown of flowers at the foot of Martí's monument in Havana's Central Park and received a brutal, highly publicized police beating. Subsequently, Echeverría attended a congress of Latin American students in Chile. There delegates promptly elected him president of their international association. Upon his return from Chile, University of Havana students elected him president of FEU once more.[69] During these months, José Antonio developed his most radical anti-imperialist voice, arguing that the primary cause of political and economic stagnation across Latin America was U.S. intervention on behalf of its own corporate and geopolitical interests.[70]

After Echeverría had openly endorsed revolution before enormous crowds and SAR organizers at the Plaza de la Luz, he consistently echoed this call with the slogan "¡A Las Armas!" (To the Weapons!) Almost simultaneously and throughout 1956, Fidel Castro continued to do the same.[71] However, Fidel boasted that he had called for armed protest *before* anyone else and unlike Echeverría, who invited citizens to support rebellion without endorsing himself as their leader, Castro overtly argued that he and his small circle of followers were uniquely qualified for this role. Although he repeated his movement's adamant rejection of "terrorism," assassination—including *tiranicidio,* the killing of the tyrant Batista—and violence against other anti-Batista activists who disagreed with his movement's positions, Fidel stated unequivocally, "We are today the *only ones in Cuba* who know where we are going and do not depend on the last word of the dictator [to get there]." Unless Batista resigned right away and handed power over to SAR's Cosme de la Torriente—a move Fidel endorsed—SAR had only one choice: to back civic resistance on a massive scale.[72]

In November 1955, just as SAR gathered oppositionists behind a program of immediate elections and an end to Batista's rule, Fidel Castro embarked on a multicity tour of the United States to reach the approximately one hundred thousand exiles living there.[73] According to Raúl Chibás, the principal organizer of Resistencia Cívica, one of two urban branches of the 26th of July Movement in Cuba, Fidel's trip to the United States capped off months of denouncing SAR's civic dialogue from Mexico.[74] On the stump in cities including New York, Union City, Bridgeport, and Miami, Fidel unvaryingly emphasized the theme of armed struggle. He had deliberately timed the latter leg of the tour to coincide with the anniversaries of José Martí's first organizational and fund-raising appearances in Tampa and Key West in the early 1890s during the run-up to Cuba's final war for independence from Spain.[75] On behalf of the now officially named El Movimiento 26 de Julio (often abbreviated M-26-7), Fidel launched his organizational network of exile supporters in New York, where Martí had lived for fifteen years, and formally unified three anti-Batista groups already in the area. In the wake of his visits, local Cubans organized revolutionary clubs to collect funds and distribute propaganda. New York's Acción Cívica Cubana featured Enma Castro, Fidel's blonde little sister, as a principal speaker and organizer (figure 16). In addition to selling highly colorful, large-size war bonds in denominations that ranged from $1 to $25, these clubs arranged high-profile protests, including ones at the United Nations (figure 17).

Significantly, Fidel prefaced the first speech of his multistop tour in New York before a crowd of approximately eight hundred men and women with a moment of silence to honor the fallen "veterans" of Moncada. A recording of one of Eddy Chibás's speeches followed.[76] But he also traced the roots of *his* revolution directly back to that of José Martí in 1895, rejecting utterly any connection or continuity with the revolution of 1933. In this way, he rendered Eddy Chibás's own connection to it as a timeless echo of Martí and despite Chibás's origins in the movements that led to revolution in 1933 as well as its legacies, he categorically condemned the generation of political leaders of 1933 as equally repugnant and ideologically contrary to the authentic Cuba founded in 1895.[77]

Fidel Castro's late 1955 U.S. tour was both resonant of the 26th of July Movement's approach in the past and prophetic of strategies its leaders would adopt over the next two years to gain the public's trust. Thus, the tour served two purposes: to drum up excitement for the 26th of July Movement under his exclusive leadership and to gloss Fidel and other chief leaders as morally driven, selfless activists who put aside all material and political ambitions for the cause of Cuba. In fact, when it came to financing the movement, there was

Figure 16. Fidel's sister Enma Castro leading a meeting in 1957 of Acción Cívica Cubana, an M-26-7 club in New Jersey, pleading for promotion of the 26th of July cause. (Ernesto Chávez Collection, courtesy of Special and Area Studies Collections, University of Florida)

no need to have made the trip at all: well before he embarked on his fund-raising tour, he had already raised substantial quantities of funds from Cubans "with means," thanks mostly to a massive letter-writing campaign headed by Melba Hernández. In Mérida, Mexico, Justo Carrillo, former president of Cuba's Agricultural Development Bank, gave him a "substantial sum." Contradicting the many claims to asceticism and poverty that Fidel had made publicly before and after leaving Cuba, these funds allowed him and his assistants to travel in style during the tour, staying in expensive hotels and traveling on the luxurious Silver Meteor train.[78]

Fidel's tour was meant to generate publicity for his movement's morality of selflessness, a discourse that lay at the heart of virtually all national heroes' historical appeal. Together with the development of a two-part strategy of prolonged rural and urban guerrilla warfare, it would be the 26th of July

Figure 17. The 26th of July Movement's network of revolutionary clubs in the United States frequently organized high-profile protests at the United Nations, such as this one in 1958, when a delegation appointed by Batista was present for a voting session. (Ernesto Chávez Collection, courtesy of Special and Area Studies Collections, University of Florida)

Movement's astute and constant public relations campaign that ultimately distinguished it from all other armed groups against Batista. Fidelista activists' consciousness of the need to create and maintain an apolitical, disinterested, morally righteous image was the key to the armed movement's success and its meteoric rise in popularity among citizens.

As he would do elsewhere from 1955 forward, Fidel also sang his own and his closest circle of followers' praises in ways that no other self-designated revolutionary leader had previously done. This included José Martí, despite the fact that Fidel clearly emulated Martí's style and claimed his legend as an ascetic, selfless defender of Cuba: "I live entirely surrendered to the struggle, and the contingencies and sacrifices of this disgraced life [*vida azarosa*] do not matter to me. . . . We all live very modestly. Here no one is a millionaire. Each one of our men in exile lives on less than it costs to sustain a horse in the army. Not one of us will ever be seen in a bar or a cabaret. . . . I can inform you today with all certainty that in the year 1956, we shall be free or we shall be martyrs. This struggle began for us on the 10th of March; it has lasted four years and will end either the last day of the dictatorship or the last day of our lives."[79] Speeches in subsequent appearances at the Flagler Street Theatre in Miami on 20 November, the same day as the SAR rally in Havana, were laced with even greater righteousness. Repeatedly, Fidel attested to the moral rectitude that the self-imposed "poverty" of the 26th of July Movement's inscribed in its leaders and the movement's character as the only *truly* revolutionary option on the island. Nobody else had the valor to offer the personal sacrifice that Cuba required.[80] Quoting Martí, he said that the only honorable thing any young man could do was serve the revolution.[81]

Fidel's particularly impassioned discourse of self-ascribed virtue was fueled in part by the mainstream Miami media's refusal to cover the story of his visit and in part by an article published in Cuba that accused Castro of "serving Batista" by effectively demonstrating that Cuba's national security *was* at constant risk.[82] Fidel accused the writer, an unknown journalist, of being a cowardly voice box for the dictator whose word proved the dictator's greatest weakness rather than his strength: Batista had to rely on defenders who had to deny they were his defenders in order to defend him.[83]

And yet, even during Castro's otherwise successful pilgrimage to the Cuban enclaves visited by Martí in the United States, the reach of Batista's publicity machine and its ability to silence his critics proved powerful. In Tampa, first the Italian Club, then the Club Cubano, and finally all other "Latin clubs" refused to allow Castro to hold his meeting there, citing its overtly political function. According to the *Tampa Sunday Tribune,* agents of Batista facilitated this decision by spreading Mafia-style rumors around Ybor City, Tampa's historically Cuban neighborhood and home of the largest cigar-making manufacturing district outside of Cuba. Anyone attending the meeting, the agents warned, could expect their family on the island to suffer retribution. Fidel also noted that Batista had paid for the Club Cubano's new roof and built a memorial to Martí on a small plot of land where Martí had stayed in a humble shack once owned by Ruperto and Paulina Pedroso, a black Cuban couple in Ybor City. In the end, the local Congress of Industrial Organizations union hall opened its doors to Fidel. But chairs sat empty; the meeting was sparsely attended by only about three hundred Cubans.[84] Nonetheless, just as Martí had received funds from Tampa's cigar makers, Fidel collected hundreds of dollars in small bills from patriots, reportedly more than in any other city.[85]

Although his speeches were laced with tones of self-congratulation and arrogance that some found unappealing, Castro attracted many adherents. In his own mind, his imprisonment, the first of many experiences that echoed those of Martí, had stripped him of his original class privilege. "Don't think that I am an eccentric or that I am becoming one," he had written his sister from prison, "it's that the habit makes the monk, and I am poor, I have nothing, I have never stolen a penny, I have never begged anyone for anything, my profession I have sacrificed for a cause."[86] But on the Isle of Pines, he had also learned the value of publicity, unconditional loyalty, and managing that very image of the selfless, penniless, would-be martyr driven by a cause. Fidel described Luis Conte Agüero as an invaluable unpaid publicity agent: through his daily TV and radio show, Conte Agüero had stoked the flames of public memory back to life with respect to the muchachos del Moncada and shared in the moral limelight as a result.[87]

Privately, Fidel Castro was far more blunt, if not cynical, in assessing strategies to move the emotions of citizens in order to encourage their admiration and trust in his leadership. For example, in no uncertain terms, he instructed members of his inner circle that police beatings made for good propaganda.[88] To Melba Hernández, he stated frankly, "Mucha mano izquierda y sonrisa con todo el mundo. Seguir la misma táctica que se siguió en el juicio: defender nuestros puntos de vista sin levantar ronchas. Habrá después tiempo de sobra para aplastar a todas las cucarachas juntas" (Lots of sleight of hand and smiles for everyone. Follow the same tactic we followed during the trial: defend our points of view without offending anyone. Later there will be more than enough time to crush all the cockroaches together at once).[89]

In many ways, his instructions to Hernández represent most clearly and concisely the pragmatism with which Fidel's inner circle of leadership and loyal supporters of the 26th of July Movement operated as they came together in Mexico over the summer of 1955 and year of 1956. Fidel wasted no time in Mexico, a central subject of many, if not most, previous accounts of the 26th of July Movement.[90] There he acquired invaluable military skills for his increasing circle of recruits from Spanish republican military veteran Alberto Bayó and equally invaluable lessons in representing the cause of Cuba's liberation for exiles in the United States from collaborators such as Mario Llerena, founding head of the 26th of July Movement's headquarters in New York.[91] He also met a Marxist intellectual doctor from Argentina, Ernesto "Che" Guevara, possibly one of the few members of his movement whom Castro respected as an equal. Guevara, together with his then wife Hilda Gadea, had been exiled to Mexico following the U.S.-backed military coup against President Jacobo Arbenz's nationalist government in Guatemala two years earlier.[92]

Deeply committed to Marxism, although adamant in his refusal to officially join the Communist Party, even when explicitly invited to do so in Guatemala, Guevara was nonetheless avowedly pro-Soviet. Since December 1955, he had established ties to the Mexican-Soviet Institute of Cultural Relations in Mexico City, where he studied Russian. When he, along with Fidel Castro, Almeida, and other would-be revolutionaries training for a return to Cuba in Mexico, was eventually arrested by Mexican authorities at the urging of Batista, Guevara fully admitted his belief in Communism. Flourishing a Soviet diplomat's card he had in his pocket, he even debated the finer points of ideology with Mexican judicial officials. During the fifty-seven days they served in a Mexican jail, Guevara and Fidel crafted the core strategy that would distinguish their movement from all others in Cuba.[93] They based this strategy on limiting military encounters with Batista's army, a force backed by the United States that would outnumber them by the thousands, and the disruption of normal economic life through allied clandestine activists in the countryside and the cities.

Together with Che Guevara, Juan Almeida, Fidel's younger brother Raúl, other survivors of the Moncada assault, and civilian activists like Mario Llerena, Fidel Castro sought the key collaboration of Frank País, a modest but brilliant committed strategist from Oriente. Hoping to link the urban network of commando units and underground cells that País had already organized throughout the region to the moncadistas' still-emergent bands of loyalists on the island, Castro hoped to connect an invasion force of armed guerrillas that would arrive by sea on the shores of eastern Oriente and make its way up the isolated mountain range of the Sierra Maestra. This idea—of bringing armed revolution to Cuba from within and from without, anchoring it in the most historically revolutionary of Cuba's provinces as well as the focal point of Batista's post-Moncada bloodbath—made the 26th of July Movement tactically unique.

Aside from their focus on urban areas, both the Auténticos and FEU's Directorio Revolucionario were far less ambitious, seeking to topple the dictator either through direct assassination or armed assaults on key points of military and political control in order to spark civilian uprisings. In both cases, the literal and symbolic decapitation of the regime was supposed to enable an internal military coup backed by a mobilized citizenry. In April 1956, the Auténticos tried and failed to achieve the latter with a conspiracy at the Goicuría military base in Matanzas that ended in disaster (figure 18).[94] It was only one of a string of efforts on the part of the Auténticos that cost thousands of dollars in caches of weapons, dozens of leaders arrested, and multiple lives lost. Yet photographs collected from planners of the Goicuría plot show a high degree of internal co-ordination with "moles" recruited among the military forces. Taking advantage of an inspection tour by U.S. military advisors, one of the plotters' allies shared photographs of nearly all interior spaces of the base, including the kitchen, the firing range, and even a group shot of the mayor's wife and the officers' wives.[95] The fact that most of the hundred members of the Auténtico commando squad died in the attack or were subsequently hunted down and killed suggests that the moles on which they counted acted as double agents, betraying the plot to the high command.[96] However, little of the Goicuría assault emerged in the press and, given the inaccessibility of Batista's military records to historians after 1959, remarkably little appears about it now, even in García-Pérez's valuable regional study of the war against Batista focused on Matanzas. After Goicuría and a steady stream of arrests of Auténticos whose homes were used to store weapons, the Auténticos' primary organization, Triple A, seemed utterly inept. Cubans often joked that it was Prío Socarrás who supplied the best rifles to Batista's armed forces.[97]

By contrast, Castro envisioned a strategy for toppling the regime that en-tailed a potentially prolonged civil war in which most of the fighting took place between urban adversaries until the guerrillas were strong enough to come down from the Sierra Maestra in Oriente province and begin conquering towns. From Fidel's base in Mexico, the most important initial factor in putting this plan into action was probably his relationship with Teresa "Teté" Casuso, the exiled widow of legendary student leader of 1933, Pablo de la Torriente Brau. Killed in combat while defending the socialist republic in the Spanish Civil War, her husband held the same saintly status as other martyrs from his circle of friends and activists of the anti-Machado generation, including Communist poet Rubén Martínez Villena and Julio Antonio Mella. Few individuals were as

Figure 18. On 29 April 1956, an officer-led uprising at the military base and barracks at Goicuría, Matanzas, failed. This photograph, taken for distribution to local and international reporters, was typical of Batista's public relations agents: rather than showing any of the uprising, bloodshed, or repression, it depicts evidence of an assault on the sanctity of an allegedly peace-loving, stable regime.

well connected politically and socially—or, more important, as discreet in their connections—as Teté Casuso.[98] Through Teté, Fidel contacted and met with Carlos Prío Socarrás, an action that clearly spoke to Fidel's willingness to put pride aside and rely solely on pragmatism in order to make his scheme work. Ironically, Prío then became the principal financier of Fidel's plan to invade Cuba from without, providing the necessary cash to buy weapons and the dubiously selected sixty-five-foot yacht *Granma* for that end.[99] As Teresa Casuso put it, Fidel had announced "to the world at large, and in writing, that he and his men would land on Cuban soil before the year 1956 went out."[100] With his personal honor on the line and his political legacy at stake, there is little doubt that Fidel would have fulfilled his claim through any means necessary, even if he had to "go begging" to official political enemies like Prío in order to secure it. Evidence of his desperation might be found in his acceptance of the *Granma* as a suitable vessel to transport nearly a hundred core revolutionaries: anyone with minimal knowledge of seaworthy vessels could tell that the yacht had been built to hold no more than thirty to forty people.[101]

Because none of this was openly discussed among Fidel's most trusted followers in Mexico, even less was known by the movement at large, let alone the Cuban public. The closest Fidel came to announcing his plan was in an article he wrote for *Bohemia* in April 1956. "We have not rested one moment in complying with the harsh and difficult duty [we alone have assigned to ourselves]," he wrote, "to restore over four years what was lost on a single day, the day of Batista's coup." Others, he added, had done nothing.[102] However, the reality was more complex than Fidel depicted it. Much as he had done in seeking the support of Prío, he relied heavily, if not mostly, on the incorporation of Frank País's already existing organizations in Oriente. Hoping to unify all effective movements under one central command he assumed would be his own, Fidel sought from José Antonio Echeverría the same endorsement and degree of cooperation he had gained from País.

From País, Fidel got everything he requested and more. From Echeverría, he received almost nothing. These very different reactions to Fidel's invitation to cooperate implied not only disagreements about tactics but, more important, distrust and discord over what collaboration with Castro might genuinely mean for the autonomy of each aligned movement in the short run and politically for Cuba in the long run. Not one of these leaders or their followers was unaware of the confusion that characterized the lines taken by Cuban politicians in recent years. On the contrary, hyper-conscious of the need to be clear, different, and men of action rather than words, Castro, País, and Echeverría attempted to force a tide of change onto citizens' understanding of what was possible for Cuba to achieve politically; they also wanted to break with the conventional wisdom of all political parties, including the Communist Party, in allowing Batista to dictate, shape, or negotiate the terms of the fight.

Divided Tactics, Divided Visions

Educated in one of Cuba's rigorous teacher-training academies, La Escuela Normal de Maestros in Santiago de Cuba, and a Sunday school teacher in Santiago's First Baptist Church, Frank País was the eldest of three sons. Born to a widowed mother, Frank was raised in an intensely religious, intensely patriotic environment. Spanish-born, Frank's mother had married his father at the age of twenty-eight. Her husband, however, a beloved reverend in the local Baptist church, was sixty-five, thirty-seven years her senior. When he died twelve years later, he left behind a large family that included the children of an earlier marriage. Frank's family always lived very simply and at times on the verge of destitution.[103] He experienced none of the material security, privilege, social experiences, and political access Fidel Castro had enjoyed in his life.

In his indispensable biography of País, the historian and longtime activist of the 26th of July Movement José Alvarez paints a portrait of him as a man shaped by reverence for God, personal humility, a profound social consciousness, and direct experience with the cruel implications of state neglect of Cuba's rural poor, particularly the local struggles of peasants for subsistence and land.[104] Aside from the strength of his loving but firm mother, Frank was also impressed at a young age by his half sister Sara País. An intellectual in the Baptist Church, Sara took him on his first visit to the capital and introduced him to politics through her own interests: at one point, she had run for (and lost) election to a seat in the House of Representatives.[105] Agustín País, Frank's younger brother, recounts a childhood in which the family began every day together by reading a chapter from the Bible.[106]

Tania de la Nuez, one of Frank's students at the local public school, remembers that in the classroom, Frank introduced the practice of La República Democrática Escolar (the Democratic Scholastic Republic), in which students elected a president, a minister of education, a minister of justice, and a minister of public health. Through such means, Frank strove to inculcate in his students the values of democracy, civic responsibility, honesty, justice, and accountability to one another. Through the symbolic "national" community of the classroom, he urged them to imagine the new, better Cuba they would one day build.[107]

At only eighteen in the fall of 1952, País was elected president of the student association of the Escuela Normal; by the following spring, he had participated in and helped organize multiple protests against the regime. On 1 May 1953, he was arrested along with dozens of teachers, students, and workers; he also received his first police beating. Then came his graduation in early July 1953. He had already built up a network of activists and counted the upper-class, MIT-educated Vilma Espín among fellow collaborators. When TV journalist Carlos Franqui traveled to Santiago to cover the protest that Frank and Vilma had arranged, events at Moncada overwhelmed all plans. The bloodbath that followed left all three of them aghast. In 1954, País founded and directed a movement called Acción Nacional Revolucionaria (ANR, Revolutionary National Action) with friends including Pepito Tey and Vilma Espín. Tey, president of the University of Oriente's branch of FEU, expanded the membership rolls by recruiting students from as far away as Camagüey and Las Villas provinces. MNR militants from Guantánamo, disappointed with the "zigzag" style of leaders like Bárcena, also joined. Within a year, the ANR movement was known for more than just issuing manifestos. Having amassed small firearms, commandos under Pais's direction had used them to attack a police station in Caney, where they killed one officer and confiscated more weapons for the cause.[108]

Over the course of 1955, the ANR raided the local elite Hunters' Club to obtain rifles, stole weapons from Triple A, and even gained first-class firearms from sympathetic allies at the U.S. base at Guántanamo.[109] By the time Fidel Castro's emissaries arrived in Oriente to request the incorporation of País's vast network of revolutionary cells of activists, they were not only disciplined and loyal to Frank, but armed and ready to go.[110]

In the summer after his return from the conference of Latin American students in Chile, José Antonio Echeverría met with Fidel Castro in Mexico, together with DR militants Fructuoso Rodríguez, Joe Westbrook, Faure Chomón, and Jan Nuiry.[111] At the time, the DR was still very small, comprised of only seven carefully selected members. Unlike the 26th of July Movement, which counted on both weapons and relatively vast funds, the DR's strength rested on the prestige, trust, and admiration that the Cuban people vested in FEU and its president Echeverría.[112] According to Lucy Echeverría Bianchi, who received her brother at the airport in Havana upon his return from Mexico, "Fidel took advantage of the popularity of the students, the honesty and the bravery of the students while he was preparing to go on the *Granma*."[113] He also may have assumed that they would concede subordination to his movement, much as Frank País had. This Fidel did not achieve.

In the name of FEU and the 26th of July Movement, Echeverría and Castro signed an ambitiously worded letter known later as the "Carta de México" (Pact of Mexico) on 30 August 1956. The plight of Cuba left them little choice than to pledge mutual commitment and cooperation in the cause of liberation. Yet knowing her brother was no fan of Fidel, Lucy remembers pointedly asking him almost immediately upon his return to Havana what he thought he had done. He answered, "Mi hermana, firmé con Dios y con el Diablo" (My sister, I just signed a contract with God and with the Devil).[114]

Not made public until October 1956, the letter was mute on precise ideological goals, although it stated in unconditional terms FEU's and M-26-7's renunciation of any party or person who continued to back general elections under Batista. It also announced firmly the mutual absolute goal of ousting the "tyranny" from power and carrying out a genuine "Cuban revolution" that would cleanse the nation of all political impunity and social injustice. Significantly, however, it appealed to the remaining "honorable and prestigious" officers of the army for support and promised them "the respect and sympathy of the Cuban revolution." Moreover, for the first time, Echeverría announced his own commitment to being one of "those who will direct" the revolution in the wake of the tyranny's fall. In effect, he claimed the equality of FEU with the self-proclaimed would-be martyrs of Moncada, demanding a right to share status and future state power with Fidel Castro. Notably, it was Castro who signed the letter first.[115]

Privately, according to the family of Echeverría, the young architect student never expected to survive the process of making war on Batista. When his brother Alfredo, a fellow activist, died in a car accident in April 1956, José Antonio was already underground, in hiding from the police. He came out, at the risk of his own life, in order to rush to his shocked and grieving family's side. According to surviving siblings Sinforiano and Lucy, Alfredo and José Antonio were so close that they could read each other's thoughts and often seemed to communicate only "through gestures and signs." From the moment they entered the University of Havana and the fight against Batista, the two brothers had indeed been inseparable, often photographed standing side by side behind prison grilles. In one picture, preserved by the family, the boys are seen lying on the street as police hit them with water hoses, Alfredo on top of his wounded and semi-conscious brother in an act of loving protection (figure 19).

When José Antonio returned to Matanzas and stood before his dead brother's body, which their mother had carefully bathed, dressed, and laid in his own bed, he could scarcely contain his emotions. Embracing his mother, he said, "Mami, no te preocupes que yo pronto lo acompaño" (Mommy, don't worry because I'll soon be joining him).[116]

Later, after the funeral, their mother led José Antonio into the sunny interior patio of their home, a large, beautiful house facing the main colonial plaza of

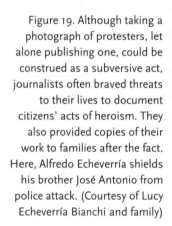

Figure 19. Although taking a photograph of protesters, let alone publishing one, could be construed as a subversive act, journalists often braved threats to their lives to document citizens' acts of heroism. They also provided copies of their work to families after the fact. Here, Alfredo Echeverría shields his brother José Antonio from police attack. (Courtesy of Lucy Echeverría Bianchi and family)

the city of Cárdenas. There, she asked him to make the act of contrition before God, according to the dictates of the Roman Catholic faith, so that he would repent for his sins in case Batista's forces killed him and he should not receive the final sacrament of last rites, recalled Lucy. "And it was then that some friends of my brother arrived and they pulled him out of the house over the rooftops; they stood one on top of the shoulders of another until they managed to pull him from the house undetected. And so it was that my mother, only three days after burying one son, bid farewell to another because she thought she would never see him again." She did not. From that moment on, José Antonio went deep underground, plotting the death of the dictator with co-conspirators of the Directorio Revolucionario. Of those closest to him, only his brother Sinforiano and José Antonio's girlfriend would see him again.[117]

From the beginning, the DR's main operating tactic had always been to decapitate the regime through selective assassination.[118] Their goal, like FEU's, was to force the flight or capitulation of the military and the reestablishment of revolutionary rule through a coalition of forces similar—but more effective and united—to the government that had taken power during the first days of the revolution of 1933. In hindsight, the Directorio Revolucionario believed that such a government, comprised of students, journalists, radical professors, and other intellectuals, might have decisively changed the rules of power if only its methods and its leaders' approach to the United States had been different. DR members justifiably blamed Batista for having collaborated with U.S. officials to undermine the revolutionary government of 1933, ultimately overturning it entirely with military support in January 1934. But they also blamed the revolutionary cabinet of 1933 led by Grau, which did not move to immediately hold elections after it assumed power but instead ruled by decree. Those in the DR were convinced that unity with civic forces, transparency of government, elections, a free press, and judicial cleansing of corrupt politicians would unite Cuba in a post-Batista age. They also counted on the majority of Batista's henchmen fleeing Cuba, as Machado's top brass had done, in order to purge the armed forces of human rights abusers and a culture of consent. Moving quickly—both to end dictatorship and institute democracy—was the DR's key to effecting long-lasting change.[119]

To jump-start support and belief in such a possibility, FEU focused on *mítines de relámpago* (improvised rallies), demonstrations that students could not publicly announce in advance because police would immediately break them up. Yet those demonstrations that did last more than a few minutes always drew dozens, even hundreds of students and average citizens to participate, as press photographs, when published, clearly showed. The FEU leaders who formed the DR considered alliances with other organized groups only to the extent of recruiting nonstudent personnel, such as Lauro Blanco, a middle-aged uncle of Vice President Pepe Puente Blanco and former member of Antonio Guiteras's Joven Cuba. Another key member was Auténtico lawyer and hombre de acción Menelao Mora, often imprisoned at the same time as José Antonio Echeverría and considered a principal architect of at least one, perhaps more, of the group's successful assassination attempts.[120]

Not surprisingly, however, Batista's supporters and publicity apparatus used Castro and Echeverría's letter from Mexico as evidence that they were legitimate heirs of the Auténticos' "gangsterism," whether within the University of Havana or without. While accurately (if surreptitiously) reporting that Fidel's 26th of July Movement was receiving contributions from Prío Socarrás in Mexico, *Gente,* the most pro-Batista and sophisticated of Cuba's many glossy magazines, accused students of having elected José Antonio Echeverría only in return for bribes from ousted president Prío Socarrás. The "Carta de México" was all the proof *Gente* needed.[121] Because of Batista's censors, however, the actual text of Castro and Echeverría's letter from Mexico had still not been made public.

Yet if Batista's publicity men were hoping to take advantage of citizens' ignorance of the contents of the letter, so were members of the DR. Long before 30 November 1956, the zero hour selected by Castro and País to launch their revolution by land and sea in Oriente, the Directorio Revolucionario's top gunners and FEU's first vice president Fructuoso Rodríguez acted first, taking center stage in the battle to strike at the heart of the dictatorship. In September, Fructuoso had become FEU's acting president because Cuban intelligence's knowledge of Echeverría's meetings with Fidel had forced him underground. *Gente* triggered the DR activists into making their first violent demonstration of opposition to the regime, however, with an editorial by the magazine's director, José Suárez Nuñez. It accused FEU of taking bribes from both the Dominican Republic's dictator Rafael Trujillo and Prío Socarrás. Such an accusation was deemed the ultimate offense to students who prided themselves on their reputation as desinteresados willing to sacrifice anything for Cuba; the magazine's defamation campaign against FEU immediately catalyzed an aggressive defensive move.

On 10 September 1956, a group that *Gente* reporters later descried as "two dozen" members of FEU patiently waited outside the production studios of Channel 2 Television to assault *Gente*'s editor in chief Suárez Nuñez when he arrived. For two uninterrupted minutes, Fructuoso Rodríguez punched the man repeatedly, saying, "Yo soy Fructuoso, y esto te lo doy de parte de Trujillo, y esto por Prío y esto por Fidel" (I am Fructuoso, and I give you this for Trujillo, this for Prío, and this for Fidel).[122] Whether Fructuoso actually said this (or what he implied if he did) remains a matter for debate, considering that *Gente* was the source of the quotation. However, one could easily interpret its meaning as contrary to that implied by the magazine. That is, rather than confirm FEU's or the DR's affiliation with either Prío or Castro, Fructuoso's brutal reply may have been intended to deny it. It was he who took the brunt of the vengeful violence that night. Once Suárez Nuñez's personal security team showed up, FEU members fled. Fructuoso chose to stay behind. He was thrown up against the wall and held down while Suárez Nuñez beat him "unconscious" until he "slid down to the floor," facing the wall.[123]

Less than a month later, its members fresh from prison, the DR struck again, this time without consulting anyone in the larger FEU group, including the underground president Echeverría. According to FEU vice president Pepe Puente Blanco, the opportunity to take out a major target in Batista's hierarchy of henchmen was seized without any planning—and it turned out better than anyone might have expected. On the night of 28 October 1956, José Fernández Cossío, Pepe's closest friend and FEU's vice president of the law school, went out with DR gunner Rolando Cubela, a medical student, and Juan Pedro Carbó Serviá, a law student. Like Fernández Cossío, the only member of FEU who owned a car, Rolando was more privileged than the majority of middle-class students attending university.[124] That night, both Fernández Cossío's car and Rolando's regular parental stipend came in handy.

The setting for the planned attack was the fashionable and expensive night-club Montmartre. Located on the second floor, the cabaret had a backdoor exit to the parking lot, which the students figured would facilitate Cubela's and Carbó Serviá's escape to the getaway car, driven by Fernández Cossío. The three hoped to target Colonel Orlando Piedra, the head of Batista's Bureau of Investigations, the primary agency charged with spying, infiltrating, and per-secuting FEU, who was a Montmartre regular. However, that night the three students got lucky: rather than encountering Piedra, they hit the jackpot. Lieu-tenant Colonel Antonio Blanco Rico, the head of Batista's most ferocious intel-ligence force, SIM, and a socialite inscribed annually in Havana's Social Reg-istry, showed up. After attending an opulent wedding earlier that night, Blanco Rico joined Lieutenant Colonel Marcelo Tabernilla, the son of Batista's chief of staff, Captain José A. Rodríguez San Pedro y López, another SIM official, and their wives for a very late night out. Although accompanied by a contingent of bodyguards, the party trusted that the power of their position would intimidate any potential attackers. They consequently valeted their cars and stationed the guards at the entrance on the first floor.[125]

Incredibly, according to an internal U.S. State Department report, only Tabernilla was armed that night and he, caught by surprise, never drew his weapon. Shortly after four o'clock in the morning, Blanco Rico's party headed toward the elevator for home and much-needed rest. At that moment, Cubela and Carbó Serviá opened fire, hitting Blanco Rico from behind with at least eight bullets and killing him instantly. When Tabernilla fell to the ground, seri-ously wounded, Captain Rodríguez San Pedro grabbed Tabernilla's pistol and pursued the assassins down the back stairs, but they escaped.[126] Immediately, Fernández Cossío phoned Echeverría and Puente Blanco to inform them of the exploit and gain their support. It was readily given: both were elated. Not only did the attack prove to the world that the regime was far from impenetrable, it showed that young Cubans like themselves, possessed of little more than a car and a few weapons, could be effective and would not be intimidated.

In response, Batista ordered extensive searches, raids, and arrests, putting all foreign embassies and the airport on lockdown, although Cubela and Carbó Serviá managed to escape, fleeing temporarily to the United States in a small boat. Brigadier General Rafael Salas Cañizares, dreaded chief of Cuba's national police, determined to make a public show of the regime's ability and will to seek revenge. Thus, he turned to the Haitian embassy, where six Auténticos, all of them participants in the abortive coup at the Goicuría military base months earlier, had sought political asylum. The Auténticos, completely ignorant of the DR's Montmartre assault, were awaiting safe-conduct passes from third countries to leave Cuba. However, because four members of FEU and the DR joined them shortly after the successful assassination of Blanco Rico, Salas Cañizares threw all respect for Haiti's diplomatic sovereignty to the wind and raided the embassy. Every Cuban inside, except for the cook, was killed. Mortally wounded by FEU asylum seekers who arrived with weapons at the Haitian embassy, Salas Cañizares also died several days later, to the delight of many of his victims in FEU.[127]

Meanwhile, País's organization and Castro's men busied themselves with final preparations for the landing in western Oriente of eighty-two men aboard the yacht *Granma* and the uprising in Santiago that they planned to take place simultaneously.[128] In the last few weeks of training, the men set up a camp north of the Mexican capital. There was little hierarchy among them; rather, respect for those who had been at Moncada predominated over new recruits. Known as an incessant reader who did little else in his free time, Che Guevara also lived by and enforced a set of bylaws that each guerrilla had promised to fulfill. These included asking for authorization to attend parties or social events. If permission was granted, late returns or sloppy behavior were not tolerated. For example, when Juan Almeida and Mario Chanes greeted Che with a raucous post-party homecoming one night, they were immediately subject to "trial." Although "acquitted" in the end, the experience taught them a humbling lesson in military discipline.[129]

Under the guidance of Spanish Civil War veteran Alberto Bayó, training proceeded easily, perhaps leaving the men overly confident and unprepared for what lay ahead. As it turned out, the first battle they fought was simply surviving the boat ride from Yucatán, Mexico, to Oriente in their overloaded yacht. The goal of "pinning down the army and police in order to give Castro and his men time to reach the hills" and allow widespread work stoppages never materialized, however.[130] Instead, the *Granma* landed five days late, leaking water and barely afloat, holding a seasick team of would-be guerrillas. Deprived of most of their military hardware, backpacks, medical supplies, and enthusiasm for the fight, the demoralized few who escaped arrest or immediate execution and made it to the mountains ultimately numbered eighteen, including Fidel. Yet many of these, as Guevara later recalled, were severely wounded.[131]

Che was himself struck by gunfire, lying on the ground and only half conscious. He later wrote, "Someone, on his knees, yelled that we had to surrender and one could hear another voice in the background, that I later discovered belonged to Camilo Cienfuegos, screaming, '*Aquí no se rinde nadie* . . . ' [Here nobody surrenders], adding a curse word at the end."[132]

Caught in the middle of the same cane field at that very moment, Mario Chanes remembers, as Che also wrote in his later account, that Fidel lay on the ground, shouting orders "as if anyone could receive or even hear them. ¿Ordenes a quién, chico?" (Orders to whom, man?) summarized Chanes, chuckling. Chanes personally pulled six wounded and exhausted fighters from the field while an "impressively brave" Faustino Pérez, Chanes emphasized, put a tourniquet on one and treated others.[133]

The days ahead promised far worse: aerial bombing raids by Batista, asthma attacks without relief for Che, dysentery for Camilo Cienfuegos, hunger, forced marches and, worst of all, betrayals by peasants who aided the rebels but subsequently blabbed to friends about their hidden stockpiles of weapons: the rebels could only stand by helplessly while Rural Guards and military police seized their hard-sought rifles, ammunition, and machine guns. Showing no sympathy, Fidel's response to the problem of lost weapons and whispering peasants combined disgust with admonition.[134] Although his adversaries were down to only a handful of men, Batista nonetheless kept one thousand soldiers in hot pursuit of the expeditionaries, arming and surely buying off peasants along the way.[135]

Frank País's network of activists, spies, and urban guerrillas fared no better. At the time of the programmed offensive, País counted on three hundred male and female activists divided into fifteen distinct cells of the 26th of July Movement.[136] Key to the plot was the takeover of Santiago's main public high school and three police stations by a large force under the command of Lester Rodríguez. País's force managed the assault on all three police stations successfully, burning one to the ground. He lost only three men in the process and all the members of his team kept their weapons.[137] Yet from the beginning, little worked out exactly as planned. At every turn, the rebels encountered a major snag. They took over the high school, intent on bombarding El Cuartel Moncada from the rooftop, only to find that their mortar launcher refused to fire. Police detained Frank and Josué País on their way to the takeover of a hardware store replete with weapons normally for sale.[138] For twenty-four hours a standoff ensued in which police eventually allowed activists to exit via the back door of the high school rather than risk accusations of yet another massacre. The army also took over the central government building of the town, establishing both "a base camp" and a center of political operations under direct military rule.[139] In the end, police arrested twenty activists, including País himself and Armando Hart, the son of a judge and a recent law graduate who had defended MNR leader Bárcena in court; far more 26th of July activists suffered automatic execution on the streets. Allowed to report on the violence in order to justify its repression, both *Prensa Libre* and *Bohemia* carried startling visual accounts of the rebels' success in bombing police headquarters. Editors also shared shockingly graphic photographs of the military's occupation of Santiago and the resulting carnage of activists, all whom wore the telltale homemade red and black armbands of the 26th of July Movement.[140]

On 4 December, the United Press International announced the discovery of the body of Fidel Castro, "identified by documents" found on his person, along with those of Raúl Castro and thirty-eight other *Granma* expeditionaries.[141] While Batista countered the accounts of Fidel's death with expressions of disbelief, the military commander of operations in Santiago responded with typical, misleading hyperbole. He denied that his men had "fired even one bullet." Instead, Díaz Tamayo claimed that soldiers had focused their attention entirely on arresting suspects and confiscating Molotov cocktails.[142] On 9 December, *Prensa Libre* reported that the army had surrounded and captured several expeditionaries, including two veterans of the attack on Moncada. A local mayor offered to negotiate terms of surrender with Fidel. The rebels, including captives, refused.[143] Symbolic of the impasse, Don Cosme de la Torriente, chief organizer of SAR's effort almost exactly one year earlier to unite the opposition and confront Batista, died of natural causes the night before.[144]

Behind Batista's Curtain: The Civil War Ahead

Over the months of November and December 1956, *Bohemia* published repeated editorials demanding an end to state violence against unarmed civilians. Yet censors required that the periodical refrain from naming the state as the primary perpetrator of "terrorism." Thus, even though *Bohemia* called for "peace" with the "progressive dignity and justice" that Cuban traditions demanded, the impact of its screaming headlines of "¡Qué Cese la Violencia Suicida!" (May Suicidal Violence End!) was necessarily muted.[145]

Other newspapers simply named those killed and reported where and how. Carlos Márquez Sterling and others kept a running count drawn from the newspapers *Crisol* and *Información* on how many unarmed citizens from Oriente and Camagüey to Santa Clara had been assassinated during the days immediately before and after Christmas 1956. With the press largely concerned with the fate of fidelista guerrillas in the hills and the public's attention distracted by the holidays, intelligence and security forces apparently felt they had the freedom to attack their closest and most vulnerable enemies with near impunity. In Holguín, Santiago, Puerto Padre, Banes, Santa Clara, the sugar mill towns of Manatí and Prestón, and El Cobre, thirty men were lynched, shot on the highway, burned alive, submachine-gunned, or tortured to death. In Havana, Güines, Luyanó, and towns of Oriente province, police brutally injured six more. A total of twelve across the country "disappeared" from police detention.[146] According to the chief military officer of Holguín, Fermín Cowley Gallegos, responsibility for the many killings in his zone of control lay with Batista and Tabernilla: Cowley Gallegos operated with senior officials' full knowledge of his actions, he said.[147] In addition, Batista was now actively preventing opponents from escaping the reach of the regime through voluntary exile by retiring their passports and effectively isolating them within Cuba, where he hoped they would find no sanctuary or place to hide.[148]

In a brief issued to the chief justice of the Cuban Supreme Court calling on it to at least condemn Batista's policies for violating the Constitution and human rights, Márquez Sterling notably pointed to a shift in the discourse of Batista's officials in asserting their right to use force. No longer simply fighting opponents who attacked the system, authorities now openly claimed they were defending the regime and the nation against "Communism." Batista's ministers even boasted about it. Yet in the same breath, they relied on an arbitrary, catch-all definition of "Communism" that had little or nothing to do with the actual party. "It doesn't matter if the incendiaries and saboteurs are or are not Communists," remarked one minister to the press, "so long as they may be delinquents there is sufficient reason to crush them like evil perverts [*alimañas*]."[149]

In fact, from early 1957 onward, the Batista administration would increasingly rely on accusations of "Communism" and the Communist backing of both the 26th of July Movement and the Directorio Revolucionario in order to gloss his use of state terror against civilians as necessary and justifiable in defense of national security. As in many contemporary and future Cold War–era military regimes supported by the United States in Latin America, state terror under Batista included arbitrary arrests, detentions, torture, executions, and distortions of truth regarding genuine armed opposition movements. Later defined as "counterinsurgency" methods, such tactics were meant to intimidate the populace into passivity and depict the most active of the opposition as ideologically bankrupt.[150] This latter objective, when successful, was intended to leave citizens feeling that there was no alternative to Batista, no better future nation-state possible. Seen from a theoretical perspective, the dictatorship's use of selective disappearance, raids on homes, and Batista's seesawing policy of imposing and then withdrawing censorship worked to keep citizens always at the sharpened end of a singular weapon wielded exclusively by the state.[151] In Cuba, however, such tactics did not succeed.

Through precise, highly visible assaults on the security of the regime and its farcical claims to popularity, first the Directorio Revolucionario and then the 26th of July Movement regularly tore through Batista's tightly woven curtain of public deception, casting a bright light onto all areas of a constructed political stage. On that stage, Batista consistently performed his role as democratic pacifier with mass support.

In the years of civil strife that eventually launched a full-fledged war against Batista in 1957, the dictator's primary adversaries in the FEU and the 26th of July Movement would rely on the integration and coordination of parallel autonomous networks of urban activists charged with secret missions to ensure the success of each movement's very different tactical strategies. As FEU leaders envisioned it, decapitating the regime and thereby inciting a social revolution would produce the flight of the worst government elements and the negotiation of renewed democracy among those who remained; for Castro and the 26th of July Movement, prolonged urban and guerrilla war would not only bring the regime to its knees but demolish all the structures that might reproduce it by neutralizing any public will to negotiate. By the dawn of 1957, upper- and middle-class, educated, and progressive leaders drawn from the ranks of Cuban youth were turning the tide of history by taking its meaning and direction into their own hands.

5

Complicit Communists, Student Commandos, *Fidelistas,* and Civil War, 1956–1957

FROM LATE 1956 THROUGH THE EARLY months of 1957, Fulgencio Batista increasingly began to augment his script of national salvation, on which he had previously relied to justify state repression, censorship, and other crimes, by peppering it with references to a Communist threat. Strategically, Batista pinned blame squarely on all opposition forces, but especially Fidel Castro's 26th of July Movement. In the wake of the near catastrophe of the *Granma* landing, Batista celebrated the fifth anniversary of his military coup with a speech at Camp Columbia in which he called Fidel Castro "an agent of the Soviet Union," insisting, "There is no doubt that the movement headed by Castro is communist and is aided by Communists."[1]

Most Cubans proved unwilling to swallow Batista's story. Indeed, as this chapter reveals, many citizens increasingly associated support for the armed opposition with *anti*-Communism and disdain for the PSP with hatred of Batista for two reasons. First, Cuba's Communists continued other traditional political parties' pattern of fighting bullets with words; and second, Batista exercised an apparent double standard in allowing the PSP to operate more freely than mainstream opponents. Rather than threatening Batista's dictatorship, the PSP actually facilitated its continuation in the eyes of many citizens and key opinion makers among the organized opposition. Yet this was not just a matter of public perception; as the following research suggests, it appears to have been a matter of some fact, at least at the national level. Batista's relationship to the PSP and, conversely, the PSP's private versus public stance on Batista's rule reflected a delicate balancing act on both sides. How this relationship came to be and what it meant for the radicalization of political alternatives to Cuba's constitutional crisis represent only small, if important and largely ignored, parts of the secret history of the making of revolutionary Cuba.

Until 1958, when Batista launched a full-on ground and air offensive against both Fidel's guerrillas and presumed peasant supporters in Oriente, his targets were primarily *clandestinos,* activists who included members of the DR, the 26th of July Movement, especially Frank País's cells in Oriente, and a spectrum of Auténtico-affiliated groups mostly financed by Carlos Prío Socarrás's seemingly bottomless bank account.[2] At the same time, PSP Communists also acted clandestinely, although they were agents of a very different kind. Charged by Moscow and the local party directorate to oppose all use of violence against Batista and stick to backing labor rights and elections, PSP militants appeared indirectly allied with Batista, possibly infiltrating and informing on M-26-7 and the DR, either on behalf of the PSP or, occasionally, for Batista's intelligence service itself.

Propelled by a shift in public attitudes toward Batista's many tactical maneuvers to intimidate citizens (including his obsessive invocations of a Communist threat) as well as citizens' views of armed assaults on batistiano officials, José Antonio Echeverría had established the Directorio Revolucionario. Until March 1957, FEU and its armed wing, the DR, upstaged Fidel Castro's 26th of July Movement on a number of levels. As head of the DR, Echeverría oversaw the actions of urban commandos in a variety of operations that directly attacked key players of the regime. However, their valiant, meticulously planned assault on the Presidential Palace in March 1957 ultimately failed to achieve its goal: the assassination of Fulgencio Batista. This, coupled with the ineffectiveness of Auténtico- and Ortodoxo-led movements and the passivity of the Communist Party, cleared the way for the 26th of July Movement to stand out in the eyes of citizens as the country's most radical and committed opposition movement. By the spring of 1957, the 26th of July Movement's growing network of urban activists and Fidel's tiny band of guerrillas in the eastern mountains of Oriente were largely the only armed opposition force left standing.

Nonetheless, the sacrifices paid by the DR's and the 26th of July Movement's activists under the command of Frank País arguably provoked the critical shift in attitude and consciousness favoring armed struggle as the *only* effective means of toppling Batista that leaders of these groups had long awaited. As we shall see, PSP operations, however minor, may well have helped corrode citizens' belief in the electoral process and the many peaceful means for pressuring the state on which they and leading resistance groups like FEU had previously relied. For this reason, it is with the history and relationship of PSP Communists to Batista that our story begins.

Cuba's Communists and the Batista Regime

From Batista's coup of March 1952 through the late fall of 1958, when the PSP dramatically switched its position and finally endorsed armed struggle, Cuba's Communists had publicly opposed all use of force and conspiracy to overthrow Batista. By the Auténticos' count, they had done so publicly no fewer than nine times by 1957.[3] Moreover, a number of lesser-known Communists and former Communists had been included in Batista's first cabinet after 1952. These included Raúl Lorenzo, minister of commerce, thought to have initially joined Batista's PAU on a party-designated mission of infiltration, influence, and information gathering. More significant were Batista's appointment of Arsenio González, militant of Santiago de Las Vegas, a nearby Havana suburb, as vice secretary of labor and of Francisco Julián García Benítez, a Communist from Holguín, to serve as a personal advisor and a member of the Consultative Council that substituted for Congress from 1952 to 1954.[4]

Perhaps because of Batista's desire to simultaneously control both labor and his image as a friend to blacks, in 1952 the PSP was the only party allowed to host national commemorations of two of Cuba's most important holidays, the anniversary of El Grito de Yara on 10 October and the death of Antonio Maceo, the black general of Cuba's independence wars, on 7 December. Given that the rest of the political establishment was forbidden to organize public events of any kind on these dates, most observers took Batista's gesture toward the PSP as indicative of mutual need and mutual, if unofficial, accord.[5]

Thus, while the violence of Batista's security forces swept the nation, the government granted the PSP license to hold its homage to Maceo in none other than the opulent, centrally located, and prestigious Teatro Nacional, a venue that accommodated thousands of spectators.[6] In this way, Batista continued the pattern of patronizing commemorative acts honoring historical figures, as he had done for the centenary of José Martí. However, the fact that he left responsibility for rendering homage to Antonio Maceo in the hands of the very party he accused of threatening the stability of the nation-state was no coincidence, although it showed a contradiction in discourse versus policy. In practical terms, this and other "favors" Batista discreetly offered the PSP benefited Batista's image and galvanized passive support for him among certain sectors of labor still dominated by the PSP, thereby greatly enhancing his ability to rule.

Importantly, on the occasion of the PSP's commemoration of Maceo, as on so many others, top Communist *dirigentes* (leaders) never crossed the line, even in criticizing Cuba's socioeconomic conditions. They never attributed the primary impediment to Cuban liberty to anything other than "the U.S. embassy," that is, the country's lack of sovereignty. "In reality," asked Aníbal Escalante, director of the PSP national paper *Noticias de Hoy,* "are Cubans today free?" His answer was definitively negative. Yet the reasons named had nothing to do with Batista, government-ordered violence, the continuing impunity of politicians and civil servants reliant on theft, fraud, and graft, or the lack of a constitutional state. In fact, Batista was nowhere to be found in the list of factors to which Escalante and other leaders assigned blame for Cuba's woes. Indeed, unlike virtually any other group that identified itself with the opposition, the PSP did not go as far as to declare the republic "dead" or even failed as a result of Batista's coup. "Cuba has not failed! The republic has not failed! The *pueblo* has not failed!" bellowed Carlos Rafael Rodríguez at the end of his speech at the commemoration to Maceo in December 1952, nine months after Batista's coup. "There is no other path besides that of General Antonio [Maceo] against imperialism!" he concluded.[7] For those cognizant of how differently the PSP had viewed the openly anti-Communist but democratically elected government of Prío de Socarrás, the organization's closed-lipped stance on Batista's flagrant violations of Cuban constitutionalism was nothing short of infuriating.

For example, *Noticias de Hoy* minced no words condemning Prío's administration in January 1952, scarcely six weeks before the coup, under a headline that fairly screamed: "El Lema del PSP es Hacer TODO PARA DERROTAR AL GOBIERNO" (The Slogan of the PSP is TO DO EVERYTHING POSSIBLE TO VANQUISH THE GOVERNMENT).[8] After March 1952 through 1957 (and even into 1958, as we shall see), one was hard pressed to find similar endorsements of the use of all means necessary to dispose of the batistiano state on the lips or in the writings of leaders of the PSP.

Two factors explain the PSP's much more aggressive call to get rid of Prío than Batista. First, there is no doubt that Prío's government had persecuted the PSP with every tool at its disposal, eliciting its enmity and condemnation.

At the rank-and-file level among unions where the PSP was strongest, the Auténticos intimidated, bribed, or simply persuaded their way to the majority of elected positions in national as well as provincial leadership between 1948 and 1952. Yet after Batista's coup, Salvador Díaz-Versón, former head of the counter-espionage and anti-Communism units of Prío's intelligence forces, maintained that ex-Communist Eusebio Mujal, the CTC's secretary-general, reversed Prío's course, returning key positions and influence among unions to the PSP. In particular, Díaz-Versón claimed that Mujal had forged a pact between Batista's PAU and the PSP that ceded five posts in the CTC's Executive Council to official (that is, known) PSP militants. The most significant of these were Faustino Calcines, a former PSP congressman, and Gonzálo Collado, who had been chief leader of the Federación Tabacalera Nacional, Cuba's largest union of tobacco workers, during longtime Communist Lázaro Peña's tenure as secretary-general of the CTC in the 1940s.[9]

Another member of Batista's cabinet after 1954 who had deep PSP roots was Pablo Carrera Justiz y de Velazco. The original director of the PSP daily *Noticias de Hoy* when Batista first legalized the party in 1938, Carrera Justiz y de Velasco had been a member of Lázaro Peña's CTC directorate in the 1940s before becoming Batista's minister of communications in 1952 and minister of defense in 1954.[10] Privately, Díaz-Versón claimed that Batista's so-called Anti-Communist Law had the unofficial backing of the PSP because he used it as a smoke screen to facilitate the repression of Ortodoxos, Auténticos, and other common enemies, not the PSP.[11]

Thus, Díaz-Versón's perspective gives a much more profound meaning to the letter cited in chapter 3 that Juan Marinello wrote to Márquez Sterling on the nature of the draconian 1953 law. In urging Márquez Sterling to condemn the law on the grounds that Ortodoxos would be its greatest victims, Marinello was not just warning him of this possibility, he was *counting* on it.

Whether or not Díaz-Versón's version of private pacts between PSP and PAU labor leaders was correct, certainly Batista's coup signified a return to power for many Communist activists in certain unions. One was the cigar makers' union of Havana; after Batista's coup, this union reversed previous electoral gains by the Auténticos and split its twenty-four-seat Executive Council nearly equally between Communists and members affiliated with either PAU or other pro-Batista parties.[12] Other Auténticos, writing privately to Carlos Hevia, additionally accused Batista of thwarting the radicalization of the labor movement against him by handing Ministry of Labor jobs over to former Communists who had become members of the pro-Batista Progressive Workers Block (Bloque Obrero Progresista) *before* the coup. Like black veterans in cities such as Trinidad who formed their own pro-Batista local clubs and new societies like "associations of housewives," these civil servants were loyal to Batista because they had been bought off. However, the collective effect was dramatic: it *demobilized* citizens on issues of labor, women's rights, and racial equality. Behind this demobilization, ironically, stood the PSP.[13]

For years, both historians of Cuba and Cuban officials have fully admitted the PSP's publicly negative view of the 26th of July Movement until the very end of the civil war in 1958 when the potentially imminent collapse of the Batista dictatorship provoked a sea change in the party's official position. Memories of the opportunism that fueled the PSP's change of heart died hard among the 26th of July Movement, especially in the first years after the revolution of 1959.[14] Equally well known to historians and fidelistas was the PSP's denigration of Castro's assault on El Cuartel Moncada in 1953 as a uselessly "putschist" act. Similarly well known was the Communists' characterization of Fidel's programmatic pamphlet *History Will Absolve Me* as an ideologically "reactionary document" representing the ignorant ideological perspective of the bourgeoisie. Perhaps two of the greatest sticking points for Castro himself were this insulting characterization of what his movement considered its premier, founding program and the PSP's pre-1959 attacks on the degree to which his followers promoted "a cult of personality" around Fidel.[15]

Yet several critical points that explain the Communists' activities and attitudes toward Batista remain largely unknown and mostly unexplored. First, what activities did the PSP actually carry out and what was their purpose? Second, how, if at all, did Batista and the PSP navigate a relationship for mutual gain? And, most important, perhaps, how did other political opponents of Batista, Cuban citizens, and U.S. officials *perceive* the PSP as a result of this relationship?

According to *Carta Semanal: Boletín de la Comisión Nacional del Partido Socialista Popular,* the weekly news bulletin printed and mailed exclusively to PSP militants from national executives of the PSP, "propaganda" defending the political policies of the Soviet Union in the world and promoting recruitment of nonmembers to the ideological or policy positions of the PSP in Cuba (through means both overt and covert) were militants' top priorities. Thus, in *Carta Se-*

manal, as in *Noticias de Hoy,* defense of Soviet leaders, promotion of Soviet policies, and reports on the growing global popularity of the USSR abounded.[16] Equally common were celebrations of the allegedly paradise-like conditions of total material and civic equality in the Soviet Union, sometimes accompanied by side-by-side comparisons with the brutality of life and racial discrimination in the United States.[17] In addition to generalized praise for Stalin, nearly every edition of *Noticias de Hoy,* from its founding to its closure by SIM in July 1953 following the Moncada attack, echoed *Carta Semanal* in its coverage of Soviet life. Both featured Edenic images, often emphasizing government-regulated cheap prices and equal access to luxury goods while remaining silent on almost all else, particularly the Soviets' decades-long practice of censorship, rationing, and methods of political "reeducation" through hard labor in concentration camps. Like many citizens of Soviet Russia themselves, Cuba's Communists knew which aspects of Soviet reality needed to be silenced in order to spread belief in Communism and inspire the Soviet-styled revolution they hoped to foment in Cuba.[18]

Carta Semanal considered propaganda the main means of influencing events and outcomes in Cuba because it shaped people's outlooks and therefore their decisions. Thus, despite Prío's allegedly unrelenting persecution of the party, it managed to print "half a million pieces of propaganda" in Camagüey province and 1.5 million pieces in Havana during the year 1950–1951 alone.[19] Significantly, while Prío was the first to interrupt the publication of the PSP's daily national paper *Noticias de Hoy* and intimidate the party by arresting Juan Marinello, when Batista shut it down altogether in 1953, that did not stop the party.[20] On the contrary, despite being officially "banned," the PSP seemed subject to special treatment compared to other political groups. For example, the publication and dissemination of *Carta Semanal* to party militants never ceased throughout the Batista dictatorship, although the publication did simplify its name to *Bulletin of Information and Orientation,* making it appear less institutionally directed.[21] Nonetheless, every edition contained an enumerated list of "Tareas de la Semana" (Tasks for the Week) and a column entitled "Vida del Partido" (Life of the Party). These sections instructed members in detail on positions to take regarding matters related to union demands as well as directions for when and where to send telegrams of protest if ever a party official, the USSR, or a specific PSP political viewpoint was criticized by officials or the media. The bulletin also told readers what to say in response to critics at the workplace or on the street, whether the mode of expression was a written tele-gram or simply a verbal response.

Such tactics, ironically, laid the groundwork for the very methods of "de-fending" Cuba's post-1959 authoritarian turn away from democratic revolution toward a one-party state led by one man. The man whom PSP advisors and militants championed after 1959 was, of course, Fidel Castro, although before he embraced the Soviet Union and adopted state Communism in 1961, the PSP had also ensured that it would survive and flourish in the revolutionary state, with or without Fidel. It did this by infiltrating the upper ranks of Fidel's armed forces to guarantee that covert PSP militants would pioneer the process that resulted in a government-controlled press, and by founding the many "mass organizations" that became the bedrock of state power.[22] Under Batista, a dictatorship firmly al-lied with the United States, however, the PSP took a back seat yet still influential role in stabilizing the regime and helping to manage civic control.

How did the PSP's national executive committee view the Batista regime and what did it envision as a solution to the violence gripping Cuba? Undoubtedly, after 1956, top PSP leaders increased the severity of their tone, condemning CTC chief Eusebio Mujal as a traitor to workers and calling Batista's govern-ment a "tyranny." They also characterized Batista's repressive tactics as well as the attacks of the armed opposition as "terror," roundly condemning both. PSP leaders saw Batista's tactics as fascistic efforts that endorsed the power of the United States by crushing the inevitability of "mass struggle." They depicted the strategies of armed opponents as erroneous methods that impeded "mass struggle," whether intentionally or not.[23] Specifically, the PSP disputed Castro's claim that those who did not join armed movements like his were doing nothing against the dictatorship: "In reality," countered the PSP, "all opposition groups, either in great or small ways, have on one occasion or the other taken measures against the government."[24]

Through most of the six years Batista remained in power, the PSP declared that the only "true Cuban solution" was to unite all the opposition, including the workers and the bourgeoisie, in "un frente único" (a united front) behind "mass struggle."[25] Although it is easy to interpret such terms as simple support for unionized battles and a general strike, the PSP had a much more specific strategy—and memory—in mind. Effectively condemning directly the actions of the Directorio Revolucionario and the 26th of July Movement thus far, the PSP's Central National Committee endorsed in the especially bloody summer of 1957 "not a putsch, not an attack on military barracks to bring about a coup [*cuartelazo*], not terrorism, but the action of the masses, which is just, as the history of our country has proven."[26] Simply put, the PSP wanted to bring about a repetition of the events of 12 August 1933, when the dictator Gerardo Machado left the country, workers rioted in the streets, unions took over sugar mills, low-ranking soldiers overthrew the heads of the armed forces and, according to *Carta Semanal*'s own historical vision, Cuba missed reproducing a social revolution like that of the Soviet Union by just a hair.[27]

Oddly, this perspective left the PSP sounding very much like many of the mainstream politicians and journalists it often criticized. Indeed, Francisco Ichaso, a regular political columnist in *Bohemia,* made a case similar to that of the PSP when it came to improving Cuba's political situation under Batista. "The best antidote against the pseudo-revolutionary *pistolerismo* [gun-toting approaches] is political mobilization," Ichaso wrote in November 1956. "The most noble civic act is to procure the expansion of the parties, that is, the instruments of democracy."[28]

Moreover, as Batista's repression increased, the PSP's long-standing insistence on being "the Party of Peace and Anti-Imperialism" seemed contradictory: nevertheless, its calls for political mobilization *without* armed confrontation deepened.[29] *Mella,* the magazine of the Communist Youth, echoed the position of *Carta Semanal* with covers that read "Unity and Mass Struggle to Detain the Terror of the Tyranny! Enough Crimes and Oppression! Machado Did Not Survive the General Strike of August 1933!"[30] At the same time, most of its political cartoons encouraged attacks on Uncle Sam, Batista's backer, rather than Batista himself as the path to change.[31]

By 1957, both the PSP's vision of a future Cuba without Batista and its logic for justifying such a future could seem downright bizarre. For example, in a July 1957 open letter addressed to Fidel Castro, Manuel Bisbé, Ramón Grau San Martín, Emilio Ochoa, José Pardo Llada, Carlos Márquez Sterling, and all other "*dirigentes* of parties and political sectors contrary to the regime of the government of the 10th of March," PSP president Juan Marinello and secretary-general Blas Roca argued that removing Batista from power invited U.S. intervention that would inevitably produce benefits for the United States. In particular, they contended that those benefits would accrue to U.S. monopolies in Cuba. For this reason alone, armed revolt and a subsequent revolution autonomous of Communist oversight and control were bad ideas. "Si mala y nefasta consideramos la intervención extranjera imperialista a favor de Batista, mala la seguimos considerando cuando tiene, pretendidamente, un fin politico no favorable a Batista" (If we consider foreign imperialist intervention on behalf of Batista bad and detestable, we consider just as bad a political end *not* favorable to Batista).[32]

Political cartoons in *Carta Semanal* were similarly contradictory. On one hand, the PSP condemned extra-judicial killings as "instruments of Batista and the CIA," while it also condemned the main strategies of the armed opposition like the burning of cane fields and the "putsch" strategy of Moncada, characterizing such tactics with Batista's term of "terrorism." Under this rubric, both Fidel's M-26-7 and the DR were not viable. Only "mass struggle for immediate demands and against the tyranny" were "instruments of a democratic victory." In short, the PSP claimed that the 26th of July Movement, the Directorio Revolucionario, and other armed groups' methods were acts of "putchismo" and "insurrections [carried out] behind the backs of the masses." They were designed to empower the middle and elite professional classes, not peasants and workers. The PSP also condemned any electoral solution arranged by Batista as just as deceptive as the tactics of armed groups against him. Nonetheless, the party *did* decide to field candidates in Batista's final 1958 elections.[33]

This kind of pragmatism formed a central strategy for the PSP. Many Cubans found its evident hypocrisy difficult to ignore. One of its most vociferous critics was, not surprisingly, a Cuban intellectual whom PSP militants loved to hate: university professor and historian Herminio Portell Vilá.[34] In 1955, Portell Vilá blasted the PSP's special treatment and, he claimed, special protection from Batista in an extensively documented article published in *Bohemia*. He began by defending himself from charges in the PSP press that he was "un alquilón de Estados Unidos" (a flunky of the United States) and *Bohemia* from accusations that it was a voice box for the indecisive, hand-wringing bourgeoisie. In fact, Portell Vilá fired back, *Bohemia* "continues to be the preferred object of hatred" for the PSP because no one could accuse it of being at the service of "dictators either of the Right or the Left," unlike—he implied—the PSP press itself. After detailing his many years fighting for the revocation of the Platt Amendment in anti-imperialist publications and representing Cuba in Latin American conferences to denounce the unrelenting interference of the United States in the region's affairs, Portell Vilá presented compelling evidence of what he perceived as Batista's deference to the PSP.[35]

How was it possible that Batista assigned a censor to every major publication in Cuba and regularly ordered the arrest and persecution of opposition journalists while the PSP was allowed to mail twelve thousand copies of *Carta Semanal* without government harassment? Given that the PSP had never printed more than six thousand copies of *Noticias de Hoy* under Prío, this boost in circulation held meaning.[36] Moreover, how could *Carta Semanal,* designated as part of the "clandestine" press, feature high-quality typesetting and circulate on two different kinds of paper: one of newspaper quality for broad dissemination in Cuba and the other on fine-quality heavy paper acquired from abroad? Such details mattered since the *real* clandestine press—when it could be found—was often hand-typed and sometimes handwritten on cheap paper of miniature dimensions to avoid detection by police. Discovering how the PSP acquired such unique high-quality paper would be easy given the availability of Cuban customs records to Batista's supposedly anti-Communist intelligence services. Yet they seemed no more interested in that question than they were in how expensive *Carta Semanal* was to produce and "where the Communists got those thousands of *pesos* given their now allegedly reduced access to civil service jobs and loss of control over the labor movement."

Moreover, even as the PSP freely published two other publications, *Boletín Semanal* and *Renovación,* without harassment, the organization consistently ignored its own exceptional treatment and claimed the higher ground among the opposition in denouncing the lack of a free press under Batista. Not only was this position inaccurate, given the disproportionately generous degree of tolerance the PSP press enjoyed, it silenced the fact that *there was no free press* in any part of the Soviet or Communist world. "Bought off by the gold of Moscow and any dictator who pays for their services," railed Portell Vilá, "[the Communists] flee from the truth as if it were soap and water" capable of revealing who they really were. "Like condemned 'zombies' they move about in the shadows; protecting themselves with anonymity, they surround themselves with secrets and they flourish in the dark."[37]

With these remarks, Portell Vilá referred to the shroud of secrecy under which PSP militants, like all Communist parties in the world outside the Soviet bloc, maintained their identity as party members and thereby carried out party-directed "tareas," or tasks.[38] Initiating events tagged as "cultural" and sponsored by institutions advocating "peace," the PSP often successfully gained people's participation and confidence in activities non-PSP-affiliates believed were ideologically neutral, rather than strategically driven.

Perhaps most problematic for the PSP was its double standard in defending Cuban sovereignty against the United States but not the USSR, and its duplicity with regard to the political intentions of many of its outwardly neutral "cultural" activities. First came its apparent blindness to the fact that supporting the Soviet Union was just as imperialistic in the minds of many Cubans as supporting the United States. Batista, by tolerating the PSP to a degree he did not allow other parties, was doing the same: courting both the Yankees and the Soviets, although one more overtly than the other. "If our government supports the imperialist policies of the antipatriotic 'Communist' party . . . we ought to have faith that our people will not allow themselves to be sheepishly convinced," wrote one citizen, who admitted to signing his manifesto with a pseudonym out of fear of reprisals. "El beso del dictador es una conquista, neguémoslo" (The kiss of the dictator is a conquest; deny him that).[39] Moreover, for all their claims of promoting "peace" and "cultural debate," PSP publications like *Por la Paz Duradera, por una Democracia Popular* (For an Enduring Peace, for a Popular Democracy) or *Mujeres Cubanas* were no more ideologically neutral than those of the Instituto de Intercambio Cultural Cubano-Soviético.[40]

But it was not simply through such high-brow activities that the PSP got its message out. It also established sewing circles for indigent girls, created popular theater groups who performed for marginalized slum dwellers, and constantly relied on discourses of peace amid civil war.[41] Through such means, the PSP regularly falsified its true goals and inheritance of pro-Soviet authoritarian values by appealing to the sympathy of the public.[42] Nonetheless, as Portell Vilá well stated, the PSP persisted in the strategy of appearing to be open and democratic when its policies and power structure were hierarchically driven, often subject to Soviet advisement, and highly centralized. It was therefore easy to accuse the PSP of failing to recognize its own pro-imperialist stripes when it came to members' admiration for the Soviet Union. Yet this evident hypocrisy represented the least important of the PSP's many weaknesses when it came to the Communists' credibility in describing themselves as genuine "opponents" of Batista.

The PSP was *not* simply interested in changing people's points of view. Unlike PAU, whose deference to the United States was infamous even if not necessarily consistent, the PSP's alleged priority of defending the sovereignty of Cuba did not include doing so against all imperial powers, just that of the United States. Although this is confirmed only for the Prío years, for which some internal intelligence reports are available to historians, the PSP undoubtedly engaged in espionage on behalf of the Soviet Union through its Cuban members. Reports of the organization's activities under Prío Socarrás suggest patterns and methods of behavior that the PSP likely continued under Batista as well, especially as it considered Batista a more amenable and pragmatic adversary than Prío.

Thus, President Prío's intelligence agencies secretly confirmed espionage activities by Cuban Communists, some of whom were Soviet agents, as well as Communists on missions for the Maoist Chinese party. For example, in February 1951, Detective Carlos Chao sent a confidential report to the minister of governance and the chief of the national secret police detailing a raid on a Chinese-owned *bodega* in Santiago de Cuba. The raid revealed publication of an underground newspaper in Chinese, propaganda posters backing the candidacy of PSP leaders in upcoming national elections, and other materials received from both the Soviets and the Chinese for dissemination in Cuba. None of these activities were technically illegal. However, the Communists' status as foreigners—none of them were either permanent residents or naturalized citizens of Cuba—made them suspicious and subject to deportation. Carlos Chao suggested that they were all spies. Indeed, at least one, Luis Lee, had managed to infiltrate the U.S. naval base at Guantánamo by getting a job there as a cook. Not surprisingly, discovery of his real purpose there—espionage—got him fired.[43]

Perhaps the most important Soviet-trained and Soviet-commissioned spy who influenced and organized the public outreach and propaganda of the PSP for decades was Fabio Grobart. A Ukrainian by birth, Grobart impressed Soviet leaders, who selected him for training in Marxist philosophy at Moscow's Political University. In 1924, Grobart had disembarked clandestinely in Havana with the task of creating intimate ties to the already radical anti-imperialist student movement led by Julio Antonio Mella and Ruben Martínez Villena, both of whom became Communist militants partly through the tutelage of Grobart. He also took responsibility for founding Cuba's first Communist cell in Manzanillo, under the leadership of Blas Roca.[44] From 1924 until Batista legalized the party in 1938, Grobart lived under five different aliases. Yet he was immensely successful in integrating himself—and thereby Soviet intelligence—into both Cuban society and the emerging vanguard of students, intellectuals, and workers comprising the anti-Machado Cuban Left. He became a naturalized citizen in 1936. Grobart's activities show evidence that the PSP exercised clandestine influence over the state in national affairs.

For instance, when Machado expelled Grobart and other Communists as spies in 1932, Grobart's longtime lover Dora Stern Vainstock managed to get the group back into Cuba on false passports she arranged by seducing the son of Ramiro Guerra Sánchez, Machado's minister of education and one of Cuba's premier historians.[45] A regular visitor to the Soviet Union in the 1940s, editor and publisher of PSP recruitment materials such as the Communist magazine *Fundamentos* and pamphlets like *Quién Puede Ser Militante Socialista?* (Who Can Be a Socialist Militant?), Grobart was considered the chief representative of Soviet-sponsored congresses and delegations in Latin America by the 1950s. Perhaps the best evidence that he was and had always been a Soviet agent, however, was the fact that from 1924 to 1950, he had never held a job in Cuba of any kind and was officially "unemployed." Yet he and his Communist wife (also unemployed), Perla Sunshine, lived in an apartment in Vedado for which they paid $90 a month in rent, a sum that surpassed most *habaneros'* monthly income at the time, even those of the professional and middle class.[46]

The significance of Grobart's infiltration of Cuba's original Communist movement and his work on behalf of the pro-Soviet party that became the PSP after 1938 lies in how his activities explain the unpopularity and wariness with which Cubans increasingly viewed the party under Batista's dictatorship of the 1950s. The party attempted to deceive Cubans into believing that many of their institutions, publications, and activities were not financed, sponsored, or subsidized by the Soviet Union when in fact they were. Indeed, it was not until June 1951 that the PSP publicly admitted, in writing, that its national newspaper *Noticias de Hoy* was not privately financed as a product of leftists' collaboration but an official organ of the Communist Party.[47] The PSP also founded a cultural club called La Sociedad Nuestro Tiempo, which produced a magazine, allegedly "free of political and religious prejudices," also called *Nuestro Tiempo,* directed by Santiago Alvarez.[48] Later, his unknown militancy in the party and success in gaining the confidence of nonparty intellectuals through the club Nuestro Tiempo for covert "tasks" earned him a position as the undisputed czar of post-1959 pro-government newsreels and documentaries in Fidel

Castro's Communist state film industry.[49] Instructed to seek out anti-imperialist activists who would lessen the appearance that the Communist Party directed its cultural and filmic activities, Nuestro Tiempo recruited radical thinkers Carlos Franqui and Guillermo Cabrera Infante until both dropped their membership upon discovering that their participation was political window dressing for the PSP and they were merely being used.[50]

Whether out of resentment or genuine ideological differences, Auténticos might have exaggerated the degree to which former Communists close to Batista remained committed or active in the party. This question remains largely unanswerable so long as historians have no access to former Soviet archives on the Cuban Communists and Batista's intelligence archives remain in the closed vaults of the current Castro-led regime's Council of State and headquarters of the Central Committee of the Communist Party. However, to say that Batista dragged his feet when it came to repressing the Communists was an understatement in the opinion of many. These included Cuban journalists, U.S. officials, and leaders of Cuba's anti-Communist movement like Salvador Díaz-Versón, Prío's former chief of military intelligence (1948–1952) and president of the Anti-Communist League of Latin America as well as its Cuba branch in the 1940s through the 1950s.

According to Luis Ortega, a friend of Batista, U.S. embassy officials had visited and persuaded Ortega to help President Prío carry out his anti-Communist campaign through Ortega's column in *Prensa Libre,* then the most widely read national newspaper in Cuba, long before Batista's coup. Delighted at the suggestion, Ortega complied, defending Prío's right to shut down *Noticias de Hoy* on the basis that it was a Soviet-financed instrument for undermining Cuban sovereignty. To his horror, however, the PSP immediately began publishing another newspaper under the title *Ultima Hora* (The Latest Update), despite the fact that the party's pariah status should have made it impossible for any landlord to rent it space for a new *taller,* or studio. "Who helped the communists find *talleres,* breaking the general rule of denying them all resources [*rompiendo la consigna general de negarles la sal y el agua*]? Well, no one more nor less than the current president of Cuba, General Fulgencio Batista y Zaldívar," Ortega wrote in an unsolicited report, apparently addressed to U.S. embassy officials in the late 1950s.[51]

When Ortega repeatedly tried to persuade him not to help the PSP, Batista explained that their mutual enmity with Prío made the Communists his allies

and friends. Despite his annoyance at the time, Ortega accepted Batista's pragmatism and later, after his coup, accepted his invitation to serve as an advisor
on his Consultative Council. Incredibly, however, Ortega's first proposal to the
council was roundly rejected by advisors closest to Batista, such as Carlos Saladrigas, his former vice president (1940–1944), and Batista himself: Ortega
had proposed the establishment of a Committee for the Investigation of Communist Activities in Cuba, modeled on the United States' infamous congressional committee of a similar name and purpose, headed by Senator Joseph
McCarthy. According to Ortega, Saladrigas characterized the creation of such a
government body as "catastrophic" to Batista's rule since so much of Batista's
control over labor and the stability of the economy rested on PSP-affiliated
members of his cabinet. These had officially joined Batista's party but secretly
or sometimes openly retained a parallel Communist militancy. They were, in
particular, minister of commerce Raúl Lorenzo and minister of labor Arsenio
González.[52]

Indeed, Ortega himself offered a clear explanation of why Batista and the
PSP needed each other: "Batista is between the sword and the wall [*entre la
espada y la pared*]. His compromises with the American government force him
to take energetic action against Communism, but the internal political reality of
the country also obligates him to make certain accommodations." An alliance
among the Ortodoxos, the Auténticos, and the PSP would be Batista's worst
nightmare because it would surely "cost him his power. . . . For their part, the
Communists are not interested in toppling Batista, but rather, on the contrary,
maintaining him in power because he is the only guarantee that they have of
being able to unleash [their usual] chaos in Cuba. Batista has created in Cuba a
climate favorable to Red agitation. They, Batista and the Communists, understand each other perfectly." For this reason, Ortega saw Batista as "a secret ally
of the Communists."[53]

Salvador Díaz-Versón went even further. For reasons that made little sense
to him, since Batista was supposedly fighting the threat of "Communism" by
arresting the opposition, selective assassination, torture, censorship, and intimidation of the public, Batista had forced Díaz-Versón into exile in the United
States. Letting him remain in Cuba would have allowed him to exploit Batista's
anti-Communist rhetoric for genuine anti-Communist ends: that is, the real repression of the party. By repressing *anti*-Communist opponents committed to
constitutional liberalism and simultaneously allowing the PSP to operate more

freely than they, Batista was radicalizing Cuba and jeopardizing citizens' belief in a democratic future based on electoral forms of government.[54] "Despite his efforts to disguise himself," wrote Díaz-Versón in a clandestinely published manifesto to the people of Cuba, "Batista is not a Latin American dictator but a Soviet dictator, and hopefully the people of Cuba and the free nations of America will comprehend this in time, before it is too late."[55]

It is impossible to say whether Ortega's and Díaz-Versón's views were widely held. Certainly, publications of anti-Communist groups such as the Asociación Cubana Pro-Democracia took easy pot shots at the PSP for being a party whose top leaders touted the glories of egalitarianism but lived the good life of Soviet-sponsored travel to Russia and promoted "jamón para todos" (ham for all), a highly bourgeois type of Communism that did not exist anywhere in the USSR, known for its ration lines and gulags.[56]

However, hatred for Batista did become increasingly associated with disdain for the Communist Party of Cuba among certain sectors such as the Colegio Médico Nacional de Cuba. In a historical memoir covering the medical association's history in the 1950s through the first two years of the revolution led by Fidel Castro, Dr. David Enrique Amado-Ledo, vice president of the Colegio Médico from 1952 to 1960, expressed how anti-Communist/anti-Batista sentiments played out. In 1956, Amado-Ledo contended, members attempted to expel all PSP militants from their ranks. Their logic rested on the basis of a mutually shared anti-Communism and the sense that the PSP was not only infiltrating its ranks but receiving special protection from Batista. Ever present in the minds of members was the undeniable reality that "all of the political leaders of the democratic parties of Cuba were being persecuted, assassinated, and forced to live in exile" while top PSP dirigentes such as Blas Roca, a regular visitor to Stalin's home, "enjoyed all the peace, care, and medical attention" they needed in Cuba, "without a care in the world." For most Cuban doctors, "It was obvious that there was at the very least a tacit pact between the bloody regime of Batista and the top levels of the Communist Party of Cuba."[57]

Possibly for the same reasons, U.S. officials proved far less confident than the U.S. public in celebrating Batista as a champion in the fight against Communism. Between 1956 and 1958, Lyman B. Kirkpatrick Jr., a top-ranking official at the CIA, made repeated trips to Cuba "to help the government establish an effective organization to fight Communism." Previously, Batista had promised secretary of state John Foster Dulles that he would put such an agency in place. However, when Kirkpatrick made his first trip to Havana in June 1956, "little had been done except to funnel some money into an organization that existed only on paper." That organization was BRAC, the Buró para la Represión de Actividades Comunistas (Bureau for the Repression of Communist Activities). Despite its aggressive title, BRAC ranked low on the totem pole of government agencies, had barely any budget, and was headed by a former army sergeant who, according to Kirkpatrick, had trouble securing interviews with the president.[58]

Worse yet, from Kirkpatrick's perspective, then U.S. ambassador Arthur Gardner had issued standing orders that no member of the U.S. Embassy have contact with anyone "in the Cuban political spectrum who opposed Batista." U.S. policy at the time was "to give full support to the Batista government," including military assistance. However, according to Kirkpatrick, the idea was more Batista's than Gardner's, and therefore a bad one. No contact with the opposition left the U.S. government deprived of critical information "about political opinions that were to form an increasingly important part of the Cuban picture." In the end, however, Gardner retained his post for another two years, a factor that greatly aided the consolidation of armed groups' "David-like" image before ominous adversaries and boosted public sympathy for armed actions in the name of a historically sanctioned, deeply ingrained cause: anti-imperialism and Cuban national sovereignty. During this time, BRAC became fully operational under director José Castaño Quevedo and directly accountable to the minister of governance Santiago Rey.[59]

Nonetheless, as foreign policy historian Thomas Paterson has shown, the CIA's position mirrored that of the U.S. government generally with regard to recognizing the depth of the crisis mounting in Cuba: passivity, complicity, and deniability remained the order of the day until December 1958, when U.S. efforts to alter its image as a stalwart Batista backer proved far too little and far too late.[60] Moreover, neither the CIA nor BRAC succeeded in persuading Batista to stop glossing *all* of his opponents as either Communists or facilitators of a Communist takeover. SIM, as Kirkpatrick noted, specialized in the "use of violence" against opponents, as did the Buró de Investigaciones. For them, BRAC was just another "weapon" in the arsenal against tactical threats to Batista's rule.[61] In real terms, these did not include Cuba's PSP, the Communists.

By contrast, most Americans were eager for easy, coherent explanations of their government's increasing interventions in Latin America as well as naively supportive of the installation of pro-U.S. dictators like Trujillo in the Dominican Republic, the Somoza dynasty in Nicaragua and, most recently, the terror-driven military state of Guatemala. The market for such narratives was clearly vast and Batista, together with his paid publicity agents in the United States, took full advantage of it. Magazines such as *Intelligence Digest* quickly fused Castro to a hemispheric Communist threat on the basis of little more than Che Guevara's ideological bent and the principle that any group's opposition to U.S.-supported dictators automatically made it "Communist."[62] In addition, U.S. magazines focused on popular culture and the Hollywood jet-set featured stories profiling a handsome, smiling Batista. That magazines such as *See* did so alongside interviews with Oscar-winning actress Anne Baxter and comedians Dean Martin and Jerry Lewis legitimated his stance among U.S. readers and diminished the explosive nature of the situation created by Batista's rule in Cuba. "He took Cuba—TWICE," read *See*'s cover-page headline on Batista. As early as January 1953, *See* described Batista precisely as he wanted the U.S. public to see him: "General Batista, friend of US, foe of Reds, teaches technique of bloodless coup d'etat." The author of the piece was the Dominican dictator Rafael Trujillo's consul general in the United States.[63] By 1956, knowledge of the violent turn that opposition to Batista had taken led the U.S. Department of Commerce to issue its own two-hundred-page glowing report on the Cuban economy, encouraging U.S. businessmen to invest in Cuba.[64]

Similarly, the "Cuban Tourist Edition" of the *Orlando Sentinel*'s *Florida Magazine* issued a thirty-two-page guide that painted Cuban reality in the pastel watercolors of progress, prosperity, and political stability, thanks to Batista, named "Man of the Week" by editors. The title of the article on Batista cheered, "Cuba Booming Under Batista and His People Applaud the Gov[ernment]."[65] Among the visible efforts to modernize Cuba that figured among Batista's greatest contributions were "fewer beggars" and "a good army." The paper noted, "Batista certainly isn't a typical Latin American in his working habits. He traces his ancestry to Cuban Indians and it shows plainly on his strong face." At the time, Florida was known not only for being one of the most racially segregated states in the country but for its long history of extra-legal executions of African Americans.[66] In the 1940s and 1950s, Florida tourist destinations such as the Saint Petersburg Alligator Farm and Central Florida were still proudly selling themselves as a place where local whites hunted alligators using black babies and small children as "gator bait." Senders of postcards celebrating the idea of

Figure 20. From the early 1900s through the 1950s, when Florida emerged as a mecca for wealthy northern tourists, local businesses sold the appeal of the state through the lens of white supremacy. (Courtesy of Special and Area Studies Collections, University of Florida)

feeding blacks to alligators hailed largely from New England, especially intellectually "liberal" cities such as New Haven, Connecticut (figure 20).[67] Given this context, Batista's success in courting Americans in high political places and using the U.S. media to broadcast his own self-designed image remains nothing short of astounding.

Daytona Beach, the city Batista and his family had called home from 1944 to 1948, aided Batista's positive image making in the United States with "Batista Day" on 25 March 1956. Launched with a twenty-one-gun salute at the airport, the four-day visit of Batista, the First Lady, and their children featured a parade through the city in honor of Batista, a speech in English that Batista had prepared himself, and a commemorative visit to Seabreeze High School, where Batista laid a wreath at the bust of José Martí.[68] Editors at the city's main paper described Batista in the most glowing of terms: "Batista has written his name into the history of Cuba, a country that has always been near and dear to Americans. . . . Batista may well turn out to be the Abraham Lincoln of Cuba. His modest background and the fight he is making to preserve Cuba as a unified

Figure 21. José "Pepe" Puente Blanco (second from left) conceived and led the
FEU's protest of Batista Day festivities in Daytona Beach, suddenly inserting young
protestors and their English-language banner into the city's celebratory parade.
(Courtesy of José Puente Blanco)

nation on its way to a 'government of the people, for the people and by the
people' establish such a parallel. Of course, like Lincoln, and all men of accomplishments, he has his enemies."[69]

Despite all the revelry, Batista's enemies were numerous enough that the
City of Daytona took extreme measures to protect him during his visit. Joined
by Batista's own intelligence forces, Daytona police placed Batista's home and
hotels where other Cubans stayed on round-the-clock watch.[70] The number of
men in Batista's personal bodyguard totaled no fewer than one hundred.[71]

Nonetheless, a group of young Cuban students led by none other than Pepe
Puente Blanco, architect of FEU's nationally televised demonstration at the
baseball stadium in 1954, managed to interrupt festivities by reenacting a very
similar protest, an operation of FEU's Directorio Revolucionario. For seven
blocks, Pepe, Gustavo Machín, José Fernández Cossío, Armando Hernández,
and Jorge Robreno carried a long banner reading, "Batista: A Dictator" before
being approached by police and fleeing the scene (figure 21). Pepe and the others went to Miami after the parade ended, only to discover that Miami's newspapers had blacked out the protest. They returned to Daytona and dropped by
the offices of the *News-Journal,* because that paper included a picture of their
protest. "We want something to show when we get back to Cuba," one of them

said.[72] After buying copies of the paper and happily providing their names to reporters—something they could not have done in Cuba—the students issued a joint statement: "We wanted Americans to know we don't like Batista. . . . We in Cuba want the Americans to know we are fighting for democracy."[73]

The paths of Daytona's political elite and the DR would soon cross again. Coinciding with the DR's successful assassination of SIM chief Blanco Rico and assault on others in late October 1956, Daytona's mayor and a delegation of important Floridians arrived in Havana to visit Batista and announce the opening of a Cuban museum in one of the two houses Batista donated to the city in 1957.[74] While the timing of these events may have happened by chance, the Directorio's commitment to pulling away the curtain to reveal Batista's dark side matched Batista's and friendly American politicians' determination to prevent that from happening.

Fighting a Moral War in Lieu of Civil War

On 24 February 1957, Herbert Matthews published his now legendary interview with Fidel Castro and report on the 26th of July Movement guerrillas ensconced in the Sierra Maestra on the front page of the *New York Times*.[75] Not only did Matthews disprove batistiano officials' claim that Fidel Castro was dead, he utterly humiliated the regime in doing so. One of a special three-part series editors assigned to Matthews, the article formed the basis of Matthews's contention that the fight for control of Cuba's future had only just begun. Batista's censorship of foreign news media had blocked the internal release of those editions of the *Times* by requiring customs officers to literally cut out the offensive articles before copies could be released and sold.[76]

Yet news of Matthews's reports quickly filtered through the cracks of Batista's censorship and catalyzed hope across Cuba. Among the arguments that Matthews made was that Fidel's movement formed only one of three wings of clandestine subversion and armed struggle: the 26th of July Movement; the still autonomous, if allied, Civic Resistance movement in cities; and the Directorio Revolucionario, mostly composed of elected leaders of FEU. "The students obviously are not seeking anything for themselves," wrote Matthews. Noting at least one member's insistence that his parents' and grandparents' experience as mambises and anti-Machado fighters made his determination to sacrifice himself for the cause unquestionable, Matthews continued, "As a whole their

traditions are anti-Communist and democratic." Contrary to traditional recol-
lections and analyses of Matthews's accounts, he was clearly most impressed
with the historical and political purity articulated by the students, particularly
José Antonio Echeverría. Nicknamed El Gordo (the Fat One) by his friends in
FEU and the Directorio, José Antonio was described by Matthews as "merely
heavy set, florid, handsome, with a mass of hair in a pompadour, prematurely
touched by gray. He is only 24 years old and an architecture student."[77]

Although repeatedly demonized after 1959 for supposedly "inventing Fidel
Castro," Matthews's three-part series actually suggested that the Directorio
Revolucionario's and José Antonio Echeverría's legitimacy far surpassed that
of Fidel Castro in the winter of 1957. They had cultivated a degree of prestige
and trust with the public unrivaled by any other oppositional group. This endowed them with the capacity to ignite public outrage against the regime and
generate support. Unafraid to die and eager for an immediate bloody end to the
dictatorial state that a guerrilla war implied, top DR leaders had been living
underground for months when they saw Matthews. They had developed a tight
bond with one another, even as the organization expanded in numbers. FEU
member Aestor Bombino, then in his last year of medical studies, spent a great
deal of time talking to Echeverría, who was hiding from the police. Lodged in
an apartment building packed with students, José Antonio successfully relied
on two brothers who were also studying medicine not only for his safety but for
the security of the highly dangerous mission that the DR was planning.[78]

Beginning in January 1957, the DR designed a commando operation involving approximately 150 men. The idea was likely born of Echeverría's conversations with Menelao Mora, an experienced Auténtico activist with whom he had
served time in prison. One group, led by Carlos Gutiérrez Menoyo, a veteran of
the Spanish Civil War, and seconded by Faure Chomón, was to gain entrance
to the Presidential Palace using three vehicles. The first of these, driven by
Mora, was a red truck labeled "Fast Delivery" on both sides: the students had
reconstructed the interior of the truck with a false floor and filled it with automatic weapons and other heavy arms. Upon arrival, members of this group of
assailants were supposed to fire their way past the presidential guard and up
the stairs to Batista's private office with the goal of assassinating him—or, as
pro-democratic activists of Latin America and the DR would have said at the
time, *para ajusticiarlo* (bringing him to justice by killing him). Meanwhile,
those of another group, led by José Antonio Echeverría, would make their way

to CMQ radio station where they would announce the killing of the dictator and subsequently converge at the University of Havana where huge caches of machine guns, rifles, and carbines had been secretly stored. Student snipers were to occupy the tallest buildings surrounding both the Presidential Palace and the University of Havana. Others were to take over the Havana airport to prevent possible escape by Batista's henchmen. Jorge Valls would lead a team to the Presidential Palace after its capture and reinforce the attack as well as participate in other operations to secure the Buró de Investigaciones, key police precincts, and other military strongholds like the headquarters of SIM.[79]

The unconditional willingness of the majority of the students and other DR recruits to participate in the task seems astounding. Samuel B. Cherson voted against the operation, warning that a failure would annihilate the DR's ability to upend the regime permanently; yet he still fully participated in the plan.[80] Similarly, Bombino, who had no knowledge of the DR's conspiracy until the night before the actual attack, had to decide on the spot when a med school classmate conveyed Echeverría's invitation to join him in "an act." If he consented, the classmate would give him the address where he would meet José Antonio that night. Without vacillation, Bombino said yes. After learning every detail of the plan from Echeverría himself, he agreed to his assignment: Bombino would ride in one of three cars that took over the CMQ radio station, wait while José Antonio transmitted the message of the DR's decapitation of the regime to the nation, and then take a carbine to the university's rooftop, where he and others would prevent the police from making their way up la escalinata by mowing them down with gunfire. "[The] night I went to the apartment, Echeverría opened the door himself and said, using a phrase very typical of him, *Mulato, mulato, yo sabía que tú no me fallabas* [Mulatto, mulatto, I knew that you would never fail me]."[81]

Yet for all these young men's evident bravery and determination, Echeverría's last acts before the zero hour spoke to his own recognition of the odds the DR faced. Although he had seen no other member of his family since he had appeared in Matanzas almost a year earlier to attend the funeral of his brother Alfredo, José Antonio's other brother Sinforiano saw him weekly, serving as a column of personal strength as well as his link to the outside. No one suspected that Sinforiano, trained in mechanical engineering, a fluent English speaker, and an employee of Sabatéz, Procter & Gamble's Cuban subsidiary, served as a primary factor in José Antonio's survival. A supplier of much-needed news and home-cooked food, Sinforiano, with his buoyant personality, sense of mission, and very Cuban sardonic sense of humor, often provided simple luxuries such as comic relief. He also lent José Antonio his car so that he, disguised, could take his girlfriend, María Esperanza, out on dates. While José Antonio certainly used Sinforiano's car for this purpose, what his brother did not know was that he also used it to transport mass quantities of weapons. A master of disguise, José Antonio managed to fool even Sinforiano. Masquerading as a bus driver, complete with a mustache, uniform, and hair that he had dyed gray, Echeverría opened the door of his safe house to Sinforiano on one occasion and subsequently dissolved into laughter when his completely duped brother repeatedly asked to speak to José Antonio.[82]

However, José Antonio Echeverría took his role and the very real possibility of his death seriously. Catholicism, Sinforiano attested, was a "living fiber" for many young Cubans who connected the multiple dimensions of their political consciousness to God, their membership in La Juventud Católica, and the Christian mission of dying in the service of Jesus's word. When Sinforiano asked his brother one day why was he doing what he was doing, José Antonio replied, using his brother's family nickname, "Vico, that's the problem with politics, that politics are managed by gangsters, *politiqueros* [scoundrel politicians], *sinvergüenzas* [shameless bastards], thieves. If we who are decent people do not participate in politics, how is this ever going to end? This will end in disaster! For that reason we must take part in politics, in order to improve the kind of people that govern our country!"

"I will never forget that," Sinforiano said solemnly in 2009. Tears filled his eyes.[83] Lucy, their sister, showed similar deep emotions when she revealed that José Antonio had received the final sacrament of last rites from Franciscan priests who had once offered him a safe house for several months.[84] For Roman Catholics, the request to receive last rites implied consciousness of imminent death and the desire to be absolved of all sins and to heal one's soul before leaving this life.

In the end, the commando teams' penetration of the Presidential Palace, the takeover of the radio station's broadcasting booth, and the convergence of key groups of participants on the grounds of the University of Havana proved remarkably successful. Led by the valiant Carlos Gutiérrez Menoyo, all but one member of the group charged with killing Batista made it into Batista's office. Shot before arriving at the palace, Faure Chomón had the "dubious distinction of crawling his way to safety" and thus surviving an otherwise increasingly doomed mission. Others demonstrated their unconditional willingness to die. Wounded as he left the Fast Delivery truck and sporting a broken, useless pair of glasses and an equally damaged machine gun, Carbó Serviá nonetheless reached the main gates, found a weapon, and proceeded up the stairs to shoot Batista.[85]

To their horror, however, the men of the commando team found that Batista was not there: only seconds before, he had gone up a hidden back staircase to the presidential family quarters on the third floor to visit one of his sons, sick and home from school.[86]

Simultaneously, although ignorant of the key commando team's failure to kill or even capture Batista, José Antonio Echeverría, Bombino, and others arrived at CMQ in three rented identical "*mamey* [salmon]-colored" Ford cars. Firing their way in and out of the transmission booth, José Antonio took the microphones of Radio Reloj at CMQ and addressed the nation as the president of FEU.[87] "¡Pueblo de Cuba!" he announced passionately, "En estos momentos acaba de ser ajusticiado revolucionariamente el dictator Fulgencio Batista. En su propia madriguera del Palacio Presidencial, el pueblo de Cuba ha ido a ajustarle cuentas. Y somos nosotros, el Directorio Revolucionario, los que en nombre de la Revolución Cubana ha dado el tiro de gracia a este regimen de oprobio" (People of Cuba! At this very moment, the dictator Fulgencio Batista has been revolutionarily brought to justice. In his very own lair of the Presidential Palace, the people of Cuba have gone to settle accounts. And we, the Revolutionary Directorate, have given the final blow to this despicable regime).[88] Incredibly, perhaps, Bombino recounted that he and others waiting in the getaway car never heard the announcement, either because the Ford rentals had no radios or because they simply were so nervous they forgot to turn the radio on.[89]

At the Presidential Palace, general mayhem broke loose as machine-gun fire sprayed the grounds from the third floor of the palace. The commando squad battled on, assisted by a group of only fifty snipers instead of the planned one hundred. Only half had shown up as the word-of-mouth method for transmitting the date and time of the battle failed to function when it was most needed.[90]

The death of José Antonio Echeverría soon followed. Having completed their task at the radio station and unaware of the plan unraveling around them, he and his fellow assailants encountered a police patrol car on the way to the university, crashing into it under a hail of bullets apparently started by "Chino" Figueredo, one of DR's commandos. All but José Antonio escaped. Shot in the leg, he attempted to assault the police car but his wound made him fall to the ground.

Having learned virtually every detail of her brother's death from key sources in the hours that followed and after the flight of Batista in January 1959, Lucy Echeverría recollected what happened next. Approached by the cop, who recognized him, José Antonio asked him, "'Are you going to kill me?' To which the man replied, 'Sí, te voy a matar pa'a que no jodas más' [Yes, I am going to kill you so you don't fuck around anymore]." Shot at point-blank range in three places, including his chest, José Antonio was left to die alone, bleeding out for over an hour. Only a group of nuns, finding him lying nearly lifeless on the ground, dared approach him to offer what little they could: spiritual comfort. The rest of the group abandoned their leader. Pale and visibly horrified, Fructuoso Rodríguez watched the murder from his position behind the giant statue of Alma Mater at the top of the university stairs. When Aestor Bombino, racing to take up his assigned position on a rooftop, saw Fructuoso, he knew immediately that something had gone terribly wrong. "'¿Fructuoso, qué pasó?' 'Mataron Al Gordo'" ("Fructuoso, what happened?" "They killed El Gordo").[91]

The Directorio Revolucionario and FEU never genuinely recovered from the death of José Antonio Echeverría. The Directorio Revolucionario had capped off the students' highly public unarmed civic struggle against Batista with the boldest and most direct assault on the dictatorship yet. For the assault on the Presidential Palace and effort to kill Fulgencio Batista, months in the planning, Echeverría had chosen 13 March, Cuba's National Day of the Architect. The selection was neither coincidental nor a boastful act, despite his own choice of a career path before state terror at the university had forced faculty and FEU to shut most departments down. In selecting 13 March, DR members had wanted to deny Batista his own self-assigned image as the "builder" and "modernizer" of Cuba's future; they wanted to set a clear symbolic path toward reconstruction, repair, and change by bringing him to justice through death. Had their plan succeeded, Echeverría and the DR would have done far more than kill the tyrant. They would have empowered a people sick of arbitrary rule, corruption, false claims to constitutionalism, and state violence against civilians. They also would have proved the vulnerability of the regime to the least likely of its enemies to succeed. Arguably more important than Castro's assault on Moncada, the DR's commando-style attack on the Presidential Palace raised the stakes for Batista as never before.

Although the DR's unexpected assault did not succeed in achieving its aims, the context in which it took place and, more important, the historically ingrained image of its authors as selfless young patriots of Cuba may well have galvanized citizens' support for armed struggle and for Fidel Castro's leadership like no other previous event. As the final chapter of this book argues, Castro and the 26th of July Movement capitalized on the consequences, impact, and example of the students' valor to forge the broader, popularly backed, and even more violent struggle that still lay ahead. With the stage now cleared of any other contender for the part of Cuba's long-awaited and much-needed selfless messiah, Fidel Castro proved more than ready and willing to take over that role. Critical to the public's acceptance and eventual embrace of him as a national, apolitical, morally righteous, and historically destined messiah were the thousands of anonymous urban agents of the 26th of July Movement and its related movement of civic resistance who stood at the frontline of the fighting. Equally significant were many heroic journalists who took on the dangers these clandestinos faced and espoused the Cuban cause of freedom and sovereignty as their own.

6

Clandestinos, Guerrillas, and the Making of a
Messiah in the Sierra Maestra, 1957–1958

THE DAY AFTER THE DIRECTORIO Revolucionario's attempted assassination of Fulgencio Batista, the press announced that the assault on the Presidential Palace had resulted in more than forty dead and eighteen wounded.[1] Those named were almost all members of Batista's military. Killed during and after the commando operation, however, were dozens more, whether shot on sight or caught and executed on the street. Coverage in *El Mundo* included images of soldiers atop armed tanks, the Fast Delivery truck used in the assault, passersby crouched behind doors, the remains of a shot-out bus, and an impressive assortment of .50 caliber ammunition belts, rifles, and machine guns the DR assailants had left behind.[2] Taking advantage of the mayhem to get rid of key opposition figures, government assassins murdered Senator Pelayo Cuervo Navarro, current president of the Ortodoxos and the much-admired brains behind many of Eduardo Chibás's legislative proposals and judicial briefs against corrupt officials.[3]

Batista's men also cracked down on suspected activists of the 26th of July Movement. First, they arrested the national director of urban action and sabotage units Faustino Pérez and then caught Carlos Franqui and Vicente Baez redhanded as they edited and printed clandestine newspapers of the movement. Interrogated and tortured, Pérez, Franqui, and Baez spent the next four months in jail.[4]

Weeks later, Batista's security forces continued the hunt for DR survivors. Although the PSP's youth division energetically protested the government's charge that Communists had collaborated with the DR and denounced the murders of Pelayo Cuervo and José Antonio Echeverría, they also held to the party line: 1957 was, in essence, no different than 1933; if opponents to the regime truly wanted to topple it, they needed to back *acciones de masa* (mass actions) and not ineffective *putschista* schemes like those of Fidel Castro and the DR.[5] In April, Batista's security forces finally found and promptly slaughtered the DR leaders Fructuoso Rodríguez, Juan Pedro Carbó Serviá, Joe Westbrook, and José Machado Rodríguez in their hideout at Humboldt 7, an apartment building facing the *malecón,* Havana's seawall. Proud to advertise the murders, police dragged their bodies into the street. Apparently operating on party orders, Marcos Rodríguez, a covert PSP activist who infiltrated the DR, had identified their location to police.[6]

No longer attempting to win hearts and minds, if it ever had, Batista's regime became a hard-line modern dictatorship in the spring of 1957 through December 1958. As Batista increasingly turned toward terror in the cities, his U.S.-supplied army and air force unleashed an all-out war against civilians in two rural regions: the countryside of Oriente dominated by Fidel Castro's guerrillas and El Escambray Mountains of central Cuba, where a small but effective force of DR fighters reconstituted themselves; each relied on the support of peasants, although DR guerrillas never benefited from the vast supply chain that Fidel's 26th of July Movement in cities could provide.[7] Yet citizens' increasing support for armed struggle did not result from great military successes by either group. Rather, the shift in consciousness brought about in the previous two years, popular backlash against the methods of the state, and sympathy for the heroic "David versus Goliath" character of activists' fight laid the groundwork for Batista's fall. No publicity campaign or rhetorical smoke screen could hide or justify Batista's militarism and brutal atrocities. In 1957 through most of 1958, moral victories rather than political or even military ones consumed the vast energies of the growing 26th of July Movement, most of which was composed of tens of thousands of faceless and nameless clandestine activists who formed a secret underground of cells across Cuba and key organizational sites abroad.[8] Until 1958, when guerrilla forces began to implement programs of social and economic reforms in the limited zones that they controlled, covert urban revolutionaries could claim most such victories. These clandestinos empowered citizens by pointing out the vulnerabilities of the state and actively avoiding civilian deaths, unlike their government adversaries.

Originally numbering ten thousand but growing to thirty thousand by 1958,

dues-paying members of the 26th of July Movement were Batista's most immediate enemies.[9] Of these, voluntary foot soldiers of the 26th of July Movement's
war in the cities totaled between one thousand and three thousand nationwide.
Called clandestinos, they were largely white professionals, journalists, skilled
workers, teachers, mothers, and students who printed and distributed an illegal
alternative press, carried out violent attacks on government officials, and set
off bombs designed to disrupt the economy and daily commercial life. Perhaps most important, they funneled supplies, hope, and critical media contacts
to Castro's small bands of guerrillas in the field. For two years, clandestinos,
the vast majority of them forgotten martyrs of the revolution, unknown to all
but Batista's security forces and their own comrades in arms, disappeared, suffered arrest, and endured beatings and torture. Meanwhile, Batista's ever more
belligerent claim that armed opponents were "Soviet agents," "terrorists," and
"Communists" diminished his credibility with all. As we have seen, this included top U.S. officials, who observed with irony how Batista tolerated Cuba's
real Communist Party, insulating the PSP from the degree of persecution his
security forces aimed at non-Communist opposition like the DR and the 26th of
July Movement. The Communists proved helpful to Batista's game of retaining
power because his relatively "softer" approach to the PSP allowed him to claim
a desire to return to constitutionalism amid the reality of a counterinsurgency
war mostly based on urban violence.

But more important than the Communists was the support of the United
States. Not until the spring of 1958 did a tiny handful of high-level State
Department officials argue that Batista should go; until July of that year, the
United States continued to provide weapons for his cause, despite statements
to the contrary.[10] Moreover, when the State Department finally came around
to realizing that Batista's regime would not survive, it encouraged the CIA to
block Fidel Castro's ascension to power at all costs. Developed far too late, the
tactic not only did not work but it revealed how little the U.S. government knew
or cared about conditions that Cuban citizens faced on the ground. Given the
United States' history of taking virtually the same route time and again since
1898, this came as no surprise.[11]

From the heights of the isolated Sierra Maestra in southeastern Cuba, Fidel
presented himself and his movement as not simply *opposed* to Communism
but the very opposite of the PSP and all other "opportunistic" political parties.
While critical of U.S. support for Batista and the economic legacies of its in-

terventionism in Cuba, he was also—as he had told Melba Hernández from prison years earlier—careful not to raise too many eyebrows or fan the flames of fear regarding the fate of U.S. investments in Cuba. In interviews and manifestos issued from the Sierra, Fidel Castro teamed fairness and moderation with invocations of national sovereignty and a strong role for a revolutionary state that would change Cubans' lives for the better. Fidel projected himself and his guerrilla followers as an ever more selfless force, increasingly purified by the trials by fire that they suffered themselves or that killed their comrades.

Getting this message out depended mostly on the activities of three affiliated wings of the revolution: Resistencia Cívica, a covert professional organization that included top advertising agents such as Emilio Guede and intellectuals like Raúl Roa; the action and sabotage units led first by Faustino Pérez and then Manolo Ray; and the 26th of July Movement's propaganda section, staffed in the cities by men like Vicente Baez and headed nationally by Carlos Franqui who, together with Enrique Oltuski, edited and distributed *Revolución (Clandestino)*, the organ of the movement.[12] In 1958, Carlos Franqui added Radio Rebelde, a secret radio station broadcasting nationally from locations in Oriente, to the 26th of July Movement's armory of media weapons, and became its national chief of propaganda. Thus, the actions, publications, and strong campaign of reaching out to people beyond Cuba's borders shattered Batista's image of the rebels as terrorists and exploded the false picture of a calm and secure haven for tourism and investment that his publicity agents painted at home and abroad.

Of course, Fidel's previous feats of leadership had already launched his image as a daring and dedicated fighter long before he arrived in the Sierra Maestra. But as his original core of eighteen men survived to see their forces grow and the authority of their troops create geographically massive liberated zones in Oriente province, Fidel Castro became a messiah for Cuba—in his own eyes and in much of the public mind. With a circulation that hovered near thirty thousand after clandestine activists released a new edition in 1958, the expanded version of the defense speech Fidel had delivered at his 1953 trial, titled *La Historia Me Absolverá*, surely found renewed resonance with many Cubans disgusted by the war.[13] For years, Fidel had been personally convinced that only he could lead the opposition to Batista. Upon launching his plot to establish a guerrilla presence in the Sierra Maestra, however, he redoubled his efforts to convince the public of his mission. Indeed, in the very first of his public manifestoes, issued in August 1955, he had declared that his movement held a special claim among the opposition on the basis of its own past actions: "the legion of martyrs" left in the wake of his assault on the Cuartel Moncada gave it that right.[14]

Yet his image as a selfless, Christ-like redeemer with similarly altruistic followers owed its origins as much to the actions of the clandestinos who withstood the brunt of the violence and constructed Fidel's messianic portrayal for Cubans and for the outside world as it did to the political strategies of the guerrillas themselves in the Sierra Maestra. "In the same way that it is false that the Sierra and 'The Twelve' were the ones responsible for the triumph, it is also a mistake to ignore the importance of the Sierra," according to Carlos Franqui, who went to the Sierra after police persecution in Havana augured certain death. Unknown but central to the guerrillas' importance was the way that they, like the clandestinos, sought to "humanize" war and violence by inviting citizens to see their actions as defensive efforts to reunite a Cuba that Batista—not the insurrectionists—had divided.[15]

Clandestinos: Fighting Batista's Batista

In the wake of the DR's assault on the Palacio, Batista sent a clear message about the hard line he planned to take in the year to come. A week earlier, his prime minister warned that the 26th of July Movement guerrillas' unexpected resurrection from the dead in Oriente augured renewed suspension of the Constitution.[16] Then, Batista began his annual 10 March celebration of his military coup by ordering the detention and interrogation of two NBC reporters on charges of being "Communists" for meeting with rebels in the Sierra Maestra. Before expelling them back to the United States, the government confiscated one thousand feet of film and dozens of still photographs.[17]

Even more symbolic of Batista's approach to the rising tide of revolution his government faced were the mass expenditures the regime incurred before and after the assault on the palace: no longer did Batista deliver solemn "state of the union"–style addresses on occasions such as 10 March or 4 September; instead, he turned them into full-fledged propaganda events, meant to convince citizens that he *already had* their support and unflinching loyalty. Thus, the banquet for 10 March 1957 required an unprecedented three thousand pieces of silverware for guests. He also announced a new propaganda team for PAP that included black intellectual David Grillo.[18] One of its first orders of business was to demonize the student movement by depicting its respectable middle-class activists as bloodthirsty criminals and bandits in disguise. After the DR's assault on the palace, defenders of Batista in the press accused the DR of violating the patrimony of the nation, by surpassing even the savagery of activists in Machado's era, *and* the sanctity of the family, by terrorizing the first lady in her own home.[19]

The United States contributed greatly to Batista's new strategy of projecting rather than courting sources of legitimacy. U.S. ambassador Gardner visited Batista the day after he survived the DR's assault on the pretext of thanking him for lowering the tax rates of the U.S.-owned Cuban Telephone Company, a business universally despised by Cuban customers and a proposed target for nationalization under the Ortodoxos' original party program. Gardner's gesture of solidarity with both the dictator and the phone company famously garnered Batista a solid-gold telephone.[20] This was followed by the official visit of Admiral Arleigh A. Berke, chief of naval operations of the U.S. armada stationed in Cuba. Berke then conferred on Batista membership in the dubiously titled "Order of Naval Merit of Cuba," apparently a spur-of-the-moment American invention.[21]

However, from March 1957 through Batista's own flight from Cuba on 31 December 1958, no one proved more dedicated or flamboyant than the dictator himself in staging a popular legitimacy he had never really had amid the steady crumbling of his regime. On 7 April 1957, he launched this strategy with the most immense rally ever held in Cuban history, gathering close to a million citizens before the balcony of the Presidential Palace and documenting the event with extraordinary photographs of jubilant masses holding banners of support (figure 22). His government also printed a special ninety-nine-page commemorative booklet that described the occasion as a "historic popular apotheosis." The document reproduced speeches, pledges, and letters of support from politicians and journalists as well as the presidents of the most important labor unions, veterans' associations, black societies, and businessmen's organizations such as the Asociación Nacional de Hacendados. Undoubtedly hoping to implicate individuals as collaborators of the regime, the booklet's editors also conspicuously printed the names of each group's leaders and, in many cases, those of every single member, even when they numbered in the hundreds. Whether they liked it or not, these people were now marked batistianos, having pledged their allegiance in a historically indelible way.[22]

Both the rally—there would be many more in the coming months—and the

Ha Sido Histórica la Apoteosis Popular del 7 de Abril de 1957

Cuando un Jefe de Estado recibe del pueblo por el que se ha desvivido, una demostración así, de personas adhesión, tiene que sentirse espiritualmente recompensado de todos los sinsabores e incomprensiones de que parece que, fatalmente, han de ser objeto los redentores de pueblos. El Presidente Batista recibe con visible emoción la aclamación imponderable.

Figure 22. Nearly a month after the Directorio Revolucionario's failed attempt to assassinate Batista in March 1957, he mobilized hundreds of thousands of his supporters, members of Cuba's umbrella federation of unions, and all civil servants in a massive display meant to "thank" him for his service in "pacifying" Cuba and, implicitly, celebrate his survival. Alfredo Sadulé, the son of Batista's chauffeur and the personal bodyguard of the dictator's wife, Marta, autographed this commemorative program of the event.

"archiving" of the event and its participants through an official government publication speak to Batista's need to meet the increasing bravado of the clandestinos. This was especially true in the capital, where authorities attempted to drown out an ever-widening chorus of rebel voices. As historian Julia Sweig has shown, based on the internal correspondence of the 26th of July Movement, at the forefront of Batista's opposition stood the clandestinos, far more than Fidel Castro and the still-tiny guerrilla band. The urban underground financed, protected, supplied, and promoted Fidel's guerrillas in the Sierra Maestra from the cities and revolutionary clubs as far away as New York, Miami, and Tampa: "Had it not been for the work of the 26th of July Movement outside of the Sierra Maestra during the first seventeen months of the insurgency, from November 1956 until April 1958, the final period, when the antidictatorial struggle gained unstoppable military and political momentum, would simply not have been possible." Reaching victory on 1 January 1959 required the clandestinos' political campaign as much or more so than a military campaign.[23]

Facilitating this process was the landmark ruling of Judge Manuel Urrutia in the district court of the province of Oriente on 14 May 1957. To the shock of the Batista regime, Urrutia ordered the release of 151 men charged with insurrection, 22 of whom were veterans of the *Granma* landing: given the unconstitutional "usurpation of and illegal retention of power by Batista and his followers, the defendants had been acting within their constitutional rights" of dissent.[24] Perhaps the most critical activist freed was Frank País. He immediately became chief coordinator of the movement for the whole of Cuba. Charged with the gargantuan task of recruiting and knitting together an urban militia that carried out its own offensives in cities against the regime while also supporting the guerrilla band in the Sierra, País established ground rules for all activists to which Fidel Castro and other leaders agreed: no clandestino or volunteer activist was allowed to go on his or her own to the Sierra Maestra without authorization from both the supreme military command and País himself, or, upon his death, his successor. By the same token, going into exile was considered desertion and, like departing the fight in the cities for the mountains, punishable by death.[25] "The city was the army and the Sierra [Maestra] was the vanguard," summarized Carlos Franqui in 2008.[26] The revolution also had to have only one face, one voice, noted Emilio Guede, and there was no question that the face and the voice had to be those of Fidel Castro.[27]

When guerrillas of the 26th of July Movement entrenched themselves in the Sierra in early 1957 and brilliant urban strategists like Frank País and his followers were later freed that May, Havana was still virtually devoid of activists. Early adherents to Frank's call included men like Marcelo Fernández, an MIT student, whose prestige, persuasiveness, and sophistication quickly impressed young men like Vicente Baez, Angel Fernández Vilá, Armando Hart, Osmani Cienfuegos Gorriarán (brother of *Granma* survivor and then guerrilla Camilo Cienfuegos), and others. Members at the time of the University of Havana–based Comité de Superación Universitaria Ramiro Valdés Dauzá, a group named for a student martyr of the early 1940s, all of these men joined Marcelo, taking charge of the propaganda section and including within it a department, largely chaired by Vicente Baez, for recruiting labor unionists. Together they produced four newspapers, *Vanguardia Obrera, Sierra Maestra,*

26 de Julio, and *Revolución.* Producing the papers, according to Franqui, was relatively easy. He used a small Multilith machine that activists transported back and forth to his apartment from the university and secret safe houses in the underground. The group never lacked for either paper or lithographic machines, thanks to Julio César Martínez, a Dominican who was able to bring them into the country with no official oversight.[28]

Distribution was far more dangerous. It happened hand to hand on the factory floor and in commercial venues. More commonly, activists dropped off a stack of clandestine newspapers right next to the bank of mailboxes in the entryways to apartment buildings. The thrill of watching an edition disappear as one by one, men and women picked up their mail stoked the fires of commitment in the papers' makers. Delight in accomplishing their mission, a kind of "pleasure of agency," propelled them to continue the fight against all odds.[29] At times, activists climbed to the top floors of buildings and tossed packets of clandestine newspapers off balconies or the roof.[30]

Yet it was also at the moment of distributing the covert press that activists were most at risk; anyone could reveal their whereabouts or identity to police.[31] Carlos Franqui, who had edited *El Aldabonazo* for the 26th of July Movement as early as August 1956, soon headed Vicente Baez's team.[32] In addition to demanding the trial and potential execution of Batista's security forces for the crimes of torture, rape, and murder, these papers detailed the embezzlement of millions of pesos in union funds by Batista's officials and covered unreported cases of detention and torture. One paper revealed the beating of Father Juan O'Farrill del Cañal, a Catholic priest whose homilies apparently inspired worshippers to reflect on the abuses of the state.[33] By 1958, *Sierra Maestra* boasted "offices" in three different locations, Havana, Miami, and Santiago de Cuba.[34]

Just as important, if not more so, were the highly creative means by which clandestinos broke through the image of unity behind Batista that his handlers began to craft after the assault on the Presidential Palace. Perhaps the most original of activists in this regard was Sergio González. Once a seminarian who aspired to be a priest, Sergio dropped his vocation entirely because participating in direct acts of violence would contradict his role as a priest. "Sergio was a man of such courage and such dignity that on one occasion on which he was being tortured alongside a group of *compañeros,* he asked Coronel Faget that they only torture him and so [his tormentors] passed all the tortures onto him. Later they assassinated him," recalled Carlos Franqui.[35]

Yet the legend of El Curita, as he was known, was rooted as much in the originality and success of his operations as in his tendency to self-sacrifice. Sergio concocted a plan to interrupt Batista's speech on 7 April 1957 before the rally of nearly a million people the government had organized on the grounds of the Presidential Palace. Going from hotel to hotel, he had registered different individuals as guests using the last name "Castro." Once checked into the room, the operative then stuffed the mattress with a large quantity of gunpowder and bullets. "When Batista began to speak," recalled Carlos Franqui, "every one of those mattresses exploded and immediately it sounded as if there was a terrible gunfight that [momentarily, at least] forced a dispersion of the rally."[36] Pulled off without a hitch, Sergio's plan was called Operation Castro Brothers.

Equally effective were many more spectacular operations designed by Sergio. One, known as La Noche de las Cien Bombas (the Night of the Hundred Bombs) consisted of manufacturing small devices that proved undetectable to most bystanders as they were moved about the city: they were made of milk bottles filled with both milk and explosive material. In order to maximize the sound of the explosions and also ensure that no one would be injured in the act, Manolo Ray, later secretary-general of the clandestinos' "action and sabotage" units nationwide, took precautions. In professional circles, Ray was widely respected for having built a bridge for the public works department as his undergraduate thesis during the Auténtico years. He also designed the underwater tunnel connecting the Bay of Havana and helped engineer the construction of the Havana Hilton in the early 1950s. In 1957, Emilio Guede recruited Ray for Resistencia Cívica. That organization's main tasks were financing operations, supporting the guerrillas by the secret sale of bonds (payable upon victory with interest by the revolutionary government), providing safe houses for urban activists, and publishing critiques of the regime in mainstream magazines such as *Bohemia*.[37] However, Ray's engineering skills soon proved more useful to allies in the action and sabotage wing of the 26th of July.

For the Night of the Hundred Bombs operation, Ray cooperated with Sergio and others to plant the bombs all over Havana. Raised by a strong mother to believe in the equal intelligence and rights of women, Ray took pride in the fact that for the task, he recruited a young woman who had been president of the Department of Education at the University of Havana and represented one of the few female leaders of FEU. Of sixty to seventy bombs placed that night (Ray asserted it was never a hundred), she alone planted more than twenty, ensuring the action's success even if the other bombs failed to explode. "Actions and sabotage were done in order to make known our presence [and intimidate the regime]," attested Ray in 2008 from his home in San Juan, Puerto Rico.[38] "We didn't place bombs with the goal of killing anyone. . . . So we wouldn't kill anyone, we placed them away from people." On the Night of the Hundred Bombs, for example, operatives exploded the bombs simultaneously at three o'clock in the morning, a time when very few people would be around. Reports in the press confirm Ray's claim, often commenting with surprise that no one had been injured or killed in violent explosions.[39] Subsequent to this success, Ray took charge, together with Faustino Pérez, of operations that burned to the ground a number of commercial buildings, a kind of operation Ray tagged as "costly" because of the amount of material involved. "These were fires that everyone could see, they would make the papers and showed that our organization was *unstoppable,* impenetrable, and it gave confidence to new members so that they would join," Ray explained. Another regular operation was littering the highways with sharp nails to burst the tires of police and army patrols as well as paralyze the economy by slowing down truck service.[40]

Only one operation, from the perspective of clandestinos, went terribly wrong: 26th of July operatives placed a bomb in the women's bathroom at La Tropicana, a nightclub that had become iconic of Batista's pandering to the U.S. Mafia and a favorite hangout for American tourists vacationing in a country whose dictatorship they rarely questioned and many chose not to see. After placing the bomb, the female activist stayed outside the bathroom door to ensure that no one entered before it went off. To her horror, a woman ignored her warning, thinking it either a joke or simply a lie. The bomb exploded, mutilating the guest. Guilt plagued the 26th of July operative for the rest of her life.[41] All of these forms of violent protest and sabotage Batista and his supporters considered "terrorism." Resistencia Cívica and the 26th of July clandestinos defined it as making Cuba more revolutionary.[42]

Resistencia Cívica and the action and sabotage units of the 26th of July in Havana considered two of their joint operations particularly successful. The first garnered the world's attention, particularly in Latin America, where people grappling with their own newly ascendant, U.S.-backed authoritarian states usually heard little about Cuban affairs. In February 1958, Ray organized the kidnapping of the world's greatest race car driver at the time, Juan Manuel Fangio of Argentina.[43] Winner of the Paris Grand Prix in 1957, Fangio was in

Havana for a similar contest that Batista had arranged to celebrate El Grito de Baire, Cuba's national holiday, on 24 February 1958. The Havana Grand Prix served a dual purpose: ramping up tourist revenues and displaying the "calm" atmosphere government publicity agents claimed now dominated major venues on the island.[44]

The operation was meticulously planned to take place before the auto race and thereby ensure that Fangio's absence would have the maximum effect. The two activists whom Manolo Ray had assigned to kidnap Fangio managed to do so with ease. Late in the evening on Sunday, the night before the race, they found Fangio conversing in the lobby of the Hotel Lincoln, where he was staying. Casually, one of the two young men approached and asked, "Are you Fangio?" When the auto racer said yes, surely expecting to sign an autograph, the man, Manuel Uziel, pulled out a .45 caliber gun and pointed it "serenely" at Fangio, saying, "You have to come with me. I am from the 26th of July Movement and nothing will happen to you." Fangio did was he was told.[45] He was housed for two weeks in the home of a Cuban woman with an American husband. National and international media outlets could not help but report on the event. More important, Ray provided regular reports to the paper *El Crisol,* keeping the story alive. "They treated me very well," Fangio said when he was finally released.[46]

In fact, Fangio's concern for himself helped his kidnappers' cause in a critical way. "When they got to the safe house, Fangio was nervous," attested Ray. "They told him not to worry, that they had nothing against him, that all we wanted was to show [the world] that we don't want Batista. He reacted very well. His only concern was that when we released him, [Batista's forces] might kill him and then they would blame us, and no one would be the wiser." Realizing that Fangio was right, two key members of Resistencia Cívica, Carlos Lechuga, a columnist for the normally pro-Batista apologist paper *El Mundo,* and Raúl Roa, arranged for Fangio to be dropped off at the Argentine embassy.[47]

Although *Bohemia*'s once valiant coverage became weaker and more abstract as the war intensified, editors characterized the kidnapping of Fangio as representative of the rebelliousness of all Cubans and a sign that citizens had simply had enough. "No se puede tapar el sol con un dedo" (One cannot hide the sun with one's finger), they wrote, a traditional Cuban phrase.[48] Agustín Tamargo titled an otherwise vague article rebuking government terror "The Hour of Truth." In it, he refuted officials' claims that journalists like him were responsible for "fomenting rebellion and swirling the pot of disorder." Rebellion, he argued, was a *reaction* to injustice, not the result of brainwashing. Cubans were not children, after all—they were patriots.[49]

The impact of such operations should not be underestimated. While censorship prevailed nationally for most of the last two years of the war, accounts of torture by police became commonplace on urban streets, attested to by the appearance of clearly tortured cadavers.[50] In addition, reports of security forces overstepping their bounds by raiding the homes of innocent citizens did more than simply compound public outrage; they validated the actions of clandestinos as defensive rather than offensive moves, undertaken to save Cuba from unspeakable savagery.

The well-documented case of Esther Lina Milanés Dantin, a fifty-year-old schoolteacher, forged new paths for recruitment, sympathy, and support among citizens for the underground network of the 26th of July. So severely did police brutalize Esther Lina during interrogation at a police station for her knowledge about an alleged weapons cache that her experience inspired the medical division of Resistencia Cívica to investigate. Doctors of the Colegio Médico Nacional then went public with their findings. Another victim arrested and questioned at the same time as Esther Lina, a young man named Enrique Zamorano, lost his ear from the severity of the blows. Esther Lina detailed her horrifying account to Emilio Guede, disguised as a doctor, from her hospital bed. The photographs doctors took of Esther Lina's wounds confirmed that she had been whipped, beaten, and punched, but they did not tell the worst part of the story. "Me introdujeron un hierro por la vagina," she told Emilio Guede, "y me dijeron: 'Habla, vieja puta, que te vamos a perforar'" (They put an iron rod into my vagina and said, "Talk, old whore, or we are going to perforate you with this").[51]

Guede and doctors affiliated with Resistencia Cívica denounced the case to Cuba's Supreme Court, the United Nations, the Organization of American States, and the International Press Society (headed by Jules Dubois). These moves eventually gained Esther Lina diplomatic asylum. But Resistencia Cívica's fearless protests also ensured that the horrors that she had endured could not be excluded from the Cuban press. *Prensa Libre* and *El Mundo* both carried denunciations of the barbarity of the case; *Bohemia* featured a full-length interview with its victim. "The tortures of a helpless teacher became the best portrait of those who ruled Cuba," concluded Emilio Guede years later.[52]

The primary reason the clandestinos' press and spectacles of protest mattered lay in the striking contradiction that they represented to the version of reality churned out by Batista's publicity machine in the United States. Beginning in 1957, Batista began issuing a weekly newsletter called *Report on Cuba* from a rented suite at the Dupont Circle Building in Washington, D.C. Businessmen like the Braga brothers, owners of the Czarnikow-Rionda Company, along with other U.S. investors with influence over U.S. policy became regular subscribers. Typical of how *Report on Cuba* described events in Cuba, the seventh edition of the newsletter opened with the following statement: "In recent months, the followers of Prío Socarrás and Fidel Castro have attempted to capitalize on one of the oldest devices in psychological warfare—the torture story. Individuals, who have allegedly undergone torture at the hands of Cuban authorities, are produced for interview by reporters. Their stories all follow the same pattern—surprise arrest in the middle of the night, psychological pressure to induce terror and physical abuse to extract confession. In every case, however, the heroic 'victim' has managed to resist these pressures, strengthened by his devotion to 'the cause.'" Such "stories," concluded the article, "are without basis in fact and are utter and ridiculous falsehoods" apparent to anyone "who takes the time to perform even the most superficial analysis." In short, they were all lies; one had to be stupid to believe them. Even more importantly, the newsletter concluded, such things could simply not be taking place because "Cuba's laws are patterned after those of the United States. Many of her police officials have been trained in the US."[53]

The same agency published a supposedly objective book on the revolutionaries in Cuba titled *Communist Activities of the Cuban Rebels.*[54] Perhaps the most convincing part of the book, given the PSP's continued resistance to endorsing armed struggle of any kind, let alone that of Fidel Castro's movement, was the following section title: "The Communists Want Cuba."[55]

Back in Cuba, Batista was once again promising to hold general elections in November 1958. His handpicked candidate for the presidency, former minister of education Andrés Rivero Agüero, had taken to repeating the mayor of Daytona Beach's analogy in describing Batista. "An example of Abraham Lincoln," contended Rivero Agüero, Batista was the only man capable of holding a nation together that the rebels wanted to tear apart.[56]

In many ways, the work of Batista's publicity agents in the United States shared a great deal of logic with Rivero Agüero's article. He compared Fulgencio Batista to an *American* president rather than José Martí and the fight against Batista's dictatorship to a reductionist view of the U.S. Civil War rather than Cuba's revolution of 1933. A radical departure from previous batistiano discourse, these were clearly arguments of last resort. The insurrection of the clandestinos, the guerrillas led by Fidel, and the growing solidarity of much of the citizenry with armed struggle were *not* going away; on the contrary, the war was intensifying with each passing day, despite Batista's public denials. In fact, although they still did not alter their position of endorsing *la lucha de masas* (mass struggle) through strikes and the actions of labor until the late fall of 1958, even the PSP had to admit that state repression had only led to more support for the rebels, not less.[57] Who were these activists? What was it like to live and survive a largely undeclared urban war? Although the answers to such questions can only be partial at best, the testimonies of top clandestinos reveal a world of purposefully unsung and hidden heroes whose courage and commitment *did* make Cuba revolutionary in new ways.

Life and Death Among the Clandestinos

Manolo Ray's successes in Havana soon prompted Faustino Pérez to ask him to head the 26th of July Movement's action and sabotage units nationwide. Clandestino members of Resistencia Cívica and Ray's units then began a practice that anonymous citizens soon joined: they started throwing helium-filled black and red balloons off rooftops and balconies, sometimes in coordinated stunts that filled Havana's skies with the colors of the 26th of July.[58] When Manolo conveyed this story to me from his home in San Juan, Puerto Rico, in late February 2009, sheer delight filled his face. Later, over lunch with his wife and collaborator Aurora, Manolo said, "That's when I knew that the rebellion and protests of *la clandestinidad* could produce more than power. They could produce mutual feelings of joy."

Echoes of joy, or at least a good sense of humor, saturated Aurora Chacón de Ray's memories of her husband's days in the revolutionary underground as well. For more than a year when Manolo was known as Batista's most wanted man in Havana, Aurora endured the pressure of being a wife with four children whose husband was likely to die at any moment and whose home was raided and sacked multiple times by Esteban Ventura, Batista's hated chief of the national police. Deeply Catholic, although married to an agnostic, Aurora relied equally on her faith and terrific acting skills to convince Ventura that she had not seen her husband in months and was disgusted by his appalling behavior. The truth was quite contrary to Aurora's dramatic, often teary-eyed testimonials in the squalid interrogation rooms of police stations.

On the occasion of the first raid, when Aurora and her children awoke to the sound of Ventura himself knocking her front door to the ground, Aurora's aunt—a lawyer and seller of 26th of July Movement bonds—ran to her servant's bathroom to flush a purseful of bonds down the toilet. Meanwhile, Aurora played the serene, if indignant, housewife. Interrogated by Ventura in the hold of the local jail more than once, Aurora focused on her rosary beads. At the jail she saw dozens of indigent lottery-ticket salesmen who relied on regular stipends from Batista in exchange for serving as a network of *chivatos,* that is, snitches and spies. The experience shocked but also educated her on the despair of the urban poor. A likely victim of precisely such chivatos, Aurora also empathized with them.

Perhaps most impressive of all, however, was Aurora's love for her husband and the daring she showed on his behalf: notified unexpectedly of Manolo's location through notes passed by strangers on the street or in Havana's many five-and-dime stores, Aurora spent whole weekends with him, encounters that she and Manolo described as deeply romantic and eternally bonding. In many ways, Manolo's survival and Aurora's gift for convincing Ventura, one of the most infamously vicious members of Batista's police, that she was innocent were nothing short of miraculous. The clear and ever present danger that clandestinos endured meant that they intentionally led double lives, telling their lovers, husbands, or wives as little as possible about their activism so that when they were detained or interrogated—a virtually inevitable occurrence—the honesty of their ignorance would, hopefully, convince authorities and ensure their release.

Manolo Ray and Aurora were married before the struggle began, but Vicente Baez had to marry his wife in secret, between two and three o'clock in the morning at the Iglesia de la Virgen de la Caridad del Cobre. Baez and his wife took no photographs of their wedding; in fact, no photographs exist of Baez throughout the course of his activism, beginning in 1952 through the end of the war. According to Baez, he chose this church to marry because its two priests, Father Eduardo Boza-Masvidal and Father Madrigal, did more for the 26th of July Movement than any others. Boza-Masvidal allowed the underground to hide weapons inside the church, and Father Madrigal went much further, "traveling to Miami on a weekly basis and returning with his cassock stuffed with weapons."[59]

The risks taken by priests like these were undoubtedly heroic acts, but so were simple actions such as meeting and discussing future operations among members of the 26th of July urban underground. Almost always clandestinos accomplished this by walking, one member beside the other, for blocks at a time and then taking turns walking and talking with another comrade until all members of a cell agreed or were duly informed. When clandestinos met as a group in safe houses, the homes always had to have a back door: in case of a police raid, the entire group could escape through the rear. Faustino Pérez saved himself from arrest more than once by jumping off a balcony or from a window, remembered Baez. In February 1957, the one time that Mario Llerena met with Frank País, Faustino Pérez, and the tiny cell of activists in Havana that País hoped to organize, Llerena left so quickly he forgot his suit jacket. Inside the pocket was his identification card. The mistake forced him into exile in New York, where until January 1958, he directed the headquarters office of the 26th of July Movement.[60] Incredibly, Manolo Ray found sanctuary in safe houses close to police stations. The strategy worked perfectly, he said, chuckling with delight: "¡Nadie se imaginaba que nosotros estabamos allí!" (Nobody would have imagined that *we* were there!)[61] Ray also counted on sympathetic labor activists allied to the Trotskyist wing of Cuba's Communist movement, a group much maligned by the pro-Stalinist core of the PSP and later jailed after Fidel Castro rose to power in 1959 and adopted Soviet-style policies of state. One such Trotskyist, Roberto Acosta Hechaverría, provided Ray sanctuary in his home for over a month. A child at the time, Acosta's son Rafael remembers fondly how Ray, secretly tucked away on the floor under Rafael's bed, entertained him nightly with bedtime stories.[62]

Years later, Manolo Ray, Emilio Guede, Carlos Franqui, and Vicente Baez all agreed in their analysis of the two greatest weaknesses the clandestine side of the 26th of July Movement faced. The first of these was the absence of open discussions of race and the exclusion of a radical statement promising the enforcement of Cuba's anti-discrimination laws after the rebels' triumph. Members of the "humble classes," Vicente Baez explained, have always been open to serving as informers for dictatorial states for two reasons: one is their poverty and the other is that they have no evidence that they would actually advance in a system stacked against them. As a result, they often prefer to work within it.

Publicly, the 26th of July Movement gave blacks little reason to hope that racial concerns would be prioritized. "In 1958, during the carnival season in Oriente province, there was a conga that said: *los negros pa'a la conga, los blanquitos pa'a la Sierra* [the blacks are for the conga line, the little whites are for the Sierra]."[63] Indeed, the 26th of July Movement guerrillas went so far as to adopt the racist image of Batista as a "monkey" on which the anti-Batista Auténtico propaganda had relied earlier. Attesting to this was Carlos Franqui, founder of Radio Rebelde. Obviously ashamed when he recounted the story, Franqui recalled that as late as the fall of 1958, el Quinteto Rebelde popularized a song whose lyrics denounced Batista as a *mono* and encouraged listeners to unite around Fidel. Still available for purchase today in collections of historic songs of the Cuban Revolution, the song is titled "Qué Se Vaya el Mono" (Monkey, Get Out of Here). The lyrics of the chorus read:

> Que se vaya el mono
> no lo quiero ver
> porque toda Cuba estamos con Fidel
>
> (Monkey, get out of here
> I don't want to see him around here anymore
> because in all of Cuba, we are with Fidel).[64]

Far more problematic, however, as Ray, Guede, Franqui, and Baez made clear, was the distrust that key guerrilla leaders, particularly Che Guevara, Raúl Castro, and even Fidel Castro himself, held for the clandestinos. Well documented and analyzed by Julia Sweig in her pioneering book, *Inside the Cuban Revolution,* these tensions derived from ideological, personal, and tactical differences. They never subsided, although they remained submerged for the duration of the war, but increased due to two factors: first, the death of Frank País in the summer of 1957, and second, the failure of a planned general strike in April 1958, an action coordinated by the 26th of July underground. País knitted together both wings of the movement because he was the person most responsible for its organization and the guerrillas' survival, an indisputable point acknowledged by Fidel. The strike mattered not only because many top guerrillas blamed clandestinos for its failure; it mattered because afterward the balance of authority and power to make decisions within the movement shifted abruptly and permanently from the urban underground to the guerrillas.[65]

Guerrilla leaders called clandestinos El Llano (the Plains), which to the latter was an insulting term implying that, in the cities, the enemy could be easily identified and therefore easily defeated. Indeed, "on the plains," so such Sierra-centric logic went, one did not necessarily even need to hide. To anyone in the urban underground, nothing could have been further from the truth. "There was never, never, never anyone whom we [the actual members of so-called El Llano] called 'del llano,'" insisted Baez. The term and the secondary status it implied was an invention not of Batista's army, but of the clandestinos' own allies in the war, the guerrillas.[66] The term was also derogatory because it implied patent disregard for the sacrifices that the clandestinos made and the dangers they suffered. Many clandestinos encountered this disregard firsthand when, quemados (literally, burned out) because they had been identified by police, the national directorate authorized them to join the guerrillas in the Sierra and, ironically, seek safe harbor there. When Baez once asked foreign television journalist Bob Taber what being in the Sierra was like versus being in the cities, he replied candidly: "Well, to tell you the truth, a herd of white elephants cannot be seen in the Sierra Maestra."[67] In other words, the dense foliage, rugged terrain, and absence of population centers and infrastructure in the Sierra meant that fighters there encountered virtually no security forces. The area's isolation insulated them from attacks because they were hard to spot; their tactical mobility only added to the naturally protective barriers of the forest and mountains.

The cities, rife not only with police but with chivatos (disguised as beggars or lottery ticket salesmen) and other paid spies, made for an entirely dangerous environment. Once a clandestino had been arrested, convicted, and sentenced to jail for revolutionary activities, there was no second chance. For this reason, activists like Baez and David Salvador, a labor leader who forged a link between the anti-Batista sectors of the CTC and the 26th of July Movement, lived in constant fear for their lives. On one occasion, when Marcelo Fernández informed Vicente Baez that Fidel doubted the propaganda section had suffered many losses, an irate Vicente had a complete list of twenty-two killed in the course of the first few months of the war sent to Fidel. The total number of people in the propaganda section never rose to more than thirty-five at the time, meaning that 80 percent of Baez's trusted comrades had been killed.[68] Others, like Enrique Oltuski, confronted doubt and disdain for the underground's efforts head-on. Although key rebel leader Camilo Cienfuegos was very much an urbanite from Havana who had spent long stretches of time abroad, especially in bohemian New York, the Argentine Che Guevara had never seen any other part of Cuba besides the Sierra. Ignorance coupled with prejudice against the "bourgeoisie" to color Che's negative attitude toward the clandestinos on whose support his life and the material comforts of the guerrillas depended. Thus, according to Oltuski, when Guevara and Cienfuegos began heading west in the late months of the war, Che's prejudice led him to believe that the PSP had been responsible for sending him critical supplies, not the clandestine members of his own movement.[69]

Beyond the material aid and logistical support clandestinos provided Fidel's rebels of the Sierra was the very specific role that the former played in building an image of the guerrillas as morally impeccable and miraculously indestructible. This they did with the aid of foreign journalists. Their reports gave the guerrillas much-needed traction in developing discourses and tactics that addressed the needs and expectations of local, national, and international audiences simultaneously.

Clandestinos primarily subverted Batista's representation of reality by disrupting the economy and undermining the sense of "normalcy" so critical to the continuation of the regime. They also made possible what national observers called Fidel Castro's immediate "apotheosis" in the first days of January 1959 by carefully cultivating the terrain of citizens' revolutionary imagination. By late 1958, clandestinos' efforts had made the mountain rebels a cause célèbre: Fidel received dozens of famous visitors to the Sierra, not just political representatives of once passive or openly hostile political parties, but prominent figures in the entertainment industry, including Havana's top cabaret stars such as Pura Pradier and her musician boyfriend (figure 23).

Most important, thanks to the clandestinos who served as contacts, guides, and guards, Castro's original guerrilla band established ties to foreign journalists, and one in particular: a Hungarian-born, self-taught, freelance photographer and former U.S. military intelligence agent in Europe, Andrew St. George.[70] However reluctant Castro portrayed his revolutionaries to be in the months he spent with St. George at his side, revolution was revolution, and both of them knew it. Making revolution acceptable for all, Cubans and Americans alike, was a primary, challenging goal—one that the clandestinos and the guerrillas took on simultaneously and in highly effective ways.

Figure 23. Pura Pradier and her boyfriend were two of many media stars who trekked to isolated, secret locations in the Sierra Maestra in shows of solidarity with Fidel Castro's guerrillas. Word—and especially images—of such visits added prestige, significance, and glamour to the rebels' domestic and international allure. (Andrew St. George Papers, courtesy of Yale University Manuscripts and Archives)

Andrew St. George and Fidel Castro's Rebels with a Cause

Fidel's guerrillas consciously imitated the methods of Cuba's nineteenth-century mambises in order to claim the fulfillment of a historically frustrated moral mission dear to the Cuban people. As detailed in the latter parts of this chapter, they also refuted the legitimacy of Batista's martial rule and political theatrics by creating a real-life alternative state and society in miniature, a simulacrum of the world that Fidel's vision of revolution would make. In transmitting glimpses of that world into the global imagination, however, Fidel and his followers presented themselves not as fearsome warriors but as honorable, serious, and likeable living legends. Their intense, unprecedented interactions with local peasants led them to act as allies of the troops but also as positive publicity agents, often before the cameras and notebooks of journalists and eyewitnesses sent by the clandestinos.

Just as Frank País had personally escorted Herbert Matthews to the Sierra

Maestra in February 1957, so clandestinos brought an unknown would-be free-lance reporter named Andrew St. George to the mountains a month later.[71] Their contribution to the process of getting the story and transmitting it to the public speaks undeniably to the capacity and centrality of clandestinos in ensuring the guerrillas' legitimation. But their invisibility in achieving this also reveals how the clandestinos themselves were inadvertently to blame for the secondary status that the guerrillas and others ascribed to them. Behind every moral victory that Fidel Castro scored in public attitudes toward the struggle stood legions of ac-tivists that made it possible, mostly by bringing foreign journalists to the Sierra and getting them out again. To put it mildly, foreign journalists were Castro's secret weapon.

The most prized of these was undoubtedly Andrew St. George. Herbert Mat-thews of the *New York Times* spent less than a day with Fidel and his men in the hills to produce his famous February 1957 cover story (and doctored pho-tograph); by comparison, St. George made six trips to the Sierra, none of them lasting less than a month, several of them as long as two.

Recalling the conditions that the eighteen surviving members of the *Granma* expedition faced in the winter of 1957 when Matthews visited the Sierra Maestra, Che Guevara pointedly remarked two years later, "The presence of a foreign jour-nalist, American [by] preference, was more important to us at the time than a mil-itary victory."[72] Indeed, Fidel personally recognized the unique role of journalists when he conferred gold medals on both Matthews and St. George as well as eleven other foreign reporters for their service to the revolution in April 1959.[73] Yet if Matthews had humiliated the Batista regime for claiming that Fidel Castro was long dead, St. George fulfilled a far more important and enduring task: he served as an imperial witness to Fidel's and his troops' paradoxical self-construction as reluctant, altruistic revolutionaries forced to defend a pure people against a barbarous tyrant. By lining up the published narratives with the much richer unedited stories St. George produced visually and orally, we discover Fidel, Raúl, and others performing roles derived from national historic myths and the mass culture of television and Hollywood movies for a singular purpose: they wanted to cast their methods of violence as well as their very real plan of economic restructuring into an acceptable, civilized, nonthreatening, and often downright entertaining light (figure 24). Doing so served the needs and expectations of both a foreign audience and citizens who might otherwise have dismissed the armed rebels as political misfits or untrustworthy radicals.

Figure 24. Andrew St. George, on his first visit to the Sierra Maestra in the spring of 1957, interviewing Fidel Castro during their initial meeting. Camilo Cienfuegos, thin and suffering from dysentery, stands behind the pair. (Cuban Revolution Collection, courtesy of Yale University Manuscripts and Archives)

At the same time, however, as St. George and his rebel collaborators knew, the real-life implications of guerrilla rule and redistributive actions were never lost on local peasants in the expanding liberated zone of Oriente, let alone nervously compliant foreign company executives or native landlords.

Living, marching, and sacrificing with the guerrillas, St. George produced thousands of unique, detailed, and emotionally moving images of guerrilla life and culture, many of which became central to the clandestine press of Fidel's movement and allied groups like Raúl Roa's Resistencia Cívica. St. George's first portrait of Fidel Castro, taken in April 1957 and titled *Christ and the Cannon,* was published no fewer than 120 times by September 1958.[74] St. George also smuggled a cropped photo taken by friend and fellow journalist Robert Taber of Fidel, Raúl, Universo Sánchez, and other survivors of *Granma* back to New York for use as background on the 26th of July Movement's colorful *bonos* (war bonds) in 1957 (figure 25); the image lives on today, emblazoned on the corner of every daily edition of the Communist Party organ *Granma.*[75]

Figure 25. In Cuba, the 26th of July Movement sold war bonds that ranged between an inch and two inches in size: this made them easier to swallow or destroy should an activist selling the bonds be caught by Batista's police. U.S. affiliates of the M-26-7 adopted the opposite approach, as this bond shows, selling delightfully colored, nearly foot-long bonds that proclaimed the triumph would happen that very year—*any* year the war bond was sold. (Ernesto Chávez Collection, courtesy of Special and Area Studies Collections, University of Florida)

Alongside one of St. George's most influential articles for *Coronet* magazine, Fidel published "Why We Fight," a manifesto subsequently reprinted in eleven different publications across Latin America.[76] By putting contemporary published accounts in dialogue with largely untouched, "raw" archival sources, this analysis discovers a different story, now mostly forgotten, than the one that the press, mainstream or clandestine, wanted to tell about rebel activities in the Sierra.[77]

St. George came to see the many Cuban spies, guides, and foot soldiers he lived with as friends, even family.[78] When Andrew and his wife Jean named their first son Andrew Fidel, Castro offered to serve as godfather and baptize him after the victory when, he assumed, St. George would naturally move his family to Havana.[79] Yet if Andrew St. George insisted on political and emotional complexity, his spin-savvy editors banked on simplicity. Revisiting the visual and textual narratives constructed through these publications while digging deeply into St. George's personal archives reveals the origins of Fidel's and the guerrillas' shared messianic mystique as a collaborative by-product of their own intentions and design.

As Fidel explained to St. George through handwritten responses in April

1957, the guerrillas faced no real enemy besides Batista and his administration; not even Batista's soldiers were to blame: "The only corrupt thing in Cuba is the tyranny [of Batista]. Because our people are wholesome and highly moral. . . . Unfortunately, before the arms of the dictatorship, one also must have recourse to arms. . . . The army is tired of . . . Batista. . . . The soldiers live under constant surveillance and the terror of the military police. We, in fighting for the freedom of all the people, also fight for the freedom of the soldiers."[80] Moreover, it was Batista, not Fidel or his movement, that put Cuba at risk of becoming pro-Communist: "The idea that we are pro-Communist is about as absurd as telling the Cuban people that I have died more than 20 times" (figure 26).[81] Not only did businessmen have more to fear from Batista's nationalization plans, remarked Fidel in two recorded interviews, but the best witnesses to the "democratic and nationalist" nature of his movement were foreign reporters like Herbert Matthews, CBS's Bob Taber and, of course, St. George himself.[82] Punctuated with dozens of photos that clandestinos helped St. George smuggle out of Cuba, Miami's *Sierra Maestra,* the 26th of July's newspaper, seconded this with a two-page spread. It reminded readers of the Communist Party's condemnation of armed protest against the dictator in the article, titled "Batista: Friend and Protector of Communists."[83]

Fidel's concern with assuaging readers' fears over possible nationalization became one of three consistent themes echoed across St. George's most influential publications. In his own essay for *Coronet* and two taped interviews, Fidel dismissed "for the record" nationalization of any investments and utilities "as a cumbersome instrument . . . that does not seem to make the state any stronger, yet enfeebles private enterprise."[84] A second theme was his consistent denial of any political ambitions: he was far too young at thirty and then thirty-one to run for president, Fidel argued; the Cuban Constitution of 1940 expressly forbade it.[85] He also needed a break after the war. "I have never thought of being President of Cuba. After we win, I am going to return to the Sierra Maestra, building roads and hospitals as we have promised."[86]

In addition, Fidel himself often presented his followers as committed but reluctant and therefore disinterested revolutionaries, soldiers who aspired to peace in the theater of the Sierra Maestra rather than war. Explaining this apparent paradox years later, he said: "We had to demonstrate before public opinion, and leave well established, that if there was going to be a war it was not going to be because the revolutionaries wanted one."[87] Thus, in his encounters with

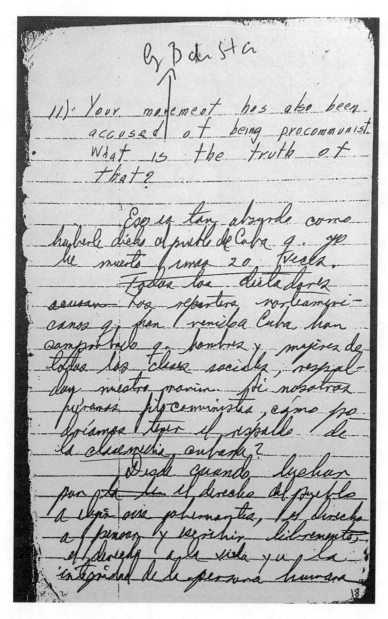

Figure 26. Andrew St. George had not mastered Spanish when he first conducted interviews with Fidel Castro in the Sierra Maestra, so he wrote down his questions in English, and Castro wrote his answers in Spanish, documenting them for the record. Fidel denied the possibility that his armed movement would establish a dictatorship or enable the formation of a Communist state. (Cuban Revolution Collection, courtesy of Yale University Manuscripts and Archives)

St. George, Fidel insisted that the rebels' struggle was not to turn the world upside down in Cuba but to restore the principles of "civilization" in the face of Batista's culture of barbarism.

For example, Fidel invented and St. George dutifully echoed far-fetched, highly fictitious claims as evidence of Batista's savagery. In St. George's first article, Fidel described the now-legendary story of Batista's soldiers torturing Abel Santamaría and providing his girlfriend Melba Hernández proof of his suffering in much more horrifying terms than any post-1959 account: St. George quoted Fidel as saying that Batista's soldiers presented Abel's testicles, not his eyes, on a plate to a horrified Melba.[88] In describing the fateful landing of the *Granma,* Fidel similarly embellished the story, explaining that eighteen survivors of the Granma "were tortured for the better part of the day and finally put to death by getting their genitals hacked off. They shrieked for a bullet, but this time the army had none."[89] A year later, St. George echoed Castro, describing the killing at the Moncada Barracks as typical of Batista's forces, "an orgy of sadism and revenge—mostly [relying on death] by castration."[90] However, in meeting batistiano fury, Fidel declared, his own forces had and would always turn the other cheek, either freeing Batista's soldiers when captured or persuading them to switch sides.

Illustrated by photos and a cover shot of Castro taken by St. George, the 26th of July Movement's official organ greatly promoted this idea. Under the title "Different Ways of Treating War Prisoners," New York's edition of *Sierra Maestra* included a picture of a government *casquito* (a helmeted soldier) standing next to a *barbudo,* a bearded guerrilla, with the caption "Batista's soldier captured by rebels, smiles assured that his life and physical integrity will be respected." Immediately below this was a photograph of a man's back, crisscrossed by scars from a severe beating. "Castro's partisan, prisoner of Batista is whipped by the men of the dictator," read the caption (figure 27).[91]

According to Manolo Ray, so successfully did the message of Batista's savagery versus Fidel's chivalry penetrate public consciousness that the movement was able to thwart Batista's censors in Cuba by openly selling postcards with similar images. Buyers then mailed them; no explanatory text was needed. It was the best free publicity the cause had yet to receive, Manolo told me in August 2008: there was no way the censors could stop the mail. "Y no nos costó ninguna gota de sangre" (And it didn't cost us even one drop of blood).[92] Six years later, I found one such postcard in an archive, featuring a man's

Figure 27. The clandestine press, distributed under censorship in Cuba and freely abroad, contended that fundamental moral differences distinguished Batista from the armed opposition. A captured batistiano soldier appears to prove this point, smiling happily beside his guerrilla captor. (Andrew St. George Papers, courtesy of Yale University Manuscripts and Archives)

back crisscrossed with the marks of an electric prod.[93] Just as Manolo Ray had described, I knew exactly what that image meant: it needed no explanation. For those accustomed to receiving tourist postcards featuring images of Cuba's sunny beaches or modern Havana skyline, the picture of a torture victim abruptly exploded expected narratives about Cuba as a hedonist, safe escape to paradise (figure 28).

The idea that Batista's men savagely whipped their rebel counterparts clearly tapped collective memories of Spanish colonial days when nineteenth-century revolutionaries like José Martí compared the political yoke that white men suffered to the dehumanizing chains of black slaves. In many other ways, however, Fidel and his followers claimed the mantle of mambises, the term used to describe Cuba's revered, often barefoot, and largely black independence fighters. At times the comparison was explicit. Resistencia Cívica, a Havana-based organization, published a centerfold of portraits of Fidel's top leaders by St. George under the title "The *Mambises* of the Sierra" in their official clandestine organ.[94] While some of the peasant recruits surely bore a ghostly resemblance to ances-

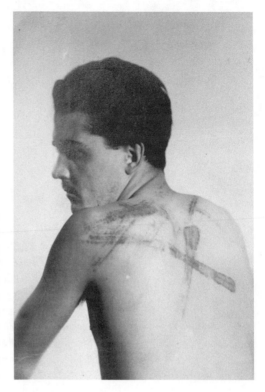

Figure 28. Symbolic of the 26th of July Movement's urban underground's means of raising awareness, this 1957 postcard featured an uncaptioned image of a civilian activist whose back displays evidence of a police beating. (Elena Kurstin Cuban Memorabilia Collection, courtesy of Special Collections, Florida International University)

tral revolutionaries, the guerrillas mostly claimed the mambises' heroic legacy through actions glossed as evidence of moral purity and impeccable honor (figure 29). In recruiting his men, for example, Fidel insisted that the simple habit of cursing, normally a favorite macho practice in Cuba, was sufficient grounds for exclusion from the rebel army. "I spent many nights watching them," said Castro of new recruits. "It is the way you do little things that really tells. When one of the boys would curse, or shout in anger, fail to obey the quiet word, I sent him home. I wanted a different army, an army of gentlemen. Not the rich or educated kind. I wanted *hidalgos,* natural gentlemen."[95]

Photographic evidence from St. George's first month-long stay with Fidel's forces in the Sierra documented the methods, culture, and selfless values of the mambises among 26th of July guerrillas; the same photographs would be reproduced repeatedly in the United States and Europe during and after the war.[96] While half of St. George's first article, published in *Look* magazine, focused on the legendary mambí method of lighting cane fields on fire, roasting and eating snakes, sleeping on the run, and setting up temporary roadblocks, the other half

Figure 29. M-26-7 guerrillas encouraged the public to make a connection between themselves and the romantic, selfless, and often penniless foot soldiers of Cuba's nineteenth-century independence wars. Andrew St. George's unstaged portraits of many peasants spoke to the authenticity of that connection. (Cuban Revolution Collection, courtesy of Yale University Manuscripts and Archives)

dealt with a less romantic side to guerrilla life.[97] First, Fidel held oath-taking ceremonies in which his original force of twelve apostles, Los Doce—really eighteen in number—asked crowds of local villagers to take pledges of "allegiance, loyalty and support" for the rebels (figure 30). As St. George noted, guajiros were mostly consigned to involuntary drudgery after taking the oath: growing crops was their *primera consigna* (first assignment); the other was bearing cargo. Fleeing the land or refusing to cultivate, Fidel made clear, were punishable acts of betrayal.[98]

Sealing this point, the rebels subsequently created a "jungle judiciary" to try local peasants who refused to take the guerrillas' side and could be accused of "banditry" for this or other offenses (figure 31).[99] For twelve days in an area called Naranjo, a five-person tribunal made up of Fidel Castro, Celia Sánchez, Camilo Cienfuegos, Juan Almeida, and Humberto Sori Marín, former vice president of the Inter-American Bar Association, presided over the "court-martial," conviction, and sentencing of dozens of men, all of whom Fidel called "bandits."[100]

Figure 30. One of many oath-taking ceremonies Fidel Castro and his original troop of eighteen men had local peasants make in the Sierra Maestra, late spring 1957. Obvious to St. George was the fact that the peasants had little choice but to swear allegiance to Fidel and his cause. (Cuban Revolution Collection, courtesy of Yale University Manuscripts and Archives)

The rebels also held "long talks with *guajiros*" to explain the process, "an essential facet of Castro's strategy."[101]

Relying on the same term that Batista used to define Fidel's men and the Spanish had used to describe mambises, Fidel defined these peasants as "bandits" for having seized resources left in the wake of a rebel encounter with government soldiers; over such resources only the rebels could claim to control, he explained. "Bandit gangs spring up wherever the government troops withdraw," St. George reported. "These outlaw 'wolf packs' are Castro's biggest headache. Unpoliced, they pillage helpless villages for money, weapons, women. 'If we don't keep order in our liberated zone,' says Castro, 'the people suffer. Our revolution is tarnished.' Prisoners shown here [in accompanying photographs] were bandit chiefs, captured after a week of relentless tracking by rebels. . . . The jungle has no prisons. The penalty for extreme crimes was

Figure 31. Castro's isolated band of guerrillas formed what Andrew St. George called
a five-person "jungle judiciary" to arrest, try, and execute dozens of men whom local
peasants accused of rape, theft, and even murder. Internationally renowned legal scholar
turned freedom fighter Dr. Humberto Sori Marín, Camilo Cienfuegos, and Celia Sánchez
joined Castro in interrogating a defendant on trial in March 1957, while René Rodríguez,
a key urban activist in Santiago, looks on. Outside the frame was Juan Almeida, a black
veteran of Fidel's Moncada attack, who served as the fifth judge. (Cuban Revolution
Collection, courtesy of Yale University Manuscripts and Archives)

death."[102] Illustrated with photographs of a confessed rapist and leader of a
twenty-two-member local gang, the article excused the rebels' "stern jungle
justice." For "mountain people and the puritanical Castro," rape was "an in-
tolerable crime."[103] Indeed, according to the article, rape was the *only* crime
meriting execution. St. George's private notes to editors and unpublished photographs told a much darker tale, however.

Clearly documented in St. George's many film reels and memos was the
dual function of the trials and the executions. First, the trials themselves served
notice to local peasants that by *acting* like a state, the guerrillas were becoming
one in practical terms, not just in words or in their own minds. Second, initial

Figure 32. Castro's armed followers had never killed anyone when they arrived in the Sierra Maestra. The executions of "bandits" tried and convicted by the jungle judiciary served to harden the men. (Cuban Revolution Collection, courtesy of Yale University Manuscripts and Archives)

execution squads, almost always led by Raúl Castro, seemed to include every available armed male member of a troop, except for Fidel and Father Sardiñas, a Catholic priest who offered sacramental last rites to prisoners before they were tied to a tree and shot (figure 32). Judging from the shocked look on many of the executioners' faces after their first execution in May 1957, the experience of killing such prisoners was meant to harden rebel troops in the general absence of encounters with Batista's soldiers, the official enemy (figure 33).

St. George's first trip to the Sierra Maestra, his subsequent collaboration with the clandestine press of the 26th of July Movement, and his 15 June 1957 story in Mexico City's splashy magazine *Mañana* clearly pleased Fidel. In a handwritten letter delivered by Dr. Miguel Angel Santos Busch in late June 1957, Fidel personally invited St. George back to the Sierra as "the rebel army's 'regular combat correspondent.'"[104] Thus, on 11 October 1957, Celia Sánchez, who used her father's home as a safe house, issued St. George a handwritten safe conduct pass and a pink paper flag labeled "Prensa" for him to wear.[105]

Ultimately, the rebels were able to extend the reach of their liberated zone to encompass most of southern Oriente province by the summer of 1958. At that time, St. George spent more than two months undertaking a two-hundred-mile guided tour of the impressively expanded rebel zone, especially Raúl Castro's Segundo Frente Frank País, or Second Front, named after the critical clandestino leader of Santiago whom police had murdered the year before. Executions had become an uncomfortable norm and Raúl Castro, according to St. George's private notes, was the rebels' "heaviest-handed executioner."[106] Fidel and Raúl's

Figure 33. Participants' stunned emotional reactions to the very first executions leave little doubt that they suddenly realized they were facing the horrors of war. (Cuban Revolution Collection, courtesy of Yale University Manuscripts and Archives)

forces had also adopted a "peculiar rebel punishment: mock execution. Though none of [the condemned] died, rebels lined them up, fired over their heads, then shouted 'One hasn't been hit!' to make each blindfolded boy think he survived by accident, [and] would get it in the second fusillade."[107] Raúl Castro had personally tied the boys to trees and directed the scene. St. George witnessed similar tactics on a march toward El Cobre. Intercepted by a rebel platoon, a "suspicious wayfarer" fell in fright when a rifle was fired over his head and Captain Rigoberto Ramirez menaced him with a pistol, "firing past his ear. . . . The threat of summary execution was rebels' only means of coercing information from suspects."[108]

In notes accompanying a "situationer" memo, a narrative describing the context in which a journalist photographed particular scenes, to NBC, St. George commented on photographs now preserved at Yale University: "Framed in red at bottom is probably the best execution sequence I ever photographed in rebel camp; for technical reasons, it was not published. The victim is a Chinese-Creole half-caste named Henrique (Quiqui) Chang, an apparently depraved sex deviate who invaded the police-less rebel area with a small gang of his own and proceeded to rack up an impressive number of rapes on peasant girls. An open-air rebel court martial convicted him of 21 confessed violations [and the death of one] protesting husband." The same sheet then described St. George's photograph of an official bulletin signed by Raúl Castro "listing suspected 'government spies' executed at Soledad Sugarmill in a single day . . . and urging other rebel field commanders to proceed against 'spies' with similar severity." Seconded by classified reports at the U.S. consulate in Santiago, the list showed thirty-nine names.[109]

Although St. George was initially sympathetic to the rebels' actions, his perspective evolved over several trips: it was not just or even mostly rapists and common criminals whom rebel judges tried and convicted but chivatos, government informers and spies, many of them women or girls. "Hunting down 'government spies'—i.e. anyone who gives army [the] time of the day—is perhaps top-priority rebel occupation," St. George wrote in an internal memo describing pictures taken during his second trip in the summer of 1957. The practice was common enough that St. George documented it frequently, often suppressing a rising sense of concern. In notes describing photographs his editors considered too bloody to publish, St. George wrote, "Suspected army spy captured by patrol is threatened with shooting and shot by accident. It's a botched but typical casualty of this family war of accidents and errors."[110]

Accidents and errors, when they affected the lives of alleged "girl spies," could be traumatic. St. George photographed "a chubby girl" as she stood "dejectedly between guards" while Juan Almeida interrogated her and local witnesses "to determine her degree of guilt" before remanding her to the rebel Judge Advocate's Office for trial and most likely death.[111] Particularly disturbing to St. George was the case of Olga Suárez, captured when rebels took the town of Bueycito, population twelve thousand. Characterized as a "a pharmacist, divorced, with three children," Olga stood accused of being a chivato, informer.[112] The woman's fate haunted St. George; although he later published her anxiety-ridden portrait in *Der Spiegel*, he refused to witness her killing (figure 34).[113]

While the vast majority of peasants may have sided with the guerrillas, tracking down and killing the local "bandits," which St. George described as Fidel's "biggest headache" was clearly bloody business. According to U.S. citizen turned guerrilla Neill Macaulay, exterminating spies—on flimsy evidence—

Figure 34. Although the evidence against her was slim and mostly hearsay, Olga Suárez faced execution by a self-appointed guerrilla tribunal. In this portrait, she struggles to compose herself only minutes before she was shot. (Andrew St. George Papers, courtesy of Yale University Manuscripts and Archives)

formed a significant part of the rebels' regular duties throughout the campaign, a fact that disturbed him for years.[114] If the identification of "chivatos" was as arbitrary as Macaulay's gruesome account suggests, it is possible that the protracted trials and methodical executions to which Fidel subjected the accused when St. George first visited his troops may have been staged for show rather than representative of the usual practices.

By the summer of 1958, the hardships of war and the creation of a revolutionary state that accepted no neutral side had quickly become facts that Andrew St. George and 26th of July guerrilla leaders neither could nor wanted to deny. However, they continued to cast local and international perceptions of the violence that shaped events in a soft, romantic light. The generosity and humanity of individual rebel soldiers clearly struck St. George. He struggled hard to document their actions and character (figure 35). Reminiscent of how clandestinos' personal sacrifices and fears remained unknown, none of St. George's most moving portraits and written descriptions of rank-and-file soldiers were ever published. At the same time, the military initiatives of Fidel and Raúl Castro

Figure 35. By 1958, the numeric expansion of rebel forces and their control of territory laid the foundations for rule in the small towns and hamlets of eastern Oriente province. Taken in early September on the vigil of the Feast of the Virgin of Charity, Cuba's most sacred patron, this image reveals how warm interactions and shared cultural values began to forge the guerrillas' legitimacy from the ground up. (Cuban Revolution Collection, courtesy of Yale University Manuscripts and Archives)

reached new heights of bravado with respect to the United States and local businesses, foreign and domestic. On one hand, they continued efforts to recruit imperial witnesses to the rebel cause through Hollywoodesque performances that St. George and others now filmed. On the other hand, they also steeped those efforts in moral and political righteousness, claiming the mantle of a Christian mission but also establishing the sovereignty of the rebel state in the Sierra Maestra with unprecedented martial fury.

Christian Disciples or Bad Boys and Glamour Girls of La Sierra Maestra?

What garnered the rebels their place on the world stage was not simply the romantic image of successful, daring warfare that they forged in the media but the practical success of their guerrilla methods, at both a symbolic and an experiential level. At first, the rebels depended on the food and hospitality of the region's impoverished peasants for their very survival. Fairly soon, however, the guerrillas began a campaign of raids on local ranches and estates from which they exacted "taxes" and other financial contributions to the revolutionary cause.[115] In exchange, the guerrillas provided receipts and bonds payable upon achieving victory, much as Cuba's historical mambises had once done.[116] As their strength and numbers grew, so did their bravado. Their army drew overt parallels to the kind of world that would result once the revolution against Batista and the "Old Republic" of U.S. manipulation, political scoundrels, and scandals was won.

By far the most important military battles of the war, in this sense, were those that took place in the first two weeks of August 1958, when the rebel army cast out all remnants of Batista's forces from the Sierra Maestra. Suffering only twenty-five deaths and forty-eight wounded, the rebels won a resounding victory in the face of overwhelming air power and ground forces. By the end of the battle of Jigue, 231 casquitos lay dead; the rebels took 422 others prisoner.[117] In a deliberate performance of genuine generosity—precisely the virtue Batista had so long claimed *he* had shown the opposition—Fidel ordered the captured POWs turned over to the Red Cross. This act alone persuaded some batistiano soldiers to stay and work for the rebel cause. One critical example was Braulio Coroneaux, a machine gunner who had defended El Cuartel Moncada during the assault led by Castro in 1953. Amazingly, Coroneaux was able to interpret the secret codes the rebels had captured from the enemy, successfully duping government military aircraft into bombarding their own battalions.[118]

Over several trips of two months each in the summer and fall of 1958, St. George documented the radical gains in political control, military power, and organizational effectiveness the rebels now enjoyed. He was clearly astonished. No longer were Fidel's men simply holding up motorists and paralyzing commercial traffic on Oriente's highways so that they could set fire to the sugarcane fields around Bayamo.[119] The rebels had opened eight field hospitals that treated injured revolutionaries and local peasants alike: "Extending medical aid to civilian population has always been rebel custom; a humanitarian gesture, it has also proved strongest political lure in an area where the ratio of hospital beds is 8,500 inhabitants for every bed, and where doctors are not seen for decades" (figure 36).[120] The rebels founded elementary schools for barefoot, half-naked children (figure 37). They established toll roads, set up agencies

Figure 36. By building hospitals and local schools in the massive liberated zone under rebel army control, the 26th of July Movement proved its commitment to transforming Cuba's long-neglected impoverished rural areas. (Andrew St. George Papers, courtesy of Yale University Manuscripts and Archives)

Figure 37. The rebels also crafted in people's hearts and minds the image
of a real-life alternative state. (Andrew St. George Papers, courtesy of
Yale University Manuscripts and Archives)

for the taxation and "military protection" of landlords, acquired a government
tank, and requisitioned wall phones from the United Fruit Company as well as
multiple jeeps from Texaco's nearby refinery.[121]

The rebels had also organized roadside *bazukero* (bazooka) teams that, according to the Havana-Santiago Bus Company, destroyed seventy brand-new
air-conditioned buses in only two months, forcing a suspension of all service.[122]
While St. George found Carlos Franqui's founding of Radio Rebelde impressive, he was bowled over by the vast communication network that formerly
vulnerable combat patrols now enjoyed. He counted thirty radio transmitters
and over a hundred shortwave receivers, some operated by female message
decoders like Magaly Montané.[123]

Most remarkable to St. George, however, was the considerable political pull
and legitimacy the rebels had achieved. Marching down a two-lane highway
with hundreds of rebels, he witnessed their occupation of thirty towns "against
half-hearted opposition."[124] Incredibly, thirty-six of forty-one sugar mills in the
area were paying taxes to the rebels by the fall of 1958.[125] Anxious "businessmen have filled rebel [coffers] but their most significant tribute was running
Santiago telephone line directly to rebel outpost. This was the contribution of
Cuban Telephone Co. (US-owned)," he wrote, "worried sick over getting its
plants around Santiago taken out by anti-telephone-company rebels, who have

already taken out hundreds of poles, dozens of miles of wiring. This is the first rebel city line since Fidel's landing two years ago and apple of their eye."[126] Of course, lost on no one was the Cuban Telephone Company's hypocritical about-face regarding Batista: this was the very same U.S. company that had once thanked him publicly for lowering its tax rates and given him a gold telephone the day after the DR's attack on the Presidential Palace.

Indeed, rebel leaders clearly delighted in regularly harassing U.S. companies, often for no apparent reason other than to show their strength and prophesy the future consolidation of Cuba's national sovereignty. The notion that U.S. investors had begun paying "tribute" to Fidel's troops was not lost on newly appointed U.S. ambassador Earl Smith, who demanded that they stop. "As Americans," Smith wrote in a private letter to U.S. businessmen, "we [have] no right to pay money to active revolutionaries who are trying to overthrow a friendly government."[127] St. George regularly witnessed rebels taking U.S.-company-owned Jeeps on joyrides, only to leave them abandoned along roads or in the countryside. They also showed their strength by invading and occupying small towns, none of which they held for more than a few hours.[128] Accompanying a rebel guard to the Texaco refinery near Santiago, St. George watched dumbfounded as a 26th of July guerrilla donned a helmet with a covered-up Texaco insignia and then honored Texaco plant managers' request that St. George refrain from taking pictures. Apparently, neither side wanted to heighten tensions with the U.S. government. Pictures of the takeover made relations between rebels and the company seem less than cordial and the guerrillas' occupation of Texaco unwelcome. "These shots escaped confiscation only by lucky accident," St. George explained.[129]

In other words, by all outward appearances, the rebels had successfully recruited Texaco's plant managers, local coffee planters, and assorted foreign and native businessmen into the ranks of the rebel army's enthusiastic supporters. Surely the involuntary nature and pragmatism of their support was not lost on St. George any more than it was on Fidel Castro himself. For this reason, St. George's careful, sympathetic documentation of the self-sacrifice of individual guerrillas and his unabashed representation of their exploits in a romantic, even glamorous light are significant. However cynically one might interpret guerrilla leaders' reliance on foreign journalists and the craft of image making, St. George witnessed heroism as well as an abiding sense of the rebels' generosity and even humor amid often dehumanizing conditions.

Figure 38. Luis Crespo deeply impressed comrades, locals, and strangers alike by adopting a disabled toddler he found abandoned in the woods. (Andrew St. George Papers, courtesy of Yale University Manuscripts and Archives)

No better example emerges in St. George's private papers and photographic record than that of Luis "El Guajiro" Crespo, one of the rebel forces' premier bomb makers, to whom St. George dedicated more than a reel of film. A survivor of the *Granma*, the thirty-three-year-old Crespo was a former sugar worker from Camagüey who had been running the rebels' main bomb factory near Fidel's headquarters for over a year. What impressed St. George, however, was the fact that Crespo had adopted a "crippled war orphan as his mascot, whom he has exercised and massaged until the boy is slowly beginning to walk." Admiringly, St. George captured El Guajiro working in his bomb shop, a small shack sitting atop a pile of 150-pound unexploded bombs dropped by Batista's air force, while his adopted son played happily nearby (figure 38).[130] In an image that reversed 1950s-style gender roles, El Guajiro is shown lovingly washing his boy on a large rock next to a stream and dousing him with Johnson's baby powder in the over-the-top way any Cuban would recognize (figure 39). Importantly, St. George wanted editors to realize that this extraordinarily generous warrior-father was *real*, not just an image. Describing a picture of Crespo mas-

Figure 39. After nearly two years of constant care and a loving routine that included massages and baths along the river, the boy learned to walk and Luis Crespo was very much his father. (Andrew St. George Papers, courtesy of Yale University Manuscripts and Archives)

saging the legs of the crippled boy, St. George insisted, "This is daily routine for rebel ancient known as 'El Guajiro' and not stunt."[131]

Other characters' self-sacrifice emerges from the archive. Examples include St. George's portrait of twenty-year-old Jack Nordeen of Chicago, a rebel guard and survivor of polio who joined Fidel's forces "to better himself." He moved along the mountain ridges "with incredible will power."[132] St. George also admired Hanibal Hidalgo, a veteran of fourteen bloody encounters with Batista's soldiers, brother of a dead rebel and son of a peasant family, all of whose members joined Castro as combatants. Laboriously, Hanibal had reengraved his own insignia onto a dead soldier's dog tag: "Let me carry this our banner to victory or die enveloped in its folds," it read. "Hidalgo conceived and engraved the motto himself but its length crowded owner's name off dogtag," St. George commented.[133]

Without doubt, it was the women in the rebel army who stood out the most.

An unpublished series of photographs documenting the lives and routines of these women seemed to ask why anyone, let alone such beautiful creatures, would want to risk their lives fighting a dictatorship in the woods. Examples included mostly forgotten and anonymous "girl guerrillas" such as a "gun-toting rebel mother of four" from Santiago; Anita, the wife of Captain Eusebio Mora, who "marched for fourteen days through the jungle to reach her husband's troop"; Alicia Marín, one of a dozen local girls who worked voluntarily as a cook; and Teresita González, a twenty-four-year-old Havana model and chief of rebel messengers who performed highly dangerous work, crossing back and forth across rebel lines.[134]

Cuban women of the revolution were not only bold but proud to express their feelings and sexuality with the men they loved: "The wives of officers, who get to yearn too hotly for their husbands' company, are sometimes permitted to join the jungle army for a few weeks—provided they are hardy enough to put up with the jungle life. Some girls, however, all but outdo the men."[135] Pride in their sexuality notwithstanding, young attractive girls barely out of puberty clearly had to put up with a lot among nearly all-male troops. A good example was sixteen-year-old "tomboy" Oniris Gutiérrez, the first woman to join Fidel's column after they set up camp in the Sierra. Fearless and smart, Oniris bathed in the river with her gun belt and holster lying beside her on the bank, pistol always cocked. She also spent an inordinate amount of time cleaning her pistol in front of the men (figure 40). Fidel, in a rare moment of undeniably Cuban-style levity, joked, "Niña, si sigues limpiando esa pistola de 22 [calibre] se te va a convertir en una 38" (Girl, if you keep cleaning that .22 caliber pistol, it's going to transform into a .38).[136]

While this remark surely ranks at the top of a running list of "salty Fidelisms" that St. George recorded, it was also among the least important; none of the comments that he recognized as highly significant ever made it into print. Editors likely feared their effect on U.S.-Cuba relations. "Let the State Department send up a man here and we'll talk things out. . . . I don't [insist on diplomatic] recognition, don't even want to hear the word, let your man come as a reporter, as a shoe salesman, a company negotiator, I'll keep his presence secret, but let him come," Fidel said.[137] When asked about Raúl Castro's decision to "[put] out an independent, anti-US political line from his command in the Sierra del Norte," Fidel balked and declared his frank disdain. Adding insult to injury, Raúl had also taken to playing the role of trickster, ordering his

Figure 40. Gun-toting teenagers like Oniris or this unidentified black recruit were not numerous among Fidel Castro's guerrillas, but they were valued for demonstrating how the 26th of July Movement embodied a frontal assault on the social and political injustice of Batista's regime. Yet not all recruits packed their own guns: according to St. George, Fidel tried to loan his telescopic rifle to virtually every man St. George photographed in order to make his troops appear far more prepared than they were. (Cuban Revolution Collection, courtesy of Yale University Manuscripts and Archives)

men to turn the water system on and off at the Guantánamo naval base, thereby demonstrating his power to make the United States anxious and uncomfortable at will.[138] What did Fidel think of Raúl's harassment of U.S. residents and U.S. installations, including the navy base? "Folly."[139]

At the time Fidel made these remarks, they carried particular weight. Dangerous tensions had emerged between Raúl's new rebel headquarters in the northern range of Sierra Cristal and the U.S. government. In June 1958, guerrillas under Raúl's command took hostage foreign employees of U.S. oil and mining companies as well as twenty-eight U.S. Marines, The story was widely reported in U.S. newspapers and forcibly ignored by the Cuban media.[140] By early July, the number of hostages totaled forty-seven U.S. citizens and three Canadians.[141] If matters were already bad enough, Raúl Castro promised they could get far worse.

Raúl's Wild West and the Great International Hostage Crisis

According to Military Order No. 30, signed by Raúl Castro, the United States was pulling strings with allied dictatorships of the region to help Batista's armed forces secure weapons the United States had publicly announced it would no longer send. Stamped "Made in the USA," bombs shipped from Trujillo's Dominican Republic and tanks supplied by the *somocista* dictatorship in Nicaragua testified to the duplicity and "criminal policy" that defined Washington's response to the Cuban war.[142] For these reasons, announced Raúl, "we are now obliged to expedite Military Order No. 30, which orders all military commanders of the Second Front, as an act of legitimate defense, to detain all American citizens within our reach."[143]

According to Mario Llerena, 26th of July Movement spokesman in New York, the guerrillas decided to take the hostages after receiving credible evidence that the U.S. government continued to ship weapons to Batista's army through the U.S. naval base at Guantánamo, despite its public declaration to the contrary only a few weeks earlier.[144] Called Operation Anti-Aircraft, the capture of the hostages represented an opportunity for the rebels to fight U.S.-issued bombs with ideas whose moral appeal they hoped would prove contagious. Completely fluent in English, Vilma Espín, a former chemistry student at MIT and head of Santiago's urban underground after the murder of Frank País, held nightly political discussions with the prisoners, apparently attempting to educate them on the social goals of the movement and thereby attenuate their complicity with imperial and national oppressors upon their release.[145] Ultimately, she served as official translator for Raúl Castro when top officials of the U.S. Consular Office in Santiago showed up to negotiate.

According to U.S. consul Park Wollam, who interviewed the Marines several days into their ordeal, "Efforts at propagandizing the men had apparently met with very little success." In fact, the Marines turned the tables on the rebels, doing some "propagandizing themselves" on the United States' behalf and "making friends around the village."[146] In his comments to St. George, Fidel characterized the hostage problem as a mere "headache." Similarly light in its assessment, a 26th of July Movement radio broadcast of the Fidel Castro Freedom Network denied any kidnapping had happened at all: "The incident was 'only a tour' to show the devastation caused by Cuban forces using United States arms against the rebels."[147] Yet despite Fidel's dismissals, there is little doubt that for U.S. officials, the kidnapping easily amounted to the greatest hostage crisis in U.S. history until that point. Attesting to this in a recent filmed interview, Robert Weicha, former CIA agent, vice consul in Santiago, and chief consul Park Wollam's partner in multiple meetings with Raúl Castro, explained that key objectives of his presence in the negotiations was to better assess conditions for a possible U.S. invasion.[148]

Similarly, in a memoir whose publication U.S. State Department officials apparently refused to authorize, Wollam dedicated five chapters typed on legal size paper to recounting the harrowing process of securing the hostages' release. For Wollam, the hostage crisis was a tipping point in the careful balancing act that U.S. officials in Santiago's consular office and intelligence network carried out with respect to the 26th of July Movement. Using U.S. leverage with Batista's regime, Wollam regularly secured the release of secret activists and more than once rescued St. George. He also put up with local American residents "haranguing" him and his colleagues "unmercifully" for dealing with the dictator. "Some of them considered it their duty to raise hell with us," he recalled.[149] "I would say more than the majority of the State Department and more than the majority of the CIA supported Fidel Castro against Batista," attested Weicha in 2010. "Mainly on the grounds of the reports of cruelty by Batista and not being legitimately elected president."[150]

After they met directly with Raúl's guerrilla leaders, however, Wollam and Weicha no longer saw the political objectives of urban activists and the top guerrillas as the same; as front-row witnesses to the gruesome crimes of Batista's regime in Oriente, U.S. officials in Santiago, unlike those in Havana, had been deeply sympathetic. In subsequent dealings with top negotiators, though, something changed.[151] Likely, U.S. officials discovered that they and the hostages were being used.

Both Wollam and Weicha quickly surmised that regardless of the open hostility and distrust of Raúl's group toward the Americans, the primary goal of the kidnappings was not political provocation or even diplomatic recognition but international publicity. Indeed, when Wollam first arrived to meet Raúl, he discovered Jules Dubois was already there. Dubois, a correspondent for the *Chicago Tribune* and president of the Inter-American Press Association, was a longtime ally of the 26th of July underground.[152] Within days, Andrew St. George and CBS-TV News reporter Eric Duerschmidt had arrived; both brought movie cameras.[153]

As Bob Weicha explained, after several days' hike and nearly a week under guard at a makeshift prison, the Columbia University–educated guerrilla Manuel Piñeiro finally showed up to guide him. Better known by the nickname Barba Roja for his fiery red beard, Piñeiro served for decades as Castro's most feared and hated intelligence chief following the revolution. After more hiking, they finally reached a rebel base near Calabaza. "And we got to the village of Calabaza and Park [Wollam] was there, and the captured engineers were there, and some of the press were already there, but Raul Castro had not made an appearance. And then [in the] afternoon, suddenly, over the mountains, it looked like Genghis Khan coming: they had about four or five Jeeps, everybody riding the hoods and fenders, holding up rifles with the 26th of July flags attached to them, and Raul came in, big, a big arrival." Undeterred by the display, Weicha persuaded Raúl to release a number of soldiers who had dysentery. "And I thought I had him, and then in came Vilma. I hadn't seen her in months. And she said, *What are you doing? What are you doing?* And so Raul explained to her the deal of releasing the sick prisoners, and she said, no, no, no, a thousand times, no, no, no. And then I had an argument with Vilma and I told her I had done a lot for the revolution and I explained to her that three of their main leaders were going to be executed, and I intervened and I got them saved and they're still alive, and that didn't even persuade her."[154]

Nonetheless, the negotiations began. For Wollam, the rebels were simply buying time as the United States pressured Batista not to bomb the area while U.S. citizens stood at risk.[155] According to Weicha, "There wasn't much heart" in the negotiations because the rebels "were receiving international publicity on this, and all the press were there, a big deal. So they'd release a prisoner one day, and release a prisoner the next day, maybe nothing for a couple days, and it was always headline news across the country." It was not until mid-July, when President Eisenhower ordered the Marines to Lebanon and the focus of the world press shifted, that all of the U.S. hostages were finally let go.[156]

In the meantime, however, Raúl, Vilma Espín, and the guerrillas of Raúl's Segundo Frente provided dramatic evidence that they were not just powerful and in control but extremely relaxed, unhurried, and thoroughly entertained by the American visitors. In a break between meetings, Barba Roja donned tennis whites and showed off his skills to Weicha on an improvised rebel tennis court (figure 41). Vilma Espín played with loaded rifles for the camera (figure 42). Raúl Castro graciously allowed his consular guests to hold his own automatic weapon for a group portrait (figure 43). Yet the rebels did not limit their strategy to intimidating U.S. officials; they illustrated the justice of their cause through the warm and friendly treatment of foreign prisoners in front of top U.S. reporters.

When CBS correspondent Eric Duerschmidt and Andrew St. George crash-

Figure 41. Manuel Piñeiro, better known as Barba Roja, dropped his studies at Columbia University to join Castro's forces in the Sierra. Intelligent, fully bilingual, and accustomed to the habits of Cuba's elite, he became a key point of contact with the CIA and Santiago's U.S. consular office during the hostage crisis provoked by Raúl Castro's detention of dozens of Marines and foreign company executives in June and July 1958. (Collection of Robert Weicha, courtesy of Glenn Gebhard)

landed an aircraft in Raúl's camp, the rebels brought out U.S. employees of the $1 million U.S. government–owned Cuban Nickel Company.[157] In addition to filming the CBS reporter filming the hostages and the rebels, St. George had the reporter film him as chatting with Raúl Castro in the doorway of a comfortable mountain cabin. Alongside them, Vilma Espín happily munched crackers as armed soldiers looked on.

St. George also filmed a group of rebels on the streets of a U.S. company town known as Mayarí Arriba after they had apparently captured the town and held it for four or five days.[158] The rebels are seen completely relaxed. In one sequence they are listening to a company commander when they seem to abruptly remember they are being filmed. Suddenly, they walk briskly down the main street of the town, six abreast, hands on their weapons, looking more like actors in a Hollywood western than revolutionaries in eastern Cuba.[159]

Most striking of all, however, were St. George's images of Duerschmidt interviewing the four unnamed hostages from the Nícaro nickel plant while they examined shrapnel and other parts of an exploded missile. The rebels ostensibly hoped to use the hostages as a way of authenticating that the bombs had

Figure 42. U.S. negotiators' first images of their rebel counterparts included former Santiago underground chief Vilma Espín. Wearing a silk blouse and a cowboy hat, Espín toyed with a loaded submachine gun for the cameras, thereby making a mockery of both Yankee and Cuban machismo. (Cuban Revolution Collection, courtesy of Yale University Manuscripts and Archives)

been dropped from U.S.-issued aircraft.[160] In a subsequent frame, Raúl Castro demonstrates the same evidence to one of the other hostages. Although unshaven and looking worn and tired, the hostages are shown to have established great camaraderie with the rebels, smoking with them, conversing with a man who appears to be a rebel doctor, and generally having a good time. Incredibly, St. George and Duerschmidt even filmed the hostages as they played a lively game of horseshoes, surrounded by smiling peasant boys and amicable armed guards. Indeed, the only image of a hostage that seems to defy the guerrilla-controlled public face of the process emerges in a sequence that St. George shot through the slats of a window. Apparently unobserved by guerrillas and hostages alike, St. George captures the worried agitation of a blond man wearing glasses as he sits thinking, alone at a table inside a cabin with an armed guard at his door.[161]

Eventually, St. George filmed the American hostages climbing into a company Jeep as they prepare to be released. As the hostages move toward the Jeep in the scene, some of their captors quickly step forward to say good-bye.

Figure 43. Posing for a group picture after successful negotiations with U.S. officials to release the hostages, Raúl Castro passed his weapon to Bob Weicha, officially the U.S. vice consul in Santiago and unofficially an agent of the CIA, in a sign of trust as well as power. Despite the smiles, clear to everyone involved was the fact that Raúl held the fate of the hostages, the image of the revolutionary movement, and U.S.-Cuba relations in guerrilla hands. (Cuban Revolution Collection, courtesy of Yale University Manuscripts and Archives)

Particularly striking in this regard, a black Cuban rebel smiles warmly as he grasps the hand of a tall, blond American. Seconds later, an older American wearing dark-framed glasses and a cowboy hat is shown gripping the hand of a white, bearded rebel officer for several seconds while he speaks seriously and respectfully to him from the front seat of the Jeep, implying a certain degree of understanding for their cause. The film ends with local officials holding a press conference on an airport tarmac, although the location of the airport is not clear.[162] One is left to wonder whether the rebels or the hostages would have been quite so friendly had the U.S. cameramen and the audiences they represented not been there at all.

Because of the challenge of finding the original presentation of the filmed news broadcast titled *Castro* (which, according to St. George, aired only in Canada shortly after the fall of Batista), the argument and selection of images included in it remain unclear.[163] Equally unclear were the purposes and destiny of St. George's films since they apparently were never used or, quite possibly, even meant for public use. Despite this, however, it seems obvious that the images both St. George and the CBS reporter shot of Vilma Espín, Raúl Castro, and the American and Canadian hostages served rebel leaders' interests and calculated needs. The daily coverage in the *New York Times* acknowledged the rebels' generosity and clearly conveyed Fidel's message that while Cuban rebels and citizens alike might blame the U.S. government for the war, they did not blame the U.S. people.[164] To prove this, Raúl's forces held an elaborate party for the hostages on the Fourth of July, even roasting a pig.[165] Even as Admiral Jerauld Wright, commander of the U.S. Atlantic Fleet, called for Raúl Castro's execution, the Associated Press's key photograph of the hostages (taken by St. George) reproduced only the fraternal image of mutual accord that Raúl and his followers had performed: Roman Cecelia, a U.S. mining engineer, smiling and chatting with his rebel captor for a global audience.[166] Later, Raúl issued an apology in which he admitted the role he assigned to journalists and their readers in the war: "I realize that this was a drastic action. I wanted these [hostages] as international witnesses to see the 26th of July Movement rebel encampment, their cause and what they are fighting for—freedom of the people."[167]

St. George's visual narratives clearly document a gregarious mixed-race and cross-class group of freedom fighters engaged in conversational and cultural exchanges with the representatives of a U.S. corporation. Rather than depict the men firing their weapons or engaging in any violence, the rebels posit themselves in a defensive role, preserving order, much like a rustic police force offering security to local residents in a frontier town. Rather than focus on the many black soldiers among the troops, the films feature lengthy close-ups of a rebel with an unexpected shock of blond hair and two women rebels, one with glamorous wavy hair, speaking unsmilingly, and the other with luminously large blue or green eyes, looking camera shy as she listens, first intently, then distractedly, to Fidel. Crowds of peasant women wearing flowered dresses carry babies; groups of round-faced children wear khaki clothes emblematic of the 26th of July guerrillas; rebel officers examine maps in order to plan strategies; a foot soldier totes a guitar as well as a machine gun.

Moreover, the leading protagonists in the films, like Vilma Espín with her mother-of-pearl button-down blouse, Raúl Castro in his ten-gallon hat, and Fidel Castro with his nerdy black-rimmed glasses, look as out of place as the

U.S. mining company employees with their linen bowling shirts, sunburns, and fancy, pleated pants. Together, they project the idea that only the most unjust of circumstances could have forced otherwise "civilized" and clearly bourgeois people to be there—in the middle of the woods. The relaxed outward countenance of the U.S. citizens shows the confidence they have gained in the secure fold of revolutionaries; it confirms their empathy for the sacrifices of their rebel hosts. Both the Cuban rebel and American citizen rebuke the barbarism of such crimes as U.S. support for Batista's bombing raids on civilian populations ensconced in the mountains. These protagonists and the generalized context of a ragged, simple people portrayed against the backdrop of forests and dust-filled towns augment the romantic, idealistic quality of these images.

Like the photographs shot during St. George's first visits to the Sierra Maestra, the discourse of these films reveals total support for the rebels' cause and therefore, their total invincibility. Viewed through the lens of St. George's camera, guerrillas' revolutionary reality showed American hostages in a war zone interacting with their captors as if all were the best of friends and on the same side. In such images, American employees of the U.S.-owned Cuban Nickel Company appear as uninformed victims of their government's hypocrisy, their eyes opened by their captors to the society suffering around them. In staging these interactions, guerrillas simultaneously authenticated the morality of the cause and the humanity of its leaders through imperial witnesses.

Obviously, guerrilla warfare in the Sierra was nothing like St. George's film or an earlier, much more romanticized CBS documentary on the rebels depicted it.[168] For example, at the time of the hostage crisis, the Nícaro mine, which the rebels had already raided in late July in order to steal a thousand gallons of gasoline, was the focal point of direct violent conflict between a large contingent of Batista's forces and the rebels. After the rebels hauled away $200,000 worth of equipment in October, the Cuban Army retaliated by occupying the mine and nearby town of Nícaro. U.S. officials reacted by dispatching an aircraft carrier and transport ship to evacuate all U.S. citizens.[169] Conflict, tension, and violence, not tranquility, trust, and friendship had long characterized the region.

Importantly, until the fall of 1958, rebels restricted the brunt of their verbal attacks, trials, and executions to local peasants, rather than confront the more obvious enemy, that is, the local landlords and members of the economic elite who were directly responsible for Batista's power and abuses in Oriente. Indeed, even when they had the chance to do so, they did not kill or harm U.S.

citizens or the U.S. Marines, whom the rebels charged with being directly allied to Batista: on the contrary, they courted, charmed, and released them, occasionally before the lens of television cameras. Just as they had done when the CBS film crew visited the Sierra earlier that year, in the fall of 1958 the guerrillas made light of resistance among any social class when St. George visited them. Tactically limiting their attacks to the property rather than the persons of the constituted regional order and discursively reducing any opposition to a smattering of confused rural "bandits" allowed the rebels to claim visually what Fidel had stated audibly to CBS reporters a year earlier: "All the people of the Sierra Maestra are with us."[170]

Messiah, Disciples, and the Hidden Heroes of Revolutionary Cuba

In the Sierra Maestra, the 26th of July Movement rehearsed—consciously and unconsciously—the revolution to come. Through tactics and imagery, the rebels forced protagonists and antagonists onto a visual stage in which *only* *they* appeared capable of moral action. Symbolic inversions of power and denials of violence flowed through messianic and apostolic images that Fidel and the guerrillas respectively presented of themselves. These images spoke loudly and deliberately of a people struggling for liberation against the greatest of odds and the most powerful of imperial states, a society that could be saved only by a great, ideologically impartial moral force embodied in the figure of Fidel Castro and his barbudos: these unmistakably manly followers, by the end of the war, showed their bravery, commitment, and the sacrifice of basic civilized comforts (such as shaving) in the length of their beards. Indeed, their beards distinguished guerrillas from clandestinos, marking the former as supposedly more heroic, more revolutionary, more like Cuba's messiah, Fidel. The legend that resulted from the guerrillas' collaboration with Andrew St. George speaks clearly of the emerging frame of historical and cultural memory within which the Batista regime was supposed to be understood and, through Fidel, finally overturned.

Undoubtedly as well, two years of collaboration had made both Fidel Castro and Andrew St. George U.S. media stars. By 1958, St. George had himself become the focal point of major magazines that discussed his exploits, daring, and even the amount of money news outlets had paid him.[171] Today it seems hard to believe that when St. George arrived as a photojournalist in the Sierra in March 1957, he was entirely self-taught and almost fully self-funded. Ironically, when

St. George pitched his work on the guerrillas to top media offices in Manhattan only months later, it was still not a story about Fidel Castro that editors wanted, but one centered on a twenty-year-old American boy named Chuck Ryan who had joined Fidel's column; St. George even included in his pitch photographs of Chuck and excerpts from his diary.[172] As fate would have it, when St. George finally did return to the Sierra for a story on Chuck, Fidel gave him the bad news that Chuck had left the previous day with "stomach problems." Happy to have someone to practice his English with, Fidel "boomed" to St. George: "I trust you'll stay for at least a month?"[173] Writing in September 1958, St. George confessed: "I felt like never going back to New York. . . . [I realized] that millions of people all over the world would see and get a clearer image from my pictures of these rebels *with* a cause. And the thought that I had helped illuminate their struggle gave me the deepest sense of satisfaction I have ever felt."[174]

If there in the Sierra Maestra, words were as important as actions to the success of 26th of July Movement's moral victory over military and political opponents, then elsewhere, outside the spaces rebels controlled, the images that clandestinos crafted of the guerrillas and that the guerrillas themselves helped stage combined the power of myth and legend to demoralize foes, convince class adversaries, and empower the masses. Arguably, Fidel and other leaders knew that the images St. George crafted spoke for them, more loudly and more clearly than the rebels could—or perhaps even wanted—to speak for themselves.

In short, this initially tiny band of eighteen armed rebels and hundreds of underground civilian activists managed to project the impossible: their own movement's ultimate political invincibility through moral means. If Fidel Castro could effortlessly claim the mantle of selfless national patriot in the immediate aftermath of Batista's flight, he did so largely because of the brilliant public relations campaign that he, a vast network of fearless clandestinos, and peasant supporters had forged in the Sierra Maestra. The guerrillas' positive, carefully constructed image of themselves garnered widespread legitimacy long before they descended from the liberated zone. As Camilo Cienfuegos and Che Guevara began the march west, they joined the DR's guerrilla force in the central mountain range of El Escambray and, finally directed by Moscow to abandon Batista to his fate and reverse their position on the war, armed PSP militants joined them. As city after city under batistiano control began to fall in their wake, Batista's departure from power and from Cuba became a fait accompli.

Revolutionary Cuba:
December 1958 and Beyond

DECEMBER 1958 REPRESENTED A MOMENTOUS month for every sector of the Cuban opposition, particularly the 26th of July Movement and its affiliate organizations of clandestinos, especially Resistencia Cívica. For a year, Batista's regime had not only been at war against domestic armed foes, real and imagined, but on the defensive with respect to its own supporters. Batista's strategy of painting all alternatives to his rule as a vote for Communism had devolved into simply "Aid to Castro is Aid to Communism." Issued in April 1958, the new slogan revealed just how tenuous Batista's grasp on power had become.[1] Edition after edition of *Report on Cuba,* Batista's primary propaganda newsletter published in Washington, attempted to convince readers by any means necessary of his own popularity and the inevitable demise of Fidel Castro's revolutionary movement. Batista's publicists accomplished this mostly through denials of any government abuse of the "Prío-Castro rebels" as well as by outright lying: the 26th of July Movement was plagued by deserters and Fidel Castro's days were numbered; fidelistas would never win in any election; Castro's closest representatives were as much in cahoots with former president Prío as their ranks were stacked with secret Communists; not only had the April 1958 strike failed but dozens more had "fizzled"; the summer tourist season had "excelled all expectations"; so opposed were Cuban workers to the war that the sugar harvest of 1958–1959 was set to be the largest on record.[2] Denial as a modus operandi did not appeal just to Batista, however.

Cuba's great sugar barons at the Czarnikow-Rionda Company mimicked Batista's optimistic outlook even as the physical and fiscal evidence of (supposedly) apolitical worker "rioting" and coordinated actions with rebel assaults piled up throughout 1958. An internal report to George Braga in May 1958 described the situation at the company's largest and most lucrative property, Central Manatí, as "very gratifying." Despite top shareholder Alfonso Fanjul's admitted "surprise at the extent of rebel operations in Manatí," he and other inspectors believed "quite strongly that none of our people are involved."[3] Yet acts of sabotage and destruction of property by "malicious individuals" had already produced a flurry of insurance claims by the company and attending increases in its corporate insurance rates.[4]

Indeed, the company's top executives concerned themselves with losses as small as a $95 horse and a $40 calf "seized and killed for food." Thus, the extent and deliberateness of destruction on plantations in Oriente, Camagüey, and Las Villas in 1958 must have seemed staggering.[5] In March of that year, the company filed claims totaling $335,837.79 for the loss by fire of forty thousand bags of raw sugar at Central Resolución.[6] However, sabotage and damage due to "strikes, riots, civil commotion, etc." in October through December 1958 were, by far, the worst. Claims filed for devastated railways, burned-out railcars, cut telephone lines, missing bulldozers, stolen trucks, and incendiary incidents at Centrales Elia, Manatí, Francisco, and Tuinuci ranged from $12,000 to $15,000 each.[7]

On 1 December 1958, the very same day that managers worried over the theft of a horse and a calf, Central Manatí served as a battleground between armed rebels apparently attempting to seize control of the plantation and locally garrisoned units of Batista's army. Despite a rebel retreat, machine-gun fire, exploding bombs, and the air force's subsequent strafing of the Central resulted in over $300,000 in losses.[8] For company executives, the fact that Batista's censors prevented such worker feats of solidarity and coordination with rebels from making the news proved comforting: appearances of normalcy kept them from losing shareholder trust and thus even more money. The company's on-site inspectors like top heir Alfonso Fanjul also preferred to look on the bright side because they were motivated by a logic that Batista officials and revolutionaries shared: in the minds of batistianos and rebels alike, harnessing citizens' *belief* that Batista's regime would either stand the test of the revolution's challenge or crumble before it remained a principal factor that would determine one of these two very outcomes.

Indeed, in the last weeks of 1958 both the rebels and Batista's supporters seemed convinced that citizens' attitudes rather than military victories remained central to Cuba's destiny. For his part, Batista gave the appearance of normalcy amid mounting chaos. In November and early December, he went so far as to inaugurate a series of public works projects in the poor working-class barrio of Casablanca on the eastern side of the Bay of Havana. These included new government-built homes and a colossal sculpture of Jesus located near the city's primary military fortification and security headquarters, La Cabaña. Although the sculpture was blessed in an official ceremony by Cardenal Arteaga, one of SIM's earliest victims following Batista's coup, only a tiny number of clergy attended the event. Those absent were demonstrating their abhorrence of the regime. "Eran Castristas" (They were Castroites), according to the bitter José Cabus, one of Batista's primary apologists and author of the work *Batista: Pensamiento y Acción,* among others.[9]

To fight Batista's theater of normalcy and Christian celebration, Resistencia Cívica and pro–26th of July Movement cells of journalists led by Carlos Lechuga launched one of their most daring and creative operations so far, a campaign known as 03C, or Cero Tres C. The acronym encoded the call for a national consumer strike during the month-long celebrations leading up to the Christmas holiday: "Zero Three Cs" meant "cero cine, cero compras, cero cabaret" (zero cinema, zero shopping, zero cabaret).[10] The campaign was brilliantly and mysteriously promoted through the print media as if 03C were a new shampoo or cosmetic product; the tagline for its advertisement was "¿Qué es 03C? Cero Tres C???" (What is 03C? Zero Three Cs???)[11] The secretary-general of the 26th of July Movement, Manolo Ray, traveled to the Sierra Maestra and explained the campaign to propaganda chief Carlos Franqui. Violeta Casals, a famous *radionovela* (radio soap opera) and cabaret star, clarified the purpose of the 03C for Radio Rebelde listeners by reading three short *décimas,* poems of a rural tradition, that connected it to the ascetic values of the revolution. These décimas defined engaging in hedonistic pleasures like going to the movies as acts of complicity with the regime's assassinations. "No niegues tu la existencia de la lucha en tu vivir. Ya te podrás divertir, pero hoy la sangre conmina: cuando el tirano asesina, ¿a qué cine vas a ir?" (Don't deny the existence of the struggle in your daily life. Soon you will get to have fun, but today, blood runs: while the tyrant murders, to what movie house could you possibly go?)[12]

Tapping citizens' sense of patriotic duty was only part of the strategy. "[We] tried to paralyze the economy so that there would be greater pressure from all sectors of the country against Batista," noted Emilio Guede, the advertising

Figure 44. The brainchild of advertising executive Emilio Guede and covert M-26-7 press activists like Vicente Baez, the December 1958 "03C" campaign had public and clandestine sides. The underground flyer explained that Cubans who enjoyed the holiday season while ignoring Batista's repression collaborated with the regime and committed treason. Activists invited all Cubans to mock the fragility of Batista's version of reality and, through a national consumer strike, to collapse the regime's authority. (Ernesto Chávez Collection, Area Studies and Special Collections, University of Florida)

executive turned revolutionary who came up with the 03C campaign. Methodically, Resistencia Cívica attempted to shift the burden of change onto the shoulders of Cuba's affluent middle and upper classes through powerful, visible, and collective protest.[13] In case Cubans' legendary reliance on *radio bemba* (lip radio), or word-of-mouth culture, proved insufficient to break through Batista's wall of terror and censorship, the group also clandestinely produced and distributed thousands of flyers that reproduced the décimas Violeta Casals read over Radio Rebelde. One side of the red and black, mini foldout flyers spelled out the meaning of the acronym 03C and invited citizens to see their acts of self-abnegation as a form of mass protest; the other side carried startling images of affluent couples enjoying themselves against a backdrop of warfare, shackled hands, and a guerrilla shot through the heart in battle (figure 44).[14]

Even as forces commanded by Camilo Cienfuegos, Che Guevara, and American DR commander William Morgan triumphed over the army in the western provinces in late December, neither guerrillas nor clandestinos like Emilio Guede believed the war had neared an end. Indeed, after rejoicing at the clear success of the 03C campaign on 26 December, Guede faced the reality that he would soon have to quit his job and go deep underground: he slept that night in his secret studio in El Vedado, surrounded by original copies of Manolo Ray's

Manual de Demoliciones del Ejército Rebelde, a guide that Ray had crafted to help the rebels blow up many of the very public works he himself had engineered.[15] Fidel Castro, meanwhile, celebrated the holidays by visiting his recently widowed mother on the family estate in Oriente.[16]

Despite all outward appearances and rebel propaganda touting the moral and historical invincibility of their cause, it was not until Fulgencio Batista finally fled Cuba that the revolutionary destiny for which so many thousands of Cubans had sacrificed their livelihoods, their personal dreams, or even their lives seemed sealed. Accompanied by his family, his handpicked would-be successor Vice President Andrés Agüero Rivero, nine members of the national police, his entire personal bodyguard (including Captain Alfredo Sadulé), their wives, and three servants, Batista touched down in the neighboring dictatorship of the Dominican Republic, headed by Rafael Trujillo. The U.S. State Department, nearly the last to abandon hope in Batista, was among the first to know.[17] According to legend and the memoir of Carlos Franqui, no one seemed initially more shocked and less prepared to make a public statement about the meaning of Batista's flight than Fidel Castro.[18]

When Batista abandoned Cuba, he left behind a citizenry that had struggled to save a wounded but resilient vision of a heroic, united, and revolutionary nation. For the previous year, Cubans, amid the many dashed hopes and violence suffered by generations past, had vested their expectations for the future in the messianic message that Fidel Castro provided them and that clandestinos' activism invited them to hear. On New Year's Day, 1959, the raw material for the story of a newly revolutionary Cuba was already there in the resilient and vibrant goal of a participatory state and socially democratic, just union. The experiences, struggles, sacrifices, and values responsible for crafting that goal did not originate on 26 July 1953, or on 13 March 1957, or on the day of Batista's coup, 10 March 1952. The essential elements for rebellion had emerged when Cubans first heard the call of Eduardo Chibás to join the Orthodox movement, cleanse the state of the financial and political impunity of its representatives, and galvanize popular energies behind a program of total sovereignty, government accountability, the amelioration of poverty, and greater racial equality. Chibás, like so many martyred leaders of Cuba, had come to embody these goals in the public's imagination. Their memories served as a national touchstone and reference point for "revolution."

Awash in the glow and euphoria that Cuba's new lease on a revolution represented that first day of January 1959 and for weeks afterward, many historical protagonists both observed and contributed to what *Bohemia* magazine would call Fidel Castro's "apotheosis."[19] Giving speeches, chatting with average citizens, and signing autographs in the company of foreign journalists in his eight-day, town-by-town journey from Santiago to the capital, Castro with his massive convoy parted open the country like a veritable sea in biblical times. For forty-five days, he remained only the head of the Ejército Rebelde, taking no post in the civilian-led revolutionary cabinet, an act that Franqui and others perceived as a strategy meant to prove his political "virginity" and altruistic stripes.[20] Undoubtedly fueled by the euphoria of popular expectations for a new era free of Batista, Fidel's reception among citizens was also highly produced, managed, and choreographed, mostly by journalist Carlos Franqui, national director of propaganda for the 26th of July Movement and advertising executive Emilio Guede, secretary of propaganda for Resistencia Cívica. Subsequently, *Bohemia* sold out its three "Liberty" editions of a million copies each; one after the other proclaimed Fidel's apotheosis in ascendant terms.

Mostly forgotten, however, is the fact that few habaneros actually knew what Fidel looked like until the activists' promotion campaign began. From their respective posts, Franqui and Guede coordinated efforts to broadcast and thereby legitimate the 26th of July leaders' assumption of government authority through all forms of media. They also recruited the country's top creative minds and commercial agents to design billboards, placards, and handbills under one unifying slogan for Fidel's triumphal arrival in Havana, convincing them to donate labor and materials for free, despite an estimated cost of $150,000, then a small fortune. Although clearly but necessarily verbose, the slogan activists devised was: "De una revolución limpia a gobernar con honradez" (From a clean revolution to the task of governing with honor). Images of Castro and his handpicked provisional president Manuel Urrutia flanked both sides of the slogan with the name 26th of July Movement stamped at its foot.[21] The citizenry seemed to accept, even celebrate, Fidel's status as a long-awaited national redeemer, even if they were not quite sure which of the revolutionaries he was. "For that reason," one *Bohemia* journalist recalled only a year later, "when his glorious entry into the capital began, the most curious chatter could be heard on the street:—That's him on the jeep!—No, Fidel is the guy on the tank with the *blond* beard!"[22]

Editors also reported citizens' confusion of Fidel with leaders who were not even members of his movement, such as Rolando Cubela, the commander of the student-led guerrilla force of the Directorio Revolucionario, a much sexier and closer approximation of the handsome, blue-eyed, fair-haired Jesus.[23] Of course, Fidel's leadership in the 1953 assault on the Moncada Barracks, the mass circulation of his eloquent defense, *History Will Absolve Me,* his 1955 fund-raising tour of the United States, and his manifestos had already launched his image as a daring politician. Yet his image as a Christ-like redeemer with similarly pure followers was the result of more than his own actions. Cuban citizens' years-long search for a messiah was responsible: they wanted a selfless man to serve the people and replace the false paternalism of Batista, the one who had proclaimed himself Cuba's "savior" on so many occasions. They wanted a messiah who would save them from Cuba's own recent history: the failed republican governments of the past, the Auténticos' betrayal, the unexpected death knell to democracy that the "martyrdom" of Eddy Chibás provoked, thanks to Batista, the unconditional support of the United States for the dictator, and the "barbarous" dictator himself, whom so many had long perceived as the devil incarnate.

Nonetheless, for large swaths of Cuban citizens, the revolutionary government still had to prove itself. Undoubtedly, feelings of euphoria and a resurgence of hope immediately replaced feelings of despair after Batista fled to the Dominican Republic and the activists of the 26th of July Movement rose to power. By all measures, these activists quickly gained the support and faith of the majority of the people by taking unprecedented action. Over the course of the first seven months of 1959, Fidel Castro and the most important leaders of the *clandestinidad* remapped and reshaped the political landscape, proving what an uncorrupted government could do. Massive investment in education, the building of tens of thousands of new homes, agrarian reform, a truly free press, the passage of hundreds of nationalist economic laws that gave unprecedented protection to the expansion of Cuban-owned industries and businesses, labor protections—all of these reforms gave credence to the idea that Cuba had indeed overturned its own history.[24] Much of the triumph, citizens surmised, was made possible only through the unique personal style and leadership of Fidel Castro: he became what Cubans wanted him to become, the savior of Cuba, a younger, dynamic Eddy Chibás incarnate and the representation of all that Cuba *might have been* had repeated U.S. interventions not robbed it of a different destiny from 1898 to 1958—at last the country had achieved the exceptionally democratic national status Cubans had long dreamed and fought for.

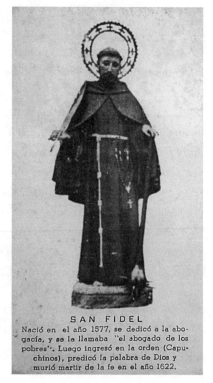

SAN FIDEL
Nació en el año 1577, se dedicó a la abogacía, y se le llamaba "el abogado de los pobres". Luego ingresó en la orden (Capuchinos), predicó la palabra de Dios y murió martir de la fe en el año 1622.

Figure 45. This prayer card to the previously little-known Saint Fidel referenced the divinely sanctioned character of Fidel Castro and his mission to save Cuba. Featured in the prayer to God on the back of the card was an invocation that God defeat the "malevolent purposes of those who accuse and attack" Cubans for their faith in the post-1959 government. (Collection of María Antonia Cabrera Aruz)

This logic helps explain the almost immediate appearance in 1959 of a prayer card to Saint Fidel, a Catholic Capuchin monk known as "the lawyer of the poor" who was born in 1577 and died in 1621 (figure 45).[25] After begging God that "the souls of our martyrs immolated for our freedom may repose in Your Glory," the prayer went on to ask that "Your Love and Your Peace reign among us; bless the Humanist Revolution that practices the doctrine of Your Son. 'LOVE YOUR BROTHER AS YOURSELF.' May it demonstrate its faith in You through its acts. Bless Comandante FIDEL CASTRO RUZ and in general all Cuban families, our lands, and the abundance of crops that we will obtain through the agrarian reform."[26] Subsequently, Fidel's messianism did not abate but increased, penetrating the public's imagination by virtual consensus.

According to the journalist made famous for being one of the first and most prestigious that Batista's security forces attacked, Mario Kuchilán, Fidel Castro was not only "the living incarnation of Jesus Christ" for most Cubans, especially peasants, but a new and improved version of him. Just as the people of Israel had witnessed "1,058 years earlier, a simple man who plainly does not

Figure 46. Originally broadcast on Telemundo, one of Cuba's eleven island television stations, this drawing of Fidel Castro, made in the style common to portraits of Jesus at the time, prompted thousands of viewers to request copies. To satisfy demand, *Bohemia* published it as a full-page image so that readers could cut it out for framing and display in their homes. (*Bohemia*, 1959)

aspire to power," so had Fidel Castro miraculously revived "in Cuba the faith of a people." Recently, Kuchilán continued, Telemundo's broadcast of an art-ist's fanciful rendition of Fidel had provoked a flood of viewer requests that the TV station provide copies of the portrait for display in private homes. With a national circulation of half a million subscribers, *Bohemia* willingly stepped in to satisfy demand. Meant to be clipped out and framed, the sketch revealed Fidel "not as he is physically but as the greater part of the Cuban people see him spiritually. . . . It is, perhaps, a fleeting lightning bolt imprisoned on paper, that extraordinary will of God to cast man in His own image. But it is not Jesus Christ, it is Fidel Castro Ruz." (figure 46).[27]

Among its contributions, this book attempts to put the messianism of Fidel

Castro that emerged in 1959 in its historical place. This popular view of Fidel as Cuba's savior did *not* form the foundation of popular faith in the revolutionary government's commitment to democracy, even as it surely endured despite signs of creeping authoritarianism and the infiltration of covert Communists to the highest ranks of military power within a year.[28] On the contrary, the majority of Cubans' expectations that the revolution could not be anything but a living democracy found their origins elsewhere, in the call to "save Cuba" that citizens heard from the lips of Eddy Chibás and that they had never forgotten throughout the years of Batista's despotism. Indeed, it was the depth of expectations for true democracy built up between 1946 and 1956 that made Cubans proclaim that the revolution led by Fidel fulfilled one hundred years of struggle against imperialism and injustice. Arguably they held this belief even before Batista fled Cuba and long before Fidel himself proclaimed the culmination of Cuban's century-long struggle for socioeconomic justice and political sovereignty in the 1959 revolution. By the time citizens began to doubt the liberating potential of the increasingly authoritarian institutions and policies Castro inaugurated in 1960 in order to centralize his rule in a one-party state, regret or even recognition that the majority of Cubans had surrendered their rights came far too late.[29]

For this reason, the new knowledge, alternative perspectives, and questions this book addresses are important. Its pages tell the story of Cubans' search for a participatory democracy, their support of a national tradition prophesying the rise of a politically altruistic messiah who would champion the Cuban cause, and their ultimate embrace of armed struggle as a solution of last resort in the face of the unyielding terror of Batista. The political culture that emerged in the mid-1940s promised that a true political messiah would one day be born in Cuba. In January 1959 and for a long time thereafter, most Cubans believed that he had been. Fidel Castro undoubtedly and deliberately embodied that image and strove to fulfill that role, albeit on his own terms and, as time went by, as he—and only he—saw fit.

However, gaining and securing a monopoly on state power over nearly six decades have had an immeasurable impact on the decline of Fidel from his initial condition of untouchable, saintly, or messianic hero. From the 1970s through the 1990s, he slowly but surely became what many Cubans see today as little more than a military dictator. Six decades of Communist rule and a monopoly on the modes and expression of citizen participation in politics have deeply affected what Cubans know about the making of revolutionary Cuba in the 1940s and 1950s, regardless of age. Control over history—particularly control over who has the *right to write* history and who can decide its meaning— has greatly ensured that the many stories of Cuban experiences from 1946 to 1958 were never told. Perhaps this book will one day be among many that explore the realities still hidden in inaccessible Cuban archives, the fading memories of protagonists, and the private collections of personal papers in Cuba and abroad.

Indeed, to this day, knowledge of many of the events and the protagonists who made the fall of Fulgencio Batista possible and justifiable in the minds of most Cubans remains taboo—or simply unknown to generations of Cubans on the island. Fidel Castro's own story has become the only one most people know and tell. Thus, the tragic fate of revolutionary heroes such as Comandante Huber Matos, who rode alongside fellow comandantes Castro and Camilo Cienfuegos on the tank that swept them—the personification of the revolution—into Havana on 8 January 1959, has remained shrouded in a dark cloud of silence and secrecy since late 1959. Such was the taboo against criticizing the revolution and citizens' collectively appointed messiah Fidel that Matos's actions represented a turning point for only a tiny minority of the 26th of July leaders, many of them revolutionary cabinet members such as Manolo Ray. Matos was sentenced to twenty years in prison in December 1959, his sole crime being a private letter of resignation written to Castro in which he denounced the promotion of Communists to posts in the revolutionary army at a time when Fidel and others continued to pledge their adherence to a non-Communist and nonimperialist path. So dangerous did Castro consider Matos's charges of the government's covert integration of Communists—former enemies of armed struggle who favored the stability of Batista—he played the role of prosecuting attorney, judge, and jury at Matos's trial. And so dangerous do the details of Matos's extraordinary act of valor and clear historical acumen remain to the Castro regime that in 2010, shortly after Matos published his autobiography from exile, the Cuban government produced its own official account to counter it: *Victoria Sobre una Traición,* by state journalist Jorge Luis Betancourt.[30]

There are many other examples of the betrayal of revolutionary principles and suppression of awareness of them. Four years after Matos's protest and imprisonment, Jorge Valls, the former student activist, follower of Bárcena, and a surviving member of the Directorio Revolucionario, was arrested and interrogated by Castro in his own private apartment for "activities against the powers of the state and leading anti-government organizations."[31] Despite the absence of proof or any public trial, Valls received a prison sentence of twenty years and forty days. Like Matos, he became a *plantado,* a prisoner who refused the government's "reeducation" programs that might have resulted in an early release because Valls considered it the ultimate act of treason: reeducation meant personal collaboration in the deliberate erasure of history and thereby Cuban national memory as whole. In that betrayal of the past and the present, Valls wanted absolutely no role.[32]

Alfredo Sánchez Echeverría, son of Aureliano Sánchez Arango, Prío's minister of education and final (notably innocent) target of Eddy Chibás's radio tirades, also suffered more than a decade in prison. Upon his release in the early 1970s, he was not allowed to remain in Cuba, despite his patriotism and deep desire to witness how Fidel had come to define "change" so radically.[33] Surviving members of the attack on the Moncada Barracks such as Mario Chanes and Gustavo Arcos suffered more than two decades as political prisoners under the Castro regime; their images were even removed from a highly circulated photograph of the moncadistas on their release from prison in 1955 (figure 47). In the doctored versions of the photograph, a suitcase remains that in the original image swings from Arcos's right hand—an artifact that Castro's censors had technical problems removing. Surviving Directorio Revolucionario guerrillas such as Comandantes Eloy Gutiérrez Menoyo and William Morgan were similarly first hailed as heroes before conspiring against Castro for transforming a sovereign revolutionary state into a Communist, pro-Soviet government. Gutiérrez Menoyo was jailed for years in Cuban prisons; Morgan, summarily imprisoned, was executed weeks before the Bay of Pigs invasion. For the curious and committed historian, the list of former heroes turned political exiles, prisoners, or forgotten ghosts of a forcibly purged, ideologically inconvenient history of revolution can begin to seem interminable. No wonder so many Cubans who experienced the horror of the 1950s and then the initial joy of 1959 asked themselves who was guilty of a greater crime against the nation: those in support of Batista who betrayed the individuals who had sacrificed their lives, livelihood, and personal tranquility to fight for political change, or those who changed the meaning and direction of change forever by toppling Batista in 1959 and then turning their backs on the hard path to sovereign, socially just, constitutional democracy in favor of one-party, one-man rule?

Many people continue to admire Fidel Castro, in the wake of his death in November 2016, or celebrate what they call "the Cuban Revolution" without accounting for the constraints that his six-decades-old regime imposed on the quality and nature of citizens' liberation. For them, such queries are inconvenient; they do not matter because it is so easy to take the empowering character of the nation-state achieved under Fidel's Communist rule for granted, especially from afar. Its championing of anti-imperialist principles in opposition to the United States allowed, as Fidel himself so often contended, Cuba's government to be judged by a distinct, often forgiving standard. From this perspective, the quest to discover the alternative nation-state Cuba might have been after 1959 had authoritarianism never triumphed is seen as either insufficiently "progressive" or simply naive. I have been accused of being both regularly throughout my career but mostly—importantly—by *non*-Cubans.

In researching this book, I discovered more than I expected about Cuba's past political culture and its implications today. What Cubans hoped to achieve *prior* to Batista's 1952 coup remains valid precisely because their aspirations reveal what Fidel Castro's authoritarianism and claims to political morality silenced over the years within the U.S./Soviet-managed frame of Cold War binaries—the "with us or against us," good guys versus bad guys, David versus Goliath narratives traditionally exploited by the *fidelista* state to justify the denial of citizens' rights and repress contestation of Communist rule. In the name of combating U.S. efforts to vanquish national sovereignty in Cuba and other nations struggling for more representative states and economies in Latin America, Fidel Castro made Cubans' pre-Batista dream of accountable, transparent, constitutional and electorally democratic government politically taboo in the first decades after Batista's fall. No longer did it suit his and his closest advisors' view of what was best for Cuba; whether Cubans had a hand in determining short-term policies or their long-term fate did not matter.

However, as this book has argued, it was Cuba's pre-Batista political culture that made the rise of a radical opposition to Batista possible and allowed the 26th of July Movement, and particularly the triumph of Fidel Castro, to succeed. Ultimately, as generations capable of remembering that dream for Cuba have died, left Cuba, or simply survived in silence in the face of the rise of a Communist state, the richness of Cuba's pre-1959 political culture, the audacity of its citizens, and the power of the people to contest the state, whatever the odds, were voluntarily forgotten as well as forcibly suppressed. Like Eddy

Figure 47. Fidel Castro and his fellow moncadistas on their release from prison
on the Isle of Pines, Mother's Day, 1955. The original photograph shown here
includes Gustavo Arcos (right foreground), wearing a suit and carrying a suitcase.
As one of many who later challenged the authoritarian Communist state ruled by
Castro, he was later excised from the image. (*Bohemia,* 1955)

Chibás before him, Castro was an exceptional leader because he recognized
just how far Cubans were willing to go to achieve national sovereignty and
thereby restore the national destiny that the United States had stolen from them
when it first occupied Cuba and changed the course of history in 1898. Embracing Communism and the Soviet model of development allowed him to harness
Cubans' will and place it in the service of Communist Party goals that they
were supposed to understand as their own.

In many ways, as popular contributions to the messianic protagonism of
Fidel Castro in Cuba's history receded over the course of the 1960s alongside citizens' control over the state, Communist officials stepped up efforts to
make him the principal guarantor of prosperity, progress, and nationhood in

the present as much as he had allegedly been in the past. Particularly after the Communist Party's promulgation of the new Cuban Constitution of 1975, few would dispute the legal means on which the state relied to achieve this, such as the criminalization of the organizing of any other party. Then the Penal Code of 1979 provided automatic sentencing for "offending the dignity of any public official" in a public manner; revisions made to the Penal Code in 1987 raised minimum sentences further: those convicted still face three to twelve months for criticizing lower-level leaders and one to three years for criticizing top state and party officials.[34] Seen against the backdrop of Batista's draconian measures, drawn up in 1953 in response to Castro's assault on the Moncada Barracks, these "revolutionary" laws remain as ironic as they are astounding.

In the historical realm, what can be said and who can say it are similarly policed. The post-1959 state has intervened decisively, dramatically, and frequently to ensure that Fidel and an increasingly reduced number of supporters in his guerrilla movement are inscribed as *the* sole saviors of Cuba from Batista. This has entailed the corresponding sidelining of other opposition groups as well as the erasure of citizens' role in promoting democracy. In a state defined by one party's monopoly on power as well as the absence of free elections and the refusal of the right to free association and assembly, it is not surprising that one of the main findings of this book is necessarily taboo: that is, the commitment of millions of citizens to seeking electoral, democratic solutions to Batista's rule from the late 1940s through 1956. Films such as the state film industry's seven-part series *Cuba: Caminos de Revolución,* begun in 2004 and completed in 2009 for the fiftieth anniversary of the flight of Batista and the rise of the 26th of July Movement to state power, clearly ignore and at times implicitly rebuke this civic quest. Moreover, as an official visual history, *Cuba: Caminos de Revolución* represents the fight to topple Batista as a continual, unfragmented struggle in which genuine rivals and critics of Castro's strategies and views, such as José Antonio Echeverría, appear as inevitable martyrs: their sacrifices and losses are mere stepping-stones leading to the rightful occupation of Fidel and his followers at the pinnacle of power in the state. Ghosts, of course, have little power to talk, let alone fight back. As many Cubans have told me over the years, historians must do it for them.

Charged with producing weekly newsreels and all major documentaries on primary political concerns at every juncture of the revolution from 1960 until his death in 1998, Cuba's legendary director and film czar Santiago Alvarez set the precedent for "defending" the revolution by identifying and repressing taboo narratives about its past and present. He repeatedly reinscribed the messianism of Fidel Castro in virtually every production that referenced or focused on the pre-1959 period. Within the realm of Alvarez's films, history itself mattered less than what often appeared as its predetermined heroic outcome: the rise and triumph of Fidel.[35] Proudly, Alvarez asserted this point near the end of his life in an interview first published in 2007. Remembering that he was a covert PSP Youth member when he initially met Castro at the wake for the student movement's first martyr, Rubén Batista, in February 1953, Alvarez remarked, "If there is really a God, he looks a lot like Fidel. Fidel is a god for me. The wisdom of night and of day, nature itself. A giant. The four-leagued giant."[36]

The fact that Castro emerged in the echo chambers of the post-1959 state as the morally righteous, uniquely endowed savior—the messiah of Cuba—he had always believed himself to be rested on the idea that the failed assault on the Moncada Barracks was Cuba's historical rebirth, a political resurrection and triumph over death. Since the revolutionary government's first celebration of 26 July as a national holiday in 1959, fidelistas have insisted that Castro's assault on Moncada was the starting point of all pertinent history, a continuation of the narrative he himself authored from the Isle of Pines prison. Recent histories of Moncada have expanded its impact exponentially, attributing to 26 July 1953 responsibility for a general coming to anti-imperialist consciousness in Latin America. According to island historian Jorge Renato Ibarra Guitart, Moncada marked "the beginning of the end for all the Latin American dictatorships."[37] In other words, it was not the flight of Batista or the taking of the state by revolutionaries of Castro's movement that changed the political stakes in the hemisphere: it was the paradoxically victorious failure of Fidel's forces at Moncada. This narrative not only robs Cubans of their past and glosses Latin American activists for change in their home countries as Fidel's followers; it denies their agency and protagonism in history.

In a related narrative as ironic as it is bizarre, the recently restored Museum of the Revolution, housed in Havana's Presidential Palace, utterly inverts the story line it once told. From the 1990s till the early 2000s, when I regularly visited the museum, its displays revealed the brutality of Batista's methods against urban clandestinos and celebrated, in a blow-by-blow account that included maps, relics, and blueprints, the Directorio Revolucionario's nearly successful assassination, led by Echeverría, of Fulgencio Batista in his office on 13 March

1957. Today, references to the assault, the DR, or even the 26th of July underground are difficult to find; instead, the entirely unrelated and geographically separate story of Castro's attack on the Moncada has seemingly colonized salon after salon, complete with a miniature three-dimensional model of the barracks lined with the tracks of each group of assailants and bloodied vestiges of the military uniforms they had used as a disguise.

Cynics might suggest that such an emphasis is intended simply to turn one of the gravest of Castro's mistakes into a triumph. Indeed, those familiar with his leadership over the course of the regime's now nearly sixty-year rule would recognize this example as only one of a pattern.[38] Still, it also explains the veritable absence of the complex, competing historical accounts of Cuba in the critical period before 1959 that lie at the center of this study. Surely, deliberate amnesia, distortions of fact, and misrepresentations of citizenship, Eddy Chibás, Batista, and the struggles for freedom during the years from 1946 to 1958 have become essential elements of official and popular historical memory in Cuba. Nonetheless, as this work has shown, fighting over memory among Cubans, like fighting over how contemporary and historical events are told, may not only be what makes Cuba *Cuban;* it may also be the hope that will launch a better, more democratic, just, and participatory political system in Cuba tomorrow.

However, for those who have led the Cuban Revolution since 1959 and for those who opposed it and supported Batista, the question of how democratic Cuba might actually be "tomorrow" remains rooted in the willingness to silence critical facts about that past that are highly inconvenient. Thus, as I write these words in the summer of 2017, Cuba stands at a monumental juncture in its history, three years after President Barack Obama and Raúl Castro took the surprise step of announcing and then inaugurating a renewal of diplomatic relations for the first time since 1961. Today, with the surprise election of President Donald Trump in the United States and the death of Fidel Castro less than three weeks later in November 2016, Cuba's present hangs in the balance as much as its future. By law, Communist Party rule remains uncontestable electorally and, in the absence of freedom of assembly, the right to strike, and a free press, unquestionable in public spaces as well as national discourse. Few examples better illustrate the marginality of citizens from state power than Fidel's transfer of power to Raúl in 2006 and Raúl's 2013 promise to pass the baton in 2018 to his handpicked successor, Miguel Díaz Canel, a Communist Party bureaucrat through whom Raúl—as continuing head of the military and intelligence forces—will still call the shots. Like 2016, 2018 may or may not be a pivotal year.

Nonetheless, however much Cuba may appear to remain the same, what Cubans now believe is possible has radically shifted. In 2016, Obama became (only) the second sitting U.S. president to visit Cuba; the other was Calvin Coolidge, who also visited a dictator, Gerardo Machado, in 1928. In contrast, however, to Coolidge's interest in bulwarking neocolonial rule, Obama addressed the Cuban people in terms that neither denied the role of the United States in historically limiting Cuban citizens' right to define their nation's political progress nor avoided discussing how the Castro brothers' one-party rule has managed, distorted, and arguably, since at least the late 1960s, patently ignored it. A product of U.S. and Cuban diplomatic negotiations, the audience that witnessed Obama's speech in person was seen on national Cuban television. It was noticeable that Raúl himself was not clapping throughout most of the speech, but the spontaneous applause of some audience members to certain lines was as shocking and inspiring to Cuban TV viewers as the presence of the U.S. president. The transcript represents something akin to a spontaneous, if coded, dialogue that expressed the ideas of many Cubans, most of whom are seldom heard:

> Before 1959, some Americans saw Cuba as something to exploit, ignored poverty, enabled corruption. And since 1959, we've been shadow-boxers in this battle of geopolitics and personalities. I know the history, but I refuse to be trapped by it. [*Applause*.] I've made it clear that the United States has neither the capacity, nor the intention to impose change on Cuba. What changes come will depend upon the Cuban people. We will not impose our political or economic system on you. We recognize that every country, every people, must chart its own course and shape its own model. But having removed the shadow of history from our relationship, I must speak honestly about the things that I believe—the things that we, as Americans, believe. As Martí said, "Liberty is the right of every man to be honest, to think and to speak without hypocrisy." . . . I believe citizens should be free to speak their mind without fear—[*applause*]—to organize, and to criticize their government, and to protest peacefully, and that the rule of law should not include arbitrary detentions of people who exercise those rights. [*Applause*.] I believe that every person should have the freedom to practice their faith peacefully and publicly. [*Applause*.] And, yes, I believe voters should be able to choose their governments in free and democratic elections. [*Applause*.] Not everybody agrees

with me on this. Not everybody agrees with the American people on this. But I believe those human rights are universal. [*Applause*.] I believe they are the rights of the American people, the Cuban people, and people around the world.[39]

Broadcast live in Cuba and around the world, stated before Raúl Castro himself, President Obama's words shook the foundations of what the majority of Cubans believed anyone could say in Cuba, perhaps most especially the president of the revolution's historic enemy, the United States.

As I discovered four months later when I traveled from Havana to Santiago and back again, family, friends, colleagues, and total strangers saw Barack Obama as one of their own. Joking, they called him "el mejor alcalde que ha tenido La Habana" (the best mayor Havana has ever had), a quip referring to how the announcement of Obama's visit prompted Raúl to suddenly order a massive restoration of infrastructure all over the city; the government repaired three-foot-deep potholes and streetlights that had not worked for years. Privately, however, Obama's words meant more to Cubans than an opportunity to indict the state. They made an American president a spokesman and an adopted hero for saying what no citizen in today's Cuba has the right to say. Obama turned the tables on history, taking the high ground and adopting the morally righteous discourse that Cuban heroes like Fidel Castro himself had employed in the past: Obama was in Cuba to make love, not war; to seek evidence of what Americans and Cubans shared, not what divided them; to forge a new, direct path toward change. Lost on no one in Cuba, it seemed, was the hope that the "change" Obama sought would not end at the diplomatic level or in the economic relations forged, as in the past, between U.S. corporate giants and Cuba's political oligarchs. *What is needed in Cuba is the same thing we needed before Fidel,* the elderly owner of a used bookstore in Santiago said to me in July 2016. What is that? I asked. *A total change of government,* he replied without skipping a beat.

For Obama in his quest to reverse the course of U.S. policy and relations with Cuba, articulating such an idea in overt terms would have been politically disastrous, evidence of yet another imperialist sleight of hand. But it was and is also an inconvenient truth. Back in the United States, most Americans I have talked to seem mainly concerned with ending the U.S. embargo against Cuba— but not so they can help promote entrepreneurialism, citizen empowerment, and access to information as vehicles of change. They want to know where I recommend they stay and which I think is the best beach. Similarly, one of the first issues to garner the U.S. media's attention in the wake of these historic accords was the demand of certain U.S. citizens that the Cuban government return the property it "confiscated" in the early weeks of 1959. Notably, the claimant to make the greatest public fuss was Carolyn Chester, none other than the daughter of Edmund Chester, Fulgencio Batista's paid publicist and the author of his most laudatory commissioned biographies.[40] Glossing the loss of her "family home" (now the residence of the Chinese ambassador) and other properties as part of the mass nationalization policies that took place two years after 1959, when U.S. aggression helped catalyze Fidel Castro's authoritarian turn, Carolyn Chester testified before a committee of the U.S. Congress on 18 June 2015. Tears streaming down her face, Chester declared, "It's very simple: we were Americans citizens, who were living, working, and investing in Cuba when the communists took over the pro-democracy government in 1959. We were not at war with Cuba and this was the first time in U.S. history that American properties were expropriated during peacetime."[41] Indeed, few island Cubans, then or now, would have agreed that Cuba was "not at war" at the time her father's properties were confiscated.

In fact, Chester's home and properties were seized by the Ministry of Ill-Gotten Goods, an agency founded in January 1959 to take back the businesses, luxury items, and homes of batistianos who had acquired them as a direct result of their ties and loyalty to a corrupt dictator and a state whose hands were clearly covered in blood. Notably, the ministry also seized the estates and goods of all immediate Batista supporters, much of which they put on display at the Cuban Capitol Building and auctioned off to finance the first social programs of the revolution. Included among these objects was the gold telephone that U.S. ambassador Gardner had given to Batista on behalf of the U.S.-owned telephone company as a celebration of Batista's willingness to let it raise rates and, more important, as a celebration of his survival of the Directorio Revolucionario's assault on the Presidential Palace the previous day.[42]

Thus returned to its historical context, Chester's story of victimization by a revolutionary government of Communists who seized family possessions "at gunpoint" simply does not add up. It is dismissive of the very real pain inflicted on citizens and the despicable attitudes that characterized Batista's and his cronies' views of the nation, its wealth, and their own eternal immunity from prosecution. Ironically, Chester's account also reads like yet another propaganda tale authored by one of Batista's favorite propagandists, Edmund Chester himself. The Ministry of Ill-Gotten Goods was not only one of the most popular agencies established in January 1959; its popularity, rightly or wrongly, was connected to the revolutionary state's six-month policy, inaugurated by Fidel Castro in 1959 under the title Operation Truth and exclusively targeting batistianos, that promised to eradicate government impunity forever from the Cuban political scene through dozens of trials and executions.[43]

Having been to Cuba nearly fifty times over the course of the past twenty years and counting on dozens of family, friends, and colleagues to educate me on "everyday" island Cubans' analysis of their country's state of affairs, I recognize how little sympathy narratives like that of Carolyn Chester and those of other former Batista supporters will garner among the Cuban public in the new era of relations between Cuba and the United States that President Obama inaugurated and, it is hoped, Trump might continue. Indeed, as many an astute member of FEU, the Directorio Revolucionario, Resistencia Cívica, or the 26th of July Movement underground have told me repeatedly from their homes in exile in both Miami, Florida, and San Juan, Puerto Rico, "El gran culpable nunca fue Fidel. Sin Batista, no hubieramos tenido nunca ese Fidel" (The great guilty one was never Fidel. Without Batista, we would never have had that Fidel).[44]

For many reasons, it is easy to say that limitations on civic freedom and public attitudes toward the legitimacy of the Cuban government are startlingly similar today to those of the Batista or even the Machado years. Yet there is little doubt that many aspects of the U.S. government have changed radically since then and even more radically since 1961. The reason for this is simple: as exemplified by Obama's reversal of policy and the overwhelming support it received in the United States, U.S. citizens' willingness to criticize and to revisit their own country's history has opened a path for analyzing the present and future. For this precise reason, the onslaught of ideas and information brought by U.S. citizens who are visiting the island in unprecedented numbers may prove impossible for the Cuban government to control. As in the 1950s, when foreign journalists played a central role in destabilizing Batista and legitimating the opposition, there may prove to be no better ally than the U.S. public when it comes to supporting change.

Indeed, as I traveled across the island in the summer of 2016, I discovered brash evidence of Cubans' thirst for information, including printed "graffiti" of

Figure 48. Painted on a nondescript wall in a small residential block near the Almejeiras Hospital in central Havana, this hand-printed and unauthorized image of Cuba's greatest nationalist and martyr José Martí reimagines him as an everyday Cuban, calling for the right of access to the Internet. Seemingly insignificant to an outsider's eyes, the image is a valiant, passionately articulated protest against the Castro regime's greatest weapon: control over knowledge, information, and the right of all citizens to news that could reshape how they perceive and relate to the Cuban state, the world, and their own lives.

José Martí wearing an "I love free Wi-Fi" T-shirt (figure 48). As occurred under Batista, ideas not regularly discussed in public venues constitute an alternative source of news—an informal but important clandestine press. For the majority of island Cubans, they represent a barometer for measuring their government's intransigence, their leaders' hypocritical self-interest, and their own impetus to demand swift, radical democratic change. That Cubans will do so by mandating revolution through electoral, unarmed, and civil means before resorting to armed struggle should surprise no one—especially the readers of this book. While Fidel Castro and his followers embraced the discourse of "love, not war" in order to contest Batista's militarization and authoritarian grip on power, Cubans today embrace not only discourses but actions that refute the authority, nature, and legitimacy of Fidel and his followers' government. *Heroes, Martyrs, and Political Messiahs in Revolutionary Cuba* serves as a reminder of how deeply the values of democracy are ingrained in Cuban political culture: the right to protest, the right to enjoy an uncensored press, the demands for racial justice and greater gender equality defined what it meant to be Cuban for most citizens of the 1940s and 1950s. Moreover, the mandate for government accountability formed a common foundation of shared morality. Just as important was the belief that Cubans who fought tyranny or simply opposed it any way that they could were everyday heroes, would-be martyrs in their own right. While today Cubans have surely abandoned all faith in political messiahs, they believe—perhaps more than ever—in themselves and the power of the individual to turn the tide of history and forge an unexpected tomorrow. However much Cuba may have changed, these ideas remain the core of who Cubans were, are, and will be.

NOTES

Introduction

1. Carlos Franqui, *Cuba, La Revolución: ¿Mito o Realidad? Memorias de un Fantasma Socialista* (Barcelona: Oceano Península, 2006), 236, 275.

2. Carlos Franqui, *Retrato de Familia con Fidel* (Barcelona: Seix Barral, 1981), *El Libro de los Doce* (Havana: Instituto del Libro, 1967), and *Diario de la Revolución Cubana* (Barcelona: R. Torres, 1976).

3. Some of the best memoirs are Carlos Franqui's *Retrato de Familia con Fidel* and his last book *Cuba, La Revolución;* Huber Matos, *Cómo Llegó la Noche* (Barcelona: Tusquets Editores, S.A., 2002); Mario Llerena, *The Unsuspected Revolution: The Birth and Rise of Castroism* (Ithaca, NY: Cornell University Press, 1978); Teresa Casuso, *Cuba and Castro*, trans. Elmer Grossberg (New York: Random House, 1961); Ruby Hart Phillips, *Cuba: Island of Paradox* (New York: McDowell, Obolensky, 1960); Juanita Castro and María Antonieta Collins, *Fidel y Raúl: Mis Hermanos, La Historia Secreta* (Doral, FL: Aguilar, 2009); Enrique Oltuski, *Vida Clandestina: My Life in the Cuban Revolution,* trans. Thomas Christensen and Carol Christensen (New York: Wiley, 2002); and the three-volume memoir by longtime Communist Lionel Soto that was published and then confiscated by Cuban intelligence forces, *De la Historia y la Memoria* (Havana: Editorial SI-MAR, S.A., 2006).

Valuable, engrossing biographies include Ilan Ehrlich, *Eduardo Chibás: The Incorrigible Man of Cuban Politics* (New York: Rowman & Littlefield, 2015); Robert E. Quirk, *Fidel Castro* (New York: Norton, 1993); Jon Lee Anderson, *Che Guevara: A Revolutionary Life,* rev. ed. (New York: Grove, 2010); José Alvarez, *Frank País: Architect of Cuba's Betrayed Revolution* (Boca Ratón, FL: Universal, 2009); Michael Sallah and Mitch Weiss, *The Yankee Comandante: The Untold Story of Courage, Passion, and One American's Fight to Liberate Cuba* (New York: Lyons, 2015); Aran Shetterly, *The Americano: Fighting with Castro for Cuba's Freedom* (Chapel Hill, NC: Algonquin Books, 2007); Miguel Hernández-Bauza, *Biografía de una Emoción Popular: El Dr. Grau* (Miami: Ediciones Universal, 1986); Celia Sánchez, *One Day in December: Celia Sánchez and the Cuban*

Revolution (New York: Monthly Review, 2013); Tom Gjelten, *Bacardí and the Long Fight for Cuba: The Biography of a Cause* (New York: Viking, 2008); John Paul Rathbone, *The Sugar King of Havana: The Rise and Fall of Julio Lobo, Cuba's Last Tycoon* (New York: Penguin Books, 2010).

4. Lillian Guerra, *The Myth of José Martí: Conflicting Nationalisms in Early Twentieth-Century Cuba* (Chapel Hill: University of North Carolina Press, 2005), and "The Struggle to Redefine Martí and 'Cuba Libre' in the 1920s," in *The Cuban Republic and José Martí: Reception and Use of a National Symbol,* ed. Mauricio A. Font and Alfonso W. Quiroz (New York: Lexington Books, 2006), 34–52.

5. See esp. Alejandro de la Fuente, *A Nation for All: Race, Inequality, and Politics in Twentieth-Century Cuba* (Chapel Hill: University of North Carolina Press, 2001); Louis A. Pérez Jr., *On Becoming Cuban: Identity, Nationality, and Culture* (Chapel Hill: University of North Carolina Press, 1999), and *The Structure of Cuban History: Meanings and Purpose of the Past* (Chapel Hill: University of North Carolina Press, 2013); Gillian McGillivray, *Blazing Cane: Sugar Communities, Class, and State Formation in Cuba, 1868–1959* (Durham, NC: Duke University Press, 2009); Ned Sublette, *Cuba and Its Music: From the First Drums to the Mambo* (Chicago: Chicago Review, 2004), 235–584.

6. Frank Argote-Freyre offers an enticing, complex portrait of Batista but ends his story in 1944. See *Fulgencio Batista: From Revolutionary to Strongman* (New Brunswick, NJ: Rutgers University Press, 2006). See also Fulgencio Batista y Zaldívar, *Respuesta* (México, DF: Manuel León Sánchez, S.C.L., 1960), *Piedras y Leyes* (México, DF: Ediciones Botas, 1961), *Cuba Betrayed* (New York: Vantage, 1962), *Gobernar es Prever* (México, DF: n.p., 1962), and *Paradojísmo: Cuba, Víctima de las Contradicciones Internacionales* (México, DF: Ediciones Botas, 1964).

7. For one of the most recent examples of this, see T. J. English, *Havana Nocturne: How the Mob Owned Cuba and Then Lost It to the Revolution* (New York: Harper, 2007).

8. Charles Ameringer, *The Cuban Democratic Experience: The Auténtico Years, 1944–1952* (Gainesville: University Press of Florida, 2000), and *The Caribbean Legion: Patriots, Politicians, Soldiers of Fortune, 1946–50* (University Park: Pennsylvania State University Press, 1996); Ramón Leocadio Bonachea Hernández and Marta San Martín, *The Cuban Insurrection, 1952–1959* (New Brunswick, NJ: Transaction Books, 1974); Julia Sweig, *Inside the Cuban Revolution: Fidel Castro and the Urban Underground* (Cambridge, MA: Harvard University Press, 2002); Antonio Rafael de la Cova, *The Moncada Attack: Birth of the Cuban Revolution* (Columbia: University of South Carolina, 2007); Michelle Chase, *Revolution Within the Revolution: Women and Gender Politics in Cuba, 1952–1962* (Chapel Hill: University of North Carolina Press, 2015).

9. Steve Cushion, *A Hidden History of the Cuban Revolution: How the Working Class Shaped the Guerrillas' Victory* (New York: Monthly Review, 2016), 13–16, 105–28.

10. Sweig, 9.

11. Quoted in Lillian Guerra, *Visions of Power in Cuba: Revolution, Redemption, and Resistance, 1959–1971* (Chapel Hill: University of North Carolina Press, 2012), 17.

12. Ibid., 43.

13. Franqui, *Cuba, La Revolución,* 90–91.

14. Aline Helg, *Our Rightful Share: The Afro-Cuban Struggle for Equality, 1886–1912* (Chapel Hill: University of North Carolina Press, 1995); Marial Iglesias Utset, *A Cul-*

tural History of Cuba During the U.S. Occupation, 1898–1902 (Chapel Hill: University of North Carolina Press, 2011); Guerra, *The Myth of José Martí*; Melina Pappademos, *Black Political Activism in the Cuban Republic* (Chapel Hill: University of North Carolina Press, 2014).

15. Guerra, *Visions of Power,* 41.

16. Louis A. Pérez Jr. has devoted many scholarly volumes to exploring the facts and the trauma of the U.S. betrayal of Cuba in 1898. Among his best are *The War of 1898: The United States and Cuba in History and Historiography* (Chapel Hill: University of North Carolina, 1998), and *Cuba Under the Platt Amendment, 1902–1934* (Pittsburgh: University of Pittsburgh Press, 1987). See also Jules R. Benjamin, *The United States and the Origins of the Cuban Revolution: An Empire of Liberty in an Age of National Liberation* (Princeton, NJ: Princeton University Press, 1990); and Philip S. Foner, *The Spanish-Cuban-American War and the Birth of American Imperialism,* 2 vols. (New York: Monthly Review, 1972).

17. Quoted in Pérez, *The Structure of Cuban History,* 153.

18. "Declaraciones de Batista a la A.P.," in *Todo Empezó en el Moncada* (México, DF: Editorial Diógenes, S.A., 1973), 11.

19. Fulgencio Batista, "Proclama al Pueblo de Cuba. Consejo de Ministros. 10 Marzo 1952," in *Batista: El Golpe,* by José Luis Padrón and Luis Adrián Betancourt (Havana: Ediciones Unión, 2013), 352–53.

20. Louis A. Pérez Jr., *Army Politics in Cuba, 1898–1958* (Pittsburgh: University of Pittsburgh Press, 1976), 131; Ameringer, *The Cuban Democratic Experience,* 182–84.

21. Chase, *Revolution Within the Revolution,* 24–25. Although Chase cites other works, perhaps those that best argue that the root of all change happened with Fidel Castro's assault on the Moncada Barracks are officially commissioned histories such as *Todo Empezó en el Moncada,* cited above, and the best-selling testimony of Haydée Santamaría, *Haydée Habla del Moncada* (Havana: Ediciones Políticas, 1967). The latter begins: "In the history of Cuba, probably there is no other date more transcendent than the 26th of July 1953, if we exclude the 10th of October 1868 [when Cubans declared independence from Spain]."

22. Padrón and Betancourt, 288.

23. Pérez, *Army Politics in Cuba,* 131.

24. Michelle Chase's groundbreaking *Revolution Within the Revolution,* documents precisely the central role of women and the forging of new forms of protest, largely thanks to women. See 16–17, 27–110.

25. Carmelo Mesa-Lago, *Cuba in the 1970s: Pragmatism and Institutionalization* (Albuquerque: University of New Mexico Press, 1978); Hugh Thomas, *Cuba; or, The Pursuit of Freedom* (London: Eyre & Spottiswoode, 1971).

26. Guerra, *Visions of Power.*

27. Guerra, *The Myth of José Martí.*

28. Michael Bustamante, "Cuban Counterpoints: Memory Struggles in Revolution and Exile, 1959–1980" (PhD diss., Yale University, 2016), 40–41.

29. This book breaks with works that portray foreign journalists as the dupes and puppets of Fidel Castro and the 26th of July Movement. See Anthony de Palma, *The Man Who Invented Fidel: Castro, Cuba, and Herbert L. Matthews of the New York Times* (New

York: Perseus Books, 2006); Humberto Fontova, *The Longest Romance: The Main-stream Media and Fidel Castro* (New York: Encounter Books, 2013); and Jay Mallin Sr., *Covering Castro: Rise and Decline of Cuba's Communist Dictator* (Washington, DC: US-Cuba Institute Press and Transaction, 1994).

30. Leonard Ray Teel, *Reporting the Cuban Revolution: How Castro Manipulated American Journalists* (Baton Rouge: Lousiana State University Press, 2015).

31. Ameringer, *The Cuban Democratic Experience* and *The Caribbean Legion;* Pérez, *Army Politics in Cuba,* 101–65; Jana Lipman, *Guantánamo: A Working-Class History Between Empire and Revolution* (Berkeley: University of California, 2008); Robert Smith, *The United States and Cuba: Business and Diplomacy, 1917–1960* (New York: Bookman Associates, 1960).

32. "The Platt Amendment," in *The Cuba Reader: The Making of a Revolutionary Society,* ed. Philip Brenner, William M. Leogrande, et al. (New York: Grove, 1989), 30–31.

33. Undoubtedly, Louis A. Pérez Jr. is a principal pioneer of the history of the Cuban repub-lic. Key works include *Cuba Under the Platt Amendment, Cuba: Between Reform and Revolution,* 4th ed. (New York: Oxford University Press, 2010), *Intervention, Revolution and Politics in Cuba, 1913–1921* (Pittsburgh: University of Pittsburgh Press, 1978). See also Guerra, *The Myth of José Martí;* Robert Whitney, *State and Revolution in Cuba: Mass Mobilization and Political Change, 1920–1940* (Chapel Hill: University of North Carolina Press, 2001); Helg.

34. Ada Ferrer provides the best account of the origins, use, and evolution of the "anti-racist" ideology of the independence wars in *Insurgent Cuba: Race, Nation and Revolution, 1868–1898* (Chapel Hill: University of North Carolina Press, 1999).

35. Helg; Guerra, *The Myth of José Martí,* 193–254; Pappademos.

36. McGillivray; Pappademos.

37. Whitney; Lionel Soto, *La Revolución del '33,* 3 vols. (Havana: Editorial de Ciencias Sociales, 1977).

38. Frank Argote-Freyre, "The Political Afterlife of Eduardo Chibás: Evolution of a Sym-bol, 1951–1991," *Cuban Studies* 32 (2001): 76–77; Robert J. Alexander, *A History of Organized Labor in Cuba* (Westport, CT: Praeger, 2002), 64–65; Pérez, *Army Politics in Cuba,* 106–8.

39. Pérez, *Army Politics in Cuba,* 101–15.

40. Ibid., 85, 104.

41. Quoted in Alexander, 78.

42. Luis Conte Agüero, *Eduardo Chibás: El Adalid de Cuba* (México, DF: Editorial Jus, S.A., 1955); Ana Cairo, ed. *Eduardo Chibás: Imaginarios* (Santiago de Cuba: Editorial Oriente, 2010); Elena Alvarez Martín, *Eduardo Chibás: Clarinada Fecunda* (Havana: Editorial de Ciencias Sociales, 2009); Hernel Pérez Concepción, *Las Luchas Políticas del Holguín Republicano, 1944–1948* (Holguín: Ediciones Holguín, 2007); and Ehrlich.

43. Handwritten mimeographed letter by Fidel Castro to José Arcadio Rodríguez Torres, 28 October 1951, in José Arcadio Rodríguez Torres, *Mi Triste Historia* (Havana: n.p., 1959), 19; Juanita Castro and Collins, 100–103.

44. Eduardo Chibás, "Yo Acuso," in *Antología Cívica de Eduardo R. Chibás: Artículos y Discursos del Formidable Fundador del Partido Ortodoxo,* ed. Hugo Mir (Havana: Edi-torial Lex, 1952), 119–22; Fidel Castro, "I Accuse (January 28, 1952)," in *Revolutionary*

Struggle, 1947–1958, vol. 1 of *The Selected Works of Fidel Castro,* ed. Rolando E. Bonachea and Nelson P. Valdés (Cambridge, MA: MIT Press, 1972), 136–43.

45. Fidel Castro, "Nuestro Partido" and "Recuento Crítico del PPC," in Cairo, 184–85.

46. "Fidel Castro ante la Tumba de Chibás (Extracto)," *Bohemia,* 18–25 February 1959, 103–4.

47. Marta Rojas, "El Asalto al Moncada," and Herminio Portell Vilá, "Tesis Sobre el Suicidio en la Historia Política de Cuba," *Bohemia,* 1 February 1959, 28, 69, 112. For a study of Cuba's abnormally high rate of suicide, see Louis A. Pérez Jr. *To Die in Cuba: Suicide and Society* (Chapel Hill: University of North Carolina Press, 2007).

1. Cuba on the Verge

1. Ramón Rey Martínez to Eduardo Chibás, 7 May 1949, Archivo Nacional de Cuba, Fondo Eduardo Chibas (hereafter ANC, FEC), fondo 176, legajo 15, expediente 406, 1.

2. Ibid., 2.

3. Chibás was constitutionally endowed with the right to present inquiries to Congress as a common citizen. The text of his complaint can be found under the heading "Al Señor President del Senado, [de] Eduardo R. Chibás Rivas, Cubano, Vecino del Edificio López Serrano, Vedado, La Habana, Manifiesto . . ." and accompanying news clippings from *El Mundo, Diario de la Marina,* and *Bohemia,* ANC, FEC, fondo 176, legajo 9, expediente 268.

4. Ehrlich, 98–99; Chibás, "Contra El Pulpo Eléctrico," in Mir, 149–51.

5. Pérez, *The Structure of Cuban History,* 15–16, 19.

6. Ibid., 150, 159.

7. Erasmo Ramean to Eddy Chibás, 22 February 1949, ANC, FEC, fondo 176, expediente 1139, legajo 39.

8. Quoted in Ehrlich, 61.

9. Pérez, *To Die in Cuba,* 65.

10. Ibid., 136–39.

11. Ibid., 315–16, 129–30.

12. Quoted in ibid., 317; see also Ehrlich, 7–10.

13. Pérez, *To Die in Cuba,* 318; Ehrlich, 16–17.

14. "El Tirito de Chibás," *La Política Cómica: Semanario Satírico Ilustrado. Organo Oficial de Liborio,* 2 June 1940, 21; Chibás shot himself on 14 November 1939. *Diario de la Marina* published a photograph of him in recovery that appears in a scrapbook of his life complied by Eva Jiménez Ruiz, "Muerte de Nuestro Adalid Eduardo R. Chibás," ANC, FEC, fondo 176, expediente 1676, legajo 47, fuera de caja.

15. "El Suicidio de Chibás (Drama Espeluznante Prohibido para Menores de Cuarenta Años)," *Prensa Libre,* 4 July 1946, 1. The author is grateful to archivist Jorge Macle for the discovery of this unique source.

16. Ibid., 3.

17. Sánchez Arango's daughter offers the most complete chronology, analysis, and compilation of documents related to the three-month public battle ending in Chibás's death. Lela Sánchez Echeverría, *La Polémica Infinita: Aureliano vs. Chibás y Viceversa* (Miami: self-published, 2004), esp. 84–89.

18. "Testamento Político de Chibás en el Primer Aniversario de Su Muerte," ANC, FEC, fondo 176, expediente 43 (pertenece al expediente 3632), fuera de caja 1.

19. Quoted in Ehrlich, 233.

20. Ibid., 235.

21. Jiménez Ruiz.

22. Ehrlich, 237.

23. Goar Mestre, "Palabras del Sr. Goar Mestre . . . 2 de Octubre de 1949," in *Universidad del Aire del Circuito CMQ. Tercer Curso. Octubre 1949–Junio 1950* (Havana: Editorial Lex, 1949), 2–3.

24. For the best biography of Mañach, see Duanel Díaz, *Mañach o la República* (Havana: Letras Libres, 2003).

25. Jorge Mañach, "Introducción al Curso," in *Universidad del Aire del Circuito CMQ*, 6–7.

26. Enrique Loynaz del Castillo, "Los Ideales Cubanos de la Fundación, ¿Están Siendo Realizados?" in *Universidad del Aire del Circuito CMQ*, 11.

27. Ibid., 16.

28. Ibid., 15–17.

29. Jorge L. Martí, "¿Está Falseada la Democracia Cubana?" and Juan Antonio Rubio Padilla, "¿Ha Habido una Revolución en Cuba?" in *Universidad del Aire del Circuito CMQ*, 19–42.

30. Carlos Márquez Sterling, "Los Partidos Politicos Cubanos: ¿Cuáles Son Sus Deficiencias?" in *Universidad del Aire del Circuito CMQ*, 93–102.

31. Rubio Padilla, 36.

32. Rafael García Barcena, "La Frustración Revolucionaria," *Bohemia,* 16 May 1948, 12, 114.

33. Raúl Roa, "Machadato a la Vista," *Bohemia,* 16 May 1948, 48–49, 83.

34. Lucilo de la Peña, "¡Cubanos, Ahora! ¡Ahora o Nunca!" *Bohemia,* 16 May 1948, 50.

35. Ehrlich, 60–61; Eduardo Chibás, "Nosotros y la Patria," in Mir, 157–58.

36. Knowledge of this appeal comes to me from my grandfather, Heriberto Rodríguez Rosado, the peasant son of a mambí captain turned top employee for Sabatés, the Cuban subsidiary of Procter and Gamble and a deeply committed Ortodoxo.

37. Ehrlich, 61.

38. "Guido García Inclán, Su Editorial de *El Periodico del Aire* [Radio] COCO, Mayo 26, 1948." ANC, FEC, fondo 176, expediente 17, legajo 2.

39. Argote-Freyre, 252–57.

40. Alberto Taboada to Eduardo R. Chibás, 28 March 1951, ANC, FEC, fondo 176, expediente 1140, legajo 39.

41. McGillivray, 240–41.

42. Juanita Castro and Collins, 115. The image of Batista holding a four-year-old smiling Raúl Castro Ruz at an event promoting his civic-military schools is widely available on the Web; for example, at http://www.latinamericanstudies.org/batista-1.htm.

43. McGillivray, 241.

44. Ameringer, *The Cuban Democratic Experience,* 32–33.

45. Ibid., 33; Guerra, *The Myth of José Martí,* 47, 71.

46. The same edition of *La Política Cómica* satirizing Chibás's first self-inflicted gunshot wound features botellas in multiple caricatures, including a cover image of a hu-

man-headed dog with a botella for a tail as he follows a cigar-smoking politician down the street, attempting to lick his rear end.

47. Ameringer, *The Cuban Democratic Experience,* 33–34.
48. Ibid., 35.
49. Ehrlich, 31.
50. Lionel Martin, *The Early Fidel: Roots of Castro's Communism* (Secaucus, NJ: Lyle Stuart, 1978), 36.
51. Ibid., 22–24.
52. Carlos Franqui, *Vida, Aventuras y Desastres de un Hombre Llamado Castro* (Barcelona: Editorial Planeta, 1988), 40–46; Ehrlich, 12–15, 28–31, 46–47.
53. Soto, *De la Historia y la Memoria,* 1:50–51.
54. Ibid., 1:29–30.
55. Gjelten, 145.
56. Ehrlich, 57.
57. Ameringer, *The Cuban Democratic Experience,* 39; Eduardo Sáenz Rovner, *The Cuban Connection: Drug Trafficking, Smuggling, and Gambling in Cuba from the 1920s to the Revolution* (Chapel Hill: University of North Carolina Press, 2008), 65–67.
58. Alberto Arredondo, "El Gobierno Ha Adoptado un Plan para que El Cubano No Pasa Hambre," *Bohemia,* 2 June 1946, 34–35.
59. "Picadillo a la Criolla. Las Manifestaciones de Hoy," *Bohemia,* 7 April 1946, 18.
60. Quoted in Conte Agüero, *Eduardo Chibás,* 466.
61. Quoted in Cairo, 54.
62. Ibid., 55.
63. Emma Pérez, *La Política Educacional del Dr. Grau San Martín* (Havana: UCar García, S.A., 1948), 21, 36.
64. Ibid., 36.
65. Ibid., 38–39.
66. Ibid., 72.
67. Ibid., front matter.
68. Ibid., 40. Manolo Castro was killed in February 1948 by rival gang members. His death implicated Fidel Castro; however, the latter accused Rolando Masferrer of the killing and Manolo Castro's murder was never solved. See "Detuvo la Policía a Cuatro Estudiantes Acusados por el Homicidio de Manolo Castro," *Diario de la Marina,* 26 February 1948, 1, 25.
69. Ameringer, *The Cuban Democratic Experience,* 50–51; Ameringer, *The Caribbean Legion,* 35–39.
70. Ameringer, *The Caribbean Legion,* 39–40.
71. Juanita Castro and Collins, 86.
72. Franqui, *Cuba, La Revolución,* 133–37.
73. Ameringer, *The Cuban Democratic Experiment,* 50; Ameringer, *The Caribbean Legion,* 9–10.
74. Ameringer, *The Cuban Democratic Experiment,* 53; Ehrlich, 28–31.
75. Ameringer, *The Cuban Democratic Experiment,* 54–55; Ameringer, *The Caribbean Legion,* 40–60.
76. Ameringer, *The Cuban Democratic Experiment,* 54–55.

77. Marta Rojas, "El Combate de Fidel por la Reinvidicación de la Campaña de la Demajagua," *Granma,* 1 April 1987, 2.

78. Quirk, 3–23; Martin, 19–28; Juanita Castro and Collins, 39–88; Georgie Anne Geyer, *Guerrilla Prince: The Untold Story of Fidel Castro* (New York: Little, Brown, 1991), 3–49. See also Patrick Symmes, *The Boys from Dolores: Fidel Castro's Schoolmates from Revolution to Exile* (New York: Vintage Books, 2007).

79. Rojas, 2; Soto, *De la Historia y la Memoria,* 1:52–53.

80. Soto, *De la Historia y la Memoria,* 1:53–54.

81. Riera, *Cuba Política, 1899–1955* (Havana: n.p., 1955), 512, 559.

82. Ibid., 53–55.

83. Martin, 19.

84. Soto, *De la Historia y la Memoria,* 1:55.

85. Mario Mencia, "Fidel Castro en el Bogotazo," *Bohemia,* 14 April 1978, 50–56; and Rojas, 2–3.

86. Rojas, 2–3.

87. "Al Grito de ¡Fuera Grau!" *Noticias de Hoy,* 4 November 1947, 1.

88. Ibid., 5.

89. Rojas, 3.

90. "30 Mil Personas Condenaron El Gobierno en la Universidad, al Grito de ¡Fuera Grau!" *Noticias de Hoy,* 7 November 1947, 1, 5.

91. "Júbilo en Manzanillo al llegar la Campana. Fué entregada al Alcalde por Medio de Acta," *Diario de la Marina,* 13 November 1947, back page.

92. Fidel Castro, "The Dignity of Our Freedom Fighters (November 6, 1947)," in Bonachea and Valdés, 132.

93. "Júbilo en Manzanillo," 1, back page.

94. Ibid., back page.

95. Arturo Alfonso Roselló, "Explica Chibás la Causa y Origen de Su Divorcio del Doctor Grau," *Carteles,* 23 May 1948, 28.

96. "Al Pueblo de Cuba," *Bohemia,* 16 May 1948, 43.

97. The author is grateful to Maikel Fariñas for pointing out the link between the Ortodoxos' cogged wheel and Cuba's *rotarios.*

98. Grupos de Propaganda Doctrinal Ortodoxa, *Doctrina del Partido Ortodoxo: Independencia Económica, Libertad Política, Justicia Social* (Havana: n.p., 1947), 1.

99. El Mazo de Hábanos to Carlos Lechuga, 3 July 1951, ANC, FEC, fondo 176, expediente 1146, legajo 39.

100. Gastón Baquero, "Chibás Considera Necesario Restitutir al Pueblo la Fe en los Hombres de Gobierno para Encauzar los Destinos de la Nación," *Diario de la Marina,* 9 May 1948, 22.

101. Ibid.

102. Ibid., 22–23.

103. Ibid.

104. Ibid.

105. See flyer from the Asociación Pro-Democracia, Grupo Azucarero, Ramiro A. Fernández Collection, Cuban Heritage Collection, University of Miami (hereafter CHC, UM), no. 5260, box 1.

106. "Hemos Venido Cerca de 300 Delegados Auténticos a Votar por Lázaro Peña," 10 April 1947, ANC, FEC, fondo 176, expediente 194, legajo 6.

107. José Ricardo, Manuel Abón Silveira, et al. to Eduardo Chibás, April 1947 and accompanying manifesto "Comisión Obrera Nacional del PRCA. Fracción de Trabajadores Auténticos del Sindicato del Central Palma," ANC, FEC, fondo 176, expediente 194, legajo 6.

108. Ibid., 251–53; Ehrlich, 39–40.

109. See political advertisement "Vergüenza contra Dinero!" *Bohemia,* 16 May 1948, 42.

110. Ehrlich, 74–75.

111. Guerra, *Visions of Power,* 40.

112. Ibid., 261n67.

113. Ibid., 85; Ameringer, *The Cuban Democratic Experience,* 75, 77.

114. Ehrlich, 84; Ameringer, *The Cuban Democratic Experience,* 81.

115. Ameringer, *The Cuban Democratic Experience,* 82–83; Ehrlich, 104–5.

116. "El Pistolerismo es el Cancer Nacional," *Bohemia,* 20 February 1949, 68–69.

117. Eduardo Chibás, "Sangre y Cieno," "Pecadores, Apostatas y Ladrones," and "¡Expulsemos del Templo a los Mercaderes y Ladrones!" in Mir, 37–76.

118. Ehrlich, 86–88; Ameringer, *The Cuban Democratic Experience,* 78.

119. O. Ruíz to Carlos Prío Socarrás, 11 May 1949, ANC, FEC, fondo 176, expediente 4–6, legajo 15.

120. "Grave Desorden Anoche, en el Parque Central," *Diario de la Marina,* 12 March 1949, 30; "Infame Ultraje de Marinos," *Noticias de Hoy,* 12 March 1949, 1, 10.

121. The current Cuban government maintains a variety of blogs featuring Chaviano's famous pictures as well as opinion pieces on the transcendence of the event. Examples are found at https://cubalagrannacion.wordpress.com/2010/09/12/las-fotografias-de-la-afrenta-de -los-marines-yanquis-a-jose-marti/; http://www.eumed.net/libros-gratis/2010f/891/ORIGE N%20DE%20DOS%20FOTOGRAFIAS%20HOY%20HISTORICAS.htm; and http:// www.somosjovenes.cu/articulo/agravio-estatua-jose-marti-final.

122. "Infame Ultraje de Marinos," 10.

123. Soto, *De la Historia y la Memoria,* 1:85–88.

124. "Un Lamentable y Bochornoso Incidente que Conmovió a Cuba," *Bohemia,* 20 March 1949, 54–57; an outtake from Butler's televised apology, in which he allegedly forgets the name of José Martí, appears in *¡Viva la República!* (ICAIC, 1972).

125. Jorge Mañach, "Si los Jueces Nos Fallan . . . (y Otras Notas de la Varia Actualidad)," *Bohemia,* 20 March 1949, 58, 89–90.

126. Quoted in Conte Agüero, *Eduardo Chibás,* 597.

127. Quoted in Cairo, 104.

128. Quoted in Conte Agüero, *Eduardo Chibás,* 599.

129. Raúl Lorenzo, "Lucha por el Liderato Oposicionista," *Bohemia,* 13 March 1949, 56, 74.

130. "¡Vergüenza contra el Dinero! Palabras que Dicen Mucho," ANC, FEC, fondo 176, expediente 17, legajo 2, p. 4.

131. Raúl Cabrera Isidrón to Eduardo Chibás Rivas, 8 June 1948, ANC, FEC, fondo 176, expediente 1105, legajo 36.

132. Victor del Pino to Eduardo R. Chibás Rivas, 7 June 1948, ANC, FEC, fondo 176, expediente 1105, legajo 36, p. 1.

133. Ibid., 2.

134. "Carta de *Bohemia* al Presidente de la República," *Bohemia,* 13 March 1949, 57.

135. Ehrlich, 98–101.

136. Padre Jaime Genescá y Rovira to Eduardo Chibás, 9 May 1949, ANC, FEC, fondo 176, expediente 406, legajo 15.

137. Emlio Maza y Rodríguez, *La Inconstitucionalidad de los Tribunales de Urgencia. Recurso Presentado ante el Tribunal Supremo de Justicia* (Havana: n.p., 1947).

138. Ehrlich, 107; "El Juicio del Ex-Senador Chibás," *Carteles,* 8 May 1949, 49–50.

139. "Cuba Entera contra el Pulpo Eléctrico," *Bohemia,* 1 May 1949, 46–47.

140. "¡Hay que Apretar las Filas!" *Bohemia,* 1 May 1949, 56.

141. Raúl Gutiérrez, "El Pueblo Opina Sobre la Condena de Chibás," *Bohemia,* 8 May 1949, 52.

142. Jorge Mañach, "Chibás en Su Castillo," *Bohemia,* 15 May 1949, 48.

143. René Felipe Bavelo Feorte to Eduardo R. Chibás, 13 May 1949, ANC, FEC, fondo 176, expediente 406, legajo 15, pp. 2–3.

144. María del Carmen Sánchez Calero to Eduardo R. Chibás, 27 May 1949, ANC, FEC, fondo 176, expediente 408, legajo 15.

145. For a particularly moving example, see Pedro Alfonso to Eduardo Chibás Ribas [*sic*], 21 May 1949, ANC, FEC, fondo 176, expediente 407, legajo 15.

146. Manuel Falcon González to Eduardo R. Chibás, 28 April 1949, ANC, FEC, fondo 176, expediente 404, legajo 15, p. 1.

147. Elena Lavrín Barinaga [?] to Eduardo Chibás, 19 March 1951, ANC, FEC, fondo 176, expediente 1140, legajo 39, pp. 2–4; Antonia García Cabello to Eduardo Chivás [*sic*], 9 March 1951, and Secretaria Particular to Antonia García Cabello, 21 March 1951, ANC, FEC, fondo 176, expediente 1139, legajo 39.

148. Gerardo Aguirre Rodríguez to Eduardo R. Chivás [*sic*], 13 May 1949, ANC, FEC, fondo 176, expediente 406, legajo 15; Rukú Reyes to Eduardo Chibás, 24 May 1949, ANC, FEC, fondo 176, expediente 408, legajo 15.

149. José Ceruto to Eduardo Chibás, 23 February 1951, ANC, FEC, fondo 176, expediente 1139, legajo 39.

150. Guido García Inlcán, "El Editorial. Carta Abierta a Eduardo R. Chibás," 19 May 1949, ANC, FEC, fondo 176, expediente 407, legajo 15.

151. Emerito Collazo to Eduardo R. Chivás [*sic*], 29 March 1949, ANC, FEC, fondo 176, expediente 408, legajo 15; Otilio Pernus Pérez to Eduardo R. Chibás Rivas, 19 May 1949, ANC, FEC, fondo 176, expediente 406, legajo 15.

152. Andrés Jiménez Vázquez to Eduardo R. Chibás, 13 May 1949, ANC, FEC, fondo 176, expediente 406, legajo 15.

153. Prof. Dr. Henrich to Eduardo Chiva [*sic*], 15 May 1949, ANC, FEC, fondo 176, expediente 406, legajo 15.

154. Gilberto García Batista to Eduardo R. Chibás, 28 April 1949, ANC, FEC, fondo 176, expediente 404, legajo 15, p. 1.

155. Benito Castillo to Eduardo R. Chibás, 21 May 1948, ANC, FEC, fondo 176, expediente 1104, legajo 36.

156. Letter from Guantánamo missing page with signature, 28 May 1948, in ANC, FEC, fondo 176, expediente 1104, legajo 36. Note that the letter is marked by the archive as folios 121–22.

157. Mario Ribadulla to Eduardo R. Chibás, 4 June 1948, ANC, FEC, fondo 176, expediente 1105, legajo 36, p. 3.

158. Charles "Carlos" Ariet Aulet to Eduardo Chibás, 5 March 1951, in ANC, FEC, fondo 176, expediente 1139, legajo 39.

159. Ibid., 48–49, 82.

160. Ehrlich, 109.

161. "El Presidente Prío Anuncia al Pueblo de Cuba la Rebaja de las Tarifas Eléctricas," *Bohemia,* 15 May 1949, 58.

162. "Otro Gran Triunfo del Pueblo," *Bohemia,* 22 May 1949, 56.

163. Dr. Carlos M. Seiglie Ferrer to Eduardo Chibás Rivas, 8 May 1949, ANC, FEC, fondo 176, expediente 406, legajo 15, p. 1.

164. Pablo Calvo Cárdenas to Eduardo Chibás, 20 February 1951, ANC, FEC, fondo 176, expediente 1139, legajo 39, pp. 1–2.

165. Luis Hamburg, "Pelea de Gallos en Holguín: 'Chibás' le Saca los Ojos a Batista," *Bohemia,* 18 February 1951, 54–55; Chase, *Revolution Within the Revolution,* 23–27.

166. The Chibás collection at Cuba's national archive includes a 121-folio file of letters, telegrams, posters, newspaper clippings, and Chibás's speeches on these events. See "Documentos Relacionados con la Aggression de la Política y el Ejército contra la Manifestación Popular Ortodoxa . . . ," ANC, FEC, fondo 176, expediente 271, legajo 90.

167. Ehrlich, 197–200.

168. Ibid., 200–205; Eduardo R. Chibás, "¡Sangre y Azucar!" *Bohemia,* 4 March 1951, 70–71, 92.

169. "Los Lamentables Sucesos del Domingo," *Bohemia,* 25 February 1951, 64–65.

170. Ibid., 60–65.

171. "Editorial. Una Sentida Apelación al Patriotismo y la Serenidad," *Bohemia,* 25 February 1951, 58–59.

172. Herminio Portell Vilá, "¡Hacia la Dictadura!" *Bohemia,* 25 February 1951, 56, 80.

173. Sánchez Echeverría, 62–83; Ehrlich, 221–31.

174. Ehrlich, 229–30.

175. Ibid., 210–18.

176. Daniel del Solar, "Jauja en Cuba: No Parece Danza sino Rumba de Millones," *Visión,* 21 August 1951, 10–11.

177. Lorenzo Pineyro González to Eduardo Chivá [*sic*], 26 February 1951, ANC, FEC, fondo 176, expediente 1139, legajo 39.

2. *El Último Aldabonazo*

1. "Testamento Político de Chibás. 16 Agosto 1952," ANC, FEC, fondo 176, expediente 43 (pertenece al expediente 3632), fuera de caja.

2. del Solar, 12.

3. Dr. José M. Fadraga to Emilio Ochoa, 21 September 1951, ANC, FEC, fondo 176, expediente 2070 A, legajo 43, p. 1.

4. Ehrlich, 238–39.

5. Pepín Sánchez, "Apuntes para la Historia. Eduardo R. Chibás, del 7 de Marzo al 27 Noviembre 1935," *Bohemia,* 11 November 1951, 60–61, 81.

6. See an example of this preserved in Cuban Heritage Collection, University of Miami, Eduardo Chibás Collection, "Ephemera."

7. Jorge Domínguez, "The Batista Regime in Cuba," in *Sultanistic Regimes,* ed. H. E. Chehabi and Juan J. Linz (Baltimore, MD: Johns Hopkins University Press, 1998), 120.

8. Quoted in Ameringer, *The Cuban Democratic Experience,* 169.

9. Padrón and Betancourt, 64.

10. Ameringer, *The Cuban Democratic Experience,* 175.

11. Fidel Castro, "I Accuse (January 18, 1952)," in Bonachea and Valdés, 136–43.

12. Ameringer, *The Cuban Democratic Experience,* 175.

13. Jorge Quintana, "Eso No Es Historia O los Capítulos Que se le Olvidaron al Señor Fulgencio Batista," *Bohemia,* 12 December 1950, 6–10, 140–41.

14. Ibid., 175.

15. As a child, I heard this joke from my grandfather Heriberto Rodríguez Rosado (1907–1992), a stalwart Ortodoxo, but it also appeared in the transcript of a live television interview with Ortodoxo Party chairman Emilio Millo Ochoa on *Ante la Prensa,* 24 August 1952. See Partido del Pueblo Cubano (Ortodoxo), *Una Entrevista y una Defensa Histórica* (Havana: n.p., 1953), 10.

16. Gladys Marel García-Pérez, *Insurrection and Revolution: Armed Struggle in Cuba, 1952–1959* (Boulder, CO: Lynne Rienner, 1998), 4; Pérez, *Army Politics in Cuba,* 126–27; Thomas, 1008–12.

17. Pérez, *Army Politics in Cuba,* 126.

18. Padrón and Betancourt, 25–30. Batista went so far as to claim that he had rejected army officers' invitation to stage a coup even earlier, in 1948, and argued, as he did on 10 March 1952, that he staved off a "self-coup" that Prío would have launched himself in order to retain the reins of power. Batista, *Respuesta,* 445–59.

19. Filmed interview with Alfredo J. Sadulé by Lillian Guerra and Abel Sierra Madero, 21 July 2014, Hialeah, FL.

20. "Confidencial. Segundo Endoso. Arch. 8, Ciudad Militar, Febrero 8 de 1952," CHC, UM, Carlos Hevia Collection (no. 5066), box folder 14, p. 1.

21. Ibid., pp. 1–2.

22. Mario Llerena, "Avance o Retroceso en la Política Cubana," *Bohemia,* 17 February 1952, 3, 119.

23. Ibid., 2.

24. Ibid., 2–3.

25. Ibid., 2.

26. According to Padrón and Betancourt (15), Prío soon regretted the decision to allow Batista's return. At the time, however, Prío even welcomed him at the Presidential Palace.

27. Filmed interview with Alfredo J. Sadulé by Lillian Guerra and Abel Sierra Madero, 24 June 2014, Hialeah, FL.

28. García-Pérez, 4–6.

29. Pérez, *Army Politics in Cuba,* 134–36.

30. See Associated Press wire cables compiled in the section titled "La Prensa Informa" in *Todo Empezó en el Moncada,* 10–15; Thomas argues for Prio's own complicity in his fall through a provocative, if unclearly documented, description of these events (775–86).

31. Filmed interview with Jorge Valls Arango by Lillian Guerra and Abel Sierra Madero, 10 July 2014, Miami, FL.

32. Ibid.

33. Matos, 31–36.

34. Ricardo Cadet, "Resumen Gráfico Nacional del 1952," *Bohemia,* 23 November 1952, 38.

35. Ibid., 39.

36. Maza y Rodríguez.

37. Fidel Castro, "Brief to the Court of Appeals (March 24, 1952)," in Bonachea and Valdés, 149–52.

38. García-Perez, 6–7.

39. Lipman, 74–98.

40. José Antonio Echeverría, "Declaración de Principios de la Federación Estudiantil Universitaria. 14 Marzo 1952," in *Papeles del Presidente: Documentos y Discursos de José Antonio Echeverría Bianchi,* ed. Hilda Natalia Berdayes García (Havana: Ediciones Abril, 2006), 13.

41. Hart Phillips, *Cuba,* 262; Cadet, 39.

42. Hart Phillips, *Cuba,* 259–64.

43. Cadet, 48.

44. Baldomero Alvarez Ríos, "Anhelamos Encauzar la Nación por un Sendero de Libertad, Progreso y Legalidad," *Bohemia,* 20 April 1952.

45. Pérez, *Army Politics in Cuba,* 129–30; Yeidy M. Rivero, *Broadcasting Modernity: Cuban Commercial Television, 1950–1960* (Durham, NC: Duke University Press, 2015), 65–66.

46. Rivero, 66.

47. Cadet, 40.

48. Ibid.

49. Hector Gómez Nocedo, *De Marzo a Noviembre, 1952–1954: Ensayo Crítico Sobre el 10 de Marzo* (Havana: Bloque Estudiantil Nacional Progresista, 1954), 10–12.

50. Ibid., 8–9.

51. Cuban Ministry of Information, *Batista—Some Call Him a Dictator. The Cuban People Tell Their True Story. What Is the Matter with Cuba?* (Havana: n.p., 1954), 19.

52. Ibid., 5; Batista, *Respuesta,* 451–56.

53. "'No Seré Candidato a la Presidencia' Afirmó de Nuevo el Gral. Batista," *Diario de la Marina,* 11 March 1953, 1; "Confía Batista que en Breve Nada Interrumpa la Ruta de las Urnas," *Diario de la Marina,* 5 September 1953, 15; Gómez Nocedo, 8–9, 11; Cuban Ministry of Information, 1.

54. "Confía Batista," 15.

55. Ibid., 1.

56. Quoted in Whitney, 128–29.

57. Fulgencio Batista, "Texto Íntegro de la Alocución del 4 de Septiembre, Pronunciada por el Coronel Batista," in *Militarismo, Anti-Militarismo, Seudo-Militarismo* (Havana: Instituto Civico-Militar, 1939), 75–76.

58. "Puntualizó Batista la Obra que Ha Hecho Desde el 10 de Marzo," *Diario de la Marina,* 5 September 1954, 18-A.

59. Pérez, *Army Politics in Cuba,* 131.

60. Quoted in Whitney, 133.

61. Edmund Chester, *A Sergeant Named Batista* (New York: Henry Holt, 1954), ix–x.

62. Ibid., 211, 225.

63. Ibid., 270.

64. Ibid., 233.

65. Ibid., 212.

66. Interview with Sadulé, 21 July 2014.

67. Ibid.

68. Hart Phillips, *Cuba,* 260.

69. Ibid.

70. Cadet, 36.

71. Dr. Manuel A. de Varona et al., "A La Nación" and "Carta Pública," in CHC, UM, Carlos Hevia Collection, box folder 15.

72. Ibid., 262; Cadet, 37.

73. Partido del Pueblo Cubano (Ortodoxo), 12.

74. Domínguez, 123.

75. For example, see photograph and caption about one such family meeting with Marta in "De la Hora de Ahora," *Carteles,* 5 February 1953, 105.

76. Interview with Sadulé, 21 July 2014.

77. "De la Hora de Ahora."

78. Rosalie Schwartz, *Pleasure Island: Tourism and Temptation in Cuba* (Lincoln: University of Nebraska Press, 1997), 140–45.

79. "'No Sere Candidato a la Presidencia,'" 24.

80. "Puntualizó Batista la Obra que Ha Hecho"; "Señaló Batista Todo lo Hecho por el País Desde el 10 de Marzo," *Diario de la Marina,* 6 September 1955, 1, 14-A.

81. Cuban Ministry of Information, 13–14.

82. Ibid., 15–16; "Erradicación de los Barrios de Indigentes," *Orientación Campesina,* May–July 1954, 36–38; and "Más de 60,000 Viviendas Campesinas Han Sido Construídas y Reparadas," *Gente de la Semana,* 13 June 1958, 20–21. The author is grateful to Abel Sierra Madero for providing the latter source.

83. Jesse Horst, "Sleeping on Ashes: Havana Slums in an Age of Revolution, 1930–1970" (PhD diss., University of Pittsburgh, in progress).

84. Philips, 264–65, 277.

85. "Editorial. A la Nación por la Cultura," *Educación Rural* (1953): 1.

86. Ibid., 12, 23–27.

87. Guerra, *Visions of Power,* 95.

88. Ibid., 2.

89. "Más de 73,000 Adultos de 18 a 90 Años Han Aprendido a Leer en la Primera Campaña de Alfabetización," *Orientación Campesina,* May–July 1954, 6–8.

90. "Unidades Móviles y Educación Rural," *Orientación Campesina,* January–February 1955, 28–31.

91. Guerra, *Visions of Power,* 77–89.

92. "Confía Batista," 15.

93. "Saludo Annual de la Flor Martiana," *Orientación Campesina,* May–July 1954, 21–35.

94. Dra. Vicentina E. Rodríguez López to Eduardo Chibás, 6 July 1951, ANC, FEC, fondo 176, expediente 1146, legajo 39.

95. Francisco Blanco and Jesús Sánchez Sordo, untitled public declaration of La Unidad Nacional Constitucional, March 1952, ANC, Fondo Carlos Márquez Sterling (hereafter CMS), fondo 69, legajo 44, expediente 2085, pp. 1–2.

96. Carlos Moore, *Pichón: A Memoir. Race and Revolution in Castro's Cuba* (Chicago: Lawrence Hill Books, 2008), 53–55.

97. de la Fuente, 243–44.

98. Ibid., 243–47.

99. Ibid., 140–49.

100. Ibid., 176–89.

101. Ada Ferrer crafted the term *anti-racism* to encompass the first iterations of a Cuban nationality in the nineteenth century that could appeal to blacks fighting for equality without alienating whites through an open endorsement of equality.

102. The original Spanish joke goes like this: "Hay dos cosas que ningún cubano en el mundo soporta: primero, el racismo; y segundo, los negros." I grew up hearing this joke in my family, particularly from my maternal grandfather, Heriberto Rodríguez Rosado. Although a peasant whose parents descended from Canary Islanders, he grew up with José Rodríguez Crespo, a mulatto half brother whom his father, a captain in Cuba's Ejército Libertador (Liberating Army), had brought back home after the war of 1895.

103. David Grillo, *El Problema del Negro Cubano*, 2nd ed. (Havana: n.p., 1953), 12, 38, 54.

104. Ibid., 19–24, 45; Matt D. Childs, *The 1812 Aponte Rebellion in Cuba and the Struggle Against Atlantic Slavery* (Chapel Hill: University of North Carolina, 2006).

105. Grillo, 59–61.

106. Ibid., 118–21.

107. Juan René Betancourt, *Doctrina Negra: La Unica Teoría Certera Contra la Discriminación Racial en Cuba* (Havana: P. Fernández y Cia., 1955), 50.

108. Ibid., 28–30.

109. Ibid., 49.

110. George Braga, "A Bundle of Relations," unpublished autobiographical manuscript, Special and Area Studies Collections, University of Florida, Gainesville, Braga Brothers Collection (hereafter SASC, UF, BBC), series 24, box 1, 132.

111. Ibid., 201.

112. "Memorandum on My Seventy-Third Birthday," Folder Miscellaneous, 1950–1953, SASC, UF, BBC, series 8, box 7, 1.

113. "The Francisco Sugar Company. Memorandum. History of the Company and Miscellaneous Data. September 30, 1963," Folder History of the Company, 1963, SASC, UF, BBC, series 97, box 2, p. 1.

114. Ibid., p. 4.

115. Braga, 203–11; see aerial maps in SASC, UF, BBC, series 22.

116. Braga, 202.

117. Bernardo Braga Rionda, "Personal and Business Experiences, Part II," outside folder, SASC, UF, BBC, series 8, box 8, p. 3 of unpaginated front matter.

118. "The Francisco Sugar Company. Charity Contributions Made by Company from 1955

to 1959, Inclusive. December 15, 1959," Folder Contributions, Gifts, Donations, 1955–1959," SASC, UF, BBC, record group 4, series 97, box 2, p. 1.

119. "Manatí Sugar Company. Traveling and Entertainment Expenses. Calendar Year 1958," Folder Manatí General, 1960–1964, SASC, UF, BBC, record group 3, series 63, box 15.

120. Braga, 162.

121. George Braga to Amado Aréchaga, 29 April 1959, Folder School on Estate, 1959–1963, SASC, UF, BBC, series 45, box 8, pp. 1–3.

122. Michael J. P. Malone to John M. González, 26 August 1958, and Dana McNally to Michael [J.] P. Malone, 31 May 1958, Folder Scholarship Juan Nicholas Evans, 1958–1960, SASC, UF, BBC, series 45, box 8.

123. See esp. Juan Nicholas Evans to George Braga, 10 December 1958, and undated Christmas card from Dana McNally to Malone describing his and his wife's visit to Juan Nicholas and discussions with his professors. See also Juan Nicholas Evans to J. M. González and George Braga, 22 October 1959, 19 Novemer 1959, 1 February 1960, 17 February 1960, Folder Scholarship Juan Nicholas Evans, 1958–1960, SASC, UF, BBC, series 45, box 8.

124. H. S. Schneider to Michael J. P. Malone, 24 November 1959, Folder Scholarship Juan Nicholas Evans, 1958–1960, SASC, UF, BBC, series 45, box 8.

125. Bourgeois (General Manager) to George Braga, Michael J. P. Malone, and Henry McC. Gross, 28 July 1958, Folder Scholarship Juan Nicholas Evans, 1958–1960, SASC, UF, BBC, series 45, box 8.

126. Juan Nicholas to George Braga, 1 February 1960 and 17 February 1960, Folder Scholarship Juan Nicholas Evans, 1958–1960, SASC, UF, BBC, series 45, box 8.

127. Memorandum from Michael J. P. Malone to Harold Schneider, 24 March 1960, Folder Scholarship Juan Nicholas Evans, 1958–1960, SASC, UF, BBC, series 45, box 8; General Alumni Association, *University of Maine Alumni Directory, 1963–1964* (n.p., 1964), 377.

128. Francisco Riverón Hernández, "Niños de la Patria," *Bohemia,* 6 November 1955, 6–8.

129. Guido García Inclán, "En la Feria de la Actualidad," *Bohemia,* 3 October 1954, 94. The author is grateful to Richard Denis for sharing his research on these dates regarding García Inclán's column.

130. For examples, see Guido García Inclán, "¡Arriba Corazones!" *Bohemia,* 13 April 1958, 118–19 and *Bohemia,* 20 April 1958, 118–19.

131. *Libro de Oro de la Sociedad Habanera* (Havana: n.p., 1946), 118, 201, 217, 375, 513, 517.

132. Joaquin Posada, "La Gran Exposición de Christian Dior en el Country Club," *Bohemia,* 21 November 1954, 73.

133. Llerena, *The Unsuspected Revolution,* 43.

134. Interview with Valls Arango, 10 July 2014.

135. "Considera la Juventud del PPC que la Línea Política Actual no Es Correcta," *El Mundo,* 26 June 1952, A7; de la Cova, 36.

136. Ramón Sotolongo to Carlos Márquez Sterling, 9 July 1954, ANC, CMS, fondo 69, legajo 43, expediente 2067, p. 3; also noted in de la Cova, 36.

137. Partido del Pueblo Cubano (Ortodoxo), 20.

138. Ibid., 12, 14.

139. Ibid., 5–6. See also "Juicio Contra Millo Ochoa" and "Discurso del Dr. Carone en Defensa de Millo Ochoa" in ibid., 23–56.

140. Cadet, 57.

141. Aracelio Azcuy, "La Fusta Sobre la Pluma," apparently censored article manuscript prepared for publication in *Prensa Libre* (14 March 1953?) and "Del Dicho al Hecho," *Prensa Libre,* 31 August 1952, CHC, UM, Carlos Hevia Collection, box folder 11, p. 2.

142. "Memorandum para el Jefe del Estado Mayor General del Ejército, Causa No. 160–952 EMG, 20 December 1952" and related documents in ANC, CMS, fondo 69, expediente 144, legajo 3.

143. Aracelio Azcuy, "Libertado del Fustazo," *Prensa Libre,* 23 August 1952, CHC, UM, Carlos Hevia Collection, box folder 11.

144. Interview with Valls Arango.

145. Llerena, *The Unsuspected Revolution,* 45–51.

146. Azcuy, "Libertad del Fustazo"; Aracelio Azcuy, *Cuba: Campo de Concentración* (México, DF: Ediciones Humanismo, 1954), 42–43.

147. Azcuy, *Cuba: Campo de Concentración,* 42.

148. Azcuy, "Libertad del Fustazo," and *Cuba: Campo de Concentración,* 44.

149. Cadet, 54.

150. Ibid., 55.

151. Ibid., 57.

152. Jesús A. Delgado, "Reliquias de Martí en el Museo Nacional. Recuerdos Personales del Apóstol," and Estebán Valderama, "Las Nuevas Monedas Cubanas," *Bohemia,* 1 February 1953, 60–61, 84–86, 96.

153. Daniel Fernández, "Constructing Legitimacy in Stone and Words During Cuba's Second Republic: Building and Contesting Batista's José Martí" (MA thesis, University of Florida, 2016).

154. Ministerio de Educación, *Unidades de Trabajo: Martí* (Havana: Comisión Nacional Organizadora de los Actos y Ediciones del Centenario y del Monumento de Martí, 1953), 7.

155. Ibid., 8–10.

156. Cadet, 45.

157. Dr. Carlos Prío Socarrás, *El Entierro Cubano de Martí: Discurso del Honorable Señor Presidente de la República, 20 Junio 1951* (Havana: n.p., 1951), 4.

158. Félix Lisazo to María Mantilla, 25 March 1954, in SASC, UF, Romero Family Papers Regarding José Martí, box 1, folder 20.

159. I gratefully acknowledge Daniel Fernández Guevara for reminding me of this important point.

160. Guerra, *The Myth of José Martí,* 198.

161. Dr. Emeterio de Santovenia Echaide to María Mantilla de Romero, 6 January 1953, in SASC, UF, Romero Family Papers Regarding José Martí, box 1, folder 6; Alfredo J. López, *José Martí: A Revolutionary Life* (Austin: University of Texas Press, 2014), 197–200.

162. Small pocketbook containing two keys noted to be to Martí's *grillos* now in SASC, UF, Romero Family Papers Regarding José Martí, box 2, folder 2.

163. All 1953 editions of the cigarette manufacturers' magazine carried special commemorative insignia and featured essays on Martí. They must have proved popular because

they continued well into the decade. See esp. "Del Homenaje a Nuestro Apóstol," *El Cigarrero,* February 1953, 10–13; G. Velarde García, "Exposición Martiana," *El Cigarrero,* April 1953, 5.

164. Soto, *La Revolución del 33;* Guerra, *The Myth of José Martí,* 44–45.

165. Julio Fernández León, *José Antonio Echeverría: Vigencia y Presencia Ante el Cincuenta Aniversario de su Holocausto* (Miami: Ediciones Universal, 2007), 136–38.

166. Azcuy, "La Fusta Sobre la Pluma," 2–3; Hart Phillips's memoir of those years, *Cuba: Island of Paradox,* gives one the impression that she and other reporters were not only intrepid but tight-lipped about any concerns with their own security as playing by Batista's rules meant denying they ever had any.

167. Azcuy, *Cuba: Campo de Concentración,* 76.

168. de la Cova, 46.

169. Azcuy, *Cuba: Campo de Concentración,* 75–77, 193.

170. Chase, *Revolution Within the Revolution,* 36–37.

171. Ibid., 22–38.

172. Ibid., 21.

173. de la Fuente, 249.

174. Luis Ortega, "Generalidades," in Azcuy, *Cuba: Campo de Concentración,* 33–34.

175. *IX Asamblea Anual de la Sociedad Interamericana de Prensa Celebrada en México. Como Asesinó Batista la Libertad de Expresión en Cuba. Informes de José Pardo Llada, Luis Ortega* (México, DF: n.p., 1953). The number of copies appears on the last page.

176. Ibid., 1, 12, 10.

177. Ibid., 11.

178. Filmed, unedited interview with Rafael Díaz-Balart by Joe Cardona and Daniel Fernández Guevara, 2002, Miami, FL. Courtesy of the filmmakers.

179. J. M. Cruz Tolosa to Carlos Márquez Sterling, 14 July 1954, ANC, CMS, fondo 69, expediente 2067, legajo 43.

180. Chase, *Revolution Within the Revolution,* 40–104.

3. Los Muchachos del Moncada

1. Filmed interview with Mario Chanes de Armas by Joe Cardona and Daniel Fernández Guevara, 2002, Miami, FL.

2. Interview with Valls Arango, 10 July 2014; interview with Chanes de Armas.

3. de la Cova, 51, 58.

4. Ibid., xxvi, 37.

5. Like Fidel, Abel Santamaría was a young Ortodoxo. The protest took place at the gravesite of Carlos Rodríguez in the Cementerio Colón in response to Batista's decree suspending freedom of assembly by Resolution No. 86 on 2 April 1952. Angelina Rojas Blaquier, *Primer Partido Comunista de Cuba,* vol. 3 (Santiago de Cuba: Editorial Oriente, 2010), 29.

6. de la Cova, xxvii.

7. Santamaría, 55.

8. For examples, see Jesús Montané Oropesa, "El Asalto al 'Moncada.' Una de las Acciones Más Heroícas de la Juventud Mundial," *Verde Olivo,* 19 July 1964, 19–22; "Men-

sajes por el 26. Actos en el Extranjero en Homenaje a Cuba," *Revolución,* 25 July 1963, 1, 5. This coverage continued annually through the 1980s, saturating every state news publication and media.

9. Santamaría, 127.

10. Partido de Recuperación Moral y Capacidad Individual, "Ya es Hora," ANC, CMS, fondo 69, legajo 44, expediente 2086.

11. "En Cuba. Policía. La Causa 459," *Bohemia,* 24 October 1954, 67–68; see also "Resolverá el Tribunal de Urgencia Hoy la Situación de los Detenidos a Causa de la Frustrada Conspiración," *Diario de la Marina,* 7 April 1953, 1, 21, 24.

12. Francisco Ichaso, "Cabalgata Política: La 'Revolución sin Revolución,'" *Bohemia,* 27 November 1955, 18, 93.

13. Lisandro Otero, "Aquel 26 de Julio. Entrevista a Haydée Santamaría y Melba Hernández," *Juventud Rebelde,* 25 July 1966, 5–6; interview with Chanes de Armas.

14. de la Cova, 49.

15. Miguel Enrique, "Pinareños en el Moncada," *Bohemia,* 22 July 1966, 12–13. de la Cova disputes this number from Artemisa, asserting only twenty-eight were from there.

16. Filmed interview with Andrés Candelario by Lillian Guerra and Glenn Gebhard, May 2008, San Juan, Puerto Rico, Yale University Manuscripts and Archives, Glenn Gebhard Collection (hereafter YUMA, GGC), New Haven, CT; de la Cova, xxvi.

17. Interview with Candelario.

18. "Los Artemisanos en el Moncada. 'Fidel Nos Escogió para la Vanguardia por Ser Buenos Tiradores," *Revolución,* 22 July 1963, 6–10.

19. de la Cova, 50.

20. Ibid., xxv.

21. Interview with Chanes de Armas.

22. Ibid.

23. de la Cova, 138.

24. Quoted in Jules Dubois, *Fidel Castro: Rebel-Liberator or Dictator?* (Indianapolis: Bobbs-Merrill, 1959), 46, 65.

25. Santamaría, 12.

26. After gathering 115 testimonies from combatants on both sides of the battle, de la Cova comes to this same conclusion: neither regret nor doubt ever seemed to have crossed the minds of the majority of participants. See xxii–xxiii.

27. Interview with Chanes de Armas.

28. Ibid.; Fidel Castro, "Relato de Fidel Castro," in *Todo Empezó en el Moncada,* 36–37.

29. Nowhere is the figure of total killed on the rebel side clear. De la Cova contends it was only sixty-one, whereas Fidel himself claimed that it was seventy and others (including Carlos Franqui) believed it closer to one hundred. Discrepancies abound because of the inaccessibility to researchers of Batista government documents, particularly the archive of SIM, and the post-1959 political inconvenience of distinguishing between those who "got lost" and were later shot and those who simply deserted the mission to face the same end. Haydée Santamaría, unlike Fidel Castro and Mario Chanes, believed that the caravan of cars that took a wrong turn once inside the barracks' grounds and got lost in Santiago did so out of "cowardice," not error or confusion. See de la Cova, 172; Santamaría, 117–19; Fidel Castro, "Relato de Fidel Castro," 36–37.

30. Franqui, *Cuba, La Revolución,* 159; see also Fidel Castro to Luis Conte Agüero, 12 December 1953, in *Cartas del Presidio: Anticipo de una Biografía de Fidel Castro,* ed. Luis Conte Agüero (Havana: Editorial Lex, 1959), 15–16. The author discussed the veracity of this account with Carlos Franqui on multiple occasions.

31. Fidel Castro to Luis Conte Agüero, 12 December 1953, 15.

32. Franqui, *Cuba, La Revolución,* 161.

33. "Opposition in Cuba Warned by Batista: President Says His Tolerance Is at End," *New York Times,* 28 July 1953, 13.

34. Juanita Castro and Collins, 112–13; interview with Chanes de Armas; de la Cova, 182–92.

35. de la Cova, 192–93.

36. R. Hart Phillips, "Batista Proves He Still Runs the Show in Cuba," *New York Times,* 2 August 1953, E4.

37. "Confía Batista," 1, 15.

38. Quoted in Dubois, 39; de la Cova gives this quote somewhat differently, stating that Fidel said that "he had not gone to Moncada to kill soldiers, but to initiate a Revolution" (192).

39. "Confía Batista," 15.

40. Kelsey Vidaillet, "Violations of Freedom of the Press in Cuba: 1952–1959," *Association for the Study of the Cuban Economy* (2006), 287.

41. Azcuy, *Cuba: Campo de Concentración,* 13–16.

42. Ibid., 17.

43. Ibid., 21.

44. Capítulo I, artículos I–II, Ley-Decreto No. 997 de 1953, *Gaceta Oficial,* 6 August 1953.

45. Capítulo I, artículo II–III, in ibid.

46. Capítulo I, artículo II, in ibid.

47. Capítulo I, artículo IV–V, capítulo III, artículo XV, in ibid.

48. Capítulo VII of this new decree modified existing articles 257–61 of the Código de Defensa Social referring to desacato, and ignored utterly the 1940 Constitution's protection of the right to criticize publicly any and all government leaders. See capítulo VII—Desacato, in ibid.

49. Título XII—Delitos Contra el Honor. Capítulo I—Defamación, in ibid.

50. Antonio Zamora Hernández to Carlos Márquez Sterling, 30 June 1953, ANC, CMS, fondo 69, legajo 44, expediente 2084, pp. 1–2.

51. Pedro Revuelta to Carlos Márquez Sterling, 11 April 1954, ANC, CMS, fondo 69, legajo 43, expediente 2069.

52. Vidaillet, 288.

53. Juan Marinello to Carlos Márquez Sterling, 19 November 1953, ANC, CMS, fondo 69, legajo 43, expediente 2065, p. 1.

54. Ibid., p. 2.

55. Oscar Fernández Trujillo and Julio Ferreiro Mora to Carlos Márquez Sterling, 4 June 1953, ANC, CMS, fondo 69, legajo 45, expediente 2105.

56. Guillermo to Carlos Márquez Sterling, 11 May 1953, ANC, CMS, fondo 69, legajo 45, expediente 2105, pp. 2–5.

57. de la Cova, 204–17.

58. See esp. the indispensable Marta Rojas, *El Juicio del Moncada* (Havana: Editorial de Ciencias Sociales, 1988); Bonachea and San Martín, 23–28.

59. Quoted in Dubois, 59.
60. Quoted in ibid., 64.
61. Ibid., 65.
62. Quoted in ibid., 68–69; Bonachea and San Martín, 27–28.
63. de la Cova, 236; Juanita Castro and Collins, 118; Fidel Castro to Melba Hernández, 17 April 1954, in Conte Agüero, *Cartas del Presidio*, 37–38.
64. Dubois, 83; de la Cova, 236–39; for the pamphlet version of the speech, see *La Historia Me Absolverá: Defensa del Doctor Fidel Castro Ruz en el Juicio por el Ataque al Cuartel Moncada—26 de Julio de 1953—ante el Tribunal de Urgencia de Santiago de Cuba* (Havana: Imp. Económico en General, 1959).
65. de la Cova, 224–25.
66. Bonachea and San Martín, 28.
67. Fidel Castro to Luis Conte Agüero, 19 June 1954, in Conte Agüero, *Cartas del Presidio*, 31, 36.
68. Mario Mencía, *Prisión Fecunda* (Havana: Editora Política, 1980), 72–77.
69. Quoted in Fidel Castro to Luis Conte Agüero, continuation of letter dated 31 July 1954, in Conte Agüero, *Cartas del Presidio*, 55–57.
70. Interview with Chanes de Armas; Juanita Castro and Collins, 118.
71. Wendy Gimbel, *Havana Dreams: A Story of a Cuban Family* (New York: Vintage Books, 1998), 116–42.
72. Ibid., 142–45; Juanita Castro and Collins, 119–23; Fidel Castro to Mirta Díaz-Balart, 17 July 1954, Fidel Castro to Luis Conte Agüero, 17 July 1954, Fidel Castro to Lidia Castro, 22 July 1954, Fidel Castro to Luis Conte Agüero, 31 July 1954, in Conte Agüero, *Cartas del Presidio*, 43–52.
73. Fidel Castro to Luis Conte Agüero, 12 June 1954, in Conte Agüero, *Cartas del Presidio*, 25–26; Mencía, 65–66.
74. Interview with Chanes de Armas.
75. Ibid.
76. Fidel Castro to Luis Conte Agüero, 12 December 1953, in Conte Agüero, *Cartas del Presidio*, 13–14.
77. Ibid., 19.
78. Ibid., 23.
79. Ibid., 21.
80. Fidel Castro to Luis Conte Agüero, 12 June 1954, in Conte Agüero, *Cartas del Presidio*, 25.
81. Jesús Rodríguez to Carlos Márquez Sterling, 28 March 1954, ANC, CMS, fondo 69, legajo 43, expediente 2065, pp. 1–2.
82. Pablo Abreu to Carlos Márquez Sterling, 9 March 1954, manifesto titled "Apoya el Frente Unido Nacional las Demandas Ortodoxas, 19 Febrero 1954," flyer titled "Segunda Conferencia Municipal de los Comités de Frente Unico por una Solución Democrática de la Crisis Cubana. Convocatoria. 10 Febrero 1954," Samuel Balbuena Gainza to Carlos Márquez Sterling, 11 March 1954, Dr. Juan M. Menocal Villalón to Carlos Márquez Sterling, 19 March 1954, ANC, CMS, fondo 69, legajo 43, expediente 2065.
83. José V. González Hernández to Carlos Márquez Sterling, 16 April 1954, ANC, CMS, fondo 69, legajo 43, expediente 2065.

84. R. Ardura to Carlos Márquez Sterling, 13 September 1954, ANC, CMS, fondo 69, legajo 43, expediente 2065p. 1.

85. Miguel A. Matos L. to Carlos Márquez Sterling, 1 July 1954, ANC, CMS, fondo 69, legajo 43, expediente 2065.

86. Félix Barreto to Carlos Márquez Sterling, 10 July 1954, ANC, CMS, fondo 69, legajo 43, expediente 2065, p. 2.

87. Goya (?) Blanco to Carlos Márquez Sterling, 26 February 1954, ANC, CMS, fondo 69, legajo 43, expediente 2065, p. 2.

88. Pedro Revuelta to Carlos Márquez Sterling, 11 April 1954.

89. Luis Fernández to Carlos Márquez Sterling, 22 June 1954, ANC, CMS, fondo 69, legajo 43, expediente 2065, p. 2.

90. Jesús Quincoces, "Manifiesto al País," Las Villas, July 1954, ANC, CMS, fondo 69, legajo 43, expediente 2065, p. 2.

91. Julio Ferreiro Mora, director de la *Revista Chic,* to Carlos Márquez Sterling, 12 July 1953, ANC, CMS, fondo 69, legajo 43, expediente 2067.

92. Silvio Lubián Muro to Carlos Márquez Sterling, 2 December 1953, ANC, CMS, fondo 69, legajo 45, expediente 2105.

93. Ramón Sotolongo to Carlos Márquez Sterling, 9 July 1954, ANC, CMS, fondo 69, legajo 43, expediente 2067, pp. 1–2.

94. Bernardo Rodríguez Cárdenas to Carlos Márquez Sterling, 5 July 1954, ANC, CMS, fondo 69, legajo 43, expediente 2066, pp. 1–2.

95. Enrique Loynaz del Castillo to Carlos Márquez Sterling, 2 May 1954, and Marina to Carlos Márquez Sterling, 19 May 1954, ANC, CMS, fondo 69, legajo 45, expediente 2106.

96. Coronel Cosme de la Torriente, "Hay que Decirlo Muy Claro," *Bohemia,* 3 October 1954, 80, 82–83.

97. Carlos Márquez Sterling to Federico Fernández Casas, 25 May 1954, ANC, CMS, fondo 69, legajo 43, expediente 2066, pp. 1–2.

98. Anardino Pérez Caito, "Miseras y Grandezas de un Partido. A Las Masas Ortodoxas del Termino Municipal de Florida. A la Opinión Pública," 7 May 1954, and Anardino Pérez Caito to Carlos Márquez Sterling and Gerardo Vazquez Alvarado, 26 May 1954, ANC, CMS, fondo 69, legajo 45, expediente 2106.

99. Federico González Cabrera to Carlos Márquez Sterling, 10 July 1954, ANC, CMS, fondo 69, legajo 43, expediente 2066.

100. "La Crónica Política," *Bohemia,* 19 December 1954, supplement, 27.

101. For examples, see José Manuel Carbonell Rivero to Carlos Márquez Sterling, 11 July 1954, Ramón Sotolongo to Carlos Márquez Sterling, 9 July 1954, Amador de los Ríos to Carlos Márques Sterling, 10 July 1954, Alfredo Don Plá to Carlos Márquez Sterling, 10 July 1954, Dr. Carlos Manuel Betancourt García, Asociación Acción Nacionalista "Por Cuba," 10 July 1954, Emeterio S. Santovenia to Carlos Márquez Sterling, 13 July 1954, Arnaldo Borrego Suero to Carlos Márquez Sterling, 16 July 1954, ANC, CMS, fondo 69, legajo 43, expediente 2067. There are literally dozens more letters like these.

102. Francisco Cairol Garrido to Carlos Márquez Sterling, 10 July 1954, ANC, CMS, fondo 69, legajo 43, expediente 2067.

103. J. M. Cruz to Carlos Márquez Sterling, 14 July 1954, ANC, CMS, fondo 69, legajo 43, expediente 2067.

104. Mario Valdivia (illegible) to Carlos Márquez Sterling, 10 July 1954, ANC, CMS, fondo 69, legajo 43, expediente 2067.

105. Emiliano Rodríguez to Carlos Márquez Sterling, 16 July 1954, ANC, CMS, fondo 69, legajo 43, expediente 2066; Emilia Martínezto Carlos Márquez Sterling, 20 July 1954, ANC, CMS, fondo 69, legajo 43, expediente 2065.

106. Carlos Márquez Sterling to Emiliano Rodríguez, 27 July 1954, ANC, CMS, fondo 69, legajo 43, expediente 2066.

107. Rodolfo Rodríguz Zaldivar, "Si Batista Dice que Me Dió Más de lo que Yo Pedía, es que Mucho le Sobraba," and "Las Urnas. Grau Tenía un Plan Perturbador que Fracas por Mis Amplias Concesiones Dice el General Batista," *Bohemia,* 10 October 1954, 72–73, 78.

108. R. Guezal, "En las Vísperas. Opinan los Abstencionistas," *Bohemia,* 31 October 1954, 56–60.

109. Delio Gómez Ochoa, Partido del Pueblo Cubano (Ortodoxo), Sección Juvenil, Comité Gestor, Holguín to Carlos Márquez Sterling, 19 July 1954, ANC, CMS, fondo 69, legajo 43, expediente 2066, p. 1.

110. Luis Ricardo Alonso, "Grau and Batista No Son un Dilema: Son Dos Negaciones," *Bohemia,* 10 October 1954, 64–65.

111. Mario G. del Cueto and Francisco D. Altuna, "El Batey: Infieron de los Trabajadores Azucareros," *Bohemia,* 17 October 1954, 58–60.

112. Guido García Inclán, "En la Feria de la Actualidad. ¡Un Poco de Humanidad!" *Bohemia,* 24 October 1954, 43.

113. Luis Aguilar León, "La Verdadera Tragedia," *Bohemia,* 3 October 1954, 32–33, 126–27; Aníbal Hernández, "Hacia la Independence Económica. Qué es el Plan de Desarrollo Económico y Social de Cuba," *Bohemia,* 10 October 1954, 12–13.

114. L. R. Alonso, "Mi Primera Medida de Gobierno Sería Devolver la Libertad a los Cubanos, Afirma Ramón Grau de San Martín," *Bohemia,* 31 October 1954, 70–71, 75–76.

115. "En Cuba. Amnistía. Presos y Exilados," *Bohemia,* 22 May 1955, 63.

116. Mario Rivadulla, "La Ortodoxía Retorna a la Calle," *Bohemia,* 30 October 1955, 25, 124.

117. R. Alvarez to Carlos Márquez Sterling, 29 October 1954, ANC, CMS, fondo 69, legajo 45, expediente 2106.

118. Rodolfo Rodríguez Zaldivar, "No Admito la Hipótesis de Perder Frente a Grau, Declara el General Batista," *Bohemia,* 31 October 1954, 72–73, 75.

119. "La Suiza de América," *Bohemia,* 10 October 1954, 67.

120. For example, see "Gráficas de Actualidad," *Bohemia,* 17 October 1954, 64–65.

121. "Ocupan Gran Cantidad de Armas," *Bohemia,* 31 October 1954, supplement 14–15.

122. Digitally recorded telephone interview with José "Pepe" Puente Blanco by Lillian Guerra, 4 December 2015.

123. Filmed interviews with Lucy Echeverría Bianchi and José "Pepe" Puente Blanco by Lillian Guerra and Glenn Gebhard, March 2009, Miami, FL, YUMA, GCC.

124. Ibid.; "Gráficas de Actualidad," 65.

125. "Gráficas de Actualidad," 65.

126. Interviews with Echeverría Bianchi and Puente Blanco, March 2009.

127. Mario Riera Hernández, "Pequeña Historia de las Elecciones en Cuba," *Bohemia,* 7 November 1954, 90.

128. "La Histórica Sesión del Tribunal Superior Electoral," and "Desde la Quinta Avenida Grau Ordena el Retraimiento," *Bohemia*, 7 November 1954, 64–66, 68–69.

129. "Desde 'Kuquine' Batista Ordena 'Elecciones de Todas Maneras,'" *Bohemia*, 7 November 1954, 70–71.

130. Rogelio Caparros, "Todo Está Preparado para las Elecciones," *Bohemia*, 31 Octubre 1954, 68–69.

131. Max Lesnik Menéndez, "La Ortodoxía Se une o Perece. La Lucha Contra Batista y La Unidad del Partido de Chibás," *Bohemia*, 21 November 1954, 57.

132. "Las Elecciones en el Interior," *Bohemia*, 7 November 1954, 79.

133. Ibid.

134. José Díaz Garrido, "Ya Ganó Castellanos la Alcaldía de la Habana," *Bohemia*, 31 October 1954, supplement 13, 76.

135. "Genovevo Desafía el Poder de Grau," *Bohemia*, 7 November 1954, supplement 8.

136. "Al Terminar los Comicios," "En Cuba: Elecciones," and "Las Elecciones," *Bohemia*, 7 November 1954, supplement 2–3, 72–74, 7–15, 80.

137. "Editorial. Victoria Pírrica," *Bohemia*, 7 November 1954, supplement 5, 81.

138. Riera, 606.

139. Ibid.

140. Ibid., 606–21.

141. Antonio, "Geografía Política," *Bohemia*, 21 November 1954, supplement 7.

142. Carlos Márquez Sterling, "El Factor Cívico en la Lucha por la Unidad," *Bohemia*, 19 December 1954, 90.

143. Jorge Mañach, "Recado Final a la Ortodoxía," *Bohemia*, 13 March 1955, 75, 96.

144. Jorge Mañach, "Las Razones de un Movimiento (Respuesta a Carlos Márquez Sterling)," *Bohemia*, 27 March 1955, 64.

145. "Movimiento de la Nación (Manifiesto)," *Bohemia*, 10 April 1955, 77–81; Francisco Ichaso, "Movimiento de la Nación," *Bohemia*, 17 April 1955, 55, 95; Emiliano Rodríguez to Carlos Márquez Sterling, 20 April 1955, ANC, CMS, fondo 69, legajo 43, expediente 2069.

146. Pedro Revuelta to Carlos Márquez Sterling, 17 December 1954, ANC, CMS, fondo 69, legajo 43, expediente 2069.

147. Mario Lecour to Carlos Márquez Sterling, 23 November 1954, and Heriberto Corona and Vanguardia Mambisa to Carlos Márquez Sterling, 24 November 1954, ANC, CMS, fondo 69, legajo 45, expediente 2106; Isidoro Bofill Vázquez to Carlos Márquez Sterling, 26 October 1954, ANC, CMS, fondo 69, legajo 43, expediente 2065.

148. Tomás Olivares del Castillo to Carlos Márquez Sterling, 2 April 1955, ANC, CMS, fondo 69, legajo 43, expediente 2069.

149. Raúl Chibás, "Raul Chibás: Some Personal Data," in Andrew St. George Personal Papers, private collection of the author, 1–2; and Raúl Chibás, unpublished manuscript authored in 1961, "Memorias de la Revolución Cubana," in Hoover Institution Archives, Stanford University, Stanford, CA, chapter 1, pp. 1–2, 7–8. Note that each chapter is numbered starting with p. 1.

150. Gabino del Monte Castillo to Carlos Márquez Sterling, 7 June 1955, and Emiliano Rodríguez to Max Lesnick [*sic*] and Mario Rivadulla, ANC, CMS, fondo 69, legajo 43,

expediente 2069; Riera, 623–24; Raúl Chibás, "Memorias de la Revolución Cubana," chapter 1, pp. 6–7.

151. Emiliano Rodríguez to Carlos Márquez Sterling, 23 January 1955 and 25 February 1955, ANC, CMS, fondo 69, legajo 43, expediente 2069.

152. Emilio Vázquez López to Carlos Márquez Sterling, 27 May 1955, and Roberto León Enrique to Carlos Márquez Sterling, 1 May 1955, ANC, CMS, fondo 69, legajo 43, expediente 2069.

153. Manuel Bisbé, "Vigencia de Eduardo Chibás," *Bohemia*, 6 February 1955, 12. Emphasis added.

4. Civic Activism and the Legitimation of Armed Struggle Against Batista

1. Rafael Guas Inclán to Carlos Márquez Sterling, 5 October 1955, ANC, CMS, fondo 69, legajo 45, expediente 2108.

2. Carlos Márquez Sterling to Raúl de Cardenas, 5 May 1955, ANC, CMS, fondo 69, legajo 45, expediente 2108.

3. Raúl Chibás, "Memorias de la Revolución Cubana," chapter 1, p. 7.

4. José Antonio Echeverría, "La Dictadura Sigue Siendo Ilegal. Diciembre 1954," in Berdayes García, 19–20.

5. Rodolfo Rodríguez Zaldívar, "Es Absurdo Decir que la Aperture del Canal Dará una Base Military a EE UU," *Bohemia*, 16 January 1955, 60–63, supplement 14–16.

6. Fulvio A. Fuentes, "El Llamado Canal Vía Cuba Constituye una Agresión Directa at Nuestra Soberanía," *Bohemia*, 16 January 1955, 64.

7. Ibid., 65.

8. Max Lesnik Menéndez, "Soberanía Humillada: Cuba Frente al Canal," *Bohemia*, 16 January 1955, 48, 78; Jorge Mañach, "Algo Más Sobre el Canal y la Soberanía (Con Vista de Unas Declaraciones del General Batista)," *Bohemia*, 23 January 1955, 4, 73.

9. Rogelio Caparros, "Lo Que Se Puede Hacer con $400,000," *Bohemia*, 30 January 1955, 20–21. Graft increasingly dominated Batista's government as did the same degree of shamelessness that its Auténtico predecessors had exhibited when it came to robbing the coffers of Cuba's social programs. The disappearance of hundreds of thousands of dollars from the retirement funds of sugar workers' unions and declining payments to pensioners were only two examples. See Mario G. Del Cueto, "Otro Escándolo en el Retiro Azucarero: Estafan $200,000 Pesos a los Jubilados," *Bohemia*, 17 April 1955, supplement 16–17.

10. José Antonio Echeverría, "Solución Económica. Debemos ir a la Fase Industrial. 13 Febrero 1955," in Berdayes García, 23–25. This editorial originally appeared in *Diario Nacional*.

11. Ibid., see editor's note, 22.

12. "Misiones Extranjeras Acreditadas para Asistir a la Toma de Posesión del Gral. Fulgencio Batista," *Diario de la Marina*, 24 February 1955, 12-A; "Toma de Posesión del Presidente de la República, Mayor General Fulgencio Batista, Programa Oficial, 24 Febrero 1955," and "Ministro de Estado en Nombre del Presidente de la República Tiene el Honor de Invitar al Sr. Alberto J. Parreño y Sra. a la Revista Militar . . . ," in

Fulgencio Batista Inauguration Collection, Special and Area Studies Collections, University of Florida.

13. "Toma de Posesión del Presidente de la República . . . ," and personal invitation to the ballet from "El Presidente de la República y la Señora de Batista," in Fulgencio Batista Inauguration Collection.

14. Marta Rojas, "Mayor Estabilidad Económica para Cuba," *Bohemia,* 7 November 1954, 75, 81.

15. Marta Rojas, "Carlos Prío Puede y Debe Regresar a Cuba," *Bohemia,* 27 February 1955, 59, 81; Francisco Ichaso, "Cabalgata Política. La Liquidación del Proceso Electoral," *Bohemia,* 28 November 1954, 41, 106–7.

16. "Apelación Pública," *Bohemia,* 28 November 1954, 62; Benito Novas, "Don Cosme de la Torriente: Una Vida Al Servicio de Cuba," *Bohemia,* 16 December 1956, 78–80, 82, 121.

17. Jorge Mañach, "La Concordia y los Presos Políticos," *Bohemia,* 16 January 1955, 51.

18. Melba Hernández, "La Concordia y los Presos Políticos," *Bohemia,* 30 January 1955, 52.

19. Melba Hernández, "Siempre Supimos que el Asalto al Moncada Culminaría en la Victoria," *Verde Olivo,* 28 July 1963, 32.

20. Mario Rivadulla, "Un Paso Hacia la Paz," *Bohemia,* 3 April 1955, 10, 115.

21. Agustín Alles Soberón y Fulvio Fuentes, "Qué Abran las Cárceles para los Presos Politicos y Regresen los Exilados," *Bohemia,* 27 March 1955, 59–62, 97.

22. Jorge Mañach, "Invitación al Paréntesis," *Bohemia,* 3 April 1955, 59, 94; "En Cuba. Amnistía. La Consigna del Momento," and Francisco Ichaso, "Cabalgata Política. Pasos Hacia la Paz," *Bohemia,* 10 April 1955, 70–71, 47, 96.

23. Quoted in Rodolfo Rodríguez Zaldívar, "Encuestas de *Bohemia.* La Juventud los 'Movimientos,'" *Bohemia,* 17 April 1955, 82.

24. Heriberto Corona Pérez to Carlos Márquez Sterling, 27 April 1955, ANC, CMS, fondo 69, legajo 43, expediente 2069, pp. 1–2.

25. "255 Mil Ejemplares," *Bohemia,* 3 April 1955, 67; Richard J. Denis, "Una Revista al Servicio de la Nación: *Bohemia* and the Evolution of Cuban Journalism, 1908–1960" (MA thesis, University of Florida, 2016).

26. Denis, 69–93.

27. Fidel Castro, "Carta Sobre la Amnistía," *Bohemia,* 27 March 1955, 63, 94.

28. "Editorial. El Gobierno y la Amnistía," *Bohemia,* 10 April 1955, 64–65, 81.

29. Luis Conte Agüero, "Sin Miedo y Sin Odio," *Bohemia,* 3 April 1955, 63, 95.

30. "En Cuba. Amnistía. Presos y Exilados," 58–65, 81–82. Menelao Mora led the Auténtico group: see "En Cuba. La Capital. El Jueves 24," *Bohemia,* 6 March 1955, 65–66.

31. "Amnistía. En Libertad Todos Los Presos Políticos," *Bohemia,* 22 May 1955, 66–71.

32. "En Cuba. Amnistía. Presos y Exilados," 59.

33. Ibid., 60.

34. "Del Moncada al Presidio y a la Libertad: 'Soy un Combatiente sin Odios Ni Resentimientos'—Fidel Castro," in "En Cuba. Amnistía. Presos y Exilados," 72–73.

35. Alberto R. Del Río, "Réplica del Coronel Del Río Chaviano Sobre los Sucesos de Santiago," in "En Cuba. Amnistía. Presos y Exilados," 38.

36. Fidel Castro, "¡Mientes, Chaviano!" *Bohemia,* 29 May 1955, 57, 94–95.

37. "Manifesto de la Ortodoxía Unida al Pueblo de Cuba," *Bohemia,* 29 May 1955, 72–73, 75.

38. Carlos Márquez Sterling, "La Paloma de la Paz," *Bohemia,* 29 May 1955, 51, 83.

39. Sociedad de Amigos de la República, "Documentos para la Historia," in *El Momento Político de Cuba: Acuerdos, Cartas y Discursos* (Havana: Editorial Lex, 1955), 19–23.

40. See letters in ibid., 25–77.

41. Cosme de la Torriente, "Discurso del Dr. Cosme de la Torriente en el Club de Leones, el día 6 de Septiembre de 1955," in Sociedad de Amigos de la República, 82.

42. "Cosme de la Torriente to Mayor General Fulgencio Batista Zaldívar, 11 Octubre de 1955," and "Cosme de la Torriente to Mayor General Fulgencio Batista Zaldívar, 19 de Octubre de 1955," in Sociedad de Amigos de la República, 101–2, 107–8.

43. "Andrés Domingo to Cosme de la Torriente, 17 de Octubre de 1955," in Sociedad de Amigos de la República, 103–4.

44. "Celebró Mitín la Oposición en la Plazoleta de Luz," *El Mundo,* 20 November 1955, A-8.

45. "En Cuba. Amigos de la República," *Bohemia,* 27 November 1955, 68–69.

46. Ibid., 71.

47. Ibid., 69–71.

48. Ibid., 70; José Antonio Echeverría, audio recording made by VCR Records and La Corona Tobacco Company of the speech and given as a gift to Echeverría's family in January 1959. Private collection of the author, courtesy of Lucy Echeverría Bianchi.

49. "Celebró Mitín la Oposición," A-1.

50. Ibid.; "Intervención en el Mitín de la Sociedad de Amigos de la República, Acto del Muelle de Luz, 19 de Noviembre de 1955," in Berdayes García, 50.

51. "Condena el Senado el Mitín de la Oposición," *El Mundo,* 22 November 1955, 1, A-8.

52. "Celebró Mitín la Oposición," A-8.

53. "En Cuba. Amigos de la República," 69.

54. José Antonio Echeverría, audio recording. Notably, Echeverría's admonitions of the provocateurs and all reference to the disruptions were edited out of the version of the speech that appeared in Echeverría's collected works, published in Cuba. See "Intervención en el Mitín de la Sociedad de Amigos de la República," 47–50.

55. "Celebró Mitín la Oposición," A-8.

56. Francisco Riverón Hernández, "Yo Acuso," *Bohemia,* 18 November 1956, 46–47; Lisandro Otero González, "Pan con una Sonrisa para los Desheredados de Cuba," *Bohemia,* 27 October 1957, 36–38; Luis Rolando Cabrera, "Dormían en el Suelo Siete Niñas y una Anciana Ciega," *Bohemia,* 16 March 1958, supplement 14–16, 83–86; Luis Rolando Cabrera, "250 Campesinos en Pie de Lucha por un Pedazo de Tierra Cubana," *Bohemia,* 2 March 1958, 46–47, 113–15; Guido García Inclán, "¡Arriba Corazones!" *Bohemia,* 18 August 1957, 118–19, and *Bohemia,* 16 March 1958, 118–19.

57. "Ya se Inauguró el Mercado de Carlos III," *Bohemia,* 17 February 1957, 81.

58. See advertisements for Perma-Strate and products by I. Posner, Inc., in *Bohemia,* 6 October 1957, 78, 79; and Mario G. del Cueto, "El Desrizamiento del Cabello," *Bohemia,* 29 September 1957, 75–78.

59. See advertisements for Fab, *Bohemia,* 11 November 1956, 83; Adams Chiclets, *Bohemia,* 15 December 1957, 48–49; Jabón Candado, *Bohemia,* 4 November 1956, 67.

60. Arroyito, "Esto Es Cuba," *Bohemia,* 1 September 1957, 78.

61. Fernando Rodríguez Abreu, "Informe al Ejecutivo Nacional de la Ortodoxía Libre," 5 August 1956, ANC, CMS, fondo 69, legajo 44, expediente 2072, pp. 1–5.

62. Case file "Tuinucu Explosion, 2/8/55," SASC, UF, BBC, record group 3, series 37, box 1.

63. Case file "Manatí Fire Railroad Crossties, 8/31/55," and "Manatí Fire 8/29/55 Railroad Crossties," SASC, UF, BBC, record group 3, series 37, box 1.

64. Arturo Mañas to Aurelio Portuondo Jr. and Cuban Trading Company, 31 October 1955, 26 December 1955, 12 January 1956, and 14 January 1955, SASC, UF, BBC, Records of Vice President Reed Clark, record group 3, series 61, box 4; Memorandum to Cuban Trading Company, 17 October 1955, SASC, UF, BBC, Labor, 1953–1960, record group 4, series 97, box 3.

65. Fernández León, 260; 278–89; José Antonio Echeverría, "Mantendremos sin Tregua Nuestra Lucha," in Berdayes García, 56–57.

66. Interview with Puente Blanco, 4 December 2015.

67. José Antonio Echeverría, "Carta Abierta de la FEU al Pueblo de Cuba, 24 de febrero de 1956," in Berdayes García, 61–63.

68. Fernández León, 260; interview with Echeverría Bianchi; Julio A. García Oliveras, *José Antonio Echeverría: La Lucha Estudiantil Contra Batista* (Havana: Editora Política, 2001), 147–64.

69. Interview with Echeverría Bianchi; for a photograph of his triumphant reception at Havana's airport upon his return, see Fernández León, 188.

70. José Antonio Echeverría, "Contra las Dictaduras de América, 9 de Marzo de 1956," in Berdayes García, 66–69.

71. José Antonio Echeverría, "Carta a Los Militares y al Pueblo de Cuba, Abril de 1956," in Berdayes García, 72–75.

72. Vicente Cubillas Jr. "Mitín Oposicionista en Nueva York," *Bohemia,* 6 November 1955, 83.

73. "Anti-Batista Cuban Comes Here to Seek Revolt Funds," *Tampa Morning Tribune,* 26 November 1955, 2.

74. Raúl Chibás, "Memorias de la Revolución Cubana," chapter 1, p. 3.

75. Ibid., chapter 1, pp. 1–2.

76. Cubillas, 60.

77. Ramon Coto, "Sirvo a Cuba. Los Que No Tienen el Valor de Sacrificarse," *Bohemia,* 20 November 1955, 82.

78. Quirk, 101.

79. Cubilla, 82.

80. Coto, 81–82.

81. Ibid., 82–83.

82. Quirk, 102; Coto, 59, 81–83.

83. Coto, 59.

84. Tom O'Connor, "Italian Club Bars Theater to Leader of Cuban Revolt," *Tampa Sunday Tribune,* 27 November 1955, 1, 22.

85. Tom O'Connor, "Cubans Here Give Funds to Aid Revolt Against Batista," *Tampa Sunday Tribune,* 28 November 1958, 1.

86. Fidel Castro to unspecified sister, 2 May 1955, in Conte Agüero, *Cartas del Presidio,* 91.

87. Fidel Castro to Jorge Mañach, 17 February 1955, in Conte Agüero, *Cartas del Presidio,* 71–73.

88. Fidel Castro to Luis Conte Agüero, 19 June 1954, in Conte Agüero, *Cartas del Presidio,* 36.

89. Fidel Castro to Melba Hernández, 17 April 1954, in Conte Agüero, *Cartas del Presidio,* 38.

90. Quirk, 86–118.

91. Llerena, *The Unsuspected Revolution,* 83–92.

92. Paco Ignacio Taibo, *Guevara Also Known as Che,* trans. Martin Michael Roberts (New York: St. Martin's, 1997), 32–78; Jorge Castañeda, *Compañero: The Life and Times of Che Guevara* (New York: Knopf, 1997), 64–91; Hilda Gadea, *My Life with Che: The Making of a Revolutionary* (New York: St. Martin's Griffin, 2009), 71–99; Bonachea and San Martín, 66–69.

93. Castañeda, 91–93.

94. Alvarez, 121.

95. Photographs of the military base of Goicuría, Matanzas, in SASC, UF, Ernesto Chávez Collection (hereafter ECC).

96. García-Pérez, 28. The author devotes only one paragraph to the event and includes no footnotes.

97. Raúl Chibás, "Memorias de la Revolución Cubana," chapter 1, p. 5.

98. Casuso, 79–100; Llerena, *The Unsuspected Revolution,* 81–83.

99. Bonachea and San Martín, 65–66; Casuso, 101–18.

100. Casuso, 111.

101. Raúl Chibás, "Memorias de la Revolución Cubana," chapter 2, p. 11. Encased under glass and under permanent guard on Havana's Prado, *Granma* looks too small even to the average tourist.

102. Fidel Castro, "El Movimiento 26 de Julio," *Bohemia,* 1 April 1956, 54.

103. Alvarez, 23–30.

104. Ibid., 39–49, 69–74.

105. Ibid., 35–37.

106. Filmed interview with Agustín País by Glenn Gebhard in *The Forgotten Revolution,* directed and produced by Glenn Gebhard (Trustees of Indiana University, 2014); unedited transcript of interview with País, collection of the author, courtesy of Glenn Gebhard.

107. Interview with Tania de la Nuez by Lillian Guerra and Glenn Gebhard, 2011, YUMA, GGC; unedited transcript of interview of de la Nuez, collection of the author, courtesy of Glenn Gebhard; Alvarez, 66–68.

108. Raúl Chibás, "Memorias de la Revolución Cubana," chapter 2, p. 2.

109. Ibid.

110. Ibid., chapter 2, p. 3; Bonachea and San Martín, 39–40.

111. Bonachea and San Martín, 69–72.

112. Interview with Echeverría Bianchi.

113. Ibid.

114. Ibid.

115. Fidel Castro Ruz and José Antonio Echeverría, "Carta de México, 30 de Agosto de 1956," in Berdayes García, 84–86.

116. Interview with Echeverría Bianchi.

117. Ibid.

118. Interview with Puente Blanco, 5 December 2015.

119. Interview with Puente Blanco, March 2009; interview with Puente Blanco by Lillian Guerra and Abel Sierra Madero, 10 July 2014, Miami.

120. Interview with Puente Blanco, 4 December 2015.

121. "La FEU en Manos de Gangsters que Pactaron en México," *Gente,* 16 September 1956, 8–9.

122. Ibid., 5.

123. Ibid.

124. Interview with Puente Blanco, 5 December 2015.

125. Interview with Puente Blanco, 4 December 2015; L. R. Cabrera, "La Trágica Muerte del Coronel Blanco Rico," *Bohemia,* 4 November 1956, 60–61, 63–66.

126. John L. Topping, Second Secretary of U.S. Embassy in Havana, to U.S. Department of State, 2 November 1956, record group 59, U.S. Department of State Records.

127. Ibid., 3–4; "Los Sangrientos Sucesos de la Embajada de Haití," *Bohemia,* 4 November 1956, 68–71; "En Cuba. Embajada. Sucedió en Haití," *Bohemia,* 4 November 1956, supplement 10–15, 80–84; "Los Funerales del General Salas Cañizares," *Bohemia,* 11 November 1956, 52–53; interview with Puente Blanco, 4 December 2015.

128. Quirk, 119–22.

129. Interview with Chanes de Armas.

130. Sweig, 13.

131. Ernesto Guevara, "Pasajaes de la Guerra Revolucionaria [1963]: Alegría del Pío," in *Obra Revolucionaria,* ed. Roberto Fernández Retamar (Havana: Ediciones ERA, 1967), 114–16. With the important exception of Mario Chanes, who was imprisoned for counterrevolution by the time of his writing, Che identifies each member of the *Granma* survivors by name. See 120–21.

132. Ibid., 116.

133. Interview with Chanes de Armas.

134. Guevara, "Pasajaes de la Guerra Revolucionaria [1963]: Alegría del Pío," 119–45.

135. "Desembarco y Persecución en la Zona de Níquero," *Bohemia,* 9 December 1956, 74–77.

136. Raúl Chibás, "Memorias de la Revolución Cubana," chapter 2, pp. 3–4.

137. Filmed interview with Carlos Franqui by Lillian Guerra, 3 October 2008, New Haven, CT, YUMA, GCC.

138. Raúl Chibás, "Memorias de la Revolución Cubana," 4.

139. Ibid., 7–8.

140. "Gráficas. Los Sucesos de Santiago," *Bohemia,* 9 December 1956, 64–73; "Siguen los Disturbios en Santiago de Cuba," *Prensa Libre,* 2 December 1956, 1–2; "Gráficas de los Sucesos," *Prensa Libre,* 4 December 1956, back page.

141. "Muerto Fidel Castro, Afirma la United Press," *Prensa Libre,* 4 December 1956, 1, 15.

142. "Desplegados por el Ejército Mil Hombres en la Sierra Maestra," and "Mis Tropas No Han Hecho un Solo Disparo en Santiago," *Prensa Libre,* 5 December 1956, 1, 2, 12.

143. "La Rebelión en Oriente. Cercados los Rebeldes; Intimados a Rendirse, Se Niegan. Gestión de Paz," *Prensa Libre,* 9 December 1956, 1–2.

144. "Murió Don Cosme Preocupado por Cuba," *Prensa Libre,* 9 December 1956, 1, 19.

145. "Editorial 2ndo. Que Cese la Vesanía Homicida," *Bohemia,* 4 November 1956, 73; "Editorial. ¡Alto al Fuego!" *Bohemia,* 9 December 1956, 53, 82; "Editorial. ¡Qué Cese la Violencia Suicida!" *Bohemia,* 30 December 1956, 51.

146. "Al Señor Presidente del Tribunal Supremo. 7 Enero 1957," ANC, CMS, fondo 69, expediente 2083, legajo 44, pp. 1–7.

147. Ibid., pp. 9–10.

148. Ibid., p. 10.

149. Ibid., p. 8.

150. For post-1959 histories that research and analyze the evolution in counter-insurgency tactics as well as their intended impacts, see Steve J. Stern, *Remembering Pinochet's Chile: On the Eve of London, 1998* (Bk. 1), and *Battling for Hearts and Minds: Memory Struggles in Pinochet's Chile, 1973–1988* (Bk. 2), (Durham, NC: Duke University Press, 2006); Gilbert M. Joseph, "What We Now Know and Should Know: Bringing Latin America More Meaningfully into Cold War Studies," in *In from the Cold: Latin America's New Encounter with the Cold War*, ed. Gilbert M. Joseph and Daniela Spenser (Durham, NC: Duke University Press, 2008), 3–46; Greg Grandin, "Living in Revolutionary Time: Coming to Terms with the Violence of Latin America's Long Cold War," in *A Century of Revolution: Iinsurgent and Counterinsurgent Violence During Latin America's Long Cold War*, ed. Greg Grandin and Gilbert M. Joseph (Durham, NC: Duke University Press, 2010), 25–28.

151. This view is based on my reading of Elaine Scarry, *The Body in Pain: The Making and Unmaking of the World* (New York: Oxford University Press, 1987), 26–59.

5. Complicit Communists, Student Commandos, *Fidelistas*, and Civil War

1. R. Hart Phillips, "Batista Charges Castro Is a Red," *New York Times*, 11 March 1957, 11.

2. Filmed interview with Alfredo Sánchez Echeverría son of Aureliano Sánchez Arango, primary leader of the Auténticos' armed groups, by Lillian Guerra, 29 March 2014, Tampa, FL; interview with Puente Blanco, 4 December 2015.

3. "Batista y el Comunismo," CHC, UM, Carlos Hevia Collection, folder 15, pp. 2–3.

4. Ibid., p. 3.

5. Ibid.; Juan Marinello, "Una Diez de Octubre de Unidad y de Lucha," and "1868–10 Octubre-1952," *Noticias de Hoy*, 10 October 1952, 1, 16; "Dan Permiso para el Acto del 'Nacional,'" *Noticias de Hoy*, 6 December 1952 1, 6; "Homenaje a Maceo. Hablarán los Líderes Populares," *Noticias de Hoy*, 7 December 1952, 1, 6.

6. "Miles de Personas Rindieron Homenaje al General Maceo," *Noticias de Hoy*, 9 December 1952, 1, 6.

7. Ibid.

8. "El Lema del PSP Es Hacer TODO PARA DERROTAR AL GOBIERNO," *Noticias de Hoy*, 29 January 1952, 1, 6.

9. Salvador Díaz-Versón to Carlos Hevia, 25 June 1953, CHC, UM, Carlos Hevia Collection, folder 15.

10. "Pablo Carrera Justiz y de Velasco," CHC, UM, Carlos Hevia Collection, folder 15.

11. Salvador Díaz-Versón to Carlos Hevia, 25 June 1953.

12. "New Communist Control. Executive Committee of the Cigar Makers Union of Havana. Comité Ejecutivo del Sindicato de Tabaqueros de la Habana," CHC, UM, Carlos Hevia Collection, folder 15.

13. Unesco [pseudonym] to Carlos Hevia, 29 March 1955, CHC, UM, Carlos Hevia Collection, folder 15.

14. Guerrra, *Visions of Power*, 62–67.

15. Fidel Castro and Janette Habel, *Proceso al Sectarismo* (Buenos Aires: Jorge Alvarez Editor, 1965), 37–38.

16. "Las Tonterías de la Propaganda Imperialista," "Resolución del Pleno del C.N. del PSP Sobre el XX Congreso del PC de la URSS," and various articles on the USSR in *Carta Semanal*, 6 June 1956, 1–2, 7–8; "Comunicado del Buró Ejecutivo del Comité Nacional del Partido Socialista Popular," and "Mentiras y Tonterías," *Carta Semanal*, 24 July 1957, 1; "Vida Internacional: La Respuesta a Bulganin," *Carta Semanal*, 22 January 1958, 5; "Vida Internacional: Crece el Apoyo a Proposiciones Soviéticas," *Carta Semanal*, 29 January 1958, 5–6.

17. "La Superioridad del Régimen Socialista en los Hechos," *Carta Semanal*, 7 August 1957, 12; "Crece la Producción en los Países Socialistas," and ""Discriminación Brutal en EEUU," *Carta Semanal*, 4 September 1957, 8.

18. For a sense of the expansive space that state repression occupied in everyday life for Soviet Russians as well as its "necessary" negation, see Orlando Figes, *The Whisperers: Private Life in Stalin's Russia* (London: Penguin Books, 2008); Eugenia Semyonovna Ginzburg, *Journey into the Whirlwind*, trans. Paul Stevenson and Max Hayward (San Diego: Harcourt Brace Jovanovich, 1967); David L. Hoffman, *Stalinist Values: The Cultural Norms of Soviet Modernity, 1917–1941* (Ithaca, NY: Cornell University Press, 2003).

19. "Medio Millón de Unidades de Propaganda Edita Camagüey," *Carta Semanal*, 14 March 1951, 1. Note that on the occasion of the fourth anniversary of the bulletin's founding and the fortieth anniversary of the PSP, a special edition of *Carta Semanal* was printed for mass distribution. See "¡Hagamos una Distribución Masiva del Número Especial de *Carta Semanal!" Carta Semanal*, 17 July 1957, 2.

20. "La Detención de Juan Marinello," *Carta Semanal*, 6 June 1951, 1; "El Rescate de 'Hoy,'" *Carta Semanal*, 27 June 1951, 1; "Vida del Partido: El Ataque Fascista Contra 'Hoy,'" *Carta Semanal*, 4 July 1951, 1–2.

21. Although the complete set of this PSP periodical is held at the Biblioteca Nacional de Cuba, access to the collection is restricted. The Ernesto Chávez Collection at the University of Florida's Special and Area Studies Collections contains a remarkably full run, starting in 1951 and ending in January 1958.

22. Guerra, *Visions of Power*, 81–92, 107–32, 147, 199–244.

23. See sections of the PSP's official manifesto titled "El Gobierno Frente a la Violencia y la Guerra Civil" and "¡Basta Ya de Tiranía," *Carta Semanal*, 12 June 1957, 1–2; "Orientación del Día: Contra el Terror," *Carta Semanal*, 18 December 1957, 1; "La Orientación del Día: Nueva Suspensión de Garantías y la Lucha Contra el Terror," and "Noticias Sobre la Situación: Continúan Asesinatos, el Terror y las Detenciones en Todo el País," *Carta Semanal*, 25 September 1957, 1; "Llamamiento del PSP: ¡Todos a la Acción de las Masas Contra el Terror del Gobierno!" and "La Lucha Contra el Terror," *Carta Semanal*, 22 January 1958, 1.

24. "Panorama Político. La Denuncia de Fidel Castro Contra el Pacto de Miami y el Pacto Necesario," *Carta Semanal*, 15 January 1958, 2.

25. See the section of the PSP's official manifesto titled "La Verdadera Solución Cubana," *Carta Semanal*, 12 June 1957, 2.

26. "Proclama del Partido Socialista Popular: Qué Hacer ante la Situación," *Carta Semanal,* 29 July 1957, 1.

27. "El Camino que Señala El PSP: Un Nuevo 12 de Agosto," and "Lucha de Masas: Celebra la Caída de Machado," *Carta Semanal,* 22 August 1956, 1–2; "12 de Agosto de 1933," and "Ingerencia No: El Camino de Maceo y Martí," *Carta Semanal,* 7 August 1957, 7, 9.

28. Francisco Ichaso, "Cabalgata Política. Unanimidad Frente a la Violencia," *Bohemia,* 11 November 1956, 50, 108.

29. "El Partido de la Paz y el Anti-Imperialismo," *Carta Semanal,* 30 May 1951, 1.

30. *Magazine Mella. La Voz de la Juventud* (no month given, 1956), cover.

31. "Suplemento Mella Gráfico. Pucho y Perrerías. 27 Noviembre," and "Luis y sus Amigos," *Magazine Mella. La Voz de la Juventud* (no month given, 1956), 1, 3.

32. Juan Marinello and Blas Roca to Fidel Castro, Manuel Bisbé, et al., 2 July 1957, ANC, CMS, fondo 69, legajo 43, expediente 2065. Emphasis added.

33. "Orientación del Día: El Camino Correcto," *Carta Semanal,* 29 May 1957, 1.

34. Soto, *De la Historia y la Memoria,* 1:137–38.

35. Herminio Portell Vilá, "La Propaganda Comunista," *Bohemia,* 24 April 1955, 10, 126.

36. Ibid., 126.

37. Ibid., 127.

38. Guerra, *Visions of Power,* 81.

39. G. A. Warner [pseudonym] to Carlos Márquez Sterling, "La Hora de Negar," undated, ANC, CMS, fondo 69, legajo 39, expediente 2000.

40. "Ref: Publicaciones Comunistas," report to Dr. Lomberto Díaz Rodríguez, Ministro de Gobernación, 26 July 1951, CHC, UM, Carlos Hevia Collection, folder 15.

41. Salvador Díaz-Versón, *El Zarismo Rojo (Rusia Avanzando Sobre América)* (Havana: Impresora Mundial, 1958), 36–46.

42. Ibid., 47–50.

43. Detective Carlos Chao to Sr. Ministro de Gobernación [Lomberto Díaz Rodríguez], "Informe Confidencial," 16 February 1951, "Los Miembros de [*sic*] Partido Comunista Chinos. En la Ciudad de la Habana," and "Nota Confirencia," CHC, UM, Carlos Hevia Collection, folder 15.

44. Sub-inspector 2nda. de la Policía Secreta Nacional Carlos Santana Pedrero to Ministro de Gobernación and Jefe de la Policía Secreta Nacional Erundino Vilela Peña, 2 November 1950, CHC, UM, Carlos Hevia Collection, folder 15.

45. Comandante S.M.E., Jefe del G.R.A.S. Clemente R. Gomez Sicre to Ministro de Gobernación, 31 October 1950, CHC, UM, Carlos Hevia Collection, folder 15, pp. 1–3.

46. Ibid., pp. 5–6. See also other secret reports on Grobart in the same file, dated 1 July 1950 and 5 April 1951. The latter document reveals that Grobart had fled before Prío could legally deport him for espionage.

47. "En Escrito Oficial la Empresa de 'Hoy' Confesó Ser Comunista," *Diario de la Marina,* 29 June 1951, 1; Aníbal Escalante to Dr. Carlos Prío Socarrás, 25 June 1951, CHC, UM, Carlos Hevia Collection, folder 15.

48. "Editorial" from the first edition of *Nuestro Tiempo,* dated 1 April 1954, in *Revista "Nuestro Tiempo": Compilación de Trabajos Publicados,* ed. Ricardo Hernández Otero (Havana: Editorial Letras Libres, 1989), 9–10.

49. Guerra, *Visions of Power,* 163.

50. Franqui, *Cuba, La Revolución,* 145–50.

51. Luis Ortega, "Batista, Aliado Secreto del Comunismo," CHC, UM, Carlos Hevia Collection, folder 15, pp. 1–2.

52. Ibid., pp. 2–4.

53. Ibid., pp. 4–6.

54. Salvador Díaz-Versón, "Al Pueblo de Cuba," 10 October 1954, CHC, UM, Carlos Hevia Collection, folder 15, pp. 1–3.

55. Ibid., pp. 4.

56. "Prefieren la Cárcel," *¡Alerta Cubanos!* April 1953, 1.

57. Dr. David Enrique Amado-Ledo, *El Colegio Médico Nacional de Cuba: La Revolución Castro-Comunista* (Miami: n.p., 1973), 26–27.

58. Lyman B. Kirkpatrick Jr. *The Real CIA* (New York: Macmillan, 1968), 156–57.

59. Ibid., 158–62.

60. Thomas G. Paterson, *Contesting Castro: The United States and the Triumph of the Cuban Revolution* (New York: Oxford University Press, 1995).

61. Kirkpatrick, 163.

62. "Report from Havana," *Intelligence Digest: A Review of World Affairs,* December 1957, 17–18.

63. Dr. Félix W. Bernardino, "He Took Cuba–Twice," *See,* January 1953, 40.

64. U.S. Department of Commerce, *Investment in Cuba: Basic Information for United States Businessmen* (Washington, DC: U.S. Government Printing Office, 1956).

65. "Man of the Week. Pres. Fulgencio Batista. He Built a Modern Cuba," *Orlando Sentinel Florida Magazine,* 3 November 1957, 6–7.

66. Equal Justice Initiative, *Lynching in America: Confronting the Legacy of Racial Terror* (Montgomery, AL: Equal Justice Initiative, 2015); Walter T. Howard, *Lynchings: Extralegal Violence in Florida During the 1930s* (Cranbury, NJ: Associated University Presses, 1995); Margaret Vandiver, *Lethal Punishment: Lynchings and Legal Executions in the South* (New Brunswick, NJ: Rutgers University Press, 2007), 23–27.

67. Fan purchased in the mid-1950s. The fan reads, "Saint Petersburg Alligator Farm. State of Florida Land of Gators" and pictures two naked black toddlers with open-mouthed alligators directly behind them; the other side shows one standing black toddler and two seated black babies over the caption "Alligator Bait." Private collection of the author. Note that the University of Florida's Special and Area Collections archive preserves several hundred postcards with this theme, most dating from the 1910s to the 1940s.

68. "Cuban Pres. Batista Arrives," and "21-Gun Salute Greets Guest of City," *Daytona Beach Evening News,* 23 March 1956, 1, 3; "Parade Heads Batista Day Gala Program," *Daytona Beach Evening News,* 24 March 1956, 1.

69. H.M.D., "An Editorial. Welcome to an Old Friend," *Daytona Beach Evening News,* 23 March 1956, 1.

70. "Batista Day Starts with Big Parade," *Daytona Beach Evening News,* 24 March 1956, 1.

71. "Batista off for Cuba After Weekend Visit," *Daytona Beach Evening News,* 26 March 1956, 1.

72. Ibid., 3.

73. Ibid.

74. "Dona el Presidente Dos Casas a la Ciudad de Daytona Beach," *Diario de la Marina*, 28 October 1957, 1, 10B; "Llegó a la Habana el Alcalde de Daytona con una Delegación," *Diario de la Marina*, 27 October 1957, 1, 8B; "Instalarán un Museo Cubano en Ciudad de Daytona Beach," *El Mundo*, 29 October 1957, A10.

75. Herbert Matthews, "Cuba Rebel Is Visited in Hideout: Castro Is Still Alive and Still Fighting in the Mountains," *New York Times*, 24 February 1957, 1.

76. R. Hart Phillips, "Censorship Ends Today, Cuba Says," *New York Times*, 26 February 1957, 12.

77. Herbert L. Matthews, "Old Order in Cuba Is Threatened by Forces of an Internal Revolt," *New York Times*, 26 February 1957, 13.

78. Filmed interview with Dr. Aestor Bombino by Lillian Guerra, February 2009, Miami, FL, YUMA, GGC.

79. Interviews with Bombino, Valls, Puente Blanco, and Echeverría Bianchi; Bonachea and San Martín, 109–11.

80. Bonachea and San Martín, 111.

81. Interview with Bombino.

82. Filmed interview with Sinforiano Echeverría Bianchi by Lillian Guerra, March 2009, Miami, FL, YUMA, GGC.

83. Ibid.

84. Interview with Echeverría Bianchi.

85. Bonachea and San Martín, 114.

86. Interview with Sadulé, 14 July 2014.

87. Interview with Bombino.

88. José Antonio Echeverría Bianchi, "Alocución al Pueblo Desde Radio Reloj. 13 de Marzo de 1957," in Berdayes García, 99.

89. Interview with Bombino.

90. Filmed interview with Jorge Valls by Lillian Guerra, March 2009, Miami, FL, YUMA, GGC; Bonachea and San Martín, 118–19.

91. Interview with Bombino.

6. *Clandestinos,* Guerrillas, and the Making of a Messiah in the Sierra Maestra

1. "Mas de 40 Muertos y 18 Heridos en el Asalto Armando a Palacio," *El Mundo*, 14 March 1957, 1, A10.

2. Ibid., 1, back page; "Varios Aspectos de los Sucesos de Ayer," *El Mundo*, 14 March 1957, A4; "Participaron 3 Grupos en el Ataque al Palacio Presidencial," *El Mundo*, 17 March 1957, A10; "El Camión Utilizado . . .," *El Mundo*, 17 March 1957, back page.

3. "Muerto Pelayo Cuervo," *El Mundo*, 14 March 1957, 1, A10; "Pelayo Cuervo fue Ajeno al Asalto, Dice O. Piedra," *El Mundo*, 17 March 1957, 1, A10.

4. Filmed interview with Vicente Baez by Lillian Guerra, 7 August 2008, San Juan, Puerto Rico; interview with Franqui.

5. "Proclamación del Comité Nacional de la JS ante los Muertos del 13 de Marzo: A Toda la Juventud Cubana," 14 March 1957, in *Cuba. Politics. File No. 11, NACLA Archive of Latin America,* reel no. 10.

6. Marcos was later tried, along with PSP accomplices Edith Buchaca and her husband

Joaquín Ordoqui, in 1964 in a series of show trials staged by Fidel Castro in order to discipline Cuban Communists and purge Soviet loyalists from state command. See Miguel A. Barroso, *Un Asunto Sensible: Tres Historias Cubanas de Crimen y Traición* (Barcelona: Mondadori, 2009); Maurice Halperin, *The Rise and Decline of Fidel Castro* (Berkeley: University of California Press, 1972), and *The Taming of Fidel Castro* (Berkeley: University of California Press, 1981); Fidel Castro and Habel; Guerra, *Visions of Power*, 294–95.

7. No in-depth history of the DR's guerrilla movement in El Escambray has yet been written, in part because of Fidel Castro's deliberate efforts to co-opt its members in the first months of 1959 and discredit those who refused to unite under his leadership. Nonetheless, the participation of American William Morgan and his rise to the rank of comandante in the DR's guerrilla force has recently inspired a number of excellent works that provide greater insight into its actions and goals. See Shetterly; Sallah and Weiss; Adriana Bosch, director and producer, *American Comandante: Cuba's Most Unlikely Revolutionary* (Public Broadcasting Corporation, 2015).

8. Chase, *Revolution Within the Revolution*, 48; Bonachea and San Martín, 264. According to the secretary-general of the 26th of July Movement's action and sabotage units, Manuel "Manolo" Ray, the figures of up to ten thousand before 1958 and thirty thousand after are inflated. As he told me in August 2008 and February 2009 interviews, the total number of activists under his orders and those of Resistencia Cívica was no more than six thousand throughout the war. Of these, three to four thousand were truly *confiable,* the most reliable.

9. Chase, *Revolution Within the Revolution*, 48.

10. Aleksandr Fursenko and Timothy Naftali, *"One Hell of a Gamble": Khrushchev, Castro and Kennedy, 1958–1964; The Secret History of the Cuban Missile Crisis* (New York: Norton, 1997), 6–8.

11. Lars Schoultz, *That Infernal Little Cuban Republic: The United States and the Cuban Revolution* (Chapel Hill: University of North Carolina Press, 2009), 13–81; William M. LeoGrande and Peter Kornbluh, *Back Channel to Cuba: The Hidden History of Negotiations Between Washington and Havana* (Chapel Hill: University of North Carolina Press, 2014), 6–41.

12. Oltuski, 91–93

13. An original second edition of the pamphlet *La Historia Me Absolverá* based on Fidel's defense speech at his trial for the 1953 assault on the Moncada barracks was printed, probably in 1958. One copy, dedicated to St. George by a member of New York's Acción Cívica, claimed that twenty thousand issues of this new edition were distributed, in addition to the ten thousand already in circulation on the island. *La Historia Me Absolverá: Discurso Pronunciado por el Dr. Fidel Castro ante el Tribunal de Urgencia de Santiago de Cuba el día 16 de Octubre de 1953* (New York: Club 26 de Julio de New York, 1957), 1, YUMA, Cuban Revolution Collection (hereafter CRC).

14. "Manifesto No. 1 del 26 de Julio al Pueblo de Cuba," 8 August 1955, YUMA, CRC.

15. Interview with Franqui.

16. "Persisten Hechos que Perturban Hondamente la Paz Pública," *El Mundo,* 5 March 1957, A4.

17. "Afirman que Habrá en Cuba, Pronto, un Nuevo Brote Revolucionario," *El Mundo,* 10 March 1957, A2.

18. "Constará de 3 Mil Cubiertos el Banquete-Homenaje a Batista," *El Mundo,* 10 March 1957, A9; "No Puede Considerarse Contienda la Situación en la Sierra Maestra," *El Mundo,* 12 March 1957, A4.

19. "Editorial. Alto a la Violencia," *El Mundo,* 15 March 1957, A6; Antonio Iraizoz, "El Gesto de Marta," *El Mundo,* 17 March 1957, A8.

20. Guerra, *Visions of Power,* 57–58; "'Gracias, Sr. Presidente . . .': Una Carta al Presidente Batista del General Edmond F. Leavey, Presidente de la International Telephone and Telegraph Corp.," *El Mundo,* 17 March 1957, A7.

21. "Viene a Cuba un Jefe Naval Norteamericano," *El Mundo,* 16 March 1957, 1.

22. *A Palacio . . .* (Havana: Ministerio de Información, 1957). Signed gift of Alfredo Sadulé to the author.

23. Sweig, 9.

24. Quoted in ibid., 12.

25. Interview with Baez.

26. Interview with Franqui.

27. Filmed interview with Emilio Guede by Lillian Guerra, May 2008, San Juan, Puerto Rico, YUMA, GGC; Guerra, *Visions of Power,* 41; Emilio Guede, *Cuba: La Revolución Que No Fue* (n.p.: Eriginal Books, 2013), 219–25.

28. Interview with Franqui.

29. Filmed interview with Manuel "Manolo" Ray by Lillian Guerra, 8 August 2008, San Juan, Puerto Rico, SASC, UF, Lillian Guerra Collection (hereafter LGC); for a discussion of how empowerment against all odds and an apparently indefatigable enemy produces "pleasure," see Elizabeth Wood, *Insurgent Collective Action and Civil War in El Salvador* (New York: Cambridge University Press, 2003), 18–19.

30. Filmed interview with Manuel "Manolo" Ray by Lillian Guerra, 28 February 2009, San Juan, Puerto Rico, SASC, UF, LGC.

31. Interview with Baez; interview with Franqui.

32. A single extremely rare copy of *Aldabonazo: Organo del M Revolucionario 26 de Julio,* 25 August 1956, may be found in SASC, UF, ECC.

33. "Sacerdote Apaleado," in ibid., 1–2; "11 Millones para Asesinatos," *Vanguardia Obrera: Con las Armas para Trabajar, Unidos Venceremos* (undated), 1–2; "Cinco Puntos para La Libertad," *Revolución: Organo Oficial del Movimiento "26 de Julio,"* 27 August 1958, 1–2.

34. Manuel García Rodríguez, *Sierra Maestra en la Clandestinidad* (Santiago de Cuba: Editorial Oriente, 1981); Two copies of *Sierra Maestra* printed in Miami may be found in SASC, UF, ECC.

35. Interview with Franqui.

36. Ibid.

37. Interview with Guede; Guede, 226–30.

38. Interview with Ray, 8 August 2008.

39. For example, see "Estallaron Anoche 5 Petardos," *El Mundo,* 5 May 1957, 1, A8.

40. Interview with Ray, 8 August 2008, and 28 February 2009.

41. Guede, 235.

42. Ibid., 230–35.

43. Eduardo Meruéndano, "Juan Manuel Fangio: El Hombre, la Velocidad y la Muerte," *Bohemia,* 24 February 1957, supplement 8, 14.

44. Guede, 235–38.
45. Interview with Ray, 28 February 2009; Fangio, quoted in "¡Exclusivo! El Sensacional Secuestro de Juan Manuel Fangio," *Bohemia*, 2 March 1958, 70–78.
46. "¡Exclusivo! El Sensacional Secuestro," 72.
47. Interview with Ray, 28 February 2009. *Bohemia*'s post-1959 report on the case confirms Ray's account and provides further details: Emma Montenegro, "Como Fué Secuestrado Fangio," *Bohemia*, 18–25 January 1959, 76–78, 104.
48. "Editorial. No Se Puede Tapar el Sol Con un Dedo," *Bohemia*, 2 March 1958, 79, 98.
49. Agustín Tamargo, "La Hora de la Verdad," *Bohemia*, 2 March 1958, 64–66.
50. Andrés Valdespino, "A la Fuerza No Se Divierte el Pueblo," *Bohemia*, 4 August 1957, 66, 95; Luis Rolando Cabrera, "El Enigma de las Tres Mujeres Muertas," *Bohemia*, 29 September 1957, 72–73, 96–98.
51. Guede, 170–71.
52. Ibid., 172–75; "Un Reportaje en Cuba. Historia de Horrores," *Bohemia*, 16 March 1958, supplement 2–3.
53. 'The Current Situation," *Report on Cuba*, January 1958, 1. Find this edition and dozens more in SCAS, UF, BBC, series 66, box 1, "Publications 1958."
54. Universal Research & Consultants, Inc., *Communist Activities of the Cuban Rebels* (Washington, DC: Universal Research & Consultants, 1958).
55. Ibid. 3.
56. Andrés Rivero Agüero, "El Ejemplo de Abraham Lincoln," *Bohemia*, 2 March 1958, 68–69.
57. "Responsabilidad Común," *Respuestas del Partido Socialista Popular*, 7 June 1957, 1, SCAS, UF, ECC.
58. Ibid; interview with Ray, 8 August 2008.
59. Interview with Baez.
60. Ibid; Llerena, *The Unsuspected Revolution*, 166.
61. Interview with Ray, 28 February 2009.
62. "An Interview with Roberto Acosta Hechaverría," in *The Hidden Pearl of the Caribbean: Trotskyism in Cuba* (London: Porcupine, 2000), 244; personal communication with Rafael Acosta Arriba.
63. Interview with Baez.
64. Quinteto Rebelde, "Qué Se Vaya el Mono," in *Kubamusika: Crónicas de la Revolución Cubana* (Kubamusika, 2011).
65. Sweig, 121–63.
66. Interview with Baez.
67. Ibid.
68. Ibid.
69. Oltuski, 194–95.
70. The best and most accurate mini-bio of St. George's activities before his arrival in the Sierra remains the editors' note beginning "Dear Reader" in the February 1958 edition of *Coronet* magazine.
71. Sweig, 13.
72. Carlos Franqui, ed., *Relatos de la Revolución Cubana* (Montevideo: Editorial Sandino, n.d.), 74.

73. Teel, xiii–xiv.

74. Andrew St. George, "A Revolution Made Me a Pro," *Popular Photography,* September 1958, 97.

75. See 26th of July Movement bonds in SCAS, UF, ECC. This collection is currently unprocessed but open to researchers under the author's supervision.

76. Andrew St. George, "A Revolution Gone Wrong," *Coronet,* July 1960, 113; see also Fidel Castro, "Why We Fight," *Coronet,* February 1958, 80–86.

77. These archival sources include the many pages of descriptive "captions" that St. George wrote in 1969, when Yale University acquired part of his collection, a rare March 1958 audio recording with Fidel, filmed outtakes from largely unknown documentaries St. George produced and, most significant, hundreds of pages of highly detailed field notes—called "situationers" and "guidance memos"—that St. George's rigorous publishers (especially at *Life, Look,* and Magnum) required him to submit for each roll of film he delivered, regardless of what editors actually chose to print.

78. The author is deeply grateful to Mrs. Jean St. George for shipping an enormous box to me this summer that contained a treasure trove of "situationers" and other documents of St. George's work in Cuba. As St. George himself explained, "I had to write 'data sheets' amounting to over 30,000 words. Big magazines are thorough, and without exact caption material complied *on the spot,* you are done for." See St. George, "A Revolution Made Me a Pro," 98.

79. St. George, "A Revolution Gone Wrong," 112.

80. Manuscript notebook of interview by Andrew St. George with Fidel Castro, YUMA, CRC, box 20, folder 1, pp. 10–11, 14.

81. Ibid., 18.

82. "El único miedo que los hombres de negocios tienen hoy en Cuba, como dijo el representante norteamericano Porter acerca de Santo Domingo, es que Batista los pida la mitad de las utilidades para él" (The only fear that businessmen have today in Cuba, as the U.S. congressman Porter said with regard to [Trujillo] in the Dominican Republic, is that Batista would demand half the [electric, water, and telephone] utilities for himself [following the model of "government ownership' under Trujillo]," wrote Fidel. See ibid., back of p. 18; audio wire recording of Andrew St. George interviewing Fidel Castro, March 1958, YUMA, CRC,. The comment can be found between minutes 21:03 and 24:35 of the recording. See similar comments in St. George, "Exclusive: Inside the Cuban Revolution," *Look,* 4 February 1958, 30.

83. "Batista: Amigo y Protector de los Comunistas," *Sierra Maestra,* July 1958, 12–13. See also back page editorial "Page Dedicated to the American People. Batista and Communism." Edition available in SASC, UF, Neill Macaulay Collection.

84. Fidel Castro, "Why We Fight," 84–85; St. George, "Exclusive," 30; Audio wire recording with comments found between minutes 19:50 and 22:00. In St. George's first article, he described Fidel's economic goals as a plan to bring FDR's "New Deal" to rural Cuba. See Andrew St. George, "How I Found Castro, the Cuban Guerrilla," *Cavalier: Action and Adventure for Men,* October 1957, 59.

85. Fidel Castro, "Why We Fight," 82; St. George, "Exclusive," 30; St. George, "How I Found Castro," 59.

86. Andrew St. George, "Castro on Eve of His Big Bid," *Life,* 14 April 1958, 27.

87. Quoted in Santiago Alvarez, "El Mar Es un Símbolo: Este Es un Lugar Sagrado," *El Caimán Barbudo,* October 1982, 16.

88. Quoted in St. George, "How I Found Castro," 56. Note that in the story, St. George uses the pseudonym of María in order to protect Melba from the trauma of having her story made public. Personal interview with Jean St. George, New Haven, CT, 6 March 2006.

89. St. George, "How I Found Castro," 57.

90. St. George, "A Visit with a Revolutionary," *Coronet,* February 1958, 77.

91. "Different Ways of Treating War Prisoners," *Sierra Maestra,* May 1958, back page. Edition found in YUMA, Andrew St. George Papers.

92. Interview with Ray, 8 August 2008.

93. Unidentified postcard in Elena Kurstin Cuban Memorabilia Collection, Special Collections, Florida International University, Miami.

94. *Resistencia: Organo Oficial del Movimiento de Resistencia Cívica,* March 1958, 4–5, box 20, folder 4, YUMA, CRC.

95. Quoted in St. George, "How I Found Castro," 56.

96. This series of images was first published in "En la Sierra Maestra: El Hombre en Quien Confía Cuba," *Mañana: La Revista de México,* 15 June 1957, 20–24; and then more extensively with a story by St. George in "Exclusive." The same images can be found "Dans la Jungle, Face aux 30,000 Hommes de Batista: Un Lecteur de Montesquieu," *Jours,* 8 March 1958, 12–17; and "J'ai Vécu la Victoire de Castro," *Paris Match,* 10 January 1959, 10–19.

97. Deeply etched into popular and official histories of Cuba's founding struggles for nation, the burning of cane fields was the principal strategy for destroying the existing colonial structures on which heroes like Antonio Maceo and Máximo Gómez had relied sixty years earlier.

98. St. George, "Photo Identification and Description," box 1, folder 1, folios 2222–4444, YUMA, CRC.

99. Ibid.; and box 1, folder 4, contact book 1, print 1, YUMA, CRC. *Manana*'s article published a photograph of the first oath-taking ceremony St. George attended; see "En la Sierra Maestra," 20.

100. St. George, "Photo Identification and Description," 1414.

101. Ibid., 1515.

102. St. George, "Exclusive," 28.

103. Ibid., 29.

104. St. George, "A Revolution Made Me a Pro," 96.

105. Safe conduct pass and flag signed by Celia Sánchez, box 20, folder 2, YUMA, CRC.

106. Document titled "Sheet: 7508/G," box 20, folder 2, YUMA, CRC. Note that the handmade "Map Sketch" to which St. George refers in the situationer memo to NBC accompanying these sheets is preserved in YUMA CRC.

107. Document titled "Sheet: Single Clip of Four Frames, Code SG1-69," YUMA, CRC.

108. The photographs of this scene can be found in box 2, folder 108, book II, print 38, YUMA, CRC. The description given by St. George in Yale's original files is quoted in the online finding aid by Lillian Guerra, *Guide to the Cuban Revolution Collection, MS 650,* http://drs.library.yale.edu/HLTransformer/HLTransServlet?stylename=yul.ead 2002.xhtml.xsl&pid=mssa:ms.0650&query=Cuban Revolution Collection&clear-styl

esheet-cache=yes&hlon=yes&big=&adv=&filter=fgs.collection:"Manuscripts and Archives"&hitPageSht.

109. This document forms part of a thick folio of sheets related to a documentary called *Behind Rebel Lines* that St. George hoped to produce; while a newsreel with his images and that title does exist, it lasts less than three minutes and does not include the majority of the images his notes describe. I received the set from Jean St. George in August 2014 and preserve it as part of a private collection. This document is titled "Sheet: C-7230/C4." Park Wollam, U.S. consul in Santiago, confirms the circulation of this list of executed at Ingenio Soledad in his unpublished memoir, p. 73, private collection of the author. The untitled typescript was apparently completed in the early 1970s upon Wollam's retirement from public service. I obtained the manuscript through Glenn Gebhard, who interviewed Wollam's widow, Jean Wollam, in Carlsbad, California, on 14 December 2009.

110. Document titled "St. George—Behind Cuban Rebel Lines—OA 35611, Sheet C-42," in Andrew St. George's personal archive, private collection of the author.

111. Document titled "St. George—Behind Rebel Lines—OA 35611, Sheet C-35," in Andrew St. George's personal archive, private collection of the author. For the photographs here described, see box 1, folder 89, book II, print 19: "Cdte. Juan Almeida Bosque and Rebel Radio and Administrative Staff," YUMA, CRC.

112. Document titled "St. George—Behind Rebel Lines—OA 35611, Sheet C-41," in private collection of the author.

113. Andrew St. George, "Cuba in Oproer," *Der Spiegel,* 17 January 1959, 26.

114. Neill Macaulay, *A Rebel in Cuba* (New York: Quadrangle Books, 1970), 10–11; filmed interview with Neill Macaulay by Glenn Gebhard, 20–21 October 2007, Los Angeles, CA, SASC, UF, Neill Macaulay Collection; Paterson, 86.

115. YUMA, group 650, "Photo Identification and Description," box 1, folder 1, folios 2222–3333.

116. Raúl Castro, "En la Universidad Popular," *Obra Revolucionaria,* 17 May 1960, 24.

117. Sweig, 173.

118. Interview with Franqui.

119. See images in box 1, folder 12, contact book 1, print 12, YUMA, CRC; see also St. George, "Photo Identification and Description," box 1, folder 1, folios 1212–1313, section titled "Sheet Y-12."

120. Document titled "St. George—Behind Rebel Lines—OA 35611, Sheet C-16," in private collection of the author. St George continues, "Here Dr. Luis [*sic;* should be Eduardo Bernabé] Ordaz examines six-year-old boy suffering from parasitism, an ubiquitous disease."

121. St. George describes photographs of the tank and telephones in a document titled "St. George—Behind Cuban Rebel Lines—OA 35611. Sheet C-57, p. 2" and the capture of an entire "motor pool of Texaco" in document titled "St. George—Behind Rebel Lines—OA 35611, Sheet C-6," in private collection of the author.

122. St. George first reported on the destruction of buses after his summer trip in a document titled "St. George—Behind Cuban Rebel Lines—OA 35611, Sheet C-30" and then again in a "General Situationer" memo dated 4 December 1958, p. 2, in private collection of the author. In the first report, he wrote, "Gutted hulk of Santiago-Habana

bus was photographed between Victoria de las Tunas and Holguín. Santiago-Habana Company claims it lost 70 of these brand new air-conditioned buses to rebel attacks in last two months, and has suspended operations."

123. Document titled "St. George—Behind Rebel Lines—OA 35611, Sheet C-4," in private collection of the author.

124. Document titled "St. George—Behind Rebel Lines—OA 35611, Sheet C-31," in private collection of the author.

125. "General Situationer" memo dated 4 December 1958, p. 3, in private collection of the author.

126. Document titled "St. George—Behind Rebel Lines—OA 35611, Sheet C-2" in private collection of the author.

127. Earl E. T. Smith, *The Fourth Floor: An Account of the Castro Communist Revolution* (New York: Random House, 1962), 148.

128. Sound recording of Andrew St. George narrating reel 3 and 5 of his films, 1969, box 21, YUMA, CRC.

129. Document titled "St. George—Behind Rebel Lines—OA 35611, Sheet C-51," in private collection of the author. I believe that in authoring the guide to St. George's photographs in Yale's Cuban Revolution Collection, I confused images of this scene with the nationalization of U.S. oil refineries in July 1960. I need to return to the original photographs I may have mistakenly dated as taking place in July 1960 in order to confirm the survival of these images St. George describes.

130. Portraits of Crespo and the boy in box 7, folder 1, YUMA, Andrew St. George Papers.

131. Descriptions from document titled "St. George—Behind Rebel Lines—OA 35611, Sheet C-21" and "St. George—Behind Rebel Lines—OA 35611, Sheet C-18," in private collection of the author.

132. Document titled "St. George—Behind Rebel Lines—OA 35611, Sheet C-15," in private collection of the author.

133. Document titled "St. George—Behind Rebel Lines—OA 35611, Sheet C-18," in private collection of the author; St. George, "Descriptions and Identifications" sheet Y-111, YUMA, CRC.

134. Document titled "St. George—Behind Rebel Lines—OA 35611, Sheet C-53," in private collection of the author.

135. Documents titled "Sheet C-2, pg. 2," "The Girls with the Guerrillas: II," and "St. George —Behind Rebel Lines—OA 35611, Sheet C-53," in private collection of the author.

136. Oniris appeared in St. George's earliest publications, particularly the second page of his *Look* magazine spread. These anecdotes come from "The Girls with the Guerrillas: II," 1. I have taken the liberty of retranslating Fidel's comment, given by St. George in English, back into Spanish. The original reads, "Girl, if you keep cleaning that .22 pistol, you're going to end up with a .38."

137. Document titled "St. George—Behind Cuban Rebel Lines—OA 35611, Sheets C-23, C-33, C-30, C-45, C-12," p. 2 of 3, private collection of the author. The document begins, "These are, with exception of frames listed below, head shots of Fidel Castro. In my notebook and on tape, I have some salty Fidelisms to go with them."

138. Llerena, *The Unsuspected Revolution*, 247.

139. Document titled "St. George—Behind Cuban Rebel Lines—OA 35611, Sheets C-23, C-33, C-30, C-45, C-12," p. 1.

140. Patterson, 160–78; Earl Smith, 140–51. See also Efigenio Ameijeiras Delgado, *Más Allá de Nosotros: Columna 6 "Juan Manuel Ameijerias" II Frente Oriental "Frank País"* (Santiago de Cuba: Editorial Oriente, 1984); Olga Miranda Bravo, *Vecinos Indeseables: La Base Yanqui en Guantánmo* (Havana: Editorial de Ciencias Sociales, 1998), esp. 122–23; and Lipman, 139–41.

141. Manuel Fajardo, quoted in Carlos Franqui, ed., *Cuba: El Libro de Los Doce* (México, DF: Ediciones Era, 1966), 76; Earl Smith 141. Fajardo claims they captured thirty-six Marines, while Ambassador Smith and historian Patterson claims the lower figure of twenty-eight. In all, Smith admitted that forty-seven U.S. citizens and three Canadians were captured that summer.

142. Circular issued by Raúl Castro titled *Denuncia del Comandante Raúl Castro ante la Juventud del Mundo. Contiene La Verdad Sobre la Detención de los Americanos. La Denuncia de la Ayuda Militar Yanqui a Batista. La Orden Militar Num. 30*, p. 4, 27 June 1958, YUMA, CRC.

143. Ibid., 5. An original copy of Orden Militar No. 30 is contained in the same collection.

144. Llerena provides photographic and documentary evidence that this was true, despite the fact that he himself became alienated from the personalistic politics of Castro at the time and resigned his post later that fall. See *The Unsuspected Revolution*, 244–45.

145. Earl Smith, 146.

146. Wollam, 81.

147. Peter Kihiss, "US Aide in Cuba Plans New Talks," *New York Times,* 5 July 1958, 7.

148. Filmed interview with Robert Chapman (alias Weicha) by Glenn Gebhard, 12 January 2010, Edenton, NC.

149. Wollam, 11.

150. Interview with Chapman, p. 6 of the transcript; sequence begins at 17:48 minutes.

151. Wollam, 34–96.

152. Ibid., 84–85.

153. E-mail communication with Jean St. George, 9 February 2006.

154. Interview with Chapman, p. 13 of the transcript; sequence begins at 35:02 minutes.

155. Wollam, 88.

156. Interview with Chapman, p. 14 of the transcript; sequence begins at 39:21 minutes.

157. Earl Smith provides this estimate of the mine's value, 149; for name and circumstances of the invitation, see Andrew St. George, sound recording, YUMA, group 650, box 21. With the help of Yale's information technology specialist Pam Patterson, I layered this recording of St. George speaking over the appropriate images that he described in 1970 as they were being projected.

158. Earl Smith reports (150) that town residents were unharmed and in fact hardly approached by the rebels during the town's occupation.

159. YUMA, group 650, reel (currently labeled) 3 and reel 5, originally in box 21. The same footage is repeated on both reels.

160. Mario Llerena provides original documents attesting to the idea that the guerrillas began to take hostages in retaliation for the U.S. government's covert efforts to rearm Batista after making public declarations to the contrary. See *The Unsuspected Revolution*, 241–46.

161. YUMA, group 650, reel (currently labeled) 5, originally in box 21.

162. Ibid.

163. St. George asserts that the documentary ran on Canadian television shortly after the fall of Batista in his interview with Lee Williams. See sound recording.

164. Emanuel Perlmutter, "Castro Expected to Act," *New York Times,* 3 July 1958, 4.

165. Peter Kihiss, "3 More Americans Released in Cuba," *New York Times,* 5 July 1958, 1, 21.

166. Peter Kihiss, "Cuban Rebels Free US Sailor; Admiral Assails Raúl Castro," *New York Times,* 11 July 1958, 1, 8.

167. Peter Kihiss, "Brother of Castro Said to Apologize," *New York Times,* 4 July 1958, 7.

168. Rivero, 129–62.

169. Patterson, 182.

170. Quoted in ibid., 85.

171. "St. George in Cuba," *Newsweek,* 3 February 1958, 63. St. George also wove many of his stories about the Sierra around his own experiences with the rebel underground and Batista's security forces in getting there and back again.

172. A copy of the four-page "pitch," titled "Memorandum: Cuba Story," can be found in St. George's personal archive, private collection of the author. The pitch includes transcripts of several entries from Ryan's diary, brought back to the States by St. George in May 1957 and preserved as an unidentified journal in YUMA, CRC.

173. St. George, "A Revolution Made Me a Pro," 98.

174. Ibid., 98, 100.

Epilogue

1. *Report on Cuba,* April 1958, 2.

2. "The Current Situation," *Report on Cuba,* January 1958, 1; "The Current Situation: The Castro Proposals," *Report on Cuba,* March 1958, 1; "The Current Situation," "The Communists Want Cuba," "Castro and Communism," and "Communists with Castro," *Report on Cuba,* April 1958, 1–2; "What the Rebels Really Want" and "The Fidelistas and Communism," *Report on Cuba,* August 1958, 1–2; "Castro's Real Fight" and "Progress in Cuba," *Report on Cuba,* September 1958, 1–2.

3. AG to George A. Braga and H.M. Gross Jr., 12 May 1958, SASC, UF, BBC, record group 3, series 45, box 9, case file "Vistors to Plantation, 1958–1959," 1–2.

4. Liverpool & London & Globe Insurance Company, Limited, to Charles R. Neidlinger, Ref: Riot Rates—Cuba, 31 October 1957, SASC, UF, BBC, record group 3, series 36, box 3, case file "Rionda Group—Riot & Civil Commotion Rate Increases 1957." See also appended correspondence.

5. Memorandum to Czarnikow-Rionda Company, Insurance Department, from the Manatí Sugar Company, 1 December 1959, SASC, UF, BBC, record group 3, series 37, box 5, case file "Manatí—Theft of Tractor TD-9 #3 w/ Plow—Returned Undamaged."

6. "Sworn Statement in Proof of Loss to Aetna Insurance Company," 1 March 1958, SASC, UF, BBC, record group 3, series 37, box 2, case file "Central Resolución: Fire 40,000 bags Gómez-Mena Sugars, 19 May 1957."

7. "Pro-forma of Proposed Proof of Loss. Statement of Loss. Loss on Property in Connection with Central Elia, October to December 1958, Due to Riots," SASC, UF, BBC,

record group 3, series 37, box 5, case file "Elia—Wooden Bridge Burned 11/3/58"; "Pro-forma of Proposed Proof of Loss. Statement of Loss. Loss on Property in Connection with Central Francisco, Camagüey Prov., Cuba, by Riots, During 1958,"SASC, UF, BBC, record group 3, series 37, box 5, case file "Francisco—Culvert Destroyed by Fire 11/2/58"; "Loss/Damage Report. The New Tuinucu Sugar Company, Inc., November 25, 1958," SASC, UF, BBC, record group 3, series 37, box 6, "Tuinucu—Sabotage—Building and Contents at Colonia Caja de Agua Destroyed by Fire 11/25/58," and Czarnikow-Rionda Company, Insurance Department to Despard & Co., Inc., R. M. Close, 23 December 1958, SASC, UF, BBC, Record group 3, series 37, box 6, case file "Manatí—Sabotage—Water Tanks 5005 & 5016."

8. Parajón e Hijo to G. F. Kohly, S.A., 19 January 1959, SASC, UF, BBC, record group 3, series 37, box 5, case file "Manatí—Store, Electric Plant & Supply Warehouse Dam-aged," and Memorandum to Czarnikow-Rionda Company, Insurance Department, from Manatí Sugar Company, 13 January 1959, SASC, UF, BBC, record group 3, series 37, box 6, case file "Manatí—Sabotage—Furniture, Fixtures, and Theatre Damaged."

9. José Domingo Cabús to Monseñor Enrique Pérez Serantes, Arzobispo de Santiago de Cuba, 4 December 1959, CHC, Fulgencio Batista Zaldívar Collection, series 2, box 16, folder 142, document 21, and José Domingo Cabús to Andrés Lago Cizur, Catedral Met-ropolitana, Santiago de Compostela, Galicia, Spain, 19 November 1961, CHC, Fulgencio Batista Zaldívar Collection, series 2, box 24, folder 297, no item number. See also José Domingo Cabús, *Batista: Pensamiento y Acción* (Havana: Prensa Indoamericana, 1944).

10. Guede, 212–13.

11. Advertisement "Qué es O3C? Cero Tres C???" *Bohemia,* 28 December 1958, 35; also pictured in Guede, 218.

12. Guede, 215; O3C in Clandestine Press, 1958, SASC, UF, ECC, p. 1 of flyer.

13. Interview with Guede.

14. O3C in Clandestine Press, 1958; also pictured in Guede, 214–17.

15. Guede, 212–13; interviews with Ray, 8 August 2008 and 28 February 2009.

16. Juanita Castro and Collins, 187–88.

17. Secret U.S. State Department flight manifest, 31 December 1958, published in Lillian Guerra, ed., "'El 10 de Marzo Fue una Herencia': Entrevista al Capitán Alfredo Sadulé, Ayudante de Fulgencio Batista. Entrevistado por Abel Sierra Madero y Lillian Guerra, el 24 de Junio y el 21 de Julio de 2014, Hialeah, Florida," *Cuban Studies* 44 (2015), 380–81.

18. Franqui, *Cuba, La Revolución,* 222–23; Juanita Castro and Collins, 187–88.

19. Guerra, *Visions of Power,* 37–106, 135–69. For additional contemporary accounts, see Angel del Cerro, "Los Panes y los Peces," *Bohemia,* 2 August 1959, 56–57, 101, and Fidel Castro's own comparison of his actions with those of Jesus Christ in "Traicionar al Pobre es Traicionar a Cristo," *Revolución,* 11 August 1960, 1, 6, 12.

20. Franqui, *Cuba, La Revolución,* 223.

21. Guede, 31–44, 69–70, 76–80.

22. Bernardo Viera Trejo, "Los Batistianos del 1ero de Enero," *Bohemia,* 10 January 1960, 48.

23. "Apoteosis en la Capital," *Bohemia,* 11 January 1959, 91–92; Julio C. González Rebull, "Por Encima del Sectarismo Está la Revolución," *Bohemia,* 7 June 1959, 88.

24. Louis A. Pérez, *Cuba: Between Reform and Revolution,* 2nd ed. (New York: Oxford University Press, 1995), 313–406; Marifeli Pérez-Stable, *The Cuban Revolution: Origins, Course and Legacy* (New York: Oxford University Press, 1993), 61–82; Guerra, *Visions of Power,* 37–74.

25. "San Fidel," private collection of María Antonia Cabrera Aruz.

26. Ibid.

27. Mario Kuchilán Sol, "Historia de un Retrato," *Bohemia,* 30 August 1959, 50–51. The author is grateful to Abel Sierra Madero for suggesting this source.

28. Guerra, *Visions of Power,* 75–169.

29. Ibid.

30. Jorge Luis Betancourt, *Victoria Sobre una Traición* (Havana: Casa Editora Abril, 2010); see also Matos; and Guerra, *Visions of Power,* 77–92.

31. Jorge Valls, *Twenty Years and Forty Days: Life in a Cuban Prison* (New York: Americas Watch Committee, 1986), iv–v.

32. Interview with Valls Arango, 10 July 2014. This view is also based on multiple conversations with Valls, both before this interview, in March 2009, and afterwards.

33. Interview with Echeverría.

34. Lillian Guerra, "Beyond Paradox: Counterrevolution and the Origins of Political Culture in the Cuban Revolution, 1959–2009," in Grandin and Joseph, *A Century of Revolution,* 220.

35. Key examples, all produced by ICAIC, the state film industry, include *Muerte al Invasor* (1961; co-directed with Tomás Gutiérrez Alea); *Fidel en la URSS* (newsreel nos. 134 and 135, 1963); *Ciclón* (1963); *Segunda Declaración de la Habana* (1966); *Mi Hermano Fidel* (1977); *El Mayo de las Tres Banderas* (1980); and *La Marcha del Pueblo Combatiente* (1980)

36. Larry Morales, *Memorias Para un Reencuentro: Conversación con Santiago Álvarez* (Havana: Ediciones Unión, 2008), 185. The author is grateful to María Antonia Cabrera Aruz for suggesting this source.

37. Jorge Renato Ibarra Guitart, "Prólogo," in *Caminos del Moncada* (Havana: Editora Historia, 2013), 9.

38. Fidel Castro certainly adopted this strategy upon the failure of his brainchild, the economically catastrophic Ten Million Ton Harvest of 1970. He also did so in the wake of the invasion of the Peruvian Embassy grounds by 10,800 Cubans in less than twenty-four hours, an event that led Fidel to open the five-month exodus of discontented citizens known as the Mariel Boatlift in 1980. See Guerra, *Visions of Power,* 290–316; and Lillian Guerra, *Patriots and Traitors in Revolutionary Cuba: Political Education, Rehabilitation and Vanguard Youth, 1961–1981* (Durham, NC: Duke University Press, forthcoming), chapter 4.

39. "Remarks by President Obama to the People of Cuba," 22 March 2016, https://www.whitehouse.gov/the-press-office/2016/03/22/remarks-president-obama-people-cuba.

40. "Americans Face Uphill Battle to Reclaim Confiscated Property in Cuba," Associated Press report, 30 March 2015, http://www.news.com.au/finance/money/americans-face-uphill-battle- . . . reclaim-confiscated-property-in-cuba/story-e6frfmci-122728526 4646. Carolyn Chester's case was also made for her on National Public Radio in a story that focused on the Chinese ambassador's home, that is, Edmund Chester's former home:

http://www.npr.org/2015/07/21/425054285/americans-seek-compensation-for-assets
-lost-in-cuban-revolution.

41. "Future of Property Rights in Cuba," in *Hearing Before the Subcommittee on the Western Hemisphere of the Committee on Foreign Affairs, House of Representatives, One Hundred Fourteenth Congress, First Session, June 18, 2015,* serial no. 114-51 (Washington, DC: U.S. Government Publishing Office, 2015), 34–35.

42. Guerra, *Visions of Power,* 57, 95, 124, 132, 213.

43. Ibid., 44–49; Michelle Chase, "The Trials: Violence and Justice in the Aftermath of the Cuban Revolution," in Grandin and Joseph, *A Century of Revolution,* 163–98.

44. This phrase "El gran culpable" also appears in the title of an analytical political memoir written by a former close associate of Batista. In a number of ways, he argues the same point from a position within the dictatorship. See José Suárez Nuñez, *El Gran Culpable: ¿Cómo 12 Guerrilleros Aniquilaron a 45,000 Soldados?* (Caracas: n.p., 1963).

BIBLIOGRAPHY

Archives

Cuba

Archivo Nacional de Cuba, Havana
- Fondo Eduardo Chibás
- Fondo Carlos Márquez Sterling

Fundación Antonio Nuñez Jiménez de la Naturaleza y el Hombre, Havana
- Fondo Personal Antonio Nuñez Jiménez

United States

Cuban Heritage Collection, University of Miami, Miami, FL
- Carlos Hevia Collection (no. 5066)
- Eduardo Chibás Collection

Hoover Institution Archives, Stanford University, Palo Alto, CA

National Archives and Records Administration (microfilm)
- General Records of the Department of State, U.S. Embassy in Havana, Correspondence 1952–1959, record group 59

Personal Collection of María Antonia Cabrera Aruz, New York, NY

Personal Collection of Lillian Guerra, Gainesville, FL

Special and Area Studies Collections, University of Florida, Gainesville, FL
- Braga Brothers Collection
- Ernesto Chávez Collection
- Fulgencio Batista Inauguration Collection
- Lillian Guerra Collection
  - Interviews with Manuel "Manolo" Ray and Aurora Chacón de Ray, 8 August 2008, 28 February 2009, San Juan, Puerto Rico
- Neill Macaulay Collection
  - Interview with Neill Macaulay, 20–21 October 2007, Los Angeles, CA,

Special Collections, Florida International University, Miami, FL
  • Elena Kurstin Cuban Memorabilia Collection
Yale University Manuscripts and Archives, New Haven, CT
  • Andrew St. George Papers
  • Cuban Revolution Collection
  • Glenn Gebhard Oral History Collection (interviews conducted by Lillian Guerra with
    Glenn Gebhard)
    ○ Aestor Bombino, February 2009, Miami, FL
    ○ Andrés Candelario, May 2008, San Juan, Puerto Rico
    ○ Robert Chapman, January 2010, Edenton, NC
    ○ Tania de la Nuez, 2011
    ○ Lucy Echeverría Bianchi, March 2009, Miami, FL
    ○ Sinforiano Echeverría Bianchi, March 2009, Miami, FL
    ○ Carlos Franqui, October 2008, New Haven, CT
    ○ Emilio Guede, May 2008, San Juan, Puerto Rico
    ○ José "Pepe" Puente Blanco, March 2009, Miami, FL
    ○ Jorge Valls, March 2009, Miami, FL

Oral History Interviews

Vicente Baez, 7 August 2008, San Juan, Puerto Rico. Conducted by Lillian Guerra.
Mario Chanes de Armas, 2002, Miami, FL. Conducted by Joe Cardona and Daniel Fernán-
    dez Guevara.
Rafael Díaz-Ballart, 2002, Miami, FL. Conducted by Joe Cardona and Daniel Fernández
    Guevara.
José "Pepe" Puente Blanco, 10 July 2014, Miami, FL. Conducted by Lillian Guerra and Abel
    Sierra Madero. 4 December 2015, 5 December 2015, telephone interviews. Conducted by
    Lillian Guerra.
Alfredo J. Sadulé, 24 June 2014, 21 July 2014, Hialeah, FL. Conducted by Lillian Guerra
    and Abel Sierra Madero.
Alfredo Sánchez Echeverría, 29 March 2014, Tampa, FL. Conducted by Lillian Guerra.
Jorge Valls Arango, 10 July 2014, Miami, FL. Conducted by Lillian Guerra and Abel Sierra
    Madero.

Government Publications

Cuba

Cuban Ministry of Information. *Batista—Some Call Him a Dictator. The Cuban People Tell
    Their True Story. What Is the Matter with Cuba?* Havana: n.p., 1954.
*La Historia Me Absolverá: Defensa del Doctor Fidel Castro Ruz en el Juicio por el Ataque
    al Cuartel Moncada—26 de Julio de 1953—ante el Tribunal de Urgencia de Santiago de
    Cuba.* Havana: Imp. Económico en General, 1959.
Ministerio de Educación. *Unidades de Trabajo: Martí.* Havana: Comisión Nacional Orga-
    nizadora de los Actos y Ediciones del Centenario y del Monumento de Martí, 1953.

United States

"Future of Property Rights in Cuba." In *Hearing Before the Subcommittee on the Western Hemisphere of the Committee on Foreign Affairs, House of Representatives, One Hundred Fourteenth Congress, First Session, June 18, 2015*. Serial no. 114-51. Washington, DC: U.S. Government Publishing Office, 2015.

Newspapers and Magazines

¡Alerta Cubanos!
Bohemia
El Caimán Barbudo
Carta Semanal
Carteles
El Cigarrero
Coronet
Daytona Beach Evening News
Diario de la Marina
Educación Rural
Gaceta Oficial
Gente
Gente de la Semana
Granma
Juventud Rebelde
Libro de Oro de la Sociedad Habanera
Life
Look
Mañana
Miami Herald
El Mundo
New York Times
Noticias de Hoy
Nuestro Tiempo
Obra Revolucionaria
Organo Oficial de Liborio
Orientación Campesina
Popular Photography
Prensa Libre
Report on Cuba
Revolución
See
Sierra Maestra
Tampa Morning Tribune
Verde Olivo

Films

American Comandante: Cuba's Most Unlikely Revolutionary. Directed and produced by
    Adriana Bosch. Public Broadcasting Corporation, 2015.

Cuba: Caminos de Revolución. Directed and produced by Instituto Cubano de Artes e Indus-
    trias Cinematográficas. Seven-part series. 2004–2009.

The Forgotten Revolution. Directed and produced by Glenn Gebhard. Trustees of Indiana
    University, 2014.

¡Viva la República! Directed by Pastor Vega. ICAIC, 1972.

Other Primary Sources

Amado-Ledo, David Enrique. *El Colegio Médico Nacional de Cuba: La Revolución Cas-
    tro-Comunista*. Miami: n.p., 1973.

Ameijeiras Delgado, Efigenio. *Más Allá de Nosotros: Columna 6 "Juan Manuel Ameije-
    rias" II Frente Oriental "Frank País."* Santiago de Cuba: Editorial Oriente, 1984.

Azcuy, Aracelio. *Cuba: Campo de Concentración*. México, DF: Ediciones Humanismo,
    1954.

Batista, Fulgencio. "Proclama al Pueblo de Cuba. Consejo de Ministros. 10 Marzo 1952."
    In *Batista: El Golpe,* by José Luis Padrón and Luis Adrián Betancourt, 352–53. Havana:
    Ediciones Unión, 2013.

———. *Respuesta . . .* México, DF: Manuel León Sánchez, S.C.L., 1960.

———. "Texto Íntegro de la Alocución del 4 de Septiembre, Pronunciada por el Coronel
    Batista." In *Militarismo, Anti-Militarismo, Seudo-Militarismo,* 75–76. Havana: Instituto
    Civico-Militar, 1939.

Berdayes García, Hilda Natalia, ed. *Papeles del Presidente: Documentos y Discursos de
    José Antonio Echeverría Bianchi*. Havana: Ediciones Abril, 2006.

Betancourt, Juan René. *Doctrina Negra: La Unica Teoría Certera Contra la Discriminación
    Racial en Cuba*. Havana: P. Fernández y Cia., 1955.

Bonachea, Rolando E., and Nelson P. Valdés, eds. *Revolutionary Struggle, 1947–1958*. Vol.
    1 of *The Selected Works of Fidel Castro*. Cambridge, MA: MIT Press, 1972.

Cabús, José Domingo. *Batista: Pensamiento y Acción*. Havana: Prensa Indoamericana, 1944.

Cairo, Ana, ed. *Eduardo Chibás: Imaginarios*. Santiago de Cuba: Editorial Oriente, 2010.

Castro, Fidel, and Jeanette Habel. *Proceso al Sectarismo*. Buenos Aires: Jorge Alvarez Ed-
    itor, 1965.

Castro, Juanita, and María Antonieta Collins. *Fidel y Raúl: Mis Hermanos, la Historia Se-
    creta*. Doral, FL: Aguilar, 2009.

Casuso, Teresa. *Cuba and Castro*. Translated by Elmer Grossberg. New York: Random
    House, 1961.

Chibás, Eduardo. "Contra El Pulpo Electrico." In *Antología Civica de Eduardo R. Chibás:
    Artículos y Discursos del Formidable Fundador del Partido Ortodoxo,* edited by Hugo
    Mir, 149–51. Havana: Editorial Lex, 1952.

Conte Agüero, Luis, ed. *Cartas del Presidio: Anticipo de una Biografía de Fidel Castro*.
    Havana: Editorial Lex, 1959.

———. *Eduardo Chibás: El Adalid de Cuba*. México, DF: Editorial Jus, S.A., 1955.

de la Torriente, Cosme. "Discurso del Dr. Cosme de la Torriente en el Club de Leones, el día 6 de Septiembre de 1955." In *El Momento Político de Cuba: Acuerdos, Cartas y Discursos*, 19–23. Havana: Editorial Lex, 1955.

Díaz-Versón, Salvador. *El Zarismo Rojo (Rusia Avanzando Sobre América)*. Havana: Impresora Mundial, 1958.

Dubois, Jules. *Fidel Castro: Rebel-Liberator or Dictator?* Indianapolis: Bobbs-Merrill, 1959.

Echeverría, José Antonio. "Declaración de Principios de la Federación Estudiantil Universitaria. 14 Marzo 1952." In *Papeles del Presidente: Documentos y Discursos de José Antonio Echeverría Bianchi,* edited by Hilda Natalia Berdayes García, 13. Havana: Ediciones Abril, 2006.

Franqui, Carlos, ed. *Cuba: El Libro de Los Doce*. Havana: Instituto del Libro, 1967.

———. *Cuba, La Revolución: ¿Mito o Realidad? Memorias de un Fantasma Socialista*. Barcelona: Ediciones Península, 2006.

———, ed. *Relatos de la Revolución Cubana*. Montevideo: Editorial Sandino, n.d.

———. *Retrato de Familia con Fidel*. Barcelona: Seix Barral, 1981.

———. *Vida, Aventuras y Desastres de un Hombre Llamado Castro*. Barcelona: Editorial Planeta, 1988.

Gadea, Hilda. *My Life with Che: The Making of a Revolutionary*. New York: St. Martin's Griffin, 2009.

Gómez Nocedo, Hector. *De Marzo a Noviembre, 1952–1954: Ensayo Crítico Sobre el 10 de Marzo*. Havana: Bloque Estudiantil Nacional Progresista, 1954.

Grillo, David. *El Problema del Negro Cubano*. 2nd ed. Havana: n.p., 1953.

Grupos de Propaganda Doctrinal Ortodoxa. *Doctrina del Partido Ortodoxo: Independencia Económica, Libertad Política, Justicia Social*. Havana: n.p., 1947.

Guede, Emilio. *Cuba: La Revolución Que No Fue*. N.p.: Eriginal Books, 2013.

Guevara, Ernesto. "Pasajaes de la Guerra Revolucionaria [1963]: Alegría del Pío." In *Obra Revolucionaria,* edited by Roberto Fernández Retamar, 114–16. Havana: Ediciones ERA, 1967.

Hart Phillips, Ruby. *Cuba: Island of Paradox*. New York: McDowell, Obolensky, 1960.

Hernández Otero, Ricardo, ed. *Revista "Nuestro Tiempo": Compilación de Trabajos Publicados*. Havana: Editorial Letras Libres, 1989.

Kirkpatrick, Lyman B., Jr. *The Real CIA*. New York: Macmillan, 1968.

Macaulay, Neill. *A Rebel in Cuba*. New York: Quadrangle Books, 1970.

Matos, Huber. *Cómo Llegó la Noche*. Barcelona: Tusquets Editores, S.A., 2002.

Maza y Rodríguez, Emilio. *La Inconstitucionalidad de los Tribunales de Urgencia. Recurso Presentado ante el Tribunal Supremo de Justicia*. Havana: n.p., 1947.

Mir, Hugo, ed. *Antología Civica de Eduardo R. Chibás: Artículos y Discursos del Formidable Fundador del Partido Ortodoxo*. Havana: Editorial Lex, 1952.

Miranda Bravo, Olga. *Vecinos Indeseables: La Base Yanqui en Guantánmo*. Havana: Editorial de Ciencias Sociales, 1998.

Ortega, Luis. "Generalidades." In *Cuba: Campo de Concentración,* by Aracelio Azcuy, 33–34. México, DF: Ediciones Humanismo, 1954.

Otulksi, Enrique. *Vida Clandestina: My Life in the Cuban Revolution*. Translated by Thomas Christensen and Carol Christensen. New York: Wiley, 2002.

Partido del Pueblo Cubano (Ortodoxo). *Una Entrevista y una Defensa Histórica*. Havana: n.p., 1953.

Prío Socarrás, Carlos. *El Entierro Cubano de Martí: Discurso del Honorable Señor Presidente de la República, 20 Junio 1951*. Havana: n.p., 1951.

Rebelde, Quinteto. "Qué Se Vaya el Mono." In *Kubamusika: Crónicas de la Revolución Cubana*. Kubamusika, 2011.

Riera Hernández, Mario. *Cuba Política, 1899–1955*. Havana. 1955.

Sánchez, Celia. *One Day in December: Celia Sánchez and the Cuban Revolution*. New York: Monthly Review, 2013.

Sánchez Echeverría, Lela. *La Polémica Infinita: Aureliano vs. Chibás y Viceversa*. Miami: self-published, 2004.

Santamaría, Haydée. *Haydée Habla del Moncada*. Havana: Ediciones Políticas, 1967.

Smith, Earl E. T. *The Fourth Floor: An Account of the Castro Communist Revolution*. New York: Random House, 1962.

Sociedad de Amigos de la República. "Documentos para la Historia." In *El Momento Político de Cuba: Acuerdos, Cartas y Discursos,* 19–23. Havana: Editorial Lex, 1955.

Soto, Lionel. *De la Historia y la Memoria*. 3 vols. Havana: Editorial SI-MAR, S.A., 2006.

Todo Empezó en el Moncada. México: DF: Editorial Diógenes, S.A., 1973.

Universal Research & Consultants, Inc. *Communist Activities of the Cuban Rebels*. Washington, DC: Universal Research & Consultants, 1958.

Valls Arango, Jorge. *Twenty Years and Forty Days: Life in a Cuban Prison*. New York: Americas Watch Committee, 1986.

Secondary Sources

Alexander, Robert J. *A History of Organized Labor in Cuba*. Westport, CT: Praeger, 2002.

Alvarez, José. *Frank País: Architect of Cuba's Betrayed Revolution*. Boca Ratón, FL: Universal, 2009.

Alvarez Martín, Elena. *Eduardo Chibás: Clarinada Fecunda*. Havana: Editorial de Ciencias Sociales, 2009.

Ameringer, Charles. *The Caribbean Legion: Patriots, Politicians, Soldiers of Fortune, 1946–50*. University Park: Pennsylvania State University Press, 1996.

——. *The Cuban Democratic Experience: The Auténtico Years, 1944–1952*. Gainesville: University Press of Florida, 2000.

Anderson, Jon Lee. *Che Guevara: A Revolutionary Life*. Rev. ed New York: Grove, 2010.

Argote-Freyre, Frank. "The Political Afterlife of Eduardo Chibás: Evolution of a Symbol, 1951–1991." *Cuban Studies* 32 (2001): 76–77.

Barroso, Miguel A. *Un Asunto Sensible: Tres Historias Cubanas de Crimen y Traición*. Barcelona: Mondadori, 2009.

Bonachea Hernández, Ramon Leocadio, and Marta San Martin. *The Cuban Insurrection, 1952–1959*. New Brunswick, NJ: Transaction Books, 1974.

Caminos del Moncada. Havana: Editora Historia, 2013.

Castañeda, Jorge. *Compañero: The Life and Times of Che Guevara*. New York: Knopf, 1997.

Chase, Michelle. *Revolution Within the Revolution: Women and Gender Politics in Cuba, 1952–1962*. Chapel Hill: University of North Carolina Press, 2015.

————."The Trials: Violence and Justice in the Aftermath of the Cuban Revolution." In *A Century of Revolution: Insurgent and Counterinsurgent Violence During the Latin American Cold War,* edited by Greg Grandin and Gilbert M. Joseph. Durham, NC: Duke University Press, 2010.

Chester, Edmund. *A Sergeant Named Batista.* New York: Henry Holt, 1954.

Childs, Matt D. *The 1812 Aponte Rebellion in Cuba and the Struggle Against Atlantic Slavery.* Chapel Hill: University of North Carolina Press, 2006.

de la Cova, Antonio Rafael. *The Moncada Attack: Birth of the Cuban Revolution.* Columbia: University of South Carolina Press, 2007.

de la Fuente, Alejandro. *A Nation for All: Race, Inequality and Politics in Twentieth-Century Cuba.* Chapel Hill: University of North Carolina Press, 2001.

del Solar, Daniel. "Jauja en Cuba: No Parece Danza sino Rumba de Millones." *Visión,* 21 August 1951, 10–11.

Denis, Richard J. "Una Revista al Servicio de la Nación: *Bohemia* and the Evolution of Cuban Journalism, 1908–1960." MA thesis, University of Florida, 2016.

Domínguez, Jorge. "The Batista Regime in Cuba." In *Sultanistic Regimes,* edited by H. E. Chehabi and Juan J. Linz, 120. Baltimore, MD: Johns Hopkins University Press, 1998.

Ehrlich, Ilan. *Eduardo Chibás: The Incorrigible Man of Cuban Politics.* New York: Rowman & Littlefield, 2015.

English, T. J. *Havana Nocturne: How the Mob Owned Cuba and Then Lost It to the Revolution.* New York: Harper, 2007.

Fernández Guevara, Daniel. "Constructing Legitimacy in Stone and Words During Cuba's Second Republic: Building and Contesting Batista's José Martí." MA thesis, University of Florida, 2016.

Fernández León, Julio. *José Antonio Echeverría: Vigencia y Presencia Ante el Cincuenta Aniversario de su Holocausto.* Miami: Ediciones Universal, 2007.

Ferrer, Ada. *Insurgent Cuba: Race, Nation and Revolution, 1868–1898.* Chapel Hill: University of North Carolina Press, 1999.

Figes, Orlando. *The Whisperers: Private Life in Stalin's Russia.* London: Penguin Books, 2008.

Fontova, Humberto. *The Longest Romance: The Mainstream Media and Fidel Castro.* New York: Encounter Books, 2013.

Fursenko, Aleksandr, and Timothy Naftali. *"One Hell of a Gamble": Khrushchev, Castro and Kennedy, 1958–1964; The Secret History of the Cuban Missile Crisis.* New York: Norton, 1997.

García Oliveras, Julio A. *José Antonio Echeverría: La Lucha Estudiantil Contra Batista.* Havana: Editora Política, 2001.

García-Pérez, Gladys Marel. *Insurrection and Revolution: Armed Struggle in Cuba, 1952–1959.* Boulder, CO: Lynne Rienner, 1998.

Geyer, Georgie Anne. *Guerrilla Prince: The Untold Story of Fidel Castro.* New York: Little, Brown, 1991.

Gimbel, Wendy. *Havana Dreams: A Story of a Cuban Family.* New York: Vintage Books, 1998.

Gjelten, Tom. *Bacardí and the Long Fight for Cuba: The Biography of a Cause.* New York: Viking, 2008.

Grandin, Greg. "Living in Revolutionary Time: Coming to Terms with the Violence of Latin America's Long Cold War." In *A Century of Revolution: Insurgent and Counterinsurgent Violence During Latin America's Long Cold War,* edited by Greg Grandin and Gilbert M. Joseph. Durham, NC: Duke University Press, 2010.

Guerra, Lillian. "Beyond Paradox: Counterrevolution and the Origins of Political Culture in the Cuban Revolution, 1959–2009." In *A Century of Revolution: Insurgent and Counterinsurgent Violence During the Latin American Cold War,* edited by Greg Grandin and Gilbert M. Joseph. Durham, NC: Duke University Press, 2010.

——, ed. "'El 10 de Marzo Fue una Herencia': Entrevista al Capitán Alfredo Sadulé, Ayudante de Fulgencio Batista. Entrevistado por Abel Sierra Madero y Lillian Guerra, el 24 de Junio y el 21 de Julio de 2014, Hialeah, Florida." *Cuban Studies* 44 (2015).

——. *The Myth of José Martí: Conflicting Nationalisms in Early Twentieth-Century Cuba.* Chapel Hill: University of North Carolina Press, 2005.

——. *Visions of Power in Cuba: Revolution, Redemption, and Resistance, 1959–1971.* Chapel Hill: University of North Carolina Press, 2012.

Halperin, Maurice. *The Rise and Decline of Fidel Castro.* Berkeley: University of California Press, 1972.

——. *The Taming of Fidel Castro.* Berkeley: University of California Press, 1981.

Helg, Aline. *Our Rightful Share: The Afro-Cuban Struggle for Equality, 1886–1912.* Chapel Hill: University of North Carolina Press, 1995.

Hernández-Bauza, Miguel. *Biografía de una Emoción Popular: El Dr. Grau.* Miami: Ediciones Universal, 1986.

Hoffman, David L. *Stalinist Values: The Cultural Norms of Soviet Modernity (1917–1941).* Ithaca, NY: Cornell University Press, 2003.

Horst, Jesse. "Sleeping on Ashes: Havana Slums in an Age of Revolution, 1930–1970." PhD diss., University of Pittsburgh, in progress.

Joseph, Gilbert M. "What We Now Know and Should Know: Bringing Latin America More Meaningfully into Cold War Studies." In *In from the Cold: Latin America's New Encounter with the Cold War,* edited by Gilbert M. Joseph and Daniela Spenser, 3–46. Durham, NC: Duke University Press, 2008.

LeoGrande, William M., and Peter Kornbluh. *Back Channel to Cuba: The Hidden History of Negotiations Between Washington and Havana.* Chapel Hill: University of North Carolina Press, 2014.

Lipman, Jana. *Guantánamo: A Working-Class History Between Empire and Revolution.* Berkeley: University of California Press, 2008.

Llerena, Mario. *The Unsuspected Revolution: The Birth and Rise of Castroism.* Ithaca, NY: Cornell University Press, 1978.

Martin, Lionel. *The Early Fidel: Roots of Castro's Communism.* Secaucus, NJ: Lyle Stuart, 1978.

McGillivray, Gillian. *Blazing Cane: Sugar Communities, Class and State Formation in Cuba, 1868–1959.* Durham, NC: Duke University Press, 2009.

Mencía, Mario. *Prisión Fecunda.* Havana: Editora Política, 1980.

Mesa-Lago, Carmelo. *Cuba in the 1970s: Pragmatism and Institutionalization.* Albuquerque: University of New Mexico Press, 1978.

Pappademos, Melina. *Black Political Activism in the Cuban Republic*. Chapel Hill: University of North Carolina Press, 2014.

Paterson, Thomas G. *Contesting Castro: The United States and the Triumph of the Cuban Revolution*. New York: Oxford University Press, 1995.

Pérez, Emma. *La Política Educacional del Dr. Grau San Martín*. Havana: UCar García, S.A., 1948.

Pérez, Louis A., Jr. *Army Politics in Cuba, 1898–1958*. Pittsburgh: University of Pittsburgh Press, 1976.

——. *Cuba: Between Reform and Revolution*. 4th ed. New York: Oxford University Press, 2010.

——. *Cuba Under the Platt Amendment, 1902–1934*. Pittsburgh: University of Pittsburgh Press, 1987.

——. *On Becoming Cuban: Identity, Nationality & Culture*. Chapel Hill: University of North Carolina Press, 1999.

——. *The Structure of Cuban History: Meanings and Purpose of the Past*. Chapel Hill: University of North Carolina Press, 2013.

——. *To Die in Cuba: Suicide and Society*. Chapel Hill: University of North Carolina Press, 2005.

——. *The War of 1898: The United States and Cuba in History and Historiography*. Chapel Hill: University of North Carolina Press, 1998.

Pérez Concepción, Hernel. *Las Luchas Políticas del Holguín Republicano, 1944–1948*. Holguín: Ediciones Holguín, 2007.

Quirk, Robert E. *Fidel Castro*. New York: Norton, 1993.

Rathbone, John Paul. *The Sugar King of Havana: The Rise and Fall of Julio Lobo, Cuba's Last Tycoon*. New York: Penguin Books, 2010.

Riera, Mario. *Cuba Política, 1899–1955*. Havana: n.p., 1955.

Rivero, Yeidy M. *Broadcasting Modernity: Cuban Commercial Television, 1950–1960*. Durham, NC: Duke University Press, 2015.

Rojas, Marta. *El Juicio del Moncada*. Havana: Editorial de Ciencias Sociales, 1988.

Rojas Blaquier, Angelina. *Primer Partido Comunista de Cuba*. Vol. 3. Santiago de Cuba: Editorial Oriente, 2010.

Sáenz Rovner, Eduardo. *The Cuban Connection: Drug Trafficking, Smuggling, and Gambling in Cuba from the 1920s to the Revolution*. Chapel Hill: University of North Carolina Press, 2008.

Sallah, Michael, and Mitch Weiss. *The Yankee Comandante: The Untold Story of Courage, Passion, and One American's Fight to Liberate Cuba*. New York: Lyons, 2015.

Scarry, Elaine. *The Body in Pain: The Making and Unmaking of the World*. New York: Oxford University Press, 1987.

Schoultz, Lars. *That Infernal Little Cuban Republic: The United States and the Cuban Revolution*. Chapel Hill: University of North Carolina Press, 2009.

Schwartz, Rosalie. *Pleasure Island: Tourism and Temptation in Cuba*. Lincoln: University of Nebraska Press, 1997.

Semyonovna Ginzburg, Eugenia. *Journey into the Whirlwind*. Translated by Paul Stevenson and Max Hayward. San Diego: Harcourt Brace Jovanovich, 1967.

Shetterly, Aran. *The Americano: Fighting with Castro for Cuba's Freedom*. Chapel Hill, NC: Algonquin Books, 2007.

Smith, Robert. *The United States and Cuba: Business and Diplomacy, 1917–1960*. New York: Bookman Associates, 1960.

Soto, Lionel. *La Revolución del '33*. 3 vols. Havana: Editorial de Ciencias Sociales, 1977.

Stern, Steve J. *Battling for Hearts and Minds: Memory Struggles in Pinochet's Chile (1973–1988) (Bk.2)*. Durham, NC: Duke University Press, 2006.

———. *Remembering Pinochet's Chile: On the Eve of London, 1998 (Bk. 1)*. Durham, NC: Duke University Press, 2006.

Sublette, Ned. *Cuba and Its Music: From the First Drums to the Mambo*. Chicago: Chicago Review, 2004.

Sweig, Julia. *Inside the Cuban Revolution: Fidel Castro and the Urban Underground*. Cambridge, MA: Harvard University Press, 2002.

Symmes, Patrick. *The Boys from Dolores: Fidel Castro's Schoolmates from Revolution to Exile*. New York: Vintage Books, 2007.

Taibo, Paco Ignacio. *Guevara Also Known as Che*. Translated by Martin Michael Roberts. New York: St. Martin's, 1997.

Teel, Leonard Ray. *Reporting the Cuban Revolution: How Castro Manipulated American Journalists*. Baton Rouge: Louisiana State University Press, 2015.

Thomas, Hugh. *Cuba; or, The Pursuit of Freedom*. London: Eyre & Spootiswoode, 1971.

Vidaillet, Kelsey. "Violations of Freedom of the Press in Cuba: 1952–1959." *Association for the Study of the Cuban Economy* (2006): 287.

Whitney, Robert. *State and Revolution in Cuba: Mass Mobilization and Political Change, 1920–1940*. Chapel Hill: University of North Carolina Press, 2001.

INDEX